THE ODES AND PSALMS

OF

SOLOMON

FACSIMILE: ODES OF SOLOMON xxvi. 13—14, xxvii., xxviii. 1—4

THE ODES AND PSALMS

OF

SOLOMON

PUBLISHED FROM THE
SYRIAC VERSION

BY

J. RENDEL HARRIS, M.A.

Hon. D.Litt. (Dubl.), Hon. LL.D. (Haverford), Hon. D.Theol. (Leiden),
Hon. LL.D. (Birmingham), Hon. Fellow of Clare College, Cambridge

SECOND EDITION
REVISED AND ENLARGED
WITH A FACSIMILE

Cambridge :
at the University Press
1911

πληροῦσθε ἐν πνεύματι, λαλοῦντες ἑαυτοῖς ψαλμοῖς καὶ ὕμνοις καὶ ᾠδαῖς πνευματικαῖς, ᾄδοντες καὶ ψάλλοντες τῇ καρδίᾳ ὑμῶν τῷ κυρίῳ.

Ad Ephes. v. 19.

οὐ γάρ ἐστιν ἡ βασιλεία τοῦ θεοῦ βρῶσις καὶ πόσις, ἀλλὰ δικαιοσύνη καὶ εἰρήνη καὶ χαρὰ ἐν πνεύματι ἁγίῳ.

Ad Rom. xiv. 17.

CAMBRIDGE
UNIVERSITY PRESS

University Printing House, Cambridge CB2 8BS, United Kingdom

Cambridge University Press is part of the University of Cambridge.

It furthers the University's mission by disseminating knowledge in the pursuit of education, learning and research at the highest international levels of excellence.

www.cambridge.org
Information on this title: www.cambridge.org/9781107497733

First published 1911
First paperback edition 2015

A catalogue record for this publication is available from the British Library

ISBN 978-1-107-49773-3 Paperback

CONTENTS

PREFACE TO THE FIRST EDITION

IT is not easy to produce a satisfactory edition of a work which has come down to us in a single document, especially when the document itself is late in date, and represents not the original text, but a version of the same, made by some unknown hand. Obscurities are sure to exist in a text so scantily attested and of such an uncertain tradition. In spite, however, of these inherent difficulties, I hope that the translation and editing of these new *Odes of Solomon* (with their associated and already known *Psalms of Solomon*) will be satisfactory ; for, although late in date, the text is very well preserved, and the translation from the Greek into the Syriac appears to have been carefully and conscientiously made. If we could come across some more traces of the newly-recovered work in the writings of the Fathers, or if, by good hap, we might find the lost Latin or a copy of the original Greek, much that is obscure in our presentation of the Odes would disappear. Meanwhile we have done our best with the material as we found it and as we were able to reinforce it : our thanks are due to scholarly friends who have assisted us with their keen revising eyes or their nimble emendating brains. My learned lady friends Mrs Lewis and Mrs Gibson have given me much assistance with the proofs : Mr Glover has criticised obscure passages and inadequate arguments : and Professor Nestle has made some brilliant suggestions for the betterment of the text, and traces of his skilled hand may be seen at several points, of which I note especially Ode 7. 12, Ode 38. 14, Ps. v. 16, Ps. vii. 4, and Ps. xvii. 31. I think it is very likely that a skilled Coptic scholar could also do something to improve either the text or the translation in those Odes which have been transferred to the text of the *Pistis Sophia*.

RENDEL HARRIS

CHETWYND
SELLY OAK
October 1909

O. S.

b

PREFACE TO THE SECOND EDITION

THE first edition of this book having been exhausted sooner than I had anticipated, I have decided not to delay the production of a new edition, which should, as far as possible, remove the errors of the former, and incorporate the results of the searching criticism to which the Odes and the manner of their presentation have been subjected.

In response to a number of appeals, I have added a facsimile of the unique manuscript from which I have worked. Then, as far as conviction ruled, I have accepted a number of textual betterments from scholars in England, France and Germany. In the case of the Psalms of Solomon, I have added the readings of the curious fragment of these Psalms, preserved in a MS. in the Cambridge University Library, to which Dr Barnes has drawn attention. In the case of the Odes, the text and the translation and the theories connected therewith have been compared with those of Harnack-Flemming, Zahn, Ungnad-Stärk, Batiffol-Labourt, Barnes, Bernard, Diettrich, Charles, Clemen, Gunkel, Haussleiter, Mead, Menzies, Nestle, Schulthess, Spitta and others. As the range of interpretation is very wide, and critical consent still seems to be somewhat remote, I have added a new section to review the work done on the Odes by the scholars referred to, and to give some estimate of its value in the most important cases. With these corrections and expansions I hope the second edition will be as welcome as and not less useful than the first.

RENDEL HARRIS

SELLY OAK
February 1911

BIBLIOGRAPHICAL NOTES

In preparing the second edition for the press, it will be convenient to give in the first place, a bibliography of the most important reviews and notices of the Odes, which I have come across: the list makes no pretence at completeness; but it will serve to indicate the currents of opinion, and special attention will be given to those articles or reviews which are important for the resolution of the problems connected with the Odes, by marking them with an asterisk.

Dr J. Vernon Bartlet in *British Weekly* for Feb. 25, 1909. (Announcement of Discovery of the Odes.)

Rendel Harris in *Contemporary Review* for April, 1909, '*An Early Christian Hymn-book.*'

J. M. Leendertz in Ἐλθέτω ἡ βασιλεία σου for May 6, 1909 (Utrecht). (Notice of Discovery etc.)

Prof. Nestle in *Kirchlicher Anzeiger für Württemberg* No. 49, 1909. (Notice of Discovery.)

Louis Mariès in *Études par les Pères de la compagnie de Jésus* for June 20, 1909. (Notice of Discovery and of Article by R. H. in *Contemporary Review.*)

Rendel Harris. *An Early Christian Psalter*, London (Nisbet and Co.), 1909. Contains the greater part of the Odes in English with a brief introduction.

Rendel Harris in *The Quest.* 1910, pp. 288—305. Text of lecture on 'An early Judaeo-Christian Hymn-book' given before the Quest Society.

G. R. S. Mead in *The Quest.* 1910, pp. 561—570. Review of Rendel Harris' *Odes and Psalms of Solomon.*

G. R. S. Mead in *The Quest.* 1910, vol. ii. pp. 166—169. Review of Harnack's *Ein jüdisch-christliches Psalmbuch.*

Harnack in *Sitzungsberichte der könig. preuss. Akademie* for 1909. No. 51. Berlin. Notice of Discovery.

'Times' Literary Supplement for Dec. 2, 1909. Brief Review.

Schürer in *Theol. Literaturzeitung* for Jan., 1910, pp. 6, 7. Review

Record for Dec. 17, 1909. (Brief Notice.)

Nestle in *Theol. Lit.-Blatt* for Jan. 7, 1910. Review of the Odes.

The Christian World for Jan. 13, 1910. Review.

W. B. Brash in *The Methodist Times* for Jan. 13, 1910. Review.

Dr James Moffatt in *British Weekly* for Feb. 24, 1910. Review.

The Athenaeum for Jan. 15, 1910. Review.

R. S. Franks in the *British Friend* for Jan., 1910. Review.

H. Ramette in *Le Chrétien Libre*, pp. 457—460. Review.

Expository Times for Feb., 1910. Editorial Notice.

Wohlenberg in *Schleswig-Holstein-Lauenburgisches Kirchen- u. Schulblatt* for Feb. 12, 1910, No. 7.

The Outlook for April 2, 1910. Review. (New York.)

Evening Bulletin for April 13, 1910. Account of Discovery. (Philadelphia.)

The Guardian for April 14, 1910. Review of *Early Christian Psalter*.

The Guardian for April 29, 1910. Review of *Odes and Psalms*.

Buonaiuti in *Rivista Storico-critica delle Scienze Teologiche* for March, 1910 (pp. 188—200). (Rome.)

Daily News for March 11, 1910. Brief Review.

'Times' Literary Supplement for April 7, 1910. *A Church Hymnal of the First Century*. Review (by Dr R. H. Charles).

H. Hansen in *Der Alte Glaube* for April 8, 1910. Review, with translation of three selected Odes into German verse.

British Weekly for April 27, 1910. Notice of Dr Harnack's book on the Odes.

Great Thoughts for May 7, 1910. Review.

*Harnack and Flemming, *Ein jüdisch-christliches Psalmbuch aus dem ersten Jahrhundert*: in *Texte u. Untersuchungen* III. 5. 4. Leipzig (Hinrichs) 1910.

Nairne in *Guardian* for June 3, 1910, p. 778. Review.

Dr Johannes Haussleiter in *Theologisches Literaturblatt* for June 10, 1910. *Der judenchristliche Charakter der Oden Salomos*.

J. M. Leendertz. *Die Oden von Salomo*. Amsterdam (Portielje) 1910.

Dr Johannes Leipoldt in *Allgemeine Evangelisch-Lutherische Kirchenzeitung* for July 8, 1910. *Die Lieder Salomos*.

Dr David S. Schaff in the *Presbyterian Banner* (America) for June 2, 1910. *A Christian Hymn-Book of the First Century*.

Dr Barnes in *Expositor* for July, 1910, pp. 52—63. *An Ancient Christian Hymn-Book*.

Dr Barnes in *Journal of Theological Studies* for July, 1910, pp. 573 sqq. *The Text of the Odes of Solomon* and pp. 615 sqq. Review of Harnack on the Odes.

*G. Diettrich in *Die Reformation* for May 8, June 5, Aug. 7, and Aug. 14, 1910. *Eine jüdisch-christliche Liedersammlung aus dem apostolischen Zeitalter.*

J. A. Montgomery in *Biblical World*, XXXVI. 93—100. The recently discovered Odes of Solomon.

A. Wabnitz in *Revue de Théologie et des questions religieuses* XIX. 351—367. *Un Psautier judéo-chrétien du 1er siècle.*

Kennedy in *Expository Times*, July, 1910, p. 444. Review of Harnack on the Odes.

Dr R. H. Charles in *Review of Theology and Philosophy* for October, 1910, pp. 220—223. Review of Harnack's book.

R. H. Strachan in *Expository Times* for Oct., 1910. *The newly recovered Odes of Solomon and their bearing on the Problem of the Fourth Gospel.*

Dr T. K. Cheyne in *Hibbert Journal* for Oct., 1910, pp. 208—212. Review of the *Odes and Psalms* and of Harnack's *Jüdisch-christliches Psalmbuch.*

The Churchman for Oct., 1910. Review.

R. Bultmann in *Monatschrift für Pastoral Theologie* Oct., 1910. *Ein jüdisch-christliches Psalmbuch aus dem ersten Jahrhundert.*

*Batiffol and Labourt in *Revue Biblique* for Oct., 1910, pp. 484—500; and for Jan., 1911, pp. 1—57. *Les Odes de Salomon.* (Not yet completed.)

F. Spitta in *Monatschrift für Gottesdienst und kirchl. Kunst* for 1910, pp. 245 sqq. : 273 sqq.

F. Spitta in *Zeitschrift für die neutestamentliche Wissenschaft* (*Preuschen's Zeitschrift*), Heft 3, 1910, pp. 193—290. *Zum Verständnis der Oden Salomos.*

F. Spitta in *Monatschrift für Pastoral Theologie* for Dec., 1910, pp. 91—101. *Die Oden Salomos und das neue Testament.*

W. Stärk in *Zeitschrift für wissenschaftliche Theologie* LII. N.F. XVII. 4.

*Prof. W. A. Menzies in the *Interpreter* for Oct., 1910, pp. 1—22. *The Odes of Solomon.*

Methodist Quarterly Review (American) for Oct., 1910. Review of the *Odes and Psalms* and of Harnack's *Jüdisch-christliches Psalmbuch.*

Bousset in *Theologische Rundschau* for Nov., 1910. Brief notice of *Odes* etc.

M. J. Lagrange in *Revue Biblique Internationale* for Oct., 1910, pp. 593—596. Notice and Review.

Dr J. H. Bernard in *Spectator* for Oct. 22, 1910. Notice of Discovery etc.

Kirsopp Lake in *Theologisch Tijdschrift* for 1910, XLV. pp. 89—92. Review.

*Dr J. H. Bernard in *Journal of Theological Studies* for Oct., 1910.

Methodist Quarterly Review (American) for Jan., 1911. Review of Harnack.

Clemen in *Theologische Rundschau*, pp. 1—19, Jan., 1911. *Die neuentdeckten Oden Salomos.*

*F. Schulthess in *Zeitschrift für die neutestamentliche Wissenschaft* (*Preuschen's Zeitschrift*), Heft 3, 1910, pp. 249—258. *Textkritische Bemerkungen zu den syrischen Oden Salomos.*

*H. Gunkel in *Zeitschrift für die neutestamentliche Wissenschaft* (*Preuschen's Zeitschrift*), Heft 3, 1910, pp. 291—328. *Die Oden Salomos.*

*Wellhausen in *Göttingische gelehrte Anzeigen* for Sept., 1910, pp. 629—642. Review.

S. Reinach in *Revue Moderniste Internationale* for Dec., 1910, pp. 457—458 (Geneva), a letter from S.R. *à propos des Odes de Salomon.*

H. Böhmer in *Kirchliche Rundschau für d. evang. Gemeinden Rheinlands und Westfalens* for 1910, pp. 215 sqq.: 238 sqq.: 266 sqq.: 297 sqq.

*Th. Zahn in *Neue kirchliche Zeitschrift* for 1910, pp. 667 sqq.: 747 sqq.

*Ungnad and Stärk in *Kleine Texte für theologische und philosophische Vorlesungen und Übungen*. Bonn, 1910. *Die Oden Salomos.*

B. Hake in *Deutsche Rundschau* Jan., 1911. *Die Oden Salomos.*

H. Hansen. *Die Oden Salomos in deutschen Nachdichtungen.* Gütersloh (Bertelsmann) 1911.

Viteau and Martin, *Les Psaumes de Salomon*. Paris (Letouzey et Ané) 1911.

* Arthur C. Headlam in *Church Quarterly Review* for Jan. 1911, pp. 272—302. Review.

Meyer: *Grosses Konversations-Lexicon*, 6. Aufl. 22. Bd. Jahres-Supplement 1909—1910.

    p. 396. *Harris*, James Rendel.... *The Odes of Solomon*, 1909.

    p. 638. *Oden Salomos*, eine Sammlung von 42 jüdischen Psalmen in christlicher Bearbeitung etc., etc.

Salomon Reinach in *Revue de l'Histoire des Religions*, 1910. (*Annales du Musée Guimet.*) *Les Odes de Salomon.*

BRIEF SUMMARY OF RECENT CRITICISMS

In the previous edition a first attempt was made to elucidate the various problems which were presented by the new book of Odes. The Psalms which were attached to them were treated in a rapid manner, as there did not seem any necessity to go over again in detail the various critical results at which scholars had arrived with regard to their origin. It is sufficient to say that no considerations have been adduced which should invalidate the reference of the Solomonic Psalms to the period of the Roman Invasion of Judæa by Pompey, and of the years that followed the desecration of the Temple[1]. With regard to these Psalms the critics have been moving in converging paths to a conclusion from which there is no appreciable dissent. With regard, however, to the Odes and their place in the history of literature and of religion, no signs of such convergence or consent are yet to be seen. On every side doubts are expressed as to the explanations which I proposed. If, for example, it was suggested that they were Judæo-Christian in origin, the contradiction comes from two opposite sides, one school affirming that they are not Christian, the other that they are not Jewish. If, again, the suggestion is made that the time of their composition is the latter part of the first century A.D., the contentions have to be met that they are (1) nearly a hundred years earlier or (2) nearly a hundred years later than the time proposed. If I suggest that the Odes frequently betray a Johannine vocabulary, but at the same time decline to recognise actual loans from the Fourth Gospel, preferring to believe that the vocabulary in question is the theological language of a time and school which are not very remote from the time and school of thought of the author of the Fourth Gospel, one has to face the objections, on the one side that the theology is not that of a Christian but of a Jewish mystic, on the other side that it is the regular Christian theology of the Church after it has been charged to saturation with the thought

---

[1] Prof. Cheyne, in the *Hibbert Journal*, expresses a hope that I shall see my way to the abandonment of the identification of Pompey with the great dragon, and to the desertion of the chronology which is marked by the allusions to his death on the Egyptian shore. I am not to be allured from so certain a piece of critical investigation into the by-paths of ancient astrology.

and expressions of St John.   On the one side there is the
alluring hypothesis that we have discovered the missing link
from which the Fourth Gospel itself depends, on the other side,
the Odes are by invisible links dependent from the feet of
St John.   Rarely has so much variety of opinion been provoked
by the publication of a new document from the lost library of
the Early Church: even the *Teaching of the Apostles* did not
evoke so many nor so varied suggestions.   Indeed, on looking
over what has been said on the subject, up to the time of the
preparation of this second edition, there does not seem to be
anything about which everyone seems agreed unless it should be
that the Odes are of singular beauty and of high spiritual value,
and that they are probably of Syro-Palestinian origin.   Well!
that is something gained, for it means that we are moving still
further away from the old belief that the origins of the Fourth
Gospel are to be sought in Alexandria and that every presenta-
tion of the doctrine of the Logos must have passed through the
moulding hands of Philo.

Let us then see what has been said on the subject of the Odes
by recent writers.   We begin, both chronologically and for other
reasons, with Dr Harnack: he was almost the first in the field[1], and
for most of us who are engaged in historical and critical investi-
gations into Christian origins and history, he is *il maestro di color
che sanno*.   Harnack's book betrays in its preface the thesis that
he means to defend, that the Odes of Solomon are a Jewish
Psalm-book composed near the beginning of the Christian era
and worked over again at no very distant date by a Christian
hand.   That is, Harnack accepts most of my arguments that
there is little or nothing in many of the Odes that is so distinctly
Christian as not to be equally well described as Jewish, and in
those cases where the Christian hand must be recognised it is
the hand of an interpolator.   Without conceding the absolute
unity of the collection, for we both agree that this unity may be
broken in one or two cases by possible later intrusions, Harnack
affirms that the general and obvious unity of style, by which the
compositions are characterised, must be qualified by regarding
the Odes as emanating from one hand or school, and passing

---

[1] He was partly anticipated by Diettrich, the first of whose remarkable articles in
Die Reformation was written and published before Harnack's work saw the light.
We shall attend to these articles later on.

through another. Like myself, Harnack does not love the hypothesis of interpolations, but it is a hypothesis to which one must sometimes resort. In particular, at the time when one great religion is passing into another, and the books are, of necessity, passing over with the migrant people, it is in the highest degree likely that Christian editions will be produced of favourite Jewish books. We have, in fact, proof positive of such transfers in the case of the *Teaching of the Twelve Apostles* and its dependence upon the Jewish *Doctrine of the Two Ways*, and in the Christian additions which can be dissected out of the text of the *Testament of the Twelve Patriarchs*. Something of the same kind, but perhaps not quite so early, has happened in the famous Christian expansions of the text of Josephus ; and, for a much less probable, but not impossible, parallel, we might refer to those attempts which have been made to dissect original Jewish writings out of the Apocalypse of John, in which case the hypothesis of Vischer that we should treat the expression 'God and the Lamb' as an interpolated expansion of the Divine Name, has a seductive simplicity which, if I remember rightly, bewitched even Harnack himself, who confesses not to love hypotheses of interpolation.

There is, however, not the least need to apologize for the use of such hypotheses, if the criticism of the text breaks down for want of them. After all, it does not mean, in the present case, more than the substitution of two authors for one : it is not a case of multiplied redaction like that which is affirmed for the Pentateuch or Isaiah. Two authors are not too many for this little book ; if two are intelligible where one is unintelligible, by all means let us have two : only let us keep in reserve the caution that it will always be easy to prove a document to be Jewish when you have dissected out of it everything that is Christian.

Certainly I have no right, *a priori*, to object to the extension which Harnack makes of my first thesis, seeing that I had already set aside certain Odes which discussed the Virgin Birth and the descent into Hades, as belonging to a relatively later stratum of thought than the main collection ; and if one may resort to the hypothesis of interjection for whole Psalms, how can one reasonably object to the hypothesis of interpolation in selected Psalms ; the interpolator has been admitted into the argument

on the greater scale, how can he be prohibited on the smaller
scale? Is it likely that the man who issues a new hymn-
book, with which he incorporates some compositions of his
own, will carefully keep his editorial hands off the rest of the
collection? Such is not the method of the modern compilers of
hymn-books, who have less reason to tamper with the texts that
they appropriate than people had in the rapidly changing beliefs
of the early centuries.

If Harnack is right, however, a curious phenomenon presents
itself. My hypothesis of a Judæo-Christian composer, who
betrays few of the external signs of Christianity, because of the
elevation of his personal experience above the levels of ritual
practices and dogmatic definitions, is replaced by Harnack by
the hypothesis of a Jewish composer who is as free from definite
traces of Judaism as my assumed writer was of the corresponding
elements of Christianity. The man who had no Eucharist (so
far as his language goes) is replaced by a man without a Passover.
The man without a doctrine of penitence is replaced by a man
who has no doctrine of sacrifice and no Day of Atonement. The
man who moves so lightly amongst the early Christian orders, as
not to refer to a bishop, while apologizing for his own priesthood
and apparently confounding deacons with evangelists, has to be
replaced by a Jew, who loves the Temple but has not a word
to say of the associated priesthood and ritual! At first sight this
looks very unlikely, and it is made more so, by the necessary
deduction that the assumed non-ritualistic, undogmatic, mystical
Jew suffered interpolation at the hands of an equally non-ritual-
istic, undogmatic and mystical Christian. At first sight, I say,
this seems to be an improbable collocation: but it is not really
so: for we start with the assumption of a mystical writer whose
affinities are not with priesthoods or sacraments: one mystic is
hereby conceded and perhaps a school: at all events, the Fourth
Gospel offers striking analogies of similar spiritual elevation and
detachment. If, however, this mystical writer be conceded, he
must be either Jew or Christian, and there is no serious difficulty
in the use by a Christian mystic of a previously existing Jewish
mystic. If such Jewish mystics existed, they must in many
cases have passed over, or evolved into Christian mystics, and
this almost makes the apparent duality of the hypothesis of
Harnack into a unity again. The parts divided are so nearly

one, that they easily re-compose into a close and ultimate connexion.

Having said so much, I hope I have made it clear that I am animated by no hostility towards Harnack's treatment of the subject. One cannot read the book in which his theory is presented without admiration for the acuteness of its criticism, and the fertility of its illustration. Whether it be right or wrong, it is certainly a notable piece of work. Let us now take one or two cases in detail, in order that we may see the hypothesis in its actual application to the supposed interpolated Odes.

In the middle of the 3rd Ode, Harnack marks an inter-polation in the 9th verse, as follows:

8. I have been united to Him, for the Lover has found the Beloved:

9. (And because I love him that is the Son, I shall myself become a Son):

10. For he that is joined to Him that is immortal, will also himself become immortal,

11. And he who has pleasure in the Living One, will himself become living.

Here Harnack's argument is that immortality comes from union with God, and that the allusion to the Son of God disturbs the sequence. He objects to my erasure of the plural points, so as to read 'Living One' for 'Life,' and thinks the parallelism is sufficient between *Life* and 'the Immortal.' Thus the Ode becomes Jewish and not Christian except in the interpolated sentence. But with regard to the erasure of the plural points, it should be noticed that they would almost certainly be added if absent, that the parallelism is improved by their absence, that the title 'the Living One' ($\dot{o}$ $\zeta\hat{\omega}\nu$) is a characteristic early name for Christ. It is involved again in Ode 8. 24, where the parallelism shows that the terms 'the Beloved,' 'the one that lives,' and 'the one that was saved (!)' all belong to Christ. Accordingly Zahn says of this passage,

> '"Wer an den Lebendigen Wohlgefallen hat." Der Parallelis-mus membrorum empfiehlt es, mit Harris das Pluralzeichen…zu ignorieren.'

The words 'has pleasure in,' if we have rightly understood the Syriac, should correspond to a Greek $\epsilon\dot{v}\delta o\kappa\acute{\epsilon}\omega$ which is again appropriate to a person, and as the account of the Baptism of Jesus shows, to a particular person.   But if the expression ' the Living One' stands (especially when we remember the Johannine 'because I live ye shall live also,' and kindred passages), then it follows that Christ is referred to in the original Ode, or the alternative to this conclusion would be that the interpolation is more extended than a single verse.   The latter alternative is very improbable.

The concluding sentence of the Ode with reference to the 'Spirit of the Lord which does not lie,' is rightly parallelled by Harnack with the ἀψευδὴς θεός of Tit. i. 2, where notice again that it is immortality that is the gift involved in God's veracity ; 'the hope of eternal life is what God promised before the world began.'   The Christian doctrine of immortality is that ' God has given unto us eternal life, *and this life is in His Son'* (1 Joh. v. 11). I see no reason to erase the reference to the Sonship in the one case which might not be applied in the other: nor any breach of continuity in a reference to the Son in one case which might not be equally affirmed in the other.

It would, of course be unfair to discuss a great hypothesis like Harnack's from the standpoint of a single interpolation : the third Ode, for example, might be Christian and be at the same time, a thing apart : but in so far as common authorship in the main body of the Odes is conceded, the proof that one of them is Christian is a proof of the Christianity of the collection.

There are other cases of interpolation in the remaining Psalms where Harnack affirms it, which need to be examined in detail. For the present, however, let us keep to this third Ode, and discuss it in the light of another hypothesis which has been brought forward.

Professor Menzies of St Andrew's University has made a variation upon Harnack's original suggestions.   He feels on the one hand the difficulty of resort to interpolation, and on the other hand the general strength of the argument that these Odes are fundamentally Jewish.   Accordingly Menzies proposes in a striking article in the *Interpreter* to discard the theory of interpolation, and explain the apparently Christian allusions from the standpoint of Judaism.   Let the reference to the Son stand : but interpret the Son as the ideal Israel, in harmony with the doctrine of the Old Testament that Israel is God's first-born son, whom

He called out of Egypt, carried in the wilderness, &c.   The third Ode now reads as follows:

> Because I love Israel (the Son of God)
> I shall myself become an Israelite (i.e. a Son of God).

The language is that of a Jewish proselyte, who has come, as the Talmud says the disciples of Hillel did, 'under the wings of the Shekinah.' Professor Menzies affirms that this note of proselytism is characteristic of the Odes, and in that way having turned the argument to his own account which I made of the proselytism of the writer, he describes the whole collection by the name of *Psalms of the Proselytes*. The advantage of this new hypothesis is obvious; it gets rid of the resort to interpolations and restores to the collection a substantial unity; it mediates between the Jewish mystics of Harnack and my own Judæo-Christian proselyte author, by the suggestion of the Jewish proselytes, and it opens up before the imagination a field of spiritual life in connexion with the propaganda of Judaism, which is almost entirely a *terra incognita*.

As I want to do justice to Professor Menzies' argument, I will try to show how it may be made to illuminate certain other passages, and in particular, let us look a little closer into this same Ode.   In the earlier part of the Ode we find the following statement:

> Ode 3. *v.* 5.   I love the Beloved and my soul loves Him;
> *v.* 6.   And where His rest is, there also am I.
> *v.* 7.   And I shall be no stranger there,
> For with the Lord Most High and Merciful, there is no grudging.

Evidently the writer is speaking of spiritual privileges into which he has been introduced by God's grace and liberality. What is this divine Rest of which he speaks? It seems natural to refer to the terms in which God's dwelling in the Sanctuary is spoken of in the Old Testament, such as Ps. cxxxii. 14, 'Here is *my rest*, here will I dwell, for I have desired it': or Ps. cxxxii. 8, 'Arise, O Lord, into *thy rest*, thou and the ark of thy strength,' or to Isaiah lxvi. 1, 'What house will ye build me, or what is the place of my rest?' God's rest is, then, the Jewish temple[1];

---

[1] We might compare Isho'dad on John xiv. 1; 'He calls mansions...the abiding rests; because all rests and enjoyments are ours in dwellings.'

and the writer of the Ode is expressing the privilege which he has obtained by his proselytism, of passing beyond the middle wall of partition, from the Court of the Gentiles to the Court of the Israelites. It is precisely the situation which St Paul describes in spiritual language in Eph. ii. 19,

> ' *Ye are no more strangers* and sojourners, but fellow-citizens of the saints, and of the household of God...the whole building groweth to *an holy temple* in the Lord.'

The reference to the Sanctuary, however it is to be explained, is a mark of the third Ode, just as it is in the much-disputed Ode which follows it. And if in the third Ode the Sanctuary (whether spiritual or literal) is the place of God's rest, in the fourth Ode, it is forcibly described as the place of God's heart. For it is God's promise to *Solomon* that 'my eyes *and my heart* shall be there continually' (2 Chron. vii. 16) which is responsible for the curious expression, 'Thou hast given Thy heart to thy believers.' Here again we see that the Temple is in the view (whether near or far) of the writer.

These instances will suffice to show the strength of Prof. Menzies' hypothesis. It enables us, as we have said, to avoid interpolation ; it emphasises the language of the proselyte which had been previously detected in the Odes; and it makes it unnecessary to explain away, as so many have done, the evident affection of the writer for the actual temple at Jerusalem[1].

I have discussed this particular Ode at length in order to give a clear idea of the theory of Prof. Menzies and the way it mediates between Prof. Harnack's view and my own. The difficulty in accepting it lies in the fact that it does not explain many of the passages which Harnack had got rid of by the theory of interpolation. The simple case of the third Ode does not find parallels in the rest of the book. How, for example, would one read the Jewish proselyte into the following passage in which Harnack had conceded a Christian element ?

---

[1] This question of the reality of the allusions to the Temple comes up most definitely in the 4th Ode, where it has to be discussed. If we do not allow a real reference to the Temple, as I am disposed to maintain, we must say with Zahn (*Die Oden Salomos*, p. 753) 'Dadurch wird klar, dass er nicht an ein von Menschenhänden bereitetes Gotteshaus mit Vorhöfen und Altären denkt, wie der alte Psalmist, sondern an ein geistliches Haus.'

Ode 31. (He opened His mouth and spake grace and joy:
And He spake a new song of praise to His name:
And He lifted up His voice to the Most High,
And offered to Him the sons that were with him.   Cf. Joh.
And His face was justified, for them had His holy Father xvii., Heb.
                                                          ii. 13.
given Him.)
Come forth, ye that have been afflicted.

Surely Harnack must be right in marking this passage as Christian: and unless the whole Ode is to be counted Christian, an interpolation must be assumed. There is no place for a Jewish proselyte here.

It seems, then, that the amendment moved by Professor Menzies to Harnack's interpretation is not of sufficient scope to cover the difficult passages. In some respects it is a brilliant suggestion, but it is inadequate. In one feature it is, I believe, nearer to the truth than Harnack's own exposition, in that it realised the traces of proselytism which are in the Odes. These are hardly appreciated by Harnack. For example, he passes very rapidly by the allusions to the Creation that does not keep Sabbath (with its obvious consequence in the de-sabbatizing of proselytes). Harnack has brushed this argument on one side, too hastily as I think, and others have followed him. His argument is as follows: the words 'do not keep sabbath' in the illustrative sentence quoted from Justin have nothing corresponding to them in the Ode; and therefore an anti-judaic polemic is not to be thought of. In fact the Ode is, like others, of Jewish origin. Upon which I remark, that the Sabbath is involved in the previous sentence that 'God rested from all his works,' and therefore a definite Sabbatic reference with regard to the motion of the luminaries was not required: and further there is no doubt that the reference to the motion of Sun, Moon and Stars on the Sabbath day is one of the chief anti-judaic arguments of the early Church. For example, take Gregory of Nyssa, *Testimonia adversus Judaeos*, 13, in a section headed περὶ τοῦ σαββατίζειν and we find that the argument against the Sabbath concludes with these words:

πῶς δὲ ἥλιος καὶ σελήνη καὶ ἄστρα τὸν
ὡρισμένον δρόμον ἐκτελεῖ καὶ τῷ σαββάτῳ;

The writer is using up earlier material in the shape of anti-judaic testimonies: and the parallelism between this particular testimony and the language of the sixteenth Ode is so striking that we must convict the Ode of an anti-judaic tendency.

Harnack fails also, as I did to some extent myself, to emphasise and interpret the repeated allusion to a circumcision that was spiritual and not carnal. It is not sufficient in such a connexion to say that circumcision of the heart is a common-place of the Old Testament and of the prophets. Why does the writer introduce it, not in the manner of exhortation, but as a personal experience, unless he is speaking *more proselytorum*? The ordinary Jewish mystic (supposing the species to have been discovered) is not likely to break out into song on this note.

Then the references made by the Odist to his being of another race need a closer examination. In Ode 41 Harnack isolates the remarkable passage contained in vv. 8—10, as an interpolation; but while admitting that the passage reminds one of the 'new creature in Christ' of whom Paul speaks, he makes the strange statement that the interpolator this time is a Jew. This Jewish interpolator is followed by a Christian interpolator in the passage from v. 12 to the end ('The Saviour who makes alive and does not reject our souls, the man who was humbled' &c.). It would surely have been simpler to admit that the language was that of a proselyte, and not to make this fantastic variation from the original Jewish author to a second Jewish interpolator, followed in his turn by a Christian annotator. The solution is too cumbrous to be the real one: but this must not be allowed to prejudice our judgment in other cases, in which the dissecting knife appears to be used with extraordinary skill. Whatever the final judgment may be as to the value of Harnack's solution, there can be no doubt that it is criticism of a very high order.

I now turn to a third hypothesis, in some ways more remarkable than either the doubtful one of Harnack or the rejected one of Menzies. In the *Journal of Theological Studies* for October 1910, Dean Bernard has launched the theory that these Odes are not Jewish (whether mystic or proselyte) nor Judæo-Christian, but simply Christian; that they are songs of newly-baptized persons, or proper to be sung over such, and that they belong to a much later date than has been supposed. Bernard suggests 150 A.D., which is the time to which Zahn and others would refer them, but I gather from him privately that he thinks this date too early, and is rather disposed to press the close of the second century as their time of composition. In some respects this solution has points of contact with Professor Menzies, for Psalms of the Baptized is a Christian way of writing Psalms of the Proselytes, in the period when baptism was adult baptism, and in that sense every believer was a proselyte. Bernard's hypothesis, however, sweeps away all that Harnack has said on the subject, and a good deal of my own reasoning. For it is clear that if the date be far on in the second century, all references to a pre-Johannine school of Christian or of Jewish thought may be swept on one side. At such a date the parallelisms with St John are equivalent to quotations, and no other explanation needs to be made of them. We are not likely to find the missing link in the ancestry of St John's Gospel from a Christian semi-liturgical book of songs at the end of the second century.

What, then, are the reasons from which Dr Bernard proceeds? For it must be said at once that the case is argued with such learning and force as to make the article to which we refer the most remarkable that has yet appeared. The case is as follows. Bernard points out that a number of striking passages in the Odes can be at once illustrated from the early baptismal rituals. For example, it seems certain that in the early Syrian Church and in the closely associated Armenian Church, baptized persons were arrayed in white robes, and crowns, or garlands, were placed on their heads. The white raiment is well known, but the crowns, which are not a feature of Western religion, as far as it is known to us, have been lost sight of. It is these crowns, according to Bernard, that are alluded to in such passages as the first Ode, ' The Lord is on my head like a crown, and I shall not be separated from Him.' The same figure recurs in the 5th, 9th, 17th and 20th Odes. The white garments are also exactly parallelled by the allusions in the Odes to the putting on of brightness or clothing oneself with light. In the Odes this bright raiment is spoken of as an exchange for ' the coat of skin' in the third chapter of Genesis ; and Dr Bernard shows that this very allusion is found in the early descriptions of Baptism, as, for instance, in the following passage from Jerome,

'Praeceptis Dei lavandi sumus, et cum, parati ad indumentum Christi, tunicas pelliceas deposuerimus, tunc induemur veste linea, nihil in se mortis habente, sed tota candida.' (Ep. ad Fabiolam, LXIV. 20.)

Dr Bernard goes on to argue that the Odes also contemplate Baptism when they refer to the 'Seal' on the one hand, and to the 'Living Water' on the other. With regard to the 'Seal,' Dr Bernard thinks he has a less strong case for identification with Baptism than with regard to the 'Living Water.' I think he entirely underestimates the value of his own argument, when he says that the references to the Seal are 'few in number, and their meaning is not as clear as is that of the Living Water.' The history of the 'Seal' is obscure, nor can it easily be said when it passed from being a mark of ownership to a sacramental sign, but that it did become a talisman is certain, and there is much to be said for the belief that this talismanic virtue of baptism is reflected upon the language of the Odes. For example, in the *Acts of Paul and Thecla* the talismanic force of baptism is implied in Thecla's words to Paul, 'Give me only the sign of God, and no temptation shall touch me.' But this is exactly parallel to Ode 4. 7, 8,

'Who is there that shall put on thy grace and be hurt? For thy seal is known &c.'

Another curious illustration may be taken from Cyprian's *Testimonia* (II. 10) where Cyprian explains that Goliath was killed by a blow on his forehead *because his head had not been sealed.* '*By this seal we also are always safe and live*[1].'

There is, therefore, much to be said for Dr Bernard's contention that the 'seal' in the Odes does sometimes refer to baptism, even if it should not turn out to be always used in this sense.

But it is just at this point that the difficulty of the interpretation lies: while it may be freely granted that the ascription of talismanic virtue to the waters of baptism is early, and that it becomes almost universal (as may be seen by its prevalence even to the present day), it must not be overlooked that *the Seal and its talismanic value are also both pre-Christian.* We need only turn

---

[1] See also a similar reference from Lactantius on p. 80 *infra.*

to the Psalms of Solomon in support of this statement. Thus in Psalms of Solomon xv. 8, we are told that 'the sign of the Lord is upon the righteous for their salvation'; and in the same way in xv. 10, 'the mark of perdition is upon the forehead (of sinners).' Granted that this may be based on the signing and sealing in the ninth chapter of Ezekiel, it is nevertheless clear that Ezekiel could be interpreted, and actually was interpreted, mystically before Christian baptism was even thought of. We must there-fore be on our guard against reading back a late baptismal gnosis into early Christian or Jewish records.

An even more remarkable case for the need of caution occurs in Bernard's identification of the dragon with seven heads in Ode 22. 5. This dragon is supposed to be latent in the waters of baptism, as originally in the river Jordan, according to a passage in Job (xi. 18) where Leviathan will take the Jordan into his mouth; Bernard quotes appropriately from Cyril of Jerusalem, *Catecheses* iii. 11:

> ὁ δράκων ἦν ἐν τοῖς ὕδασι κατὰ τὸν Ἰώβ, ὁ δεχόμενος τὸν Ἰορδάνην ἐν τῷ στόματι αὐτοῦ.

To the various allusions to this dragon who lurks in the midst of the waters which Bernard collects from the Eastern Baptismal rituals, I add the following passage of Bar Ṣalibi from his commentary on Matthew[1]:

> 'Baptizatus est...ut confringeret caput draconis spiritalis qui in aquis reptabat, quem etiam olim immersit per Pharaonem.'

Here is again the dragon lurking in the water of Jordan whose head is broken when Christ is baptized: and I find that Bar Ṣalibi has taken this passage from an earlier Syriac writer, Moses Bar Kepha; for in a MS. of that writer in my possession, in which the meaning of baptism is discussed, there occurs the following passage:

> ܒܕ̈ܝܢ ܢܝܐܝ ܕܒܬܘ ܘܐܝܬܝܗ ܐܬܚܝܕܬܐ ܡܛܠ ܡܟܐ ܕ̣ܘ ܘ ܕܐ̣ܪܣ ܣܐܒ ܘ ܟܦܩܗ ܩܦܣܐ ܒܓܘ ܡܝ̈ܐ ܩܣܘܡ.

i.e. 'And again, it was in order that he might bruise the head of the spiritual dragon because he lurked in the waters: in the

---

[1] *l.c.* in trans. p. 98.

same way as erst he typically drowned that dragon, by means of Pharaoh the Egyptian, in the Red Sea.' In this way Bernard's argument is re-inforced, so far as the belief is affirmed (especially the belief of Oriental Christians) that the devil lurks in the waters of baptism, and requires to have his head broken (i) by Christ, (ii) by the insufflation and chrism of the water.

But here again caution would be wise; for the dragon with seven heads is not a Christian conception arrived at by applying baptismal gnosis to the Old Testament; we see him again in the *Psalms of Solomon*, where by almost every critic he is recognised as the equivalent of Pompey and not of the devil or his counterpart the Leviathan of Job: he appears also in the Apocalypse certainly at a time anterior to the development of any baptismal gnosis: and when we look more closely at the language of the twenty-second Ode, we get quite a different kind of dragon from the mystical one of Bernard (*Draco aquatilis Bernardi*). He is indeed a water-snake; but his nearest zoological representative lies in quite another direction than the book of Job or even the ninety-first Psalm. For this dragon has a *wicked poison* which has to be eliminated, and *when his heads have been broken, the roots have to be destroyed*. So it is a *bona fide* hydra which is in the imagination of the Odist. One has only to recall the story of Hercules and the Lernaean Hydra, the battle with the hydra-heads, the searing of the roots, and the ravages wrought by the poison of the creature, to make it a fair suggestion that Bernard has mistaken the species, and that what he saw was really a *Hydra spiritalis Harrisii*, an older form zoologically than the ecclesiastical specimen to which Dr Bernard introduced us. The baptismal metaphors may turn out to have been borrowed from an earlier stratum of Christian thought, as well as from the Old Testament.

Perhaps the most striking of Dr Bernard's illustrations will be found in the quotations which he brings to bear on the obscurities at the beginning of the 24th Ode, where the abysses cry out with terror at the Baptism of the Lord. Dr Bernard observes that ' all Eastern Baptismal rites bring in the idea that the waters were terrified at the coming of Christ for Baptism.' The Scriptural basis for this belief is Ps. lxvii. 17, 18, 'The waters saw thee and were afraid, the abysses were troubled.' Bernard gives many striking patristic and liturgical parallels for these beliefs ; and, taken all together, they make a very strong impression.   His whole argument must be carefully studied.   I have only touched on a few points in the briefest manner.

If it should turn out that there is good ground for Dr Bernard's contention, the whole question of the date will have to be re-considered, and, in part, the history of the baptismal rite will have to be re-written. It will not follow, even then, that the date of the Odes is as late as Dr Bernard suggests.   Take, for instance, the single point, which he so forcibly expounds, that the baptized in early ritual wore crowns.   A reference to Hermas will show that there was a controversy in the early Church of the West as to whether baptized people should be crowned or not, and it is decided in the negative, because the crown belongs properly to the Martyrs.   Thus in Similitude VIII (the great willow) the angel gives slips of willow to be planted by the believers, and scrutinizes the result of the planting.   Those who put forth shoots and bring forth fruit are crowned with garlands of palm. Those who put forth shoots without fruit are not crowned ; but all alike have the white raiment and the seal.   The meaning of this is that all baptized people are not crowned ; the crown belongs to the martyrs, 'those who have wrestled with the devil and overcome him.'   And the suggestion arises that the garlanding of baptized people which Dr Bernard detects in the Eastern rituals was discontinued in the West at a very early period, or never definitely adopted.

Something of the same kind goes on with regard to another form of honour.   The Odist speaks of becoming one of the men on the right hand, whatever may be covered by that term (cf. Ode 19, 'They who receive in its fulness are the ones on the right hand'). And in the Visions of Hermas we have a scene in which he wishes to sit at the right hand of the Church, but is refused that position, because that place belongs to those who have actually suffered for the name.   So Hermas (see the account in Vis. III) has to sit on the left hand.   It seems clear that there has been a transfer of some kind of honour from the ordinary believers to the Martyrs.   The case is like the previous one.

I should not, therefore, be surprised to find that Bernard's case for a late dating of the Odes will have, even from his own point of view, to be revised.   He will certainly be in difficulties over the interpretation of the references to the Sanctuary in the fourth Ode, which are too definite and too Jewish to be got rid of. Perhaps we shall see more clearly the essential Judaism of this Ode, if we examine a little more closely the proof of the unchangeableness of the Sanctuary which the Rabbis deduce from Exod. xv. 17. We shall be able to show that this passage of Exodus was actually in the mind of the writer, and that he is commenting on the following sequence:

εἰσαγαγὼν καταφύτευσον αὐτοὺς εἰς ὅρος κληρονομίας σου.
εἰς ἕτοιμον κατοικητήριόν σου ὃ κατηρτίσω, Κύριε.
ἁγίασμα, Κύριε, ὃ ἡτοίμασαν αἱ χεῖρές σου.
Κύριος βασιλεύων τὸν αἰῶνα καὶ ἐπ᾽ αἰῶνα καὶ ἔτι.

Let us see how Philo would comment on this passage: the treatise *De Plantatione* § 47 sqq. introduces the text as above: he begins with an explanation in terms of the Stoic philosophy, that the highest life is that which is in accordance with nature and that this is what is meant by being planted in the mountain of the Lord's inheritance. He then reverts from his philosophical speculations to the earlier doctrine that the sanctuary was made, as a reflexion from holy things, an imitation of an archetype; after which he continues as follows:

'But in order that no one should suppose *that the Creator has need of any of the things that are made*, he subjoins the following most necessary addition, "Reigning for eternity and beyond eternity," for *a king is in need of no one, but his subjects are in everything in need of him!*'

It will be seen that this at once explains why the Ode which began with 'No man changeth thy holy place,' should go on with 'Thou hast given us thy fellowship, it was not that thou wast in need of us, but that we are in need of thee.'

Philo and the Odist are both working over the same Rabbinical gnosis on the fifteenth chapter of Exodus. And it is from the Jewish side of Philo's mind and not from the Hellenistic and philosophical, that the parallel is made. We see, then, that it is right to ascribe a Jewish background to the fourth Ode. In fact, the weak point of Bernard's argument lies just there, that the Jewish background of the Odes is too patent to be neglected. The ultimate origin of the coats of light in place of coats of skin must be Jewish: the mere allegorisation of Genesis by Christian hands·is insufficient to explain a belief which, as I have shown, can be illustrated from the great Jewish and leading Gnostic teachers, and is perpetuated in the Kabbala and in folk-lore. *A Christian allegorisation of Genesis cannot be responsible for all this.* At the same time, it is well known that all the early Christian teachers used up Genesis by the way of gnosis and allegory in their teachings of redemption by Christ.

In this way it will be seen that Jewish expositions are necessary to the right understanding of the references to the unchangeable sanctuary, whatever meaning be attached to it: even if a reference to Jerusalem's fortunes be denied or to any other temple, the explanation of the fixity of the sanctuary is to be sought in Jewish writers, as I think I have pointed out.

While I am writing on this point a remarkable confirmation comes to light of the early belief in the pre-existence of the Sanctuary at Jerusalem, and its consequent inviolability, which I hold to underlie the language of the opening verses of the fourth Ode. In an odd quarter, too, the evidence alluded to makes its appearance. The last number of *Anthropos* (Heft i. 1911) contains an account by the Carmelite father Anastase Marie, of Bagdad, of his recovery of the sacred books of the Yezidees from their hiding place in the mountain of Sinjar, in the Mesopotamian plane between Mosul and Aleppo, about due south from Mardin. These Yezidees, commonly known as devil-worshippers, appear to have been originally devoted to the worship of the Demiurgos as against that of the true God, and they represent the survival of an early Oriental sect, perhaps of Jewish origin. For however much they may disown the Jews in these newly-found documents, and affirm their racial priority to them, it is clear that they believed in the pre-existence of Jerusalem, as the following passage will show:

Yezidi Black-book (*Anthropos l.c.* p. 37):

XVII. 'The Lord then descended to Jerusalem, and ordered Gabriel to bring a little earth from the four cardinal points of the earth[1]. He did so. To this earth he added air, fire and water, and thus created the first man. He gave him a soul, taken from his own almightiness. He ordered Gabriel to put Adam in Paradise, etc.'

[1] Which four points are, according to early Fathers, latent in the four letters of the name of Adam.

Here the pre-existence of Jerusalem to the creation of man is clearly involved. We have an excellent parallel to the doctrine that 'thy holy place thou didst design before thou didst make (other) places[1].'

All of this makes a late date impossible, nor will the position of honour given to the Odes in the *Pistis Sophia* be explicable, unless the early date of the Odes be conceded, or unless Dr Bernard succeeds in lowering the date of the *Pistis Sophia* as well as that of the Odes.

I have stated Bernard's case rapidly, with inevitable omission of many of his striking parallels and illustrations, and without trying to break the force of his criticism by drawing attention to its exaggerations. Dr Bernard does not seem to be aware (or was not aware, until I drew his attention to it) that his case had been anticipated. In a series of articles published in *Die Reformation* Dr Diettrich had anticipated Bernard in detecting references to baptismal customs and had equally anticipated Harnack in the assumption of a Jewish background for the Odes. In the first of the series of articles, published as far back as May 1910, Diettrich held that the later stratum was definitely Christian and the earlier was Essene ; but, after the first article was out, he had read Harnack's criticisms and reviewed the whole matter more closely, coming to the conclusion that the later Odist was not an orthodox Christian but that he belonged to a little-known group of Eastern heretics whom Diettrich proposed to identify. It is unfortunate that the separate articles appeared in such an out-of-the-way corner, and that they were too summarily set aside as fantastic by those German critics who read them. Diettrich had the advantage, from his studies on the *Nestorian Baptismal Liturgy*, of recognizing any parallels that might exist between the Odes and the Ritual, just as Bernard was helped by Conybeare's publication of the *Ritual of the Armenians*. Moreover, his excellent Syriac scholarship contributes frequently to the right understanding of the meaning of some difficult passages. Whether Bernard and Diettrich have reached the final explanation of the parallels between the Odes and the Eastern Rituals is the matter that has now to be decided. In a recent criticism in the *Theol. Tijdschrift* Mr Lake

---

[1] Is it possible that the original language of the Ode was 'thy holy place thou didst design *before thou madest man*'?

has thrown out, independently, the same suggestion as Diettrich
and Bernard, that the Odes are not a case of 'Mystic' but of
'Sacramental Mystic'; that is the problem that at present is
before us.   The remaining question, after this problem is solved,
will be the residual Judaism of the Odes.   If Bernard is right
that the Odes are all Christian, and late as well as Christian, the
Jewish background has to be denied or explained away: if
Diettrich is right that the Odes are strongly coloured by
Essenism, then much of Bernard's argument will be weakened;
the 'white robes' in which the singer is assumed to be clad, will
be Essene drapery, and the songs before sunrise, which Bernard
refers to the Easter baptisms, will be illustrated from the well-
known solar adorations of the ascetics of the Jordan valley and
the Dead Sea.   I reserve my own judgment as to whether such
explanations are at all required.   They may all be vitiated by
over-subtlety.   I do not, however, wish to spoil so interesting a
debate by summing it up prematurely.

Of the many other tracts and discussions which have
hitherto appeared, it must suffice to refer briefly to two or
three.

The revision of the Syriac text by Schulthess in Preuschen's
Zeitschrift is excellent, and contains some of the best things
that have been said linguistically and with reference to the
translation.   I am pleased to find that, while recognizing the
excellence of Flemming's translation (as I myself am forward
to do) he points out that my renderings are not always to be
rejected for Flemming's.   Some of the differences between us
were due to unfortunate misprints or transcriptions, which I
have done my best to remove in the present edition.   With
Schulthess should be taken the valuable reviews of my book
and of Harnack's by Wellhausen in the *Göttingische gelehrte
Anzeigen* for September 1910.   As was to be expected, the
criticism of the text is searching and the interpretations pro-
posed are acute.   W. will not allow that the Odes are Jewish;
even the reference to the unchangeable sanctuary is to be
treated as ideal, and the Odes furnish no definite historical date.
They know nothing of the Law, but only of the yoke of Love.
Their idea of God is as un-Jewish as possible; the initiation
by circumcision is replaced by that through the Spirit.   The
community to which the writer belongs is grounded on inward,

rather than outward, fellowship. The transitions in the Odes from the speaking believer to the speaking Christ are illustrated by Bacchic parallels. While the Odes are as little to be classed as Gnostic as the Fourth Gospel itself, they show some Gnostic tendencies, and W. suggests that we might compare the Mandaean hymns, which I have not yet been able to do.

A number of other criticisms lie before me. In the same number of Preuschen's *Zeitschrift* to which I have referred for Schulthess' discussion of the text of the Odes, there will be found an article by Spitta (one of several which he has written), in which, according to his *métier*, he dissects the Odes into Jewish and Christian elements, and arrives independently at conclusions not differing very widely from those of Harnack. This is followed by a very interesting article by Gunkel, who discards Harnack's hypothesis in favour of a reference to a heretical Christian sect, to which there was a secret initiation, as betrayed by the language of Ode 8, which Bernard explains by the theory of *disciplina arcani*. Finally Preuschen himself promises to prove that the Odes are the work of the great Gnostical Mystic Valentinus. It is not difficult to imagine some of the arguments that will be brought forward. It is clear that it will be some time before these investigations are concluded and the final grains of truth gathered from the miscellaneous heap of opinions.

Meanwhile, we ought not to lose sight of the spiritual value of the recovered document, which cannot be seriously affected by the variety of the solutions that may be offered as to the time and place of its production. Dr A. C. Headlam's article in the *Church Quarterly Review*, which has just come to my hands, expresses this duty, in a very able and sympathetic discussion.

SUPPLEMENTARY NOTE ON RECENT CRITICISMS.

In the pages that precede I have attempted to give some view of the critical debate that has been in progress with regard to the right interpretation and correct chronology of the Odes. It has been difficult to obtain a correct representation of what is really a moving picture. As I left the matter in the foregoing summary Dr A. C. Headlam's article in the *Church Quarterly Review* had just appeared and had delighted me by its appreciation of the spiritual value of my book of songs, and by its just handling of many of the points that had to be decided. It also seemed to me to be very judicious in its estimate of what one may call the Baptismal Parallels of Dean Bernard, for while recognising much that was forcible in the criticism, Headlam also suggested that the elevated tone of the writer's experience implied a certain priority over the highly evolved Gnosis to which Bernard drew attention. The baptismal cult was, in fact, reposing upon an earlier stratum, and there was no need to chronologically depress the Odes to the level, say, of the Nestorian Liturgy. As the Odes themselves would say, "That which is earlier shall not be changed by those that are younger than itself." Dr Headlam's actual language is as follows.

"The writer of the Odes is thinking primarily of the new life he is experiencing and not of Baptism. No doubt he had been baptized. No doubt Baptism may have provided language to express his own spiritual experience, but it is not of Baptism that he is thinking. Further, in some cases this reference to Baptism is forced and unreal. It would be far truer to say that language which is here as elsewhere used of the Christian life as a whole was quite naturally introduced into baptismal services and songs and so obtained a specialized. use. This particular development of his theory on which Dr Bernard insists is probably more than doubtful."

There has also just reached me an article by S. Reinach in the *Revue de l'Histoire les Religions* (*Annales du Musée Guimet*) for 1910, in which there is contained a brilliant survey of the question of the Odes, expressed with the acuteness and insight that one would naturally expect from such a quarter. I have no wish to re-analyse the analysis of M. Reinach, but there is one passage in which he appears to say something like what we just now quoted from Headlam. On p. 15 of the reprinted article which M. Reinach has kindly sent me, after discussing Bernard's hypothesis in detail, he says:

> "Dans l'hypothèse où les Odes de Salomon auraient été adoptées par l'Église chrétienne, ou par telle partie judaïsante de cette Église, on comprendrait que cette littérature dont le mérite n'est pas médiocre, eût exercé de l'influence sur le langage métaphorique usité pour le sacrement de baptême."

If I understand this rightly, it runs parallel to Dr Headlam's suggestion, but at the same time runs farther, into the *terra incognita* of the history of baptismal symbols, and into a branch of literature that corresponds to it, and is itself equally unknown. M. Reinach does not commit himself to any definite position, but makes a half promise that when the translators have come to some closer agreement as to the rendering, and the interpreters are a little nearer to one another and to the meaning, he may return to the subject again. As far as I am concerned, he will be sure of a hearty welcome.

It is clear that M. Reinach is right that we have to go a good way in the acceptance of the Bernard parallels ("les ressemblances si ingénieusement signalées"). Accordingly I pick up the threads of the argument again, and turn once more to the loom.

It was suggested a little way back that the treatment of the dragon with seven heads was too exclusively made from the standpoint of the Baptismal ritual, and that there was in the figure a pre-Christian origin (as shown by the Psalms of Solomon) and perhaps a pagan parallel of great antiquity, for which the closest correspondence would be found in the Lernaean Hydra of Hercules. This, at all events, helped us to explain the destruction of the wicked poison of the dragon, and of his roots. Thus there would be more dragons involved than the

Leviathan who would swallow up the Jordan, or the Pharaoh who pursues the Israelites in the Red Sea.

To be quite fair to Bernard's hypothesis, we will show that the *virus* of the dragon in the midst of the waters was actually exorcised in the waters of baptism, according to early Christian belief, and we shall also suggest that the dragon in the Jordan still exists in the local folk-lore.

For the first of these points it is sufficient to refer to Cyprian *Ep.* lxviii (Hartel, p. 764), where Cyprian says definitely:

> "diaboli nequitiam pertinacem usque ad aquam salutarem ualere, in baptismo autem *omne nequitiae suae uirus* amittere, quod exemplum cernimus in rege Pharaone":

here we have the baptismal parallel to the language of Ode 22 "Thy right hand destroyed his wicked poison." Cyprian continues with the argument that serpents and dragons lose their poison when they pass from dry places into waters:

> "nam si scorpii et serpentes qui in sicco praeualent, in aquam praecipitati praeualere possunt sua uenena retinere, possunt et spiritus nequam, qui scorpii et serpentes appellantur et tamen per nos data a Domino potestate calcantur, permanere ultra in hominis corpore, in quo baptizato et sanctificato incipit spiritus sanctus habitare."

Perhaps this contribution to the history of the virus of the dragon may not be unacceptable to Dr Bernard.

The second point, as to the existence of a folk-lore belief in the dragon that lurks in the Jordan, was gathered from my own experience. I was one day, when travelling in the East, planning to rid myself of the discomforts of travel by a bath in the Jordan, the river being at that time in flood. It was certainly a dangerous experiment, even for a good swimmer, and I was deterred from it by the natives who used, amongst other more valid arguments, the statement that there was a whale in the waters into which I proposed to plunge. The whale was, of course, the Biblical *tannin* (Arabic *tinîn*), and can be equated with *serpent* or *dragon* or *sea-monster*. The Palestinian folk-lore, therefore, retains the belief that there is a dragon in the Jordan. I have no means of deciding whether this belief is older or younger than the belief of the baptismal rituals: but it should certainly be connected with it.

In order to test Bernard's hypothesis more closely, for the value of a hypothesis depends on the number of things it explains, I propose to try whether it will help us to understand the very difficult thirty-eighth Ode.

The opening of this perplexing and discontinuous Ode has perplexity and discontinuity of its own:

"I went up into the light of truth as if into a chariot:
And the truth took me and led me and guided me across pits
and gulleys:
And from the rocks and the waves it preserved me:
And it became to me a haven of salvation."

Here we have a chariot flying across pits and ravines, after which we have, what is not usual in chariot riding, the risk of rocks and waves, and finally the chariot arrives—in harbour. This is perplexing. Is it impossible that the chariot can be a ship?

The Syriac word (markebā) which we have translated "chariot" does sometimes mean "ship," as the lexicons will show (v. Payne Smith *ad voc.*). This rendering is probably due to Arabic influence, for in Arabic *markab* means *inter alia* a ship (as a reference to the story of Sindbad the Sailor will show). Perhaps the Odes have been translated into Syriac at a later age than the golden age of Syriac literature, and then the word we are discussing is an Arabism. Let us, then, translate it as *ship*. We are now on the way to the rocks and waves and haven at the close of the passage. The "pits and ravines" must now be marine and not terrene: they are the gaping and yawning depths of the sea sailed over: so we translate:

"I went up into the light of Truth, as into a ship:
And the Truth took me and led me and guided me over the
hollows and yawning depths (of the sea):
From the rocks and the waves it preserved me:
And it became to me a haven of salvation."

That is certainly much more reasonable than going to sea in a chariot. The perplexity and discontinuity of the opening is gone.

But what is the ship? Does he mean the Ark? If so, we are again in contact with a baptismal symbol, for the earliest figure borrowed from the Old Testament to illustrate baptism is the Ark of Noah, in which few, that is eight, souls were saved by water (1 Pet. iii. 20).   And Justin carries on the argument by quoting (*Dial.* 138) a passage which he says comes from Isaiah, to the effect that God says to Jerusalem, "At the flood of Noah I saved thee": and this mystery of human salvation took place at the flood, says Justin.   We should, therefore, naturally expect that a person who is writing a book of baptismal hymns would not neglect the typology of the Ark of the Flood.

But here also the difficulty will be felt that the mode of criticism is perilously near the line of over-subtlety and unrestrained imagination.   A poet who was working up baptismal symbols would probably not neglect Noah's Ark, but would he express himself so obscurely? and would the "disciplina arcani" cover such obscurity?   Perhaps Dr Bernard will tell us when he writes next on the subject.

CORRECTION

P. 121, l. 33, *for* See Preface to this edition *read* See above, pp. xxv sq.

INTRODUCTION

The present volume contains an important addition to our knowledge of the literature which immediately anticipates or directly follows the time of Christ. It contains, on the one hand, a hitherto unknown version of the Psalms of Solomon, a collection which has often been studied, from the standpoints both of the higher and lower criticism, and which is, by common consent, referred to the middle of the first century B.C. ; and on the other hand it presents a new collection which I have called, for the sake of distinction, and in harmony with the references in ancient writers, by the name of the Odes of Solomon ; they are here edited and translated from a Syriac MS. in my own possession : and it will probably be no rash prediction to say that their value and antiquity will be at once recognized by students and critics, and that they will be assigned, either wholly or in part, to the first century of the Christian era. The reasons for this belief will appear presently, but, apart altogether from the question of a half-century more or less in the dating of a document, it lies outside controversy that the new Odes are marked by a vigour and exaltation of spiritual life, and a mystical insight, to which we can only find parallels in the most illuminated periods of the history of the Church. They differ, in this respect, by the whole breadth of the firmament, from the extant Psalms of Solomon, with which they are associated in our MS. In these there is little originality, and not much hope : the hard experiences through which Jerusalem passed at the hands of the Romans in the Invasion of Pompey have left a gloom over the sky even in the moments of temporary relief and in the time of exultation over the fall of the great oppressor : what life and light there is may be traced to the severe morality of the traditional Pharisees, and to the Messianic hopes for whose development their times of affliction were the appropriate and necessary nidus; and so far are they from religious originality in the expression of personal or national experience, that many of the Psalms in question are little more than centos and expansions from the canonical Hebrew Psalter. In the Odes, on the other hand, we have few quotations or adaptations from previous writings, whether Jewish or Christian ; there is little that can be traced to the Old Testament, almost nothing that is to be credited to the Gospels or other branches of the Christian literature. Their radiance is no reflection from the illumination of other days : their inspiration is first-hand and immediate ; it answers very well to the summary which Aristides made of the life of the early Christian Church when he described them as indeed 'a new people with whom something Divine is mingled.' They are thus altogether distinct from the extant Psalms of Solomon which are bound up with them in our MS. Whatever we may have to say of these latter is limited to the interest which arises in the discovery of an Eastern Version of a book whose Greek text is peculiarly difficult to edit, and whose original Hebrew text has altogether disappeared. We shall show that the new Syriac version is itself a translation of the Greek ; we shall point out in what ways, if any, it serves to the betterment of the Greek text, and whether it gives any assistance to the detection of the lost Hebrew text.

Our chief interest, however, will be with the Odes. We shall discuss the quotations and fragments of these which are found in early Christian writers : we shall try to determine the limits of time within which the composition of the Odes must lie, as well as the locality or Church from which they emanate : we shall try to find out also how they became attached to the Psalms, and whether they were originally composed in Greek ; and we shall add a brief commentary and notes to the Odes as translated. In this way we hope to clear up some perplexities in the historical tradition, while leaving, no doubt, a number of unsolved problems to those who shall follow after us.

The MS. from which our texts come is a paper one of quite
The Syriac a late period : its age may be between three and
MS. four hundred years : but as it is imperfect both at the beginning and ending, and so has lost both its preface and colophon, we cannot tell how it was described by the person who made the copy, nor can we say anything definite about the date. It has been lying on my shelves for some time, perhaps

for as long as two years, along with a heap of leaves from various Syriac MSS. written on paper, which came from the neighbourhood of the Tigris. In spite of its relatively late date, the text is a good one: it is carefully, if somewhat coarsely written, and is furnished with occasional vowels in the Nestorian manner, to which there have been added, probably by a later hand, sundry Greek vowels in the Jacobite manner. As we have said it is incomplete both at the beginning and the end: we can, however, make out pretty clearly what the original MS. was like.

The book is arranged in quires of ten leaves: of the first quire three leaves are missing: these three leaves contained the first and second Odes and the beginning of the third Ode. The Odes then run continuously till the fourth quire, where they stop on the verso of the fourth leaf: thus the Odes occupy roughly thirty-four leaves. Then the extant Psalms begin: they occupy the remaining six leaves of the fourth quire (say six leaves *plus*), the fifth quire, and the sixth quire, of which the last leaf is gone, *plus* whatever was needed to complete the book from a seventh quire: and since the extant portion of the Psalms in our Syriac MS. takes us up to Ps. xvii. 38 there is not much to add from a seventh quire. Suppose we say that the Psalms occupied twenty-six leaves, and that three more leaves are required to complete the text, we have then approximately

> Odes = 34 leaves
> Psalms = 28 leaves
> or Psalms and Odes = 62 leaves[1].

Now let us turn to the accounts given us by ancient writers Psalms of the extent of the books in question: first of all and Odes we know that the 18 Psalms of Solomon once compared. stood in the great Codex Alexandrinus: for in the index to the MS. we find as follows:

> Ἀποκάλυψις Ἰωάννου
> Κλήμεντος ἐπιστολὴ αʹ
> Κλήμεντος ἐπιστολὴ βʹ
> ὁμοῦ βιβλία—
> Ψαλμοὶ Σολομῶντος ιηʹ.

[1] I have made a slight correction here, following Harnack's estimate of the missing matter.

Here the eighteen Psalms stand just outside the accepted Christian books of the N.T., in the very penumbra of canonicity. Next turn to the *Synopsis Sanctae Scripturae* which passes under the name of Athanasius: here we find as follows, after the enumeration of the *Antilegomena* of the Old Testament:

σὺν ἐκείνοις δὲ καὶ ταῦτα ἠρίθμηνται·

Μακκαβαϊκὰ βιβλία δ'

Πτολεμαϊκά

Ψαλμοὶ καὶ ᾠδὴ [l. ᾠδαὶ][1] Σολομῶντος

Σώσαννα.

Here we find the Psalms in the company of the Odes, and forming a part of the disputed writings of the Old Testament: from the supplementary manner in which they are introduced, following an unknown book on Egyptian history, we may perhaps describe their position as the penumbra of uncanonicity, or, rather of deuterocanonicity. The Psalms and Odes are here (say in the sixth century) definitely grouped together.

Next take the Stichometry of Nicephorus, the Patriarch of Constantinople in the beginning of the ninth century: here we find as follows:

1. Three books of Maccabees.
2. The Wisdom of Solomon.
3. Ecclesiasticus.
4. The Psalms and Odes of Solomon, containing 2100 verses (στίχοι ͵βρ').
5. Esther.
6. Judith.
7. Susanna.
8. Tobit.

Here we find our two books again grouped together, and very well placed amongst the Apocrypha of the Old Testament: they do not seem to have lost any dignity between the sixth and ninth centuries; and they have been carefully measured, after the manner of books which are likely to be transcribed and whose contents must therefore be estimated on some recognized scale.

---

[1] Zahn tries to justify the singular, by reference to the LXX. of 1 K. viii. 53 οὐκ ἰδοὺ αὕτη γέγραπται ἐν βιβλίῳ τῆς ᾠδῆς;

In the same connexion we have a list of books which is found attached to the *Quaestiones et Responsiones* of Anastasius the Sinaite, and is commonly known as the Catalogue of the Sixty Books. After the sixty canonical books, we have a list of nine deuterocanonical books, and then a list of twenty-five definitely apocryphal writings; amongst these last we find

    8. Ἀνάληψις Μωϋσέως.

    9. Ψαλμοὶ Σολομῶντος.

    10. Ἡλίου ἀποκάλυψις. etc.

Here we cannot be certain whether Psalms means Psalms and Odes, nor is any estimate made of the extent of the composition. The book is not in such good company as it is in the Catalogue of Nicephorus.

Assuming the correctness of the statement that the Odes and Psalms contain 2100 verses, let us now turn **Stichometry.** to the Greek texts of the eighteen Psalms, and see what the scribes say about their compass. The Vatican MS. (Cod. R of Gebhardt's edition of the Psalms) says that the book contains στί ψν' : the Copenhagen MS. (Cod. H) says ἔπη ͵α ; and the Paris MS. (Cod. P) says ἔπη τριάκοντα. Here, as Gebhardt says, Cod. P has misread Δ as Λ'; so we have two statements as to the length of the book. One statement says *verses*, the other *verses of Homer*, but since that is what verses mean in a stichometric reckoning, there is no discrepancy here except in the numbers. If we imagine that the scribe of Cod. R has misread the sign for 900, ϡ, as ψ, we have 950 verses for R, which agrees closely with the reckoning in Cod. H. Suppose we say then that the 18 Psalms equal 950 verses. But then we are told by Nicephorus that the Psalms and Odes together make 2100 verses: we have then the ratio of Odes to Psalms 1150 to 950 or 23 to 19. Our estimate of the relative lengths in the Syriac was 34 to 28 or 17 to 14. The former estimate is 1·21 to 1, the latter 1·21 to 1, which is so exact as to make the verification that our new Odes are those of which Nicephorus and the other Canonists speak, so far as statistics can make the demonstration.

It will be observed that Nicephorus has divided the Solomonic literature into two parts, the Canonical books, viz.: Proverbs, Ecclesiastes and Canticles, and the Antilegomena which include the Wisdom of Solomon, perhaps Ecclesiasticus, and the Psalms and Odes of Solomon; that is, there are three canonical books of Solomon, and at least two sub-canonical books. We put it in that way, because there is evidence in some quarters that Ecclesiasticus was also reckoned amongst the books of Solomon. If, however, it is not so reckoned, we have five books of Solomon.

Now let us turn to the Cheltenham Stichometry as published by Mommsen[1].

Here we have the Solomonic writings introduced as follows:

Psalmi David CLI. v̄er. V̄.

Salomonis v̄er. V̄ D.

profetas maiores v̄er. X̄V̄I. CCCLXX. numero IIII.

This is a little perplexing; at first sight it seems as if the Cheltenham list had only one book of Solomon, or several books reckoned as one, and that the total extent of this book or books is 5500 verses.

The five Solomonic Books of the Church.

But, as Preuschen[2] has suggested, the real reckoning for Solomon has got into the next line, and we should read

Salomonis lib. v. ver. V̄ĪĪ. CCCXX.

profetas maiores numero IIII.

If this restoration be correct, we should have the Cheltenham list in evidence for five books of Solomon, but without any clue to the identification of the five books, or any means of comparison with the stichometry of the Psalms and Odes as given by Nicephorus.

Now, that Preuschen is correct as regards the numbers may be seen from the fact that the figure 7320 agrees with the count which we find in Vulgate MSS.[3]   For here we have

Proverbs	1740	verses
Ecclesiastes	800	,,
Canticles	280	,,
Wisdom	1700	,,
Ecclesiasticus	2800	,,
Total	7320	,,

1 Mommsen, *Zur lateinischen Stichometrie* in *Hermes*, Bd xxi. pp. 142—156. Cf. Sanday in *Studia Biblica*, iii. pp. 217—303.

2 Preuschen, *Analecta*, p. 138 ff.   3 Sanday, *l.c.* p. 266.

This justifies Preuschen's restoration, and shows that five books of Solomon were reckoned amongst the Canonical and deuterocanonical books, but the Psalms and Odes of Solomon are not amongst the five. For our purposes, therefore, we may dismiss the Cheltenham catalogue. The date of this catalogue is soon after A.D. 359, and it is North African in origin: we may say that at this date the Psalms of Solomon were not recognized in Carthage.

The very same thing follows from the consideration of the list of Canonical Scriptures contained in the Acts of the Council of Carthage in 397, for the entry in the list of Canonical Books,

Salomonis libri quinque

can hardly be referred to any other grouping than that which we have already described. The tradition of the Church is steady that there are *five* books of Solomon. Thus we find in Innocentius, writing at the beginning of the fifth century,

'prophetarum libri sexdecim, *Salomonis libri quinque*, Psalterium[1],'

and in Cassiodorus, writing at the middle of the sixth century[2],

'Psalterium librum unum; Salomonis libros quinque *i.e.* Proverbia, Sapientiam, Ecclesiasticum, Ecclesiasten, Canticum Canticorum';

and so in other places. Isidore of Seville, in the early part of the seventh century, divides the five Solomonic writings into groups of three and two respectively, and explains that the two which he detaches (Wisdom and Ecclesiasticus) were really the works of Jesus the son of Sirach, but have been credited to Solomon on the ground of style[3]:

'Duo quoque illi egregii et sanctae institutionis libelli, Sapientiam dico et alium qui vocatur Ecclesiasticus; qui dum dicantur a Jesu filio Sirach editi, tamen propter quandam eloquii similitudinem Salomonis titulo sunt praenotati[4].'

---

[1] *Ad Exsuperium* (Galland, *Bibl.* vol. viii. pp. 561 ff.).

[2] *De instit. div. litt.* c. xiv.

[3] Isidore, *De ordine libb. S. Script.*, *P.L.* lxxxiii. 155 ff.

[4] For the persistence of the tradition as to the five Solomonic books, see Nestle, *Zeitschrift f. altt. Wiss.* (1907), 27, 294 ff.

There are no further references that I know of to the Psalms or Odes of Solomon in the lists of canonical books which have come down to us, unless there should be a cryptic allusion to them in the new book of Psalms written for Marcion, which the Muratorian Canon condemns (Saec. ii.—iii.), or the ψαλμοὶ ἰδιωτικοί which the Council of Laodicea (c. 360 A.D.) prohibits from being used in the Church[1]. In the latter case we have the opinion of John Zonaras in favour of the identification. But Zonaras in the twelfth century was probably, like ourselves, engaged in speculation. On the other hand, if we might describe ψαλμοὶ ἰδιωτικοί as meaning Psalms of personal experience, the term would exactly suit our collection of Odes.

Having now proved that we have the two books of Solomonic
Lactantius and the Odes. Psalms and Odes in substantially the same compass that they were known to the ancient Stichometers, we now pass on to consider what light is thrown on the matter by actual quotations from the book of Odes which are extant. We begin with a passage from Lactantius, which was first noticed by the learned Whiston[2]. In the *Divine Institutes* (Bk iv. c. 12) we have the following passage:

> 'Salomon in ode undevicesima[3] ita dicit: Infirmatus est uterus Virginis et accepit foetum et gravata est, et facta est in multa miseratione mater virgo.'

And in the *Epitome* of the *Divine Institutes* the passage is introduced by the words *Apud Salomonem ita scriptum est*. These references to a 19th Ode betray a knowledge of the book from which the quotation was taken: on turning to the 19th Ode in our collection we find the very words quoted by Lactantius, the actual Syriac text being as follows:

---

[1] Origen's Canon, as contained in Euseb. *H. E.* vi. 25, has an entry of three Solomonic books, Proverbs, Ecclesiastes and Canticles; with regard to this last he says Ἄσμα ᾀσμάτων, οὐ γὰρ ὡς παραλαμβάνουσί τινες, Ἄσματα ᾀσμάτων. But this is only an alternative title which Origen condemns; it has no suggestion in it of other Songs or Canticles. [In the Latin Vulgate of Sixtus V (1590) the title was first *Canticum* and is everywhere in the headings of the pages pasted over as *Cantica* (Nestle).] Origen is expressly enumerating the twenty-two books of the Hebrew Canon. The alternative title for Canticles is actually found in the *Synopsis* of Chrysostom, in John of Damascus (*De fide orthodoxa* iv. 17) and elsewhere.

[2] *Authentick Records*, i. 155.

[3] So in the Cambridge MS. Gg. 4. 24 and in all MSS. in the apparatus of Brandt's edition; but in the MS. Kk. 4. 17 of the same University the reference is wanting.

ܥܠ ܪܝܫܐ ܕܩܘܕ̈ܠܬܐ
ܘܕܡܟܬ ܒܥܠܗ ܘܐܬܬܠܝܬ.
ܘܗܘܬ ܐܡܪ ܕܠܐܕܬܐ ܒܪ̈ܘܬܐ ܣܡܝܠܐ.

The only discordance is in the first word of the passage,
which is certainly wrong in the Latin[1], and very difficult to
interpret in the Syriac. It is clear, however, that Lactantius is
working from a book of Odes arranged in the same order as
ours : if he had both Psalms and Odes in his collection, then the
Odes preceded the Psalms.   And further, since Lactantius
quotes in Latin, the book was extant in a Latin translation in
his time ; for when Lactantius quotes Greek books, as in the
case of the Sibylline verses, he quotes in Greek and does not
offer a translation.   From which it appears that by the begin-
ning of the fourth century the Odes of Solomon must have been
translated into Latin[2].

Ryle and James in their edition of the eighteen Psalms of
Solomon drew attention, following Whiston, to this passage of
Lactantius, and made the correct inference from it that there
must have been more Solomonic matter at one time accessible
to Christian scholars than the eighteen Psalms.   And since the
Ode quoted by Lactantius is undoubtedly Christian, they sug-
gest that the original collection of Psalms of Solomon was
fitted with an Appendix of Odes of Solomon, the added matter
being approximately equal in length to the original collection,
and either Christian or marked by distinctly Christian inter-
polations.   So far they were undoubtedly right, as our MS.
incontestably shows.   Only our book presents the matter of the
Appendix in a different light : here it is the Odes that have the
first place and the Psalms that are appended ; and possibly this
was also the case with Lactantius' book of Solomon.   We shall
show, presently, that there is reason to believe that the two
books came together in both orders, in different lines of tradition,

---

[1] I am inclined to believe it is simply a mistake for 'insinuatus.' Just above
Lactantius says, 'Descendens itaque de caelo sanctus ille spiritus dei sanctam virginem
cujus utero se *insinuaret* elegit.'   Harnack points out, by reference to Rönsch, *Itala
u. Vulgata* p. 371 that the word *infirmatus* is only used of sick people in the time of
Lactantius.   The Ode expressly denies sickness to the Virgin.   For further sugges-
tions see notes to text and translation.

[2] We shall show later that there is some probability that Lactantius has been
influenced by our fourth Ode in a passage of *Div. Inst.* iv. 27.

and that there was current not only a book of Odes and Psalms
but also a book of Psalms and Odes[1].

And now let us pass on to a more interesting question, the

The Odes and   existence of extracts from the Odes of Solomon in
the Pistis   that curious Gnostic book, preserved in the Coptic
Sophia.   (or more exactly, Thebaic) language, and known
as the *Pistis Sophia*. These extracts will be important, not
only because they give us, in the form of a version, a good deal
of matter that coincides with what we have recovered from the
Syriac, but because they present this matter at an earlier time
than that of Lactantius, from whom our first quotation was made,
and the writer who made these quotations in the latter part of
the third century was not only quoting from the Odes of Solomon,
but from those Odes as forming a part of his accepted Biblical
text. We shall endeavour to make these points clear, and also
to show that in the Biblical text from which the writer quoted
the Odes of Solomon were preceded by the Psalms of Solomon.
If we can establish these points, the antiquity of the Odes will
be made out, for it is on the one hand clear that they are
traditional companions of the Psalms of Solomon for a con-
siderable length of time and on the other hand it is quite
improbable that a book written, say, as late as the end of the
second century, should be a part of the accepted Egyptian
canon in the latter part of the third century[2]. To get into the
canon at all, in any of the great centres of Christian life, a
book must have a measure of antiquity on its side : those
books which secured such canonicity, Clement's *Epistle*, or
Barnabas' *Epistle* or the *Shepherd* of Hermas, obtained their
position by the presumption of antiquity, and even then were
not easily rooted in the positions that they acquired, as the history
of the Canon will show. Let us, then, try to establish the points
to which we have referred above : and first with regard to the
date of the *Pistis Sophia* from which the extracts have been
made.

The best investigation into the *Pistis Sophia* is the one

---

[1] Note that the five apocryphal Psalms published by Wright from the Syriac in
Proc. S. Bibl. Arch. for 1887 have nothing to do with our collection.

[2] [Harnack puts the point equally strongly: *Die Oden Salomos* p. 9: 'dass irgend
eine Provinzialkirche ein nach der Mitte des 2. Jahrhunderts entstandenes Schriftstück
in das A.T. aufgenommen hat, ist ganz unwahrscheinlich.']

made by Harnack in Bd vii. of his *Texte u. Untersuchungen* in 1891. His treatise is divided into five sections : (i) the relation of the *Pistis Sophia* to the N.T. ; (ii) the relation of the *Pistis Sophia* to the O.T. ; (iii) the biblical exegesis of the author; (iv) its general Christian and catholic elements; and (v) a discussion of the character, origin, time and place of production of the work in question. Under this last head Harnack comes to the conclusion that the book is of Egyptian origin, and that it was written in the second half of the third century ; that its Gnosticism is Ophite in character, and betrays an origin in a Syrian rather than an Egyptian school ; *i.e.*, it is an imported Gnosticism developed on Egyptian soil, and that the actual school from which it emanated can be detected from allusions made by Epiphanius in his treatise on Heresies. He tells us of certain Gnostics who had a Gospel according to Philip, from which he makes a quotation which is quite in the manner of the *Pistis Sophia*, in which Philip appears as the principal scribe of the discourses ; they had also *inter alia*, books called the *Longer* and *Shorter Questions of Mary* : and as a large part of the *Pistis Sophia* is taken up with questions addressed to Jesus by Mary Magdalene and her women friends, it is natural to regard at least a part of the *Pistis Sophia* (as we call it) as coinciding with the books spoken of by Epiphanius. But since Epiphanius gives us an extract from the *Longer Questions* which cannot be identified with the Pistis Sophia (it is in fact, to judge from the extract, an obscene book, though it has many points of contact with the *Pistis Sophia*, which definitely contradicts its obscenity), we are led to the conclusion that the *Pistis Sophia* is identical, either wholly or in part, with the *Shorter Questions of Mary*.

In discussing these Gnostic heretics, Epiphanius tells us that in his early youth he came under their influence in Egypt, and that he was mercifully preserved from entanglement with them. He read their books, understood the sense of them, and then, like the virtuous Joseph from the house of Potiphar, he made his escape from their seductions and denounced the sect to the bishops of the province, and had the heretics expelled from the city in which he had met them. (See Epiphanius, *Haer.* 26, c. 17, 18.)

We thus succeed in locating in Egypt a group, or rather two

related groups of heretics, who may be described as Ophites or as Sethites (Epiphanius uses several names to describe the same groups); to one of these bands of Egyptian heretics the *Pistis Sophia* may be referred : and we thus get a fairly accurate idea of the place, time and character of the people to whom the book must be referred.

It must not be supposed that all of Harnack's arguments under these heads are valid. For instance on p. 101 he shows that the Gnostic writer uses an Egyptian calendar, for he makes Jesus to be transfigured before His disciples on the 15th of the month Tybi, when the moon is full; this suggests the use of an Egyptian calendar: and then he goes on to say that Egypt is also betrayed by the fact that the book quotes the Gnostic *Odes of Solomon*[1], which are probably of Egyptian origin, and allude to the inundation of the Nile. It is instructive to enquire how the *Odes of Solomon* came to be suspected of Gnosticism, and of references to Egyptian events.

The Odes not Gnostic and not Egyptian.

Amongst the passages quoted by the Coptic writer from the *Odes of Solomon* there is one which can be identified at once with the sixth Ode in our collection ; it describes a great overflow or inundation of the water of life, which has for its first objective point, if not its actual point of departure, the Temple at Jerusalem, and which flows out over all lands, bringing healing and strength.

The Psalm is a very beautiful one, and thoroughly Christian. But because it happens to describe the breaking out of the waters by the Greek word ἀπόρροια, which the Coptic has carefully transliterated, and because this is a favourite word in the *Pistis Sophia* to describe a Gnostic Emanation, it has been assumed that the Ode was Gnostic and that the illustration of the efflux was borrowed from the rising waters of the Nile. In support of this it may be urged that the waters were fought by a professional class of water-restrainers, and that those who

---

[1] [As soon as Harnack came to the knowledge of the complete collection of Odes, he withdrew the Gnostic epithet : see p. 103 note 2. 'Häretisch-Gnostisches ist auch nicht zu finden. Früher, als man nur fünf kannte und diese in der Beleuchtung der Pistis Sophia, habe ich, wenn auch nicht ohne Bedenken, an Gnostisches gedacht. Allein, wie auch Harris richtig gesehen hat—die vollständige Sammlung zeigt, dass der Verfasser nicht zu den Gnostikern gerechnet werden kann (oder nur so, wie auch Johannes zu ihnen gehört).']

drank of them were, according to the Coptic, a people who lived on the dry sand.   It might, therefore, be maintained that this language suited Egypt better than Palestine.   It is difficult, however, to see how Jerusalem comes in, if the scenery of the Ode is Egyptian, and it would have been better to express the matter more cautiously, as was done by Ryle and James in their first attempt on the problem of the Odes.   Their language was as follows[1]: 'Ode iii. (*i.e.* the third of the quoted Coptic Odes) is also Christian, and the employment of the term ἀπόρροια seems to stamp it as Gnostic.   But we cannot see that there is anything unmistakably Gnostic in the doctrine.   The imagery employed is that of Ezek. xlvii.[2], and of our Lord's words concerning the living water: and the thing described appears to be the preaching of the Gospel, which no human effort can avail to hinder, and which brings life and health to a thirsty heathen world.   If our theory of these Odes is correct, we have here a hymn of the second century at latest, and one filled with Johannine phraseology and ideas.'

Thus far Ryle and James; and I think we must say that their judgment is a sound one.   There is no reason to take ἀπόρροια in a Gnostic sense, nor do the remaining Psalms of our collection encourage the belief in a Gnostic origin : they are as Gnostic as the New Testament, no more and no less.   Of course I do not mean that the author of the *Pistis Sophia* will take this colourless view of ἀπόρροια.   His business is to write a book dealing with Gnostic philosophy, and with the Effluxes and Emanations that cause the different strata of the spiritual world : so he will naturally employ the word ἀπόρροια in his own sense, and will build a castle of cloudy words upon it.   But we have no reason to follow him in any such architecture nor even to accept his foundation.   Consequently we do not regard Harnack's case as made out with regard to the Gnostic character of the Odes of Solomon.   If Gnostics could write such beautiful praises of God as we have in our recovered volume, we can only say 'Would God all the Lord's people were Gnostics!'   But this they never were nor ever can be in the Valentinian, or Ophite or Sethian sense.   With this deduction from the argument,

---

[1] *l.c.* p. 160.

[2] [This should not be so strongly stated : we shall see later that the real parallel is with the 35th chapter of Isaiah.]

Harnack's general inferences from the Ode which we have been discussing are so just that we are tempted to examine his analysis a little more closely.

Let us, in view of the importance of the matters at issue, The sixth Ode not Gnostic. set down a translation of the sixth Ode as it stands in Syriac, and see what Harnack says by way of interpretation.

'As the hand moves over the harp, and the strings speak, so speaks in my members the Spirit of the Lord, and I speak by his love. For he destroys everything foreign, and everything that is bitter: thus it was from the beginning and will be to the end, that nothing should be His adversary, and nothing should stand up against Him. The Lord has multiplied the knowledge of Himself, and is zealous that those things should be known, which by His Grace have been given to us[1]. And the praise of His name He gave us: our spirits praise His holy Spirit.

'For there went forth a stream and became a river great and broad: it flooded and broke up everything, and it brought [water] to the Temple: and the restrainers of the children of men were not able to restrain it, nor the arts of those whose business it is to restrain waters: for it spread over the face of the whole earth and filled everything; and all the thirsty upon earth were given to drink of it: and thirst was relieved and quenched: for from the Most High was the draught given. Blessed then are the ministers of that draught who are entrusted with that water of His: they have assuaged the dry lips and the will that had fainted they have raised up: and souls that were near departing they have caught back from death; limbs that had fallen they straightened and set up: they gave strength for their coming (?) and light to their eyes: for every one knew them in the Lord and they lived by the water of life for ever. Hallelujah.'

The first thing that we notice when we transcribe the Ode is that the passage in the *Pistis Sophia* is only an extract; nearly half of the Ode has been neglected. Consequently the word ἀπόρροια which is supposed to be the key to the character of the Psalm, is not in its opening sentence at all, but has been

---

[1] Cf. 1 Cor. ii. 12.

caught up by the Gnostic writer out of the middle of it. It is certainly not the key-word. The Psalmist (or Odist) is telling in very beautiful language the power of the Lord and the scope of His Gospel. There is nothing Gnostic about this living water : there is not, even, anything Ecclesiastic about it, though Harnack wished to interpret it of the water of Baptism[1] : one might as well say the fourth chapter of John's Gospel was Gnostic and that when the Lord promised the Samaritan woman the water of life, he wanted to baptize her ! I submit that the interpretation of the Ode is affected (i) by regarding it in its entirety, (ii) by regarding it in connexion with the main body of the Odes : and that when this is done, the supposed Gnosticism of the Ode vanishes away. Harnack, in fact, did not positively commit himself on the point, and the greater part of his judgment is valid : thus on page 43 he says :

'Das Lied ist ohne Zweifel christlichen Ursprungs und damit ist auch die christliche Herkunft der vier übrigen Oden, als zu einer Sammlung gehörig, erwiesen.' I should not go quite so far, nor quite so fast as that. 'Ferner weist die Ode auf Ägypten : denn offenbar hat der Verfasser das Bild der grossen Fluth von der Überschwemmung des Nils genommen, der bis über die Häuser steigt, und das durstige Wüstenland tränkt.' This, as I have said, is extremely doubtful : Harnack tries to make it easier by suggesting that ναός should be corrected to λαός, which would get rid of the Temple at Jerusalem, but it is not a necessary emendation. The Temple is, as we shall see elsewhere, very much in the field of view of the Odist. 'Endlich scheint mir auch der gnostische Ursprung sehr wahrscheinlich, wenn auch nicht sicher.' Here Harnack is wisely hesitant.

The Odes probably Christian.

Again on page 45 Harnack sums up the case for the five Odes incorporated in the *Pistis Sophia* : (i) that the composer found them in his collection of Old Testament writings ; (ii) that they are of Gnostic origin : but he adds at once that the Gnostic character does not stand out clearly, and that the Christian piety of the Ode is powerfully expressed and not discoloured by Gnostic language : a statement which is much

---

[1] [Harnack withdrew this interpretation in his complete study of the Odes. See p. 32. 'An die Taufe ist nicht zu denken !' Bernard, as we shall see, would retain and emphasise the baptismal allusion.]

strengthened when we read the Ode in its entirety and not merely the part excerpted in the *Pistis Sophia*.

Further Harnack admits (p. 46) that if the Odes are Gnostic, their Gnosticism is separated by a deep gulf from that of the *Pistis Sophia*; which is certainly a just statement: and that, since at the time of the composition of the *Pistis Sophia* the Odes must have been of considerable antiquity, we may perhaps refer them to the first half of the second century. With this I have little fault to find; only I suggest that they may be 50 years earlier than Harnack's upper limit[1].

In order to understand more clearly what the writer of the *Pistis Sophia* has been doing with the matter that he has borrowed from the Odes of Solomon, we must try to get a better understanding of the Gnostic book itself. At first sight this is a very repellent task, for the book appears to be mere useless jargon. Harnack evidently thought as much when he first began to study it, for he says:

Use of the Odes in the Pistis Sophia.

'In der That kann man kaum etwas Verwirrteres und Ermüdenderes lesen als diese mit den Ausgeburten der gnostischen Phantasie bedeckten Blätter, die bei flüchtigerem Studium zum Zwecke der Verbreitung des systematischen Blödsinns geschrieben zu sein scheinen.'

The impression that the writer is busied with the propagation of systematic imbecility is certainly the result of a cursory or preliminary study; but there is method in the madness and meaning in the aberration, and after a while one begins to pick up threads of continuity and to see what the writer is aiming at. And then the underlying Christianity begins to assert itself through its Gnostic superincumbent weight. Let us see if we can get at the writer's argument.

Jesus is sitting with His disciples, male and female, on the Mount of Olives. It is the twelfth year after the Resurrection; for

---

[1] The same arguments are repeated by Harnack in his *Chronologie der altchrist. Literatur*, ii. 193, where he discusses the date of the *Pistis Sophia* and the related Gnostic writings in the Codex Brucianus. Here again he dates the *Pistis Sophia* in the second half of the third century, following the lines of his previous investigation. He remarks again on the use of the Odes of Solomon as an ancient book ranking with the Old Testament, but says they are of Gnostic origin: 'Die fünf Oden Salomos, die das Buch neben den alt-testamentlichen Psalmen zitiert, sind selbst gnostischen Ursprungs, und werden doch wie alte Urkunden behandelt. Wir haben hier also einen Gnostizismus, der über einem älteren auferbaut ist.'

eleven years Jesus has been teaching His disciples the mysteries
of the Kingdom of God : at the end of that time He has ascended
to the place of the Prime Mystery (which is the Gnostic expres-
sion for the Supreme God); this ascension took place while
they were sitting with Him on the Mount of Olives.   He was
suddenly transfigured before them.   A Light-Power, or Glory of
the Supreme Being, descends from the twenty-fourth or highest
mystery and surrounds Jesus with splendour.   The disciples
were amazed and terrified at the sight.   While they gazed on
Him, Jesus ascended into Heaven.   After a while Jesus, out of
compassion for their fears, for they thought the end of all things
was at hand, descended again and appeared to the disciples.
He begins to teach them further the secrets of the Kingdom.
He explains to them their own miraculous births, the miraculous
birth of John the Baptist and His own incarnation.   He tells
them the story of His ascent through the various heavens and
the orders of spiritual beings, 'thrones, dominations, princedoms,
virtues, powers.'   They proceed to interrogate Him on various
points.   The company consists of Peter, John, Andrew, Philip,
Thomas, Matthew, James, Bartholomew and Simon the Kanaan-
ite: Mary the Magdalene and Mary the Mother of Jesus, Martha
and Salome are all mentioned.   The chief place is given to the
enquiring women, especially to Mary Magdalene, the lowest place
to Simon Peter.   Between Mary Magdalene and Peter there is
something like a feud.   Peter complains that the women talk
too much and that the men don't get a chance: and Mary
complains that Peter hates our sex and wants to suppress us.
Jesus mediates gently between them: advises Mary to make
place for the brethren; but when the dispute breaks out again,
Jesus definitely takes the side of the women, and Peter is sup-
pressed[1].   The meaning of this is that there has been a conflict
over the place of women in the ministry of the Church: it is
even possible that the hostility of Peter may imply the attitude
of the Roman Church towards the prophesying woman of the
early centuries.   At all events there has been an acute situation

---

[1] The crisis in the feud between the men and women will be found in *P.S.* 161.
' Progressa Maria dixit: mi domine, meus νους est νοερος omni tempore, ut progrediar
omni vice: dicam solutionem verborum, quae dixit, ἀλλα timeo Petrum, quod ἀπειλει
mihi et odit nostrum genus.   Haec δε quum locuta esset, dixit ei primum μυστηριον:
unumquemque qui impletus fuerit πνευματι luminis, ut progressus proferat solutionem
horum, quae dico, nullus κωλυσει.'

created, which has found its reflection in the Gnostic circles in which our book was produced.

Jesus answers a number of enquiries as to the worlds through

The sorrows of Sophia.

which He has passed, and then we come to what is the kernel of the first part of the book, the account of the sorrows of Sophia, or, as she is called in the book, *Pistis Sophia*. Jesus relates how He found Sophia sitting below the thirteenth Aeon. She was mourning over her inability to rise further. Her path was blocked by fearful forms, named προβολαὶ αὐθαδοῦς or *Emanations of the Self-willed*. They and the rulers of the upper regions prohibit her advance and ascent. One of them had the face of a lion, half flame and half darkness. They chase poor Sophia back into Chaos. But in the midst of her affliction, she sees Jesus passing by, and to Him she addresses a series of Repentances and Hymns. Jesus relates these successively to His disciples. The method of the composition must now be carefully studied: we shall find the key in the lock.

Sophia makes her penitence, let us say, from one of the canonical Psalms. But in using this, she carefully alters every possible term in a Gnostic sense: instead of God, she says Prime Mystery or Light of Truth; instead of my adversaries, she says the Emanations of the Self-willed; by a series of

Gnostic Targums in the Pistis Sophia.

substitutions of this kind she turns the Psalm into a Gnostic Targum, in which you can only detect the original by the expressions which remain unaltered and by the general tenor of the confession. When Jesus has reported to the disciples what Sophia has said, He turns to the disciples and asks, 'Who knows what Sophia said?' It is a game of guessing. Mary Magdalene or some other of the company springs forward, begs permission to speak, and then says, 'This is what your Light-Power (the Light-Power is a substitute for the Divine Name) prophesied through David in the 69th Psalm,' or whatever the portion of Scripture may be that has been selected for disguise. Jesus gives an approbation and a blessing to the successful guesser. Sometimes, to make the matter still clearer, the Gnostic Targum is gone over again in detail with the text and explained sentence by sentence, so that we have the matter treated three times over: viz. the LXX. text, the Gnostic Targum, and the detailed commentary upon the text with the Targum. It is of the utmost importance that the method of the composition should be clearly grasped : if this is understood, the major part of the *Pistis Sophia* will become intelligible. To make this quite clear we will transcribe a short passage: here is an extract from one of the first prayers of repentance which Sophia utters[1]:

Serva me propter ἀρχοντας, qui oderunt me : *nam tu scis afflictionem meam* et cruciatum meum, et fractam meam vim, quam abstulerunt a me. *Sunt coram te* qui plantarunt me in haec mala omnia. Χρω iis κατα voluntatem tuam. Vis mea prospicit e medio χαους atque e medio tenebrarum. *Exspectavi* meam συζυγον, ut veniens pugnaret pro me, et haud venit. Atque exspectaveram, ut veniens daret mihi robur, *et haud reperi eam.* Et quum quaererem lucem, *dederunt mihi* caliginem : et quum quaererem meam vim, *dederunt mihi* ὕλην. Nunc igitur, lumen luminum, caliginem et ὕλην duxerunt super me προβολαι αὐθαδους. *Sunto iis insidiae* et involvunto eas ; et *retribuas* iis, *ut* σκανδαλιζωσιν, ne veniant in τοπον sui αὐθαδους. *Manento in tenebris, ne videant lucem.* Contemplantor χαος omni tempore, neve intuentor in altitudinem. *Adduc in eas suam vindictam et apprehendito eas tuum iudicium.*

Probably without the aid of the Virgin Mary, who in this case is the successful guesser, one could have identified the following verses of the 68th (69th) Psalm :

19. ἕνεκα τῶν ἐχθρῶν μου ῥῦσαί με·

20. σὺ γὰρ γινώσκεις τὸν ὀνειδισμόν μου· καὶ τὴν αἰσχύνην μου καὶ τὴν ἐντροπήν μου. ἐναντίον σου πάντες οἱ θλίβοντές με.

21. ὀνειδισμὸν προσεδόκησεν ἡ ψυχή μου καὶ ταλαιπωρίαν· καὶ ὑπέμεινα συλλυπούμενον, καὶ οὐχ ὑπῆρξεν, καὶ παρακαλοῦντα καὶ οὐχ εὗρον.

22. καὶ ἔδωκαν εἰς τὸ βρῶμά μου χολήν, καὶ εἰς τὴν δίψαν μου ἐπότισάν με ὄξος.

23. γενηθήτω ἡ τράπεζα αὐτῶν ἐνώπιον αὐτῶν εἰς παγίδα· καὶ εἰς ἀνταπόδοσιν καὶ εἰς σκάνδαλον.

24. σκοτισθήτωσαν οἱ ὀφθαλμοὶ αὐτῶν τοῦ μὴ βλέπειν· καὶ τὸν νῶτον αὐτῶν διὰ παντὸς σύγκαμψον.

25. ἔκχεον ἐπ' αὐτοὺς τὴν ὀργήν σου. καὶ ὁ θυμὸς τῆς ὀργῆς σου καταλάβοι αὐτούς.

Now if we go over the Penitence of Sophia, with these texts

---

[1] *P. S.* ed. Schwartze and Petermann, p. 50 of MS.

from the Psalms, we shall easily pick up out of the Penitence the *disjecta membra Psalmistae.*

I have italicized some of the words, which are either unchanged or almost unchanged. The rest, as I have said, is Gnostic Targum.

The importance of the underlying equivalence of the Targum and text is evident. We are dealing with Biblical matter; Psalm after Psalm is treated in this way, and sometimes short passages of the Gospels are similarly treated. It is not even necessary that the discourse be limited to a single Targum. Sometimes two or three occur of short passages. For us, however, the important thing is that the Odes of Solomon are treated just like the Canonical Psalms, with which they stood in an equal honour in the Bible of the author of the *Pistis Sophia.* This position of unassailed honour and un-doubted confidence marks the antiquity and the prestige of the Odes of Solomon. And as there is no such thing as a Gnostic Bible, these Odes cannot be Gnostic Odes, as was at first surmised.

It is clear, moreover, that in editing the portions of the Odes which occur in the *Pistis Sophia* we shall have to edit the Targums as well as the texts. We must print the excerpted matter in double form, and in cases where there is a detailed commentary, in triple form. And in this way we can finally make a Coptic apparatus to the Syriac text of the Odes.

One curious result will be arrived at almost immediately. The second of the passages taken from the Odes of Solomon by the author of the *Pistis Sophia* is definitely stated to be from the nineteenth Ode. It does not find any place in our collection. Neither does it agree, except in its opening sentence, with its Targum. On the other hand the Targum does agree with the fifth of the Syriac Odes. It is easy to see what has happened. The Targum was made on the fifth Ode, but when the author came to transcribe the Ode on which he had been commenting, he took out of his Psalter another Ode with a similar opening. This must, then, be one of the missing Odes at the beginning of our book. And since it is numbered 19, it will be the first of our collection, and will have followed directly on the eighteen extant Psalms of Solomon. The Gnostic author had, therefore,

The missing first Ode recovered.

both the Psalms and the Odes in his Bible; and the Psalms stood before the Odes, and not as in our MS. and perhaps in Lactantius' Bible, after the Odes: this is an important discovery, and the study of the text with its Targum has led to the recovery of part of the missing matter at the beginning of our MS.

To make this clear I transcribe the Targum side by side with the Syriac text, in order to show their coincidence:

The Hymn of Sophia as contained in the Gnostic Targum of the *Pistis Sophia*, 115, 116.

Incepit ὑμνεύειν vis εἰλικρινης luminis, quae in σοφιᾳ. Ὑμνεύουσα δε meae vi luminis, quae est *corona eius capiti*, cecinit ὑμνον δε dicens, Lumen est corona meo capiti et haud ero absque ea, ut ne privent me προβολαι αὐθαδους et, *quum motae fuerint* ὑλαι *omnes, ego δε haud movebor, et quum perierint* meae ὑλαι omnes, ut maneant in chao, *quas videbunt* προβολαι αὐθαδους, *ego δε haud peribo, quod* lumen *est mecum, atque etiam ego ero cum* lumine.

The Syriac Odes of Solomon, Ode 5, ad fin.

For my hope is upon the Lord, and I will not fear: and because the Lord is my salvation, I will not fear: and he is a garland on my head, and I shall not be moved: Even if everything should be shaken, I stand firm, and if all things visible should perish, I shall not die: because the Lord is with me and I am with Him.

Hallelujah.

Remembering the method of composition of the Targum, there can be no doubt that it is the fifth Ode which is being commented on. It is equally clear that the Ode which is set as the text to the Targum and which is introduced as the 19th Ode of Solomon does not coincide with it.

It runs as follows[1]:

Dominus super caput meum sicut corona, neque ero absque eo (ea). Plexerunt mihi coronam veritatis, et ramos in me germinare fecit. Nam non similis est coronae aridae quae non germinat; sed vivis super caput meum, et germinasti super caput meum: fructus tui pleni et perfecti sunt, pleni salute tua.

Clearly this is not the right Psalm, except as regards the opening sentence. Probably the mistake arose in the first instance with the Targumist who copied a line out of a wrong Ode, and thus made the way for copying the whole Ode from a

---

[1] Schmidt's rendering in *Texte u. Untersuch.* vii. 2. 37.

wrong place. The inference is that we have recovered the missing first Ode.

It is not uncommon in our book of Odes for the openings to be similar or to be repeated. The most striking example will be the short 27th Ode, which appears again almost bodily at the beginning of the 42nd Ode. The coincidences are important, as suggesting the same hand at different parts of the book.

As our object is not so much the interpretation of the *Pistis* *Sophia*, as the elucidation of the Syriac Odes, we must collect the matter which is quoted from the Odes in the *Pistis Sophia*, in order that the texts may be compared. It will be convenient to do this in one place, rather than under the heading of the separate Psalms that may be quoted. For the text of the Odes, we have two translations, that of Schwartze-Petermann, and that which is emended from the original translation (Woide-Münter) by Schmidt, and is given in Harnack's *Texte u. Untersuchungen*, Bd vii. We may quote these as S.-P. and W.-M.-S. We print these translations side by side. It is to be observed that Schmidt did not revise the Gnostic Targums when correcting the text of the Odes for Harnack, no doubt because their importance was not sufficiently recognized. But he went on to publish a complete translation into German of the *Pistis Sophia*, as well as of other Gnostic books preserved in Coptic. We shall have to refer to this enlarged and emended translation, but I do not think it necessary to give the German text of the quoted and commented Odes in full[1]. [A complete German revision has been made by Schmidt for Harnack's edition, and will be found pp. 14—20.]

The Odes in the Pistis Sophia collected.

ODE 1.

The text is introduced as follows:

Respondens δε Maria, mater Jesu, dixit: Mi domine, tua vis luminis ἐπροφητευσε de his verbis olim per Salomonem in eius decima nona ode et dixit:

---

[1] There has also been a French edition by Amélineau, which has been employed by Mead in his English edition of the *Pistis Sophia*. But as Amélineau is impossible in his paleography, and, I believe, an unsafe guide in other respects, I do not refer to him. I am not engaged upon the *Pistis Sophia*, except indirectly.

Schmidt's German edition appeared in 1905 under the auspices of the Prussian Academy of Sciences, with the title *Koptisch-Gnostische Schriften*.

S.-P. p. 116.

Dominus super meum caput sicut corona, neque ero absque eo. Plexerunt mihi coronam ἀληθειας. Et fecit tuos κλαδους germinare in me, quod non tulit coronam aridam, haud germinantem, ἀλλα vivis super meum caput et progerminas super me : tui καρποι pleni sunt et perfecti, pleni sunt tua salute.

W.-M.-S. pp. 37, 38.

Dominus super caput meum sicut corona, neque ero absque eo (ea). Plexerunt mihi coronam veritatis, et ramos tuos in me germinare fecit. Nam non similis est coronae aridae, quae non germinat, sed vivis super caput meum, et germinasti super caput meum : fructus tui pleni et perfecti sunt, pleni salute tua.

ODE 5.

The Gnostic Targum on the closing verses of this Ode has been already given : I repeat it for completeness below : the Targum on the rest of the Ode, and the text corresponding to it, are also found in the *Pistis Sophia*, as indicated. The text is introduced as follows :

Factum δε est, quum Jesus finisset dicere haec verba suis μαθηταις, progressa Salome dixit : mi domine, mea vis ἀναγκαζει me ad dicendam solutionem verborum, quae dixit πιστις σοφια. Tua vis ἐπροφητευσεν olim per Salomonem dicens :

S.-P. p. 114.

Manifestabo me tibi, domine, quod tu es meus deus. Ne sine me, domine, amplius, quod tu es mea ἐλπις : dedisti mihi meum ius gratis [P tuum iudicium] et servor a te : labuntor persequentes me, neve vidento me. Nubes caliginis obtegito eorum oculos atque nebula ἀερος, esto caligo iis, neve vidento diem, ut ne prehendant me : esto impotens eorum consilium, et quae deliberarunt, veniunto in eos : meditati sunt consilium neve esto [P et non factum est] iis. vicerunt [P et vicerunt] eos validi, et quae pararunt collapsa sunt infra eos. Est mea ἐλπις in domino, et haud timebo, quod tu es meus deus, meus σωτηρ.

W.-M.-S. p. 37.

Gratias tibi agam, quia tu es deus meus. Ne relinquas me, domine, quia tu es spes mea. Dedisti mihi iudicium gratis, et liberatus sum a te. Cadant persequentes me, et non videant me. Nubes fumi tegat oculos eorum et nebula aeris obtenebret eos, neve videant diem, ne prehendant me : consilium eorum fiat inefficax, et quae consultarunt, veniant super eos : meditati sunt consilium, neve succedat illis. Et vicerunt eos potentes[1], et quae praeparaverant malitiose, descenderunt in eos. Spes mea est in domino, et non timebo, quia tu es deus meus, servator meus.

[1] Schmidt, ' Und sie sind besiegt, obwohl sie mächtig sind.'

ODE 5.

The Gnostic Targum. S.-P. p. 113.

Cecinit ὑμνον et clamavit sursum ad me dicens: ὑμνευσω sursum *ad te, lumen,* quod volo venire ad te, ὑμνευσω *tibi, lumen, nam tu es meus* servator. *Ne sine me* in chao, libera me, lumen altitudinis, *nam tu es,* cui ὑμνευω. *Misisti mihi tuum* lumen a te et *servasti* me. Duxisti me in τοπους superiores chaus. Collabuntor [P *delabuntor*] igitur in τοπους inferiores chaus προβολαι αυθαδους, *quae persequuntur me,* neve veniunto in τοπους superiores *ut videant me. Et magna caligo obtegito eas, et venito iis obscura caligo; neve vidento* me in lumine tuae vis, quam misisti mihi ad servandam me : *ut ne prehendant* iterum *me; et eorum consilium quod excogitarunt* ad auferendam meam vim, *ne fiat illis,* et sicut [P κατα modum, quo] dixerunt mihi, auferre meum lumen mihi, aufer suum quoque loco mei ; et dixerunt auferre meum lumen totum, neque poterant auferre id, quod tua vis luminis est mecum propterea quod consilium ceperunt sine tuo statuto, lumen, propter hoc non potuere auferre lumen meum, quod ἐπιστευσα lumini, *non timebo, et* lumen *est meus servator, neque timebo.*

S.-P. 115, 116.

Ὑμνευουσα δε meae vi luminis, quae est corona eius capiti, cecinit ὑμνον δε dicens, Lumen est *corona meo capiti, et haud ero absque ea*[1], ut ne privent me προβολαι αυθαδους et, *quum motae fuerint* ὑλαι omnes, ego δε *haud movebor, et quum perierint* meae ὑλαι omnes, ut maneant in chao, *quas videbunt* προβολαι αυθαδους, ego δε *haud peribo, quod lumen est mecum, atque etiam ego ero cum lumine.*

ODE 6.

The text of this Ode is introduced as follows :

Progressus Petrus dixit: mi domine, de solutione verborum quae dixisti, tua vis luminis ἐπροφητευσε olim per Salomonem in eius ᾠδαις.

S.-P. 131.	W.-M.-S. *l.c.* p. 38.
Egressa ἀπορροια facta est magnum flumen latum : attraxit eos omnes, et conversam super	Egressa est emanatio et facta est magnum flumen dilatatum. Attraxit eos omnes et conversa est

---

[1] Schmidt, 'und nicht werde ich von ihm weichen.'

templum haud potuerunt capere in clausis et in locis aedificatis, neque potuerunt capere eam τεχναι capientium illos. Duxerunt eam super terram totam, atque prehendit eos omnes. Biberunt versantes super arenam aridam. Eorum sitis soluta est et exstincta, quum dedissent iis potum ab excelso. Μακαριοι sunt διακονοι potus illius, quibus concredita est aqua domini. Converterunt labia arida, sumserunt vigorem animi [P in me] hi, qui erant soluti: prehenderunt (i.e. confirmarunt) ψυχας, eicientes halitum, ut ne morerentur: erexerunt μελη collapsa: dederunt robur suae παρρησια, atque dederunt lucem suis oculis, quod isti omnes cognovere se in domino, atque servati sunt aqua vitae usque ad aeternum.

super templum[1]. Non potuerunt eam capere in locis munitis et aedificatis: neque potuerunt eam capere artes eorum qui intercipiunt (aquas). Duxerunt[2] eam super omnem terram, et ipsa comprehendit eos omnes. Biberunt qui habitabant in arena arida: sitis eorum soluta est et exstincta, cum daretur illis potus ab Altissimo. Beati sunt diaconi potus illius, quibus credita est aqua domini. Converterunt labia, quae arida erant, accipiebant gaudium cordis, qui soluti erant: comprehenderunt animas, halitum inmittentes, ne morerentur. Restituerunt membra quae ceciderant, dederunt robur parrhesiae eorum, et lucem oculis eorum. Nam omnes illi se cognoverunt in domino et salvati sunt per aquam vitae aeternam[3].

ODE 6.

The Gnostic Targum.   S.-P. pp. 128—130.

Ego igitur et altera vis, exiens a me, necnon ψυχη quam accepi a Sabaothe αγαθω, venerunt ducentes se invicem, *factae sunt* απορροια una luminis, existens lumen quam maxime. Vocavi Gabrielem desuper ab αιωσιν atque etiam Michaelem per κελευσιν mei patris, primi μυστηριου introspicientis, dedi eis απορροιαν luminis, feci eos descendere in chaos, ut βοηθωσι πιστει σοφια et uti ferrent vires luminis, quas abstulerunt ab ea προβολαι αυθαδους, ut auferrent eas ab illis et darent πιστει σοφια; et tempore, quo duxerunt απορροιαν luminis desuper in chaos, resplenduit quam maxime in chao toto et *dilatata est* in eius [P eorum] τοποις omnibus; et quum vidissent magnum lumen απορροιας illius προβολαι αυθαδους, timuerunt super se invicem, atque απορροια illa extraxit iis vires omnes luminis, quas abstulerunt a πιστει σοφια *neque* ετολμησαν προβολαι

---

[1] Schmidt, 'gegen den Tempel.'   [2] Schmidt, 'er wurde...geführt.'
[3] Schmidt, 'Wasser ewigen Lebens.'

αὐθάδους *prehendere* ἀπορροιαν luminis illius in chao tenebrarum, *neque prehenderunt eam* τεχνη αὐθάδους dominantis in προβολας. Et Gabriel et Michael attulerunt ἀπορροιαν luminis in corpus ὕλης πιστεως σοφιας et iniecerunt in eam lumina eius omnia, quam [P quae] abstulerunt ab ea, atque accepit lumen totum σωμα ὕλης [P + eius]: atque etiam acceperunt lumen eius vires omnes, quae in ea, hae quae acceperunt suum lumen et cessarunt indigere luminis; nam acceperunt suum lumen, quod abstulerunt ab iis, *propterea quod dederunt lumen iis a me.* Et Michael et Gabriel, qui διηκονησαν mihi, duxerunt ἀπορροιαν luminis in chaos daturam iis μυστηρια luminis: *his concredita est* ἀπορροια luminis: hanc, quam dedi iis, intuli in chaos. Et Michael et Gabriel non sumserunt quidquam luminis sibi in luminibus πιστεως σοφιας, quae abstulerunt a προβολαις αὐθάδους. Factum igitur est, quum ἀπορροια luminis intulisset in πιστιν σοφιαν suas vires omnes luminis, quas abstulerunt [P abstulit s. abstulerat] a προβολαις αὐθάδους facta est lux tota, atque etiam vires luminis, quae sunt in πιστει σοφιᾳ, quas haud abstulerunt προβολαι αὐθάδους, hilares redditae sunt iterum et impletae sunt luminis, et lumina, quae iniecerunt in πιστιν σοφιαν, vivificarunt σωμα eius ὕλης, in qua nullum lumen, *haec quae peritura* est aut haec quae perit, et *constituerunt* eius vires omnes, *quae erant solvendae,* et dederunt iis vim luminis[1]. Factae sunt iterum, sicut erant ab initio. Atque etiam exaltatae sunt in αἰσθησει luminis, et vires omnes luminis σοφιας *cognovere se invicem* per ἀπορροιαν luminis, *et servatae sunt* a lumine ἀπορροιας *illius.*

I have indicated some of the points where the Ode crops out: the broad stream of water has been replaced by an ἀπορροια of light, and this makes it difficult to follow the sequence of the Ode, satisfied thirst having been replaced by illumination. But the detailed commentary which follows will make it all clear.

ODE 6.

The detailed Commentary. S.-P. 131—135.

Peter explains the meaning of a prophecy which the *vis luminis* had formerly made through Solomon.

Audi igitur, mi domine, proferam verbum in παρρησιᾳ κατα modum quo tua vis ἐπροφητευσε per Salomonem: "ἀπορροια

---

[1] Schmidt, 'und sie nahmen sich eine Lichtkraft u.s.w.'

egressa facta est magnum flumen latum," quod est ἀπορροια
luminis dilatata est in chao, in τοποις omnibus προβολων αυθα-
δους ; atque verbum iterum, quod tua vis dixit per Salomonem,
"*attraxit eos omnes, duxit eos super templum*," quod est hoc,
attraxit vires omnes luminis a προβολαις αυθαδους quas abstule-
runt in [a] πιστει σοφιᾳ, et iniecit eas in πιστιν σοφιαν altera
vice ; atque verbum rursus, quod tua vis dixit, "*haud potuerunt
capere eam [loca] clausa neque loca aedificata*," quod hoc est:
προβολαι αυθαδους haud potuerunt prehendere ἀπορροιαν luminis
in septis tenebrarum chaus, atque verbum iterum, quod dixit:
"*duxerunt eam¹ super terram omnem, et implevit res omnes*," quod
hoc est: quum Gabriel et Michael duxissent eam [P eam super]
σωμα πιστεως σοφιας, intulit in eam lumina omnia, quae
abstulerunt ab ea προβολαι αυθαδους atque splenduit [pr. factum
est lumen] σωμα eius ὑλης; atque verbum, quod dixit: "*biberunt
versantes in arena arida*," quod est, acceperunt lumen quae sunt
omnia in πιστει σοφιᾳ quorum lumen abstulerunt (*i.e.* abstulerant)
prius² (*i.e.* antehac); atque verbum quod dixit "*sitis eorum
soluta est et exstincta*," quod hoc est: eius vires cessarunt
indigere luminis, quod abstulerunt [P *om.* quod abstulerunt],
quoniam dederunt (*i.e.* datum est) *iis* lumen [P + suum], quod
abstulerunt ab iis. Atque iterum κατα modum [P + quoque] quo
dixit tua vis, "*dederunt iis potum³ ab excelso*," quod hoc est:
dederunt lumen iis ex ἀπορροιᾳ luminis, quae exiit a me, primo
μυστηριῳ, et κατα modum, quo dixit tua vis: "μακαριοι sunt
διακονοι *potus illius*," quod est verbum, quod dixisti: Michael et
Gabriel, διακονησαντες, duxerunt ἀπορροιαν luminis in chaos,
atque etiam duxerunt eam sursum. Dabunt iis μυστηρια lumi-
nis altitudinis, *quibus concredita est* ἀπορροια luminis, atque etiam
κατα modum, quo dixit tua vis: "*verterunt* labia arida," quod
hoc est: Gabriel et Michael haud sumserunt sibi e luminibus πισ-
τεως σοφιας, quae eripuerunt προβολαις αυθαδους, ἀλλα iniecerunt
ea in πιστιν σοφιαν; atque iterum verbum, quod dixit: "*acceperunt
vigorem⁴ in me qui sunt soluti*," quod est hoc: aliae vires omnes
πιστεως σοφιας, quas haud abstulerunt προβολαι αυθαδους, valde
praeditae sunt vigore⁵ et impletae lumine a suo socio lumine,
quod iniecerunt ea in illas. Et verbum, quod tua vis dixit:

---

¹ Schmidt, 'er wurde...geführt.'   ² Schmidt, 'früher genommen war.'
³ Schmidt, 'es wurde...gegeben.'   ⁴ Schmidt, 'Herzensfreude.'
⁵ Schmidt, 'sind sehr fröhlich geworden.'

" *vivificarunt* ψυχας *eiicientes halitum, ut ne morerentur*," quod hoc est: quum iniecissent lumina in πιστιν σοφιαν vivificarunt σωμα eius ὕλης a quo lumina sua abstulere prius, hoc, quod erat periturum. Atque iterum verbum, quod tua vis dixit: "*constituerunt* μελη *quae collapsa sunt, aut ut ne collaberentur*," quod hoc est: quum intulissent in eam eius lumina, constituere (*i.e.* erexere) eius vires omnes, quae erant dissolvendae; atque etiam κατα modum, quo tua vis luminis dixit: "*dederunt robur earum* παρρησιᾳ"; quod hoc est: receperunt iterum illorum lumen atque factae sunt, sicut fuerunt prius: atque etiam verbum, quod dixit "*dederunt lumen eorum oculis*," quod hoc est: acceperunt αἰσθησιν in lumine et cognoverunt ἀπορροιαν luminis, quod pertineat ad altitudinem. Atque etiam verbum, quod dixit: "*isti omnes cognoverunt se in domino*," quod hoc est: vires omnes πιστεως σοφιας cognovere se invicem per ἀπορροιαν luminis: atque etiam verbum, quod dixit, "*servati sunt aqua vitae usque ad aeternum*[1]," quod hoc est: servatae sunt per ἀπορροιαν luminis totius: atque verbum, quod dixit: "*attraxit eos omnes* ἀπορροια luminis *et attraxit eos super templum*[2]," quod est: quum ἀπορροια luminis accepisset lumina omnia πιστεως σοφιας, et quum eripuisset ea a προβολαις αὐθαδους, iniecit ea in πιστιν σοφιαν, atque conversa est, exiit a chao, [3]ascendit in perfectionem [P vel " super te "] quod tu es templum[3]. Haec est solutio verborum omnium, quae dixit tua vis luminis per oden Salomonis. Factum igitur, quum primum μυστηριον audisset haec verba, quae dixit Petrus, locutum est ei: εὐγε, μακαριος Petre, haec est solutio verborum quae dixerunt [*i.e.* dicta sunt].

ODE 22.

This Ode is introduced as follows:

Respondens δε primum μυστηριον dixit: κελευω tibi, Mathaee, ut proferas solutionem ὕμνου, quem dixit πιστις σοφια. Respondens δε Mathaeus dixit: de solutione ὕμνου quem dixit πιστις σοφια tua vis luminis ἐπροφητευσεν olim in ᾠδη Salomonis:

S.-P. pp. 155, 156.	W.-M.-S. p. 39.
Qui deduxit me in locis excelsis super caelum, et duxit me	Is, qui duxit me deorsum e locis altis, caelestibus, et duxit me

---

[1] Schmidt, 'Wasser ewigen Lebens.'

[2] Schmidt, 'riss alles an sich, und zog (?) es über den Tempel.'

[3-3] Schmidt, 'und kam über Dich, der Du der Tempel bist.'

sursum in locis quae in funda-
mento inferiori: qui abstulit ibi
haec, quae in medio, et docuit me
ea, qui dispersit meos inimicos, et
meos ἀντιδικους, qui dedit mihi
ἐξουσιαν super vincula ad solvenda
ea, qui ἐπαταξε serpentem cum
septem capitibus meis manibus.
Constituit me super eius radicem,
ut evellerem eius σπερμα atque tu
eras mecum, adiuvans me, in omni
loco circumdedit me tuum nomen.
Dextra tua perdidit venenum
huius, qui dicit malum. Tua
manus stravit viam tuis πιστοις.
Redemisti eos e ταφοις et trans-
tulisti eos e mediis cadaveribus.
Sumsisti ossa mortua, induisti iis
σωμα et qui haud movent se,
dedisti eis ἐνεργειαν vitae. Via
tua facta est perniciei expers,
atque tua facie duxisti [P tua
facies. Duxisti] tuum αἰωνα in
perniciem, ut dissolverentur omnes
et fierent novi, et uti tuum lumen
sit duplicatum [P fundamentum]
iis omnibus. Construxisti tuam
opulentiam per eos et facti sunt
habitaculum sanctum.

in loca, quae in fundamento in-
feriori. Is, qui abstulit ibi haec,
quae in medio sunt, et docuit me
ea. Is, qui dispersit inimicos
meos et adversarios meos. Is,
qui dedit mihi potestatem super
vincula ad solvenda ea. Is qui
percussit serpentem septem capita
habentem manibus meis: con-
stituit me super radicem eius, ut
exstinguerem semen eius. Et tu
eras mecum, adsistens mihi. Omni
in loco circumdedit me nomen
tuum. Dextra tua perdidit vene-
num male loquentis. Manus tua
planavit viam fidelibus tuis. Liber-
asti eos e sepulcris et transtulisti
eos e medio cadaverum. Accepis-
ti ossa mortua, induisti iis corpus,
et, qui non movent se, dedisti eis
ἐνεργειαν vitae. Via tua facta est
expers perniciei, et etiam facies
tua: duxisti aeona tuum in per-
niciem[1] ut dissolverentur omnes
et renovarentur. [2]Et ut lumen
tuum duplicaretur iis omnibus[2],
superstruxisti divitias tuas super
eos, effecti sunt habitaculum
sanctum[3].

ODE 22.

The Gnostic Targum. S.-P. 153—155.

Pergens δε adhuc πιστις σοφια, ὑμνευσε rursum ad me
dicens: " ὑμνευω sursum ad te hoc. Tuo statuto eduxisti me ab
αιωνι excelso, qui supra caelum, et deduxisti me ad τοπους in-
feriores, atque etiam tuo statuto liberasti me e τοποις inferioribus,
et per te abstulisti ὑλην ibi, quae est in meis viribus luminis, et vidi
eam, atque tu dispersisti a me προβολας αὐθαδους, quae affligebant
me et erant inimici mihi, atque dedisti mihi ἐξουσιαν ut solverer

[1] Schmidt, 'Du hast Deinen Aeon über das Verderben geführt.'
[2-2] Schmidt, 'und Dein Licht ihnen allen Fundament sei.'
[3] Schmidt, 'Du hast Deinen Reichtum auf sie gebaut.'

e vinculis προβολων Adamae, *et* ἐπαταξας *serpentem basiliscum cum septem capitibus.* Proiecisti [P eiecisti] eum *meis manibus, et constituisti me super eius* ὑλην. Perdidisti eam, ut ne σπερμα suum surgeret inde ad hoc tempore, atque *tu* es qui *eras mecum,* dans mihi vim in his omnibus, et tuum lumen *circumdedit me* in τοποις omnibus, et per te reddidisti προβολας omnes αὐθαδους impotentes, quod abstulisti vim sui luminis ab eis *et direxisti meam viam* ad educendam me ex chao, et transtulisti me e tenebris ὑλικαις et abstulisti meas vires omnes ab iis, [1]quarum lumen abstulere[1]. Iniecisti in eas lumen purum, et meis μελεσιν omnibus, quibus nullum lumen, dedisti lumen purum ex lumine altitudinis, et direxisti viam iis, et lumen tuae faciei *factum mihi est* vita, *pernicie vacua.* Duxisti me sursum super chaos, locum (τοπον) chaus et perniciei, *ut dissolverentur omnes* ὑλαι, quae in eo, quae sunt in τοπῳ illo, *et uti fiant novae* meae vires omnes tuo lumine, et *ut tuum lumen sit in iis omnibus.* Posuisti lumen tuae ἀπορροιας in me. Facta sum lumen purgatum." Hic iterum est secundus ὑμνος quem dixit πιστις σοφια.

ODE 22.

The detailed Commentary.

Matthew then goes on to show in detail the parallelism between the Ode of Solomon and the hymn of the *Pistis Sophia.*

S.-P. pp. 156—160.

Haec, igitur, mi domine, est solutio ὑμνου quem dixit πιστις σοφια. Audi igitur, dicam eam ingenue. Verbum quod tua vis dixit per Salomonem : *"qui deduxit me e locis excelsis quae super caelum, atque etiam duxisti me sursum in locis, quae in fundamento inferiori,"* ipsum est verbum, quod dixit πιστις σοφια : ὑμνευω sursum ad te hoc. Tuo statuto duxisti me ex hoc αἰωνι excelso, qui super caelum, et duxisti me in τοπους inferiores, atque etiam servasti me tuo statuto, duxisti me sursum in τοποις inferioribus. Et verbum, quod tua vis dixit per Salomonem : *"qui abstulit ibi haec, quae in medio, et docuit me ea,"* ipsum est verbum, quod dixit πιστις σοφια : atque etiam per te abstulisti[2] ὑλην quae in media mea vi, et vidi eam : atque etiam verbum,

---

[1-1] Schmidt, 'deren Licht genommen war.'

[2] Schmidt, 'hast...reinigen lassen.'

quod tua vis dixit per Salomonem: "*qui dispersit meos inimicos et meos* ἀντιδίκους," ipsum est verbum, quod dixit πιστις σοφια: et tu es, qui dispersisti 'a me προβολας omnes αὐθαδους quae affligebant me, et quae erant inimici mihi; et verbum, quod tua vis dixit: "*qui dedit mihi suam* σοφιαν *super vincula ad solvenda ea*": ipsum est verbum, quod dixit πιστις σοφια; [+ et P] dedit mihi suam σοφιαν ut solverer e vinculis προβολων illarum; et verbum, quod tua vis dixit: "*qui* ἐπαταξε *serpentem cum septem capitibus meis manibus et constituit me super eius radicem, ut evellerem eius* σπερμα," ipsum est verbum, quod dixit πιστις σοφια: et ἐπαταξας serpentem cum septem capitibus meis manibus et constituisti me super eius ὑλην, perdidisti eum, ut ne eius σπερμα surgeret inde ab hac hora; et verbum, quod tua vis dixit: "*et tu mecum eras, adiuvabas me*," ipsum est verbum, quod dixit πιστις σοφια: et tu eras mecum, dans vim mihi in his omnibus; et verbum quod tua vis dixit: "*et tuum nomen circumdedit me in omni loco*," ipsum est verbum, quod dixit πιστις σοφια: et tuum lumen circumdedit me in eorum locis omnibus; et verbum, quod tua vis dixit: "*et tua dextera perdidit venenum huius qui dicit malum*," ipsum est verbum, quod dixit πιστις σοφια; et per te factae sunt impotentes προβολαι αὐθαδους, quod abstulisti lumen vis suae ab iis; et verbum, quod tua vis dixit: "*tua manus stravit viam tuis* πιστοις," ipsum est verbum, quod dixit πιστις σοφια; direxisti meam viam ad educendam me e chao, quod ἐπιστευσα tibi; et verbum, quod tua vis dixit: "*redemisti eos e* ταφοις *et transtulisti eos e mediis cadaveribus*," ipsum est verbum, quod dixit πιστις σοφια: et redemisti me e chao et transtulisti me e tenebris ὑλικαις quae ipsae sunt προβολαι caliginis, quae in chao, e quibus suum lumen abstulisti; et verbum, quod tua vis dixit: "*sumsisti ossa mortua, induisti eis* σωμα, *et hi, qui non movent se, dedisti iis* ἐνεργειαν *vitae*," ipsum est verbum, quod dixit πιστις σοφια: et abstulisti meas vires omnes, in quibus nullum lumen, et [*om.* et P] indidisti eis lumen purum, et meis μελεσιν omnibus, in quibus nullum lumen movetur, dedisti eis lumen vitae tua altitudine; et verbum quod tua vis dixit: "*tua via facta est pernicie vacua et tua facies*," ipsum est verbum, quod dixit πιστις σοφια: et direxisti viam [+tuam P] mihi, et lumen tuae faciei facta[1] mihi est vita, pernicie vacua; et verbum, quod tua vis dixit:

---

[1] factum P.

"*duxisti tuum* αἰωνα *in perniciem, ut dissolverentur ut fierent novi omnes*," ipsum est verbum, quod dixit πιστις σοφια : [1]duxisti me, tuam vim, in chaos et in perniciem[1], ut dissolverentur ὑλαι omnes, quae sunt [+ sursum P] in τοπῳ illo, et ut fierent novae meae vires omnes lumine'; et verbum, quod tua vis dixit, "*et tuum lumen duplicatum* [P *fundamentum*] *est*[2] *iis omnibus*" : ipsum est verbum, quod dixit πιστις σοφια : et tuum lumen est in iis omnibus : et verbum quod tua vis luminis dixit per Salomonem : "*posuisti* [3]*tuam opulentiam*[3] *in eo, et factus est habitaculum sanctum*": ipsum est verbum, quod dixit πιστις σοφια : firmasti lumen tuae ἀπορ-ροιας super me, et facta sum lumen purum.   Haec igitur, domine mi, est solutio ὑμνου, quem dixit πιστις σοφια.

ODE 25.

The text of this Ode is introduced as follows :

Respondens δε primum μυστηριον dixit Thomae : κελευω tibi, ut proferas solutionem ὑμνου, quem ὑμνευσεν sursum ad me πιστις σοφια. Respondens δε Thomas dixit : mi domine, de ὑμνῳ quem dixit πιστις quod liberata est a chao : tua vis luminis ἐπροφητευσεν olim per Salomonem, filium Davidis, in eius ῳδαις :

S.-P. p. 150.	W.-M.-S. *l.c.* p. 39.
Servatus sum e vinculis. Fugi ad te, domine, quod fuisti mihi dextra servans me, atque servans me et adiuvans me, ἐκωλυσας pugnantes contra me, neque apparuerunt, quod tua facies mecum erat servans me tua χαριτι. Affecta sum ignominia coram multitudine, atque proiecerunt me. Fui sicut plumbum coram iis. Facta mihi est vis a te adiuvans me, quod posuisti lucernas ad dexteram mihi et ad sinistram mihi, ut ne quidquam circa me esset luminis expers. Ἐσκεπασας me sub umbra tuae misericordiae et fui super vestes	Liberatus sum e vinculis. Fugi ad te, domine : quia fuisti mihi ad dextrám, salvans me. [Et salvans me] et adiuvans me, prohibuisti adversarios meos, neque se manifestaverunt, quod tua facies mecum est, liberans me gratia tua. Accepi contumeliam coram multitudine, et eiecerunt me : fui sicut plumbum coram iis. Fuit mihi robur per te adiuvans me. Quia posuisti lucernas ad dextram meam et ad sinistram meam, ne neutra parte luminis expers essem. Texisti me sub umbra gratiae tuae et [4]superavi vestimenta pellicea[4]. Dextra tua

1-1 Schmidt, 'Du hast mich, Deine Kraft, über das Chaos hinaufgeführt und über das Verderben.'

2 Schmidt, 'ist ihnen allen Fundament (geworden).'

3-3 Schmidt, 'Deinen Reichtum.'

4-4 Schmidt, 'ich wurde überhoben den aus Fellen gemachten Kleidern.'

pelliceas. Tua dextra exaltavit me et abstulisti infirmitatem a me: Factus sum validus tua veritate, purgatus tua δικαιοσυνῃ. Remoti sunt a me pugnantes contra me, et iustificatus sum tua χρηστοτητι, nam tua quies est ad aeternum aeternitatis.

exaltavit me, et abstulisti infirmitatem porro a me. Fui corroboratus veritate tua, purgatus iustitia tua. Procul remoti sunt a me adversarii mei, et iustificatus sum iustitia tua, quia requies tua est in saecula saeculorum.

ODE 25.

The Gnostic Targum. (S.-P. 148, 149.)

Pergens δε iterum in sermone primum μυστηριον dixit μαθηταις: Factum est, quum duxissem πιστιν σοφιαν sursum in chao, exclamavit iterum dicens: "*Servata sum* in chao, et soluta e *vinculis* caliginis. *Veni ad te,* lumen, *quod fuisti* lumen ex omni parte mihi *servans me, et adiuvans me.* Et προβολας αὐθαδους *quae pugnant contra me,* ἐκωλυσας tuo lumine, *et haud potuerunt adpropinquare mihi, quod erat* tuum lumen *mecum, et servabat* me tua [P me in tua] ἀπορροιᾳ luminis, quoniam γαρ προβολαι [P + αὐθαδους] affligentes me abstulerunt meam vim a me, *iniecerunt me* in orcos (chaos Plur.) nullum lumen habentem. *Fui sicut* ὑλη gravis *coram iis.* Atque post haec vis ἀπορροιας venit mihi a te servans me. Splenduit *ad sinistram mihi et ad dextram mihi;* et circumdabat me, ex omni parte mihi erat, *ut ne ullum* μερος quo fui, essem [P *esset*] *sine lumine, et* obtexit [P *obtexisti*] *me* lumine tuae ἀπορροιας et purgasti in me omnes meas ὑλας malas, *et fui super* meas ὑλας omnes propter tuum lumen [1]et tuam ἀπορροιαν luminis. Ista *exaltavit me*[1] *et abstulit* me προβολαις αὐθαδους θλιβουσαις me. Atque fui confisa tuo lumini, nec non lumen purum [P lumini puro] tuae ἀπορροιας, *et remotae sunt a me* προβολαι αὐθαδους quae affligebant me, et facta sum lux tua magna vi, quod tu servas omni tempore.

ODE 25.

The detailed Commentary.

Thomas explains that he will interpret openly the words of the Pistis Sophia, and proceeds to speak ἐν παρρησίᾳ, as follows:

[1-1] Schmidt, 'und Dein Lichtabfluss ist es, der mich erhöht...hat.'

S.-P. 150—153.

Verbum igitur, quod tua vis luminis dixit per Salomonem: "*Servatus sum e vinculis. Fugi ad te, domine,*" ipsum est verbum, quod dixit πιστις σοφια: soluta sum e vinculis caliginis, veni ad te, domine [P lux]: et verbum, quod dixit tua vis: "*Fuisti mihi dextra servans me et adiuvans me*"; ipsum iterum est verbum, quod dixit πιστις σοφια: factus es lumen ex omni parte mihi et adiuvans me: et verbum quod tua vis luminis dixit "*ἐκωλυσας pugnantes contra me, et haud apparuerunt*" ipsum est verbum, quod dixit πιστις σοφια: et προβολας αὐθαδους quae pugnant contra me, ἐκωλυσας tuo lumine, et haud potuerunt adpropinquare mihi": et verbum, quod tua vis dixit, "*quod tua facies mecum erat servans me tua χαριτι,*" ipsum est verbum, quod dixit πιστις σοφια: quod tuum lumen erat mecum servans me tua ἀπορροιᾳ luminis: et verbum quod tua vis dixit, "[1]*contemnor eorum multitudine et proiecerunt me*[1]," ipsum est verbum, quod dixit πιστις σοφια; afflixerunt me προβολαι αὐθαδους et abstulerunt meam vim a me, et contemta sum coram iis et proiecerunt me in chao expertem luminis. Et verbum, quod tua vis dixit: "*fui sicut plumbum coram iis,*" ipsum est verbum, quod dixit πιστις σοφια: quum abstulissent mea lumina a me, facta sum sicut ὑλη gravis coram iis. Et verbum, [+ rursus P] quod tua vis dixit, "*et facta mihi est vis a te adiuvans me,*" ipsum [+quoque P] est verbum, quod dixit πιστις σοφια: et post haec vis luminis venit mihi a te servans me": et verbum quod tua vis dixit: "*posuisti lucernas ad dextram mihi et ad sinistram mihi, ut ne quidquam circa me esset luminis expers,*" ipsum est verbum, quod dixit πιστις σοφια, Tua vis luminis [P + splenduit] ad dextram mihi et ad sinistram mihi et circumdans me ab omni parte, ut ne quidquam circa me esset luminis expers: et verbum quod tua vis dixit: "*ἐσκεπασας me umbra tuae misericordiae,*" ipsum iterum est verbum, quod dixit πιστις σοφια: et obtexisti me lumine tuae ἀπορροιας; et verbum quod tua vis dixit: "[2]*fui super vestes pelliceas*[2]," ipsum iterum est verbum, quod dixit πιστις σοφια: et eiecerunt a me meas ὑλας omnes malas, et [3]elevavi eas[3] tua lumine; et verbum, quod tua vis dixit per Salomonem: "*tua dextra exaltavit me et abstulit infirmitatem*

[1-1] Schmidt, 'ich wurde verachtet im Angesichte vieler und hinausgestossen.'
[2-2] Schmidt, 'ich wurde überhoben den aus Fellen gemachten Kleidern.'
[3-3] Schmidt, 'ich erhob mich über sie.'

a me," ipsum est verbum, quod dixit πιστις σοφια : et tua ἀπορροια luminis haec est, quae exaltavit me tuo lumine, et abstulit a me προβολας αὐθαδους θλιβουσας me ; et verbum, quod tua vis dixit: "*factus sum validus tua veritate et purgatus tua* δικαιοσυνῃ," ipsum est verbum, quod dixit πιστις σοφια : facta sum valida. tuo lumine et sum lumen purgatum tua ἀπορροιᾳ : et verbum, quod tua vis dixit : "*remoti sunt a me pugnantes mecum*," ipsum est verbum, quod dixit πιστις σοφια : remotae sunt a me προβολαι αὐθαδους, hae quae affligebant me, et verbum quod tua vis luminis dixit per Salomonem : "*et iustificatus sum tua* χρηστοτητι, *quod tua quies est ad aeternum aeternitatis*" : ipsum est verbum, quod dixit πιστις σοφια : servata sum tua χρηστοτητι quod tu servas unumquemque. Haec igitur, o mi domine, est solutio tota μετανοιας quam dixit πιστις σοφια quum servata esset in chao et soluta est e vinculis caliginis.

These, then, are the extracts and comments on the Odes of Solomon which are contained in the Pistis Sophia.

We will now examine what light they throw on the original form of the text, and we will also enquire as to the language in which the book was originally circulated.

Original
language of
the Odes.

We begin by comparing the Odes quoted in the Coptic book with their Syriac equivalents.

The presumption is that the Coptic is a direct translation from the Greek : the number of Greek words that are embedded in the Coptic at once suggests this, and it is natural to carry back these Greek words into the text from which the Coptic is derived.

A little caution is necessary, for it will be remembered that Greek words are often used in the Coptic to redeem the language from its linguistic poverty, and it will also be found that the Coptic does not always directly transliterate a Greek word : it sometimes translates by another and more familiar Greek word. But with some reserve of this kind, the Greek elements in the text are sufficient evidence that the book was taken from the Greek to the Egyptian language ; and we know that the Psalms and Odes had a wide circulation amongst Greek-speaking peoples. The *Pistis Sophia*, in which the Odes are embedded, dates from the third century, and the author of the *Pistis* had, as we have shown, the Odes bound up with his Canonical Psalter ; at the time intimated there was no Coptic

[Thebaic] Bible from which the extracts could have been made; so we may be sure the Odes were taken from a Greek Bible, and, with almost equal certainty, that the *Pistis Sophia* itself was a Greek book. Detailed examination leads to the same result.

Suppose we examine the parts of the sixth Ode which we have preserved both in Coptic and in Syriac: this is the Ode in which Harnack thought we could detect both Gnostic and Egyptian elements, the supposed Gnostic feature being the use of the word ἀπόρροια, and the supposed Egyptian feature being a sudden inundation, which sweeps over a whole country and defies professional attempts to regulate it. Near the end of the Ode is a beautiful passage describing the way in which the ministers of the water of life have assuaged the thirst of the world: they have given ease to dry lips, strength to paralysed wills and weak limbs. Then the writer adds

> "Members which had fallen they made straight and set up. They gave strength for their coming and light to their eyes."

There is something awkward about this word 'coming': and when we turn to the Coptic we find

> "Restituerunt membra quae ceciderant. Dederunt robur παρρησία eorum et lucem oculis eorum."

This is almost as unintelligible as the former; what does he mean by 'strength for freedom of speech'? However we have found out that the Greek behind the Coptic read τῇ παρρησίᾳ αὐτῶν; and it is not difficult to infer that the Syriac has rendered a Greek text τῇ παρουσίᾳ αὐτῶν. Now which of these is correct? Neither of them makes good sense. But if we write

> τῇ παρέσει αὐτῶν or τῇ παραλύσει αὐτῶν
> "they gave them strength for their paralysis,"

we can make the passage intelligible, and explain both the Coptic and Syriac readings[1].

[1] The key to the passage is Is. xxxv. 3 = Heb. xii. 12; ἰσχύσατε...γόνατα παραλελυμένα (Is.), and cf. τὰ παραλελυμένα γόνατα ἀνορθώσατε (Heb.).

For a similar confusion between παρουσία and παρρησία we may compare the words of Valentinus, quoted in Clem. Alex. *Strom.* ii. 22: εἷς δέ ἐστιν ἀγαθός· οὗ παρρησία ἡ διὰ τοῦ υἱοῦ φανέρωσις, where Grabe, *Spic.* 2 conjectures παρουσία.

This suggests that the Syriac as well as the Coptic has a Greek text behind it. We shall examine this point more in detail presently.

We are not limited to the occurrence of the single Greek word παρρησία (whether it be the right word or only a corruption); nor to the favourite word ἀπόρροια which the Pistis Sophia has caught at, on account of its Gnostic associations.

The Syriac tells us that the flood could not be restrained by the professional restrainers, nor by the arts of those who make the management of floods their business. The Coptic text tells us

> haud potuerunt capere in clausis et in locis aedificatis, neque potuerunt capere eam τεχναι capientium illos.

Here the Syriac is somewhat at variance from the Coptic, but it is clear that 'capere' stands for the Syriac 'restrain,' and that τεχναι is the Greek word for the Syriac 'arts of the restrainers.'

The Gnostic Targum has also worked in τεχναι in the following form :

> neque ἐτόλμησαν......prehendere ἀπορροιαν......neque prehenderunt eam τεχνῃ......

Here 'prehendo' is the same as 'capio,' and stands for the Syriac 'restrain.' Τεχναι seems to come from the original Greek. I should have said that ἐτόλμησαν came from the same source, if it were not that the text and the comment have 'potuerunt' in harmony with the Syriac.

Another bit of the original Greek is picked up in the clause which answers to the Syriac,

> 'Blessed are the ministers of that draught.'

Here the Coptic gives us, Μακαριοι sunt διακονοι potus illius, and the Comment, as well as the Targum, explains that the ministers are Michael and Gabriel, οἱ διακονήσαντες. So that we can restore the words Μακάριοί εἰσιν οἱ διάκονοι οὗτοι to the Greek. And so in other cases.

But this raises the question whether the Greek is the last stage. Were the Odes written in Greek? Or may we say, as for the eighteen Psalms, that they were translated into Greek from an original Hebrew? The possibility must at all events be kept in mind. But we can only advance by slow stages. The next step should be to confirm the suggestion that the Syriac has been translated from a Greek base by discussing the case for the eighteen Psalms.

Here we should naturally expect dependence on the Greek.

The Syriac of the 18 Psalms depends on the Greek. For it is now clearly made out, as Ryle and James have shown, that the original Hebrew of these Psalms was done into Greek at a very early period. For the Greek version of the 11th Psalm is used by the author of the book of Baruch in his fifth chapter, and this chapter is quoted at length by Irenaeus. So it would be unreasonable to put the Greek of the eighteen Psalms later than the middle of the first century, when it is employed by Baruch writing, probably, not later than the end of the first century.

So the Greek of these Psalms is available for translation into Syriac at a very early date; we have to determine from the evidence before us whether it was so translated from the Greek. Let us see whether the Syriac confirms any conjectures either in Greek or in Hebrew that the editors have thought necessary to the understanding or betterment of the text. It does not confirm Hilgenfeld's brilliant suggestion of ὁρίων for ὁρέων in Ps. ii. 30: the Syriac has 'mountains' and agrees with the Greek tradition. In Ps. ii. 20 Gebhardt's emendation of κατέσπασεν to κατεσπάσθη is confirmed by the Syriac ܐܬܥܩܪܐ, which is rather a free translation. In Ps. v. 4 Gebhardt conjectures

οὐ γὰρ λήψεταί [τις] σκῦλα παρὰ ἀνδρὸς δυνατοῦ

and the word added is confirmed by the Syriac, which adds ܒܪܢܫܐ (a son of man, a man): but then the Copenhagen MS. has σκῦλα ἄνθρωπος, and the Syriac might just as well be a translation of this.

In Ps. viii. 3 Hilgenfeld's emendation

καὶ εἶπα [ἐν] τῇ καρδίᾳ μου

is not confirmed by the Syriac, which follows the MSS. in omitting ἐν.

In Ps. x. 1 Fritzsche made a striking emendation to the first couplet,

Μακάριος ἀνὴρ οὗ ὁ κύριος ἐμνήσθη ἐν ἐλεγμῷ,
καὶ ἐκυκλώθη ἀπὸ ὁδοῦ πονηρᾶς ἐν μάστιγι

by reading ἐκωλύθη for ἐκυκλώθη.

The Syriac confirms this conjecture, which Gebhardt has
discarded in favour of a misunderstood Hebrew text. If this is
not a successful emendation on the part of a scribe, the Syriac
at this point takes precedence of the existing Greek texts: but
that does not mean that it is not dependent on a Greek text.

In Ps. xvi. 9 the Greek text

$$\tau\grave{a}\ \mathring{\epsilon}\rho\gamma a\ \tau\hat{\omega}\nu\ \chi\epsilon\iota\rho\hat{\omega}\nu\ \mu o\upsilon\ \kappa a\tau\epsilon\acute{\upsilon}\theta\upsilon\nu o\nu\ \mathring{\epsilon}\nu\ \tau\acute{o}\pi\omega\ \sigma o\upsilon$$

is altered in the Syriac to $\mathring{\epsilon}\nu\acute{\omega}\pi\iota\acute{o}\nu\ \sigma o\upsilon$ which seems a better, as
well as an easier reading.

In Ps. xvii. 16 [14] where Gebhardt has emended

$$[\kappa a\theta\grave{\omega}\varsigma\ \kappa a\grave{\iota}\ \tau\grave{a}\ \mathring{\epsilon}\theta\nu\eta\ \mathring{\epsilon}\nu\ \tau a\hat{\iota}\varsigma\ \pi\acute{o}\lambda\epsilon\sigma\iota]\ \tau o\hat{\upsilon}\ \sigma\theta\acute{\epsilon}\nu o\upsilon\varsigma\ a\mathring{\upsilon}\tau\hat{\omega}\nu$$

for $\tau o\grave{\upsilon}\varsigma\ \theta\epsilon o\grave{\upsilon}\varsigma\ a\mathring{\upsilon}\tau\hat{\omega}\nu$ of Cod. R the Syriac reads 'to their gods'
with the rest of the Greek MSS.

In Ps. xvii. 23 [21] Gebhardt emends

$$\epsilon\mathring{\iota}\varsigma\ \tau\grave{o}\nu\ \kappa a\iota\rho\grave{o}\nu\ \mathring{o}\nu\ \epsilon\mathring{\iota}\lambda o\upsilon\ \sigma\acute{\upsilon},\ \mathring{o}\ \theta\epsilon\acute{o}\varsigma$$

for the current Greek

$$\epsilon\mathring{\iota}\varsigma\ \tau\grave{o}\nu\ \kappa a\iota\rho\grave{o}\nu\ \mathring{o}\nu\ \epsilon\mathring{\iota}\delta\epsilon\varsigma\ [\mathring{\iota}\delta\epsilon\varsigma,\ o\mathring{\iota}\delta\epsilon\varsigma,\ o\mathring{\iota}\delta a\varsigma].$$

The Syriac has ܕܝܢ ܚܙܐ, which answers most nearly to $\epsilon\mathring{\iota}\delta\epsilon\varsigma$.

This is one of the places where Felix Perles found a trace of
the original Hebrew, which had been corrupted from יָעַדְתָּ to
יָדַעְתָּ, i.e. from 'thou hast appointed' to 'thou hast known.'
Most of the proposed emendations seem to me to be more
ingenious than necessary. The Syriac, at all events, does not
endorse them.

In Ps. xvii. 32 [30] the Syriac renders $\mathring{\epsilon}\nu\ \mathring{\epsilon}\pi\iota\sigma\acute{\eta}\mu\omega$ by ܚܝܠܬܢܐ,
which throws light on the same expression in Ps. ii. 6, where the
Syriac seems to have left the words untranslated, but there
Felix Perles conjectured that they stood for an original Hebrew
בְּגָלוּי. The Syriac seems, while itself following the Greek in
Ps. xvii. 32, to support this restoration of Perles for the Hebrew
in Ps. ii. 6.

In Ps. xvii. 37 [33] Gebhardt has added conjecturally the
word $\lambda a o\hat{\iota}\varsigma$ in

$$\kappa a\grave{\iota}\ \pi o\lambda\lambda o\hat{\iota}\varsigma\ [\lambda a o\hat{\iota}\varsigma]\ o\mathring{\upsilon}\ \sigma\upsilon\nu\acute{a}\xi\epsilon\iota\ \mathring{\epsilon}\lambda\pi\acute{\iota}\delta a\varsigma\ \epsilon\mathring{\iota}\varsigma\ \mathring{\eta}\mu\acute{\epsilon}\rho a\nu\ \pi o\lambda\acute{\epsilon}\mu o\upsilon.$$

The Syriac has 'and he shall not hope in a multitude for the
day of war,' and so does not favour the emendation. So far,
then, as these passages go, there is not much ground for taking
the Syriac outside the grouping of the Greek MSS., and erecting

it into a separate authority. There are one or two passages to be considered in which the Syriac gives us either an independent conjecture, or something nearer to the original text.

In Ps. i. 6 the difficult

$$\kappa \grave{a} i \; o\grave{v}\kappa \; \mathring{\eta}\nu\epsilon\gamma\kappa a\nu$$

Singular readings of the Syriac. of the MSS. is replaced by ܐܣܟ ܪܠܐ, and the sentence connected with the previous $\epsilon\mathring{i}\pi a\nu$ by omission of the intervening matter, so as to read

'And they spake what they did not understand';

whether this was arrived at in the first instance by substituting $\mathring{\epsilon}\gamma\nu\omega\kappa a\nu$ for $\mathring{\eta}\nu\epsilon\gamma\kappa a\nu$ is not quite clear: but the whole treatment of the text is too drastic to allow us to believe that the Syriac is the original. Another suggestion is that the Syriac translator read $\kappa a\grave{i} \; o\grave{v}\kappa \; \mathring{\epsilon}\gamma\nu\omega\nu$, and took it for a 3rd person plural instead of a 1st person singular.

In Ps. ii. 29 [25] the difficult

$$\tau o\hat{v} \; \epsilon\mathring{i}\pi\epsilon\hat{i}\nu \; \tau\grave{\eta}\nu \; \mathring{v}\pi\epsilon\rho\eta\phi a\nu\acute{i}a\nu \; \tau o\hat{v} \; \delta\rho\acute{a}\kappa o\nu\tau o\varsigma$$

appears in the Syriac as ܐܣܘܝܣܠ which makes excellent sense, from whatever quarter it is derived. Perles conjectures that the original Greek was $\tau a\pi\epsilon\iota\nu o\hat{v}\nu$: it is just conceivable that the Syriac might stand for a translation of this.

In Ps. ii. 41 [37] for

$$\epsilon\mathring{v}\lambda o\gamma\eta\tau\grave{o}\varsigma \; \kappa\acute{v}\rho\iota o\varsigma \; \epsilon\mathring{i}\varsigma \; \tau\grave{o}\nu \; a\mathring{i}\hat{\omega}\nu a \; \mathring{\epsilon}\nu\acute{\omega}\pi\iota o\nu \; \delta o\acute{v}\lambda\omega\nu \; a\mathring{v}\tau o\hat{v}$$

the Syriac has the equivalent of $\mathring{v}\pi\grave{o} \; \tau\hat{\omega}\nu \; \delta o\acute{v}\lambda\omega\nu \; a\mathring{v}\tau o\hat{v}$, and a glance at the previous line of the Greek will show that $\mathring{\epsilon}\nu\acute{\omega}\pi\iota o\nu$ has been accidentally borrowed from there, so that we may replace $\mathring{v}\pi\grave{o} \; \tau\hat{\omega}\nu$ on the faith of the Syriac, which at this point establishes a better Greek text.

In Ps. iv. 25 [21, 22] for

$$\kappa a\grave{i} \; \pi a\rho\acute{\omega}\rho\gamma\iota\sigma a\nu \; \tau\grave{o}\nu \; \theta\epsilon\acute{o}\nu \cdot \; \kappa a\grave{i} \; \pi a\rho\acute{\omega}\xi\upsilon\nu a\nu$$
$$\mathring{\epsilon}\xi\hat{a}\rho a\iota \; a\mathring{v}\tau o\grave{v}\varsigma \; \mathring{a}\pi\grave{o} \; \tau\hat{\eta}\varsigma \; \gamma\hat{\eta}\varsigma$$

the Syriac reads

$$\kappa a\grave{i} \; \pi a\rho\acute{\omega}\rho\gamma\iota\sigma a\nu \; [\text{ܐ ܝܪ}] \; \tau\grave{o}\nu \; \theta\epsilon\acute{o}\nu \cdot$$
$$\kappa a\grave{i} \; \pi a\rho\omega\rho\gamma\acute{i}\sigma\theta\eta \; [\text{ܐܬܢܕܢܐ}] \; \mathring{\epsilon}\xi\hat{a}\rho a\iota \; \kappa\tau\acute{\epsilon}.$$

Here the translator seems to have taken a slight liberty with his text, by translating the same word in two different ways, unless we prefer the explanation that παρωξύνθη stood in his copy, instead of παρωργίσθη.

In Ps. viii. 23 [20] the clause

$$\text{ἀπώλεσεν ἄρχοντας αὐτῶν καὶ πάντα σοφὸν}$$
$$\text{ἐν βουλῇ}$$

has for its last words

ܟ̈ܠܒܐ ܦܝܫܝܢ ܠܛܘ

'because he is wise in counsel';

it is, however, only a blunder in the Syriac text itself: read ܣܘܠ for ܠܛܘ and you have the equivalent of the Greek.

The same thing has happened in Ps. x. 9 [8], where the Syriac reads

'The salvation of the Lord is upon the house of Israel
for an eternal Kingdom':

a very slight change restores ܠܡܣܟܢܘܬ for ܠܡܣܟܢܘ and gives us the Greek σωφροσύνην as in Codd. H (R). This must, in its turn, be corrected to εὐφροσύνην with Codd. J L C.

Here the Syriac follows a corrupt Greek text, and has itself been corrupted. For more violent changes in the Syriac we may take the following:

Ps. ii. 37 [33]

$$\text{εὐλογεῖτε τὸν θεόν, οἱ φοβούμενοι}$$
$$\text{τὸν κύριον ἐν ἐπιστήμῃ·}$$
$$\text{ὅτι τὸ ἔλεος κυρίου ἐπὶ τοὺς φοβουμένους}$$
$$\text{αὐτὸν μετὰ κρίματος.}$$

The Syriac reads ἐν σχήματι for ἐν ἐπιστήμῃ: but the parallelism shows that the Greek is right, and perhaps the Syriac ܐܣܟܡܐ should be corrected to ܣܘܟܠܐ.

In Ps. v. 8 [6] for μὴ βαρύνῃς τὴν χεῖρά σου ἐφ' ἡμᾶς the Syriac has

ܠܐ ܬܬܚܕܘܪ ܐܝܕܟ ܡܢ

'let not thy hand be delayed from us';

which appears to answer to

$$\text{μὴ βραδύνῃς τὴν χεῖρά σου ἀφ' ἡμῶν,}$$

the error being due to a false transcription of the Greek. For the correctness of the Greek, we may compare Ps. Sol. ii. 24 and the Biblical parallels cited by Ryle and James [Judg. i. 35 : 1 Sam. v. 6 : Ps. xxxi. (xxxii.) 4].

In the difficult passage Ps. xv. 8, 9 [7]

λιμὸς καὶ ῥομφαία καὶ θάνατος ἀπὸ δικαίων μακρὰν,
φεύξονται γὰρ ὡς διωκόμενοι πολέμου ἀπὸ ὁσίων,

the Syriac boldly says in the second clause, that

'they shall flee as death flees away from life.'

Perles compares Lev. xxvi. 36

καὶ φεύξονται ὡς φεύγοντες ἀπὸ πολέμου

which suggests that ἀπὸ has dropped from our text, and gives the original Hebrew.

The Syriac variation is very vivid, but I am afraid it is an evasion of a difficult text : the parallelism would be spoilt by saying that 'death flees from the righteous, as death flees from life.' The Greek seems to be right as it stands, and to mean 'they shall flee from the saints as fugitives of war [are wont to flee].'

In Ps. xvii. 11 [9] Gebhardt edits

οὐκ ἠλέησεν αὐτοὺς ὁ θεός.
ἐξηρεύνησεν τὸ σπέρμα αὐτῶν
καὶ οὐκ ἀφῆκεν αὐτῶν ἕνα.

The Syriac has a series of imperatives, or of futures equivalent to imperatives : so that we ought to have in the Greek, if that were the original of the Syriac,

οὐκ ἐλεήσεις αὐτούς, ὁ θεός.
ἐπίσκεψον [? ἐξερεύνησον] τὸ σπέρμα αὐτῶν,
καὶ οὐκ ἀφήσεις αὐτῶν ἕνα,

and since the MSS. have ἐλεήσει and two of them have ἐξερεύνησον we may, by the Syriac, bring the Greek into closer agreement with what must have been its original form.

So far, then, our investigation has not taken us sensibly out of range of the Greek MSS. There are one or two obscurities still to be cleared up, but the above are the principal cases. Here is one microscopic, but significant error. In Psalm v. 16 the Syriac translator has definitely blundered over the word οὗ in

καὶ οὗ ἐστιν ἡ ἐλπὶς ἐπί σε,
οὐ φείσεται ἐν δόματι.

Here he reads the first ου as a negative, and is obliged to discard the second. Cod. R also reads οὐκ for the first ου.

We may, then, conclude that the Syriac translator of the Psalms has worked from a Greek text; and we will presently try to find out its nearest affinity amongst the existing MSS.

In one or two cases the translator makes very successful paronomasiae in his translation, such as might almost deceive the very elect into a belief that he had recovered a play on words of the original Hebrew.

For example in Ps. xi. 6, 7 [5]

οἱ δρύμοι ἐσκίασαν αὐτοῖς ἐν τῇ παροδῷ αὐτῶν,
πᾶν ξύλον εὐωδίας ἀνέτειλεν αὐτοῖς ὁ θεός.

For the second line the Syriac reads

ܡܢ ܟܠ ܐܝܠܢܐ ܕܪܝܚܐ ܒܣܝܡܐ ܐܪܝܚ ܠܗܘܢ ܐܠܗܐ

As it does not seem possible that ܐܪܝܚ can be a direct translation of ἀνέτειλεν we are almost obliged to believe that the writer has introduced a paronomasia: 'every tree of sweet breath God caused to breathe upon them.' It cannot be original, for as Perles points out[1], Baruch read ἐνέτειλεν (cf. Bar. v. 8, πᾶν ξύλον εὐωδίας τῷ Ἰσραὴλ προστάγματι), and this can only be a variant of ἀνέτειλεν.

Another similar case will be found in Ps. ix. 9 [5]

ὁ ποιῶν ἐλεημοσύνην θησαυρίζει ζωὴν
αὐτῷ παρὰ κυρίῳ,

which the Syriac renders by

ܗܘ ܓܝܪ ܕܥܒܕ ܙܕܩܬܐ ܣܐܡ ܚܝ̈ܐ ܕܢܚܘܪ ܣܝܡ ܠܗ
ܠܘܬ ܡܪܝܐ.

As this ܣܝܡ ܣܐܡ cannot be a Hebrew form of speech, we are obliged to admit that the play on words is due to the ingenuity of the translator.

Now let us see whether we can get a rough idea of the place which the Syriac text of the Psalms of Solomon occupies amongst the Greek MSS.

Relation of the Syriac text of the 18 Psalms to the Greek MSS.

The edition of Ryle and James is based upon four MSS. of which the chief is the very beautiful Copenhagen MS. But since the other three (at Paris, Vienna and Moscow respectively) have been shown by

[1] *Zur Erklärung der Psalmen Salomos,* p. 9.

Gebhardt to be derived from the Copenhagen MS., the text of Ryle and James is reduced to a single authority, for the other three may be neglected.

To this MS. Gebhardt adds four more, one from the Vatican, two from Mount Athos, and one from Monte Cassino. We have thus eight MSS. as follows:

C = Codex Casanatensis 1908.
H = Codex Hauniensis 6: (the Copenhagen MS.).
J = Cod. 555 of the Monastery at Iveron.
L = a MS. in the Monastery of the Laura.
M = a Moscow MS.: Library of the Holy Synod 147.
P = Paris Gr. 2991 A.
R = Vatican Gr. 336.
V = Vienna: Theol. Gr. 11.

The relations between these eight MSS. Gebhardt reduces to the following scheme:

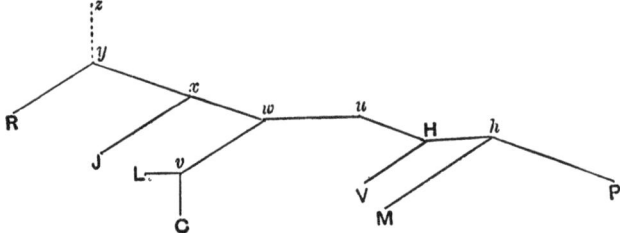

Here z is the archetype: y, x, w are uncial MSS. which make connecting links between the existing texts, and v, u and h are similar links in the shape of minuscule MSS.

The first thing we notice is that in numbering the Psalms, H proceeds as follows:

Psal. Sol. 1 = a'
.... 2 = β'
.... 3 = ... thus missing one in the count.
.... 4 = γ'
.... 5 = δ'
.... 6 = ϵ'
.... 7 = ς'
.... 8 = ζ'
.... 9 = θ' thus missing a numeral:

after which the count is regular.

This error in the numbering of Ps. 5 has led its copy V astray, which has no number by the first hand, but has a wrong number δ' on the margin by a later hand.

Now turn to the Syriac MS.; we have

Psal. Sol. 1 = Psalm 43 of the Syriac.

.... 2 = ... 44 ....

.... 3 = ... 45 ....

.... 4 = ... 47 ....

&c. = &c.

all the numbers being now one in excess.

It will be seen that the Syriac numeration has gone wrong very nearly at the same place as Cod. H, and in correcting an error in one direction, the scribe has made a continuous line of errors in another direction. This suggests that Syr. and H are not very widely removed from one another. Now let us examine some special readings.

In Ps. i. 3 we have

R L Syr. for πολλὴν⎫
J H πολὺν ⎭ .

In Ps. i. 4 we have

R J L Syr. against H (διέλθοι).

In Ps. ii. 1 we have L H Syr. for κατέβαλε ⎫
R J for κατέβαλλε⎭ '

this suggests that the Syriac comes on the diagram somewhere between x and w.

In Ps. ii. 24 [22]

ἱκάνωσον, κύριε, τοῦ βαρύνεσθαι χεῖρά σου
ἐπὶ Ἰερουσαλὴμ ἐν ἐπαγωγῇ ἐθνῶν.

Here ἐπαγωγῇ is clearly right, but some MSS. have ἀπαγωγῇ: the Syriac has it correctly: thus the MSS. divide R J L and Syr. against H.

In the same connexion it is somewhat perplexing to find both R and Syr. in what seems to be a common error, reading 'Israel' for 'Jerusalem.' One would have expected the same reading to turn up in J, but perhaps it was corrected by the scribe. If Gebhardt's diagram is correct, it looks as if R and Syr. might be the original reading and not an error at all.

In Ps. iv. 3 R and the Syriac are together in reading ἁμαρτωλῶν against J L C H (ἁμαρτιῶν).

In Ps. iv. 10 [8] we have J L C H Syr. (νόμον μετὰ δόλου) against R (μόνον μετὰ δούλου).

In Ps. viii. 24 [21] the Syriac seems to involve

ἁ with R against ἁς of J L C H.

In Ps. viii. 26 [22] Syr. and R are again together in reading ἐμίανεν.

In Ps. xvi. 12 the Syriac omits a clause by homoioteleuton, in company with L.

In Ps. xvii. 8 [6] the Syriac reads ἀλλάγματος with R J L against H (ἀλαλάγματος).

In Ps. xvii. 23 [21] the Syriac reads εἶδες with R J L against H and the rest.

These are the most striking of the non-singular readings of the Syriac, and they show clearly that the version belongs to an earlier strain of text than Cod. H, and that its place is with the group R J L, being perhaps intermediate between J and L. The singular readings and free translations on the part of the Syriac give us no assistance in regard to the grouping of the MSS., and we must leave the matter in the approximate manner explained above.

It must be clear from the foregoing that we cannot expect to get any nearer to the original language of the Psalms by means of the Syriac. The original Hebrew must be sought in the emendations to the Greek text made by Wellhausen, Geiger, Ryle and James, and Perles. [Dr Barnes has discovered in the Cambridge University MS. Add. 2012 (a volume containing two short works of Bar Hebraeus followed by a collection of prayers), the Syriac text of the Psalm of Solomon xvi. 6—13. The Psalm, which is wrongly numbered as the 59th in our collection, is actually numbered 58, which shows that the arrangement in our MS., viz. Odes and Psalms numbered continuously, beginning with Odes, is not unique. I have added the readings of this fragment, Cod. C, to the text.]

Let us turn in the next place to the Odes, and see whether we can trace their linguistic history. Here we have no Greek text extant, but we have the Coptic text of certain Odes and there are Greek words embedded; we have also traces of a Latin version, which we may assume, provisionally, to have been made from the Greek; and we have the Syriac version.

The Syriac text of the Odes taken from the Greek.

In Ode 6, *v.* 16, we have tried to explain the variation between a Coptic = παρρησία and a Syriac = παρουσία by reference to a misread Greek word.

We can frequently detect Greek compounds in their awkward Syriac substitutes; for example, in Ode 7, *v.* 26, 'excellent beauty of the Lord' is an attempt to render the Greek μεγαλο-πρέπεια[1]. The constantly recurring ܐܠ ܘܢܒܐܠ, 'without corruption,' stands for ἄφθαρτος and ἀφθαρσία.

A good instance is in Ode 9, *v.* 3, where the literal rendering

'His thought is everlasting life,
And without corruption is your perfection'

probably stands for

καὶ ἐν ἀφθαρσίᾳ τὸ τέλος ὑμῶν,

and should therefore be translated,

'And your end is immortality.'

A somewhat similar case is the frequently repeated ܐܠ ܚܣܘܡ which stands for the Greek ἄφθονος, ἀφθόνως[2]. An interesting example will be found in Ode 11, *v.* 6, where we read that 'speaking waters touched my lips from the fountain of God without grudging' (*i.e.* abundantly). In the passage just quoted I was at first tempted to emend 'the speaking waters' to 'waters of a flood,' but it is clear that this must not be done: the expression is the same as in Ignatius *ad Rom.* 7, ὕδωρ ζῶν καὶ λαλοῦν, which Lightfoot too hastily altered to ζῶν καὶ ἀλλόμενον and thus made a direct Johannine parallel. For 'talking water' there are sufficient literary and folk-lore parallels.

Lightfoot quotes from Jortin [*Eccl. Hist.* i. 356] the reference to Anacreon 11 (13),

δαφνηφόροιο Φοίβου λάλον πιόντες ὕδωρ,

for the expression 'talking water' and for the prophetic inspiration that was supposed to be produced by drinking it: but objects to Jortin's inference that, as there was one of these 'speaking' fountains at Daphne, the famous suburb of Antioch,

---

[1] We may compare with the LXX. of Ps. lxvii. (lxviii.) 34 and the Peshitta.

[2] An interesting parallel to this series of translations will be found in Irenaeus (247) where the Latin text shows a double translation: '*sine invidia largiter* donans hominibus.'

Ignatius may have borrowed his image from thence. Lightfoot thinks the reference doubtful, even if the text were correct. It seems clear, from the language of the Ode, that the text, about which Lightfoot hesitated, is correct, and I think we may say that the Greek text lies behind the Syriac[1]; as to the interpretation, that may require a little further deliberation.

We may now pass on to discuss briefly the question of the Unity of Authorship? unity or multiplicity of the authorship of the Psalms. Do they come from a single hand or are they a collection made up out of various authors extending over a period of time? It is natural that we should be on our guard against a too hasty belief that the whole of a collection like the present one comes from a single workshop: for we have before our eyes the example of the traditional authorship of the Canonical Psalter, where the authors to whom the compositions are referred are far too few and where the Psalms are often referred to periods when it is impossible to believe the compositions can have been extant.

In the case before us, however, we can apply a number of

---

[1] Lightfoot was quoting Jortin by way of Jacobson. A reference to Jortin himself shows that Lightfoot has not done justice to Jortin, whose statement of the case for λαλοῦν and against ἀλλόμενον is admirable. I transcribe a part of it: 'The expression, ὕδωρ λαλοῦν, resembles the *vocales undae* which inspired the Poets and Prophets.

Statius, *Silv.* i. 11. 6,
> Et de Pieriis vocalem fontibus undam.

An oracle of Apollo Delphicus given to Julian, and preserved by Cedrenus:
> Εἴπατε τῷ βασιλεῖ, χαμαὶ πέσε δαίδαλος αὐλά.
> Οὐκέτι Φοῖβος ἔχει καλύβαν, οὐ μάντιδα δάφνην,
> Οὐ παγὰν λαλεοῦσαν, ἀπέσβετο καὶ λάλον ὕδωρ.
> ....

In these verses, which, to do them justice, are elegant, Apollo, to raise Julian's compassion, deplores the silence of his oracles, and of *speaking streams*. In the first line read βασιλῆι.

Anacreon xiii.,
> Οἱ δὲ Κλάρου παρ' ὄχθαις
> Δαφνηφόροιο Φοίβου
> Λάλον πιόντες ὕδωρ
> Μεμηνότες βοῶσιν.'

Then after discussing the passage in Ignatius and its variant readings, he shows that the Greek Menaeum had both readings, and goes on to say, against Le Clerc, that 'the λαλοῦν ὕδωρ must not be altered: it is sufficiently confirmed by the citations of Cotelerius in this very note where he is inclined to reject it, and it is more elegant and proper than Le Clerc imagined.' References to Antioch and Daphne follow.

Our seventh Ode shows the fitness of the Ignatian expression. It is not necessary to assume any connexion, either of place or authorship, with the Ignatian letters.

tests as to style and matter, and I think it will be evident that the majority of the Odes do come from a single hand. They are so often cast in the same mould, both as regards ideas and expressions, that we are obliged to recognize kinship in the separate compositions[1]. Moreover the very elevation of the thoughts of the Odes is an index of a single personality : even if we cannot identify him, we are sure that the writer was a rare spirit, and rare spirits do not agree with multiplied authorship. When our Odist is at his best, he is certainly one and not many. A good way to test for unity of authorship is to group together those Odes which have the same ideas similarly expressed.

For example, we are all familiar with the expression in the Epistle to the Hebrews (Heb. xiii. 15) in which we are told to offer to God through Christ the fruit of our lips in a continual sacrifice of praise. This expression is borrowed from Hosea xiv. 3 according to the Septuagint, or perhaps from the Hebrew of Is. lvii. 19. The expression is one which is already employed in the extant Psalms of Solomon, where we find as follows :

Ps. Sol. xv. 5 [3]

ψαλμὸν καινὸν μετ' ᾠδῆς ἐν εὐφροσύνῃ καρδίας,
καρπὸν χειλέων ἐν ὀργάνῳ ἡρμοσμένῳ γλώσσης,
ἀπαρχὴν χειλέων ἀπὸ καρδίας ὁσίας καὶ δικαίας.

Here the expression has caught the fancy of the Psalmist, who works it into a parallel between ' fruits ' and ' firstfruits.'

In the Odes it is a very favourite expression, as the following instances will show :

> Ode 8. ' Let your love be multiplied from the heart and even to the lips, to bring forth fruit to the Lord, living fruit, holy fruit, and to talk with watchfulness in His light.'
> Ode 12. ' Like the flow of waters flows truth from my mouth, and my lips show forth His fruit.'
> Ode 14. ' Teach me the Odes of thy truth, that I may bring forth fruit in thee.'
> Ode 16. ' His love has nourished my heart, and even to my lips His fruits He was pouring out.'

---

[1] A good parallel case would be the modern recovery of the works of the seventeenth century poet Traherne.

The recurrence of the theme 'the fruit of the lips' suggests that this group of Psalms should be credited to a common author.

The sixteenth Ode from which we just quoted is one of a group that begins with a similitude, something like those which we find in the Songs of Degrees in the Canonical Psalter. For instance we have:

> Ode 14. 'As the eyes of a son to his father, so are my eyes, O Lord, at all times towards Thee.'

The parallel to this is Ps. cxxiii. 2, 'As the eyes of servants to the hands of their masters, and as the eyes of a maid to the hand of her mistress, so are our eyes to the Lord our God.'

Very similar is Ode 15.

> 'As the sun is a joy to them that seek for its day break, so is my Joy the Lord,' with which we may compare Ps. cxxix. (cxxx.) 6, 'more than they that watch for the morning.'

Ode 16 begins something in the same way:

> 'As the work of the husbandman is the ploughshare: and the work of the steersman is the guidance of the ship: so also my work is the Psalm of the Lord: my craft and my occupation are in His praises.'

With these three Odes we may probably take Ode 28:

> As the wings of doves over their nestlings, and the mouths of their nestlings towards their mouths, so also are the wings of the Spirit over my heart.'

Suppose we group these four together, viz. 14, 15. 16, 28: of these we have already 14 and 16 in the group 8, 12, 14, 16: so the six Odes 8, 12, 14, 15, 16, 28, belong together and have a common authorship.

Next let us try the association and repetition of ideas: one of the harshest symbols employed by the Odes is the figure of milk from the breasts of God: we have the following coincidences:

> Ode 8. 'My own breasts I prepared for them that they might drink my holy milk and live thereby.'
>
> Ode 14. 'With thee are my breasts and my delight.'

Ode 19 contains a parallel in extended form in which Christ is the cup that contains the milk from the breasts of the Father.

With this we must probably take

Ode 35. 'I was carried like a child by its mother, and he gave me milk, the dew of the Lord.'

The same connexion between the milk and the dew of the Lord is found in Ode 4

'Distil thy dews upon us and open the rich fountains that pour forth milk and honey.'

Here then is a group of Odes, 4, 8, 14, 19, 35, which appear to belong together: but of these 8 and 14 are in the previous group, which must now be enlarged to

4, 8, 12, 14, 15, 16, 19, 28, 35

In this way then, we may form the Odes into groups, as a preliminary test for authorship. Here are some more suggestions for grouping.

In Ode 6 we begin with

'As the hand moves over the harp, and the strings speak, so speaks in my members the Spirit of the Lord.'

From the use of an opening similitude, it may be suggested that this belongs with the similitudes in Odes already quoted: but the actual figure of the hand and the harp recurs: the very next Ode has

Ode 7. 'They shall go forth to meet Him and shall sing to Him with the harp of many notes':

and this Ode also opens with a similitude.

In Ode 14 we have

'Open to me the harp of thy Holy Spirit, that with all its notes I may praise Thee, O Lord.'

In Ode 26

'His harp is in my hands and the Odes of His rest shall not be silent.'

These four odes may be taken together, and attached to the previous group, which now contains

4, 6, 7, 8, 12, 14, 15, 16, 19, 26, 28, 35.

Ode 7 and Ode 10 are connected by the use of a curious expression, 'the traces of the Light'; thus

> Ode 7. 'He set over it the traces of His Light.'
> Ode 10. 'The traces of the Light were set upon their heart.'

Ode 4 and Ode 8 are connected by their reference to the seal of God which is set on His creatures:

> Ode 4. 'Who is there that shall put on thy grace and be hurt? For thy seal is known.'
> Ode 8. 'On their faces I set my seal' &c.

Ode 3 and Ode 8 are connected by the fact that both of them speak of Christ as (a) the Beloved, (b) the Living One.

Ode 3 and Ode 17 have a common feature in that they speak of believers as the members of Christ.

Odes 1, 5, 9 (?), 17 and 20 (?) contain the doctrine of the crown of life which does not wither.

Odes 17, 21, 40 and 41 speak of the transfiguration of the face of the believer: e.g.

> Ode 17. 'I received the face and the fashion of a new person.'
> Ode 21. 'The exultation of the Lord increased on my face.'
> Ode 40. 'My face exults with His gladness.'
> Ode 41. 'Let our faces shine in His light.'

We have now, tentatively, grouped together Odes

> 1, 3, 4, 5, 6, 7, 8, 9 (?), 10, 12, 14, 15, 16, 17, 19,
> 20 (?), 21, 26, 28, 35, 40, 41.

No doubt other coincidences and parallels may be detected: the net result of this is the recognition that the majority of the Odes come from a single hand, or if we prefer it, from the same school. The doubtful member, in my judgment, is Ode 19 which is far too grotesque to be by the same hand as the other compositions. It appears to me to be an imitation of the other Psalms that speak of the breasts of God. It is tritheistic as well as grotesque. There will be some short Psalms that do not readily furnish material for identification, but even these short Odes will sometimes be capable of grouping; thus the figure of the Cross in prayer is found in Ode 27, and reappears in a longer composition Ode 42. It is very difficult, however, to believe that this 42nd Ode belongs to the main body of the collection.

Setting aside such small compositions and such as are late or discordant, I believe it will be found that the internal evidence will throw nearly all the Odes together, and that those which are thus grouped will be found to be Christian compositions, although at first sight many of them might seem to be Jewish, or not definitely marked one way or the other. Their internal parallelisms enable us to say with confidence that they are either Christian or at least Judaeo-Christian compositions.

Several of the longer Odes do not admit of grouping with the others : amongst these we note

> Ode 22, which contains an account of the victory over the dragon with seven heads.
>
> Ode 23, which records the descent from heaven of a mysterious letter, inscribed with the name of the Trinity.
>
> Ode 38, which records the preservation of the writer from various errors and deceits.
>
> Ode 39, which explains the dangers which attend the rapid rise of great rivers, and how the believers walk firmly on their waves, following the footsteps and example of Christ.

These are also, in all probability, Christian ; but the question of their authorship must be reserved and examined in detail.

We now proceed to examine the historical allusions in the book of Odes.

The first thing that strikes us is the poverty of historical background compared with that in the extant Psalms of Solomon. In these known Psalms it is impossible to miss the historical situation which provoked them : they were made under the stress of national exigency, and the troubles stand out from the Psalms with their dates on them. Pompey is written large over several of the Psalms, and when Rome is not expressly mentioned it is distinctly felt. The great dragon of the Psalms of Solomon is a classified specimen. We can tell him a mile away.

Not only so, but when the history is recognized, the theology

Historical allusions in the Odes.

also becomes patent. The Pharisaism of the Psalms is transparently clear, and the Messianism that went with it. So that it was with justice that some critics labelled the compositions Psalms of the Pharisees. That does not mean that all these Psalms are necessarily by one hand nor that all of them are decidedly marked. Some of them are, in fact, colourless, and in that sense, dateless: but the collection, as a whole, is identified, both historically and theologically. The case of the Odes is very different. If there are any national disasters behind the songs, they have been lost in the songs. There is not a sad note, and there is hardly a vindictive note in the whole collection. And on the theological side, the leading characteristic is experience, and not dogma: and experience is much harder to date than dogma, and shows fewer of the weather-marks of evolution. Sometimes, indeed, the expressions of the Odists rise to such a height that they catch from the object of their Faith something that is everlasting rather than evolutionary. It is difficult to date a man who has disclosed the fact that he is supremely happy and that God has made his face to shine with the light of heaven. The only way in which we could date such a phenomenon would be to say that, if he is not an isolated specimen, the songs must proceed from some time of general spiritual elevation; and since it is historically verifiable, that the experimental time of the bloom of Church life is the first age (for one hardly expects to find people generally rejoicing with 'an unspeakable and glorified joy,' say, in the time of Constantine), then these hymns or odes must belong to the first days of the Church: but even that way of dating them is somewhat indefinite.

When we go in search of special historical details, we do not get a very rich harvest. The most important cases must be carefully examined. The first case is Ode 4, which has a reference to a proposal or suggestion to change the Sanctuary of God from Jerusalem to some other position, and it is a noble protest from a standpoint, which at least in part is a Jewish standpoint, against the suggestion. The Ode begins as follows:

The proposal to found another Sanctuary.

> No man, O God, changes thy holy place: and it is not possible that he should change it and put it in

another place: because he has no power over it: for thy
sanctuary was designed before thou didst make other
places: that which is the elder shall not be altered by
that which is younger than itself.'

Now here it is clear that some change in the value of the
Sanctuary at Jerusalem is threatened at the hands of man.   The
writer does not mean the same thing as the author of the
seventh of the extant Psalms of Solomon, where he prays God
not to remove His tabernacle from amongst them, lest the enemy
should tread the inheritance of the Sanctuary.   It is at the hands
of man that the Sanctuary is threatened, and the writer is
confident that the Lord himself has never changed and never will
change.

His thoughts turn to the origin of the holy place.   That
holy place had a pre-existence and a corresponding eternity:
it was a 'Sanctuary from the beginning.'   Here we are certainly
face to face with Jewish beliefs ; the writer of the Ode may be
shown on other grounds to be a Christian, but on this point he
is betrayed as having Jewish sympathies.   And his views with
regard to the Temple are not merely Jewish in a general sense,
but highly evolved.

The first theories of the Heavenly Sanctuary appear to have
been almost Platonic in character: there was a pattern in the
mount: according to that pattern or idea the visible thing was
fashioned ; but the idea was eternal, and pre-existent.   This
Platonic idea underwent change at the hand of later Rabbins,
who came to teach that the actual Sanctuary had been created
before other things, and had been caught away to Heaven and
disappeared.

Accordingly we find in the Apocalypse of Baruch, c. 4, that
the Lord explains the doctrine of the Sanctuary to the prophet,
in language which depreciates the earthly sanctuary :

> ' Dost thou think that this is that city of which I said,
> On the palms of my hands have I graven thee?   It is not
> this building which is now built in your midst: it is that
> which will be revealed with Me, that which was prepared
> beforehand here from the time when I took counsel to
> make Paradise, and showed it to Adam before he sinned,

but when he transgressed the commandment, it was removed from him, as also Paradise.'

Here, then, we have the view of a first-century writer who is amazed at the desolation of Zion, and like our Odist, is concerned with the problem of the deserted Sanctuary: he concludes that it has been caught away, as Paradise was. The real city of God is that which was made at the beginning ; like Paradise, it was only here temporarily : what is left is not the real thing.

Now our Odist does not go so far in despair as the writer of the Apocalypse, of whom he may have been a contemporary. He believes the Sanctuary was made at the very beginning before other things, but still holds to the belief that Jerusalem is the Holy City and the Temple the true Sanctuary. He does not go so far even as the Epistle to the Hebrews, in drawing a distinction between the tabernacle which the Lord pitched, and that which was made by man.

His position appears to be very closely that of the great Jewish Rabbis, who taught the pre-existence of the Sanctuary and its priority to the rest of the works of God, and who do not appear to have explained this pre-existence according to the theory of Ideas, for in that case where would the priority have been of the Temple amongst other works of God ? Their method of teaching can be seen from

Bereshith Rabbah, 20 :

> ' Seven things were created before the world : Thorah, Gehenna, the Paradise of Eden, the Throne of Glory, *the Sanctuary*, Repentance and the Name of Messiah.'

Very nearly to the same effect is the dictum of Rabbi Meir in *Pirqe Aboth* vi. 10 :

> ' Five possessions possessed the Holy One, blessed is He, in His world and they are these : Thorah, one possession : Heaven and Earth, one possession : Abraham, one possession : Israel, one possession : *the Sanctuary*, one possession.'

The Scriptural proofs of these statements are important : the case of the Sanctuary is proved as follows :

> ' The Sanctuary, whence is it proved ? Because it is written, " The place, O Lord, which thou hast made for

thee to dwell in, the Sanctuary, O Lord, which thy
hands have established" (Exod. xv. 17): and it saith,
"And he brought them to the border of his Sanctuary,
even to this mountain, which his right hand had
possessed"' (Ps. lxxviii. 54).

That will suffice to show the nature of the Scripture proofs
employed: and it is clear that the same beliefs were in the mind
of the writer of our Ode. The question then arises as to the
situation which provoked his expression of faith.

In the case of the Apocalypse of Baruch, to which we have
referred as a parallel, it is clear that it is the desolation of
Jerusalem by Titus which is the historical background: and it
is some similar situation which is reflected in this fourth Ode.
Only the language in this latter case seems to imply that some
deliberate suggestion or attempt had been made by man to
move the Sanctuary: and against this the writer protests. The
agent who makes or suggests the change cannot be the Roman
conqueror: he might carry away the holy vessels, but that does
not remove the Sanctuary, any more than it was moved in the
days of Nebuchadnezzar. So it must be a suggestion coming
from Jewish or quasi-Jewish quarters. And the difficulty lies in
this: it is hardly possible that in the time of the last Jewish
wars, any body of Jewish believers could have cherished the
thought of a temple anywhere else than at Jerusalem. If the
temple was gone, it was gone back to Heaven and to God: it was
not to be sought elsewhere. It is not easy to believe that in
A.D. 70 or in A.D. 135, under the hand of Titus, or at the time
of Bar Cochba, the Jews would have thought of another temple.

For this reason I suggest that the writer is referring to an
attempt which had been made in earlier days to provide an
alternative Sanctuary to that at Jerusalem.

We know of at least three such attempts to change the
Holy Place; one, the Samaritan temple on Gerizim, another the
Sanctuary at Assouan, whose officials were in friendly relations
with both Jerusalem and Gerizim, the third the temple of Onias
at Leontopolis in Egypt, said to be actually modelled on the
temple at Jerusalem, and designed as a substitute for it. Of
these the Sanctuary on Gerizim was destroyed by John
Hyrcanus in B.C. 128; the Sanctuary at Assouan was wrecked

by the Egyptians, after the retreat of Cambyses; the temple of
Onias actually outlasted the temple at Jerusalem, and was
destroyed in A.D. 73 by the Roman general Paulinus in con-
sequence of the fears of the Romans that this temple also might
become a rallying point for sedition and revolt. And I have
suggested that it is the destruction of this temple, and not the
Jerusalem temple, that provokes the protest of the fourth Ode.
Unless it can be shown that there is a probability that some one
actually proposed building a new temple, soon after the great
Jewish disasters, elsewhere than at Jerusalem, it seems to me
that this is the likeliest solution: and it furnishes an exact
historical date.

There can be no doubt as to the writer's affection for the
temple at Jerusalem: but he does not wail or lament: he is satis-
fied with the unchangeableness of God and the immutability of
His promises. If he had been a Jew, he could not have displayed
such equanimity: compare, for example, the language of the
Apocalypse of Baruch or of Fourth Ezra, to see how the real
Jew would feel. It may be inferred that the writer of the
Ode is a Judaeo-Christian. If his date was not, as I suggest,
soon after A.D. 70, the only other possible date seems to be soon
after A.D. 135[1].

The importance of the temple at Leontopolis, in connexion
with the desecration of the temple at Jerusalem by Antiochus
Epiphanes, as a factor in the decentralization of the Jewish
religion, is indicated by Harnack in his *History of Dogma.*

'The spread of Judaism in the world, the secularization and
apostasy of the priestly caste, the desecration of the Temple,
the building of the Temple at Leontopolis, the perception
brought about by the spiritualizing of religion in the Empire of
Alexander the Great, that no blood of beast can be a means
of reconciling God—all these circumstances must have been
absolutely dangerous and fatal, both to the local centralization
of worship, and to the statutory sacrificial system[2].'

In view of this luminous statement, it is not difficult to

---

[1] The desecration of the Temple by Pompey in B.C. 63 is not a possible situation;
for no serious interruption of the Temple Worship took place, and therefore no acute
religious problem was provoked. Nor can our Odes be referred to so early a period.
We have shown that they belong, almost entirely, if not absolutely, to the Christian
period.

[2] Harnack: *l.c.* i. 69 note, Eng. trans.

imagine the resentment of a Palestinian Jew against Leonto-
polis, nor the expression of such resentment in song, when the
offensive institution had been swept away.

We shall get a good idea of the theological position of the
writer amongst the early Christian sects and schools, if we
contrast his position with (i) that of the Ebionites on the one
hand, and (ii) that of the author of the epistle of Barnabas on the
other. Irenaeus tells us, for example, that the Ebionites per-
severe in the customs of the law and in the Jewish mode of life,
and adore Jerusalem as if it were the house of God[1]. Without
pressing too closely the language of Irenaeus concerning the
Ebionites, which may be coloured by polemical exaggeration,
there is certainly a common ground between the writer of the
fourth Ode and the Ebionites, in their affectionate religious
attachment to the ancient Sanctuary.

Now turn to the sixteenth chapter of the very anti-judaic
epistle which passes under the name of Barnabas. Barnabas
begins by telling us that the poor wretches (sc. the Jews) are
in error about the temple, which they take to be a house of God.
They have almost consecrated God in a shrine, as the Gentiles
do. He then quotes prophecies to show the vanity of the Jewish
belief. In the course of these quotations he has to explain
Isaiah xlix. 17, 'Behold those that have destroyed this temple
shall build it again,' and affirms that this is actually taking place
at the hands of the Romans, who had wrecked the temple
because the Jews had made war against them. But instead of
drawing the Ebionite conclusion from this (to us) obscure
historical allusion, he flies off to prove that the only real temple
of God is a redeemed soul. It is clear that the writer of the
fourth Ode, while accepting the spiritual interpretation of life,
would never express himself like Barnabas.

As Dr Taylor says[2], 'those who felt with Barnabas would
have looked with disfavour upon the rebuilding of the temple
at Jerusalem.' [For a further discussion of the Unchangeable
Sanctuary see what is added in the preface.]

There is another way in which we can see that the position
of the writer of the fourth Ode is not that of the normal
Christian of Gentile extraction. One of the commonest exercises

[1] Iren. (ed. Mass. 105).
[2] *Pirqe Aboth* : ed. ii. p. 153.

of the early Christian was the demonstration to the orthodox Jew by means of Testimonies from the Old Testament—that his religion was no longer acceptable to God. From the traces of these early collections of Testimonies which have come to light, it is easy to see that they involved special statements under the heads 'that the Jews were to lose Jerusalem,' and 'that the old temple should pass away and a new one take its place.' The new temple was to be a spiritual one, but whether the new temple was Christ or the believer, is not quite clear. The writer of the fourth Ode is prepared with spiritual interpretations of the older religion, he spiritualizes the priesthood (if it be the same hand as wrote Ode 20) and perhaps the rite of circumcision (cf. Ode 11), but he is not prepared to say that the old Sanctuary was to pass away. His position, therefore, is an intermediate one, not wholly Gentile, though with strong Gentile leanings, and, as we said above, much nearer to the doctrine of the Ebionites than to that of the epistle of Barnabas.

In connexion with the foregoing argument, it may be proper to examine the references made in the Odes to the prevalence of wars, and to determine whether the writer is speaking of actual wars or only of spiritual conflicts. When we read the eighteen Psalms of Solomon, the noise of war is common ; we can see the engines moved up for the siege, we can hear the thud of the battering rams. These Psalms open in affliction : 'instead of peace,' says the writer, 'there was heard the sound of war.'

Possible reference to wars which have occurred.

'Distress and the sound of wars,' so another Psalm begins, 'mine ears have heard, the sound of the trumpet, and the noise of slaughter and destruction.' When this writer says war he means war, and there is no alternative. But the case is not so clear in the Odes. The references to war are few, and obscure.

In Ode 8 we have :

> 'The right hand of the Lord is with you, and He is your helper : and peace was prepared for you, before ever your war was.'

How shall we explain this allusion ? Does it simply mean that the Divine foresight had seen to the end of the man's spiritual troubles and had designed for him

Predestined Peace.

the happy issue out of them? The objection to this is (i) that it is somewhat forced ; (ii) that the language is evidently addressed to a community of persons who have passed through affliction together ; and are spoken of as those who have been despised, whose righteousness has now been exalted. But if it is addressed to a community, the distresses can hardly be spiritual: and it is possible, though I should not like to affirm it positively, that the persons addressed are those Judaeo-Christians at Pella, who escaped from the siege of Jerusalem by flight, in harmony with the evangelic precepts. The Ode to which we have been referring finds a striking parallel in Ode 9, where we have as follows:

> ' For I announce to you peace, to you His saints : that none of those who hear may fall in war, and that those again who have known Him may not perish......There have been wars on account of the crown. Put on the crown in the true covenant of the Lord. And all those who have conquered shall be written in His book. For their book is victory.'

Is this spiritual or carnal warfare? the concluding sentences sound like the language of the Apocalypse, ' To him that overcometh,' and in that case, are spiritual. But the opening sentences sound like an exemption from actual strife and its dangers: and this might again be compared with the condition of the Judaeo-Christians at Pella.

When we turn to Ode 29 we have again allusion to victory over one's enemies, and to war made by the word of the Lord. But as this Ode is definitely Christian, and its language is parallel to the vigorous expressions of Paul about the casting down of imaginations and the bringing of every thought into the captivity of obedience to Christ, we may be sure that the warfare and the victories are spiritual. Examine the following sentences :

> ' From the mouth of death he drew me back, and I laid my enemies low, and He justified me by His grace : for I believed in the Lord's Messiah.'

These are certainly spiritual statements: justification by grace through faith in Christ is the record of spiritual experience, and the victories must be interpreted in the same sense: and so must the following :

cf. Ps. cx. 2
cf. 2 Cor.
x. 5

' He gave me the rod of His power :
that I might subdue the imaginations of the peoples :
    and the power of the men of might to bring them
    low :
to make war by His word,
and to take victory by His power :
And the Lord overthrew my enemy by His word :
and he became like the stubble that the wind carries
    away.'

So far, then, as this 29th Ode is concerned, it is a Christian
and a spiritual product, and relates to a warfare that is not
carnal.

We come now to a much more difficult Psalm of conflict,

The fight with the Dragon. the story of a triumph over a dragon with seven
heads.

In the twenty-second Ode the Lord is praised because

' He overthrew by my hands the dragon with seven
heads :

Thou hast raised me up over his roots, that I might
destroy his seed :

.   .   .   .

Thy right hand destroyed his wicked poison, &c. &c.'

Then follows an account of the raising of an army of dead
bodies, something like the scene in Ezekiel's valley of dry
bones.

The Ode is a striking one and attracted the attention of the
author of the *Pistis Sophia*, who found in the dragon with seven
heads one of the Emanations that threatened the upward pro-
gress of Sophia. When Sophia escapes from these Emanations,
she does it to the music of the ninety-first Psalm, in which it is
promised that the believer shall tread on the lion and the dragon.
And the *Pistis Sophia* says (p. 140):

'Conculcabat προβολην cum facie basilisci serpentis, *cui
septem erant capita* ; et conculcabat vim cum facie leonis et
cum facie δρακοντος. Feci πιστιν σοφιαν manere stantem
super προβολην αυθαδους, quae habet faciem basilisci ser-
pentis, *cui sunt septem capita.*'

and (p. 147)

'Atque verbum quod tua vis luminis dixit per Davidem: meabis super serpentem et basiliscum...... super hos, qui sunt facie serpentis, et super hos, qui facie basilisci serpentis, *quibus septem sunt capita.*'

And then the Ode of Solomon is quoted and commented on. The *Pistis Sophia*, therefore, has annexed this dragon with seven heads and given him a spiritual interpretation. We may say that the dragon was the cause of the quotation of the Ode. As far as natural history goes, he is a lay figure. But is this the original idea? We remember that in the eighteen Psalms of Solomon, the dragon is palpable and tangible: he is Pompey himself, and not a spiritual force or opposing influence.

Then there is an even closer parallel to our Ode, in the almost contemporary twelfth chapter of the Apocalypse; a dragon with seven heads and ten horns persecutes the woman who brings forth the man-child. And the same dragon appears to be intended in the seventeenth chapter, where it is ridden by the mystical Babylon that makes war with the saints. The dragon stands for the power of Antichrist[1], exhibited especially in the adverse action of imperial Rome. This, then, is the nearest parallel to the situation in our Ode.

Now the situation cannot be reduced to an actual war, as when Rome subdues Jerusalem under Pompey, for in these wars Rome always wins: so it must be some other form of conflict, either the passive resistance and triumph of the saints in times of persecution, or the conflict between truth and error, which results in the defeat of heretical teaching.

The Odist refers to the conflict as a personal one carried on from place to place by himself:

'Thou hast raised me up over his roots to destroy his seed: thou wast there and didst help me; and in every place thy name was blessed by me: thy right hand destroyed his wicked poison.'

This is the story, not of a persecution, but of a conflict

---

[1] Thus Irenaeus, in denouncing the Gnostic leaders, such as Simon Magus, and Carpocrates, calls them expressly the precursors of the dragon, who is by his magic going to cast down from Heaven the third part of the stars; that is, Simon and Carpocrates are rehearsals of the coming Antichrist. See Irenaeus (ed. Mass. 164).

between truth and error: and the dragon with seven heads stands, not for a world-power nor an aggressive world-ruler, but for the Antichrist who is spreading the poison of false doctrine and must be confuted from city to city. A parallel situation would be the conflict between Peter and Simon Magus in the Clementine Homilies. Who this Antichrist is, in the mind of the writer, or what is the special form of error that is combated, we have not sufficient information to decide: and for that reason must leave the historical situation somewhat obscure.

The next Ode to be discussed, in the hope of finding some points of contact with history, is the twenty-third: and it is the most difficult of all the Odes to interpret, and quite unlike any of the other compositions in the series.

After some opening sentences, affirming that Joy, Grace and Love are the marks of the elect of God, we are informed that a letter was mysteriously sent down from heaven to earth, as if it had been shot from a bow. People rushed to read it; but it was talismaned by a seal, which none dared to break. Like the tables of the law, it was wholly written by the finger of God and the name of the Trinity was on it.

The mysterious letter.

A mysterious wheel (?) protects the letter from venturesome or hostile hands. This wheel with the sign upon it went down to the feet, along with the head. Perplexing as this language is, it appears to be explained of Christ's descent into Hades: for in Ode 42, where there is an account of Christ's under-world triumph, we are informed that death cast Him up, and *let go the feet with the head.* Christ is the head, and the feet are those members of His who are imprisoned in Hades. This explains our statement about the head going down to the feet. It seems, then, that the mysterious letter has something in it relating to the *Descensus ad Inferos.*

We may compare it with the little book in Apoc. v., which is sealed so that no one can open it, and read it: here there are seven seals, which are to be broken successively. Another suggestive parallel would be the letter in the Bardesanian Hymn of the Soul, which is sent to rouse the King's Son in Egypt[1].

---

[1] See *Acts of Thomas* for the Hymn, and the translation of it in Burkitt, *Early Eastern Christianity.*

This letter was also talismaned with a powerful seal:

'This was my letter, sealed with the King's own seal on the cover,

Lest it should fall in the hands of the fierce Babylonian Demons.'

It flew rapidly as an eagle:

'High it flew as the Eagle, King of the birds of the heaven,

Flew and alighted beside me, and spoke in the speech of my country.'

Such flying letters are not uncommon in Apocryphal literature: one such is sent by Baruch to Babylon, and carried by an eagle. The machinery is not unlike that in our Ode.

We have not, however, succeeded in finding a historical situation for this Ode and the implied document.

It does not seem to belong to the main body of the collection; it may, however, be connected with the forty-second Ode, and both of them may belong to a later period than the rest of the book.

We referred above to the suggestions furnished in Ode 22 of a conflict with Antichrist in the form of some heretical teaching, whose poison was being widely diffused. This suggestion finds some further confirmation in Ode 38, where the writer refers to his pursuit of Truth and the protection which it gave him from the poisons and plagues of Error. He came across a mysterious Bridegroom and Bride, who are corrupting the whole world, and giving them to drink from a cup which, in Circean manner, makes away with their understanding. The Odist escapes by Divine Grace, and by his passion for Truth. But who are these that furnish the blandishments that our writer succeeds in resisting? It cannot be the language of a mere crusader in favour of celibacy, though we know there was a strong tendency in the early Church, especially in the East, to regard all married life as a form of corruption that was to be avoided. But here a mysterious Bridegroom and Bride spread a seductive table before the world, and after they have intoxicated their victims, they forsake them as soon as they have robbed them of their understanding. This can hardly be the language of a general hostility to

The deceiver and his bride.

marriage. And it seems more natural to regard the seducers in the Ode as real people, who are bewitching the world. One thinks of 'thy wife Jezebel' in Apoc. ii. 20, of Simon Magus, and his 'lost sheep' Helena, or some other of the many Antichrists with whom the Church had to contend in the first and second centuries. The description in the Ode is too shadowy for a more exact identification.

In one passage in the Odes the writer speaks of himself in

Jew or Gentile?

language which suggests that he was by birth a Gentile, and that he was looked upon by those to whom he had joined himself with astonishment. The Ode to which we refer is the forty-first, where in the midst of a noble strain of Christian exultation and confession of Christ and the great day that has dawned in Him, we find:

> 'Let us exult with the joy of the Lord. All that see me will be astonished: for I am from another race: the Father of Truth remembered me.'

The writer is explaining his position in a Christian community as a Gentile amongst Jews. He explains his faith in a Saviour who 'makes alive and does not reject our souls.'

The language suits the first century better than the second, and the Church in Palestine better than that in Asia Minor, Greece or Egypt

In another Ode, Christ Himself makes something like an

Christ receives Gentiles.

apology for the reception of the Gentiles. Thus in Ode 10:

> 'I was strengthened and made mighty and took the world captive......The Gentiles were gathered together who were scattered abroad. *And I was unpolluted by my love*......They became my people for ever and ever.'

There can be no doubt that this Ode is Messianic, and that, to put it in the lowest possible terms, it is explanatory of the coming in of the Gentiles   No such explanation, or, if we prefer it, apology, would be natural in Corinth or in Ephesus. It belongs farther East, and seems to me to savour, in any case, of the first century. Certainly the Gentile could not feel himself isolated, nor have to be apologized for in the great Churches of the West, nor in the second century, when Gentile bishops began to appear in Jerusalem itself.

There is another direction in which the writers of the Odes

The coat of skin.

show a curious contact with Judaism.

It is well known that the teaching of the earliest Christians and of the philosophically minded Jews of the first century made a special study of the story of creation in the first chapters of Genesis, which they systematically allegorised. We have a statement of Anastasius the Sinaite that all the early Christian exegetes, from Papias onward, interpreted the Hexahemeron, or Six days of Creation, by reference to Christ and the Church[1]. And those who did not make this direct mystical reference, especially the great Alexandrines, followed Philo in a general allegorisation of the narrative. Many of these explanations, whether Jewish or Christian, are well known. But there is one case which is more obscure. The clothing of Adam and Eve with coats of skins at the time of their expulsion from Paradise was a point that required explanation, and taxed the ingenuity of Philo himself. In his *Questions upon Genesis* he first apologizes for the homely occupation attributed to the Most High, and argues that at any rate simple leather garb is superior to purple and fine linen, and then he boldly breaks away from the literal explanation and says that the coat of skin simply means the human body, which is the receptacle for the Mind and the Life which God had already created.

Now this interpretation is not confined to Philo[2], for there is a steady stream of Rabbinical opinion which has coloured the folk-lore of Eastern Europe that Adam had before his fall a nature clothed in light, like God Himself 'whose robe is the light,' and that after his fall the light was replaced by the ordinary integument. It will be interesting to trace this belief, which agrees with that of Philo so far as to make the coat of skin to be the human body, and to see whether it has left its mark on early Christian circles of thought.

The origin of the belief appears to be indicated by a various

[1] See Routh, *Rell.* i. 15.

[2] We find it, for example, in the Encratite Cassianus in the second century, according to the testimony of Clement of Alexandria (*Strom.* iii. 14), χιτῶνας δὲ δερματίνους ἡγεῖται ὁ Κασσιανὸς τὰ σώματα.

reading of the passage, Gen. iii. 21, which is credited to a MS.
belonging at one time to Rabbi Meir[1], viz. that instead of

כתנות עור = coats of skin

we should read

כתנות אור = coats of light.

We could then translate the passage, 'And for Adam and his
wife Jahveh Elohim had made coats of light and had clothed
them.' It is quite possible that this may be the origin of the
Rabbinical conceit as to the 'Light-Body' of Adam. And
the opinion is strongly reflected upon European folk-lore. It
appears also in Gnostic circles: for we find in the Bardesanian
Hymn of the Soul which is embedded in the *Acts of Thomas*,
that the Prince who forgets the Imperial Palace whence he
came, in his journey to Egypt to find the Pearl of great price,
had left behind him in the homeland the robe of glory with
which he had been adorned. The account tells us

> 'They took off from me the glittering robe, which in
> their affection they had made for me, and the purple toga
> which was measured and woven to my stature.'

He puts on the disguise of an Egyptian dress and forgets his
race and his country. When the young Prince comes to himself
in the far country, he gets possession of the pearl, and promptly
strips off from him the filthy and unclean dress in which he was
clad. On his way home, the robe came to meet him; it fitted
him closely and seemed to be a mirror of himself. It was, in
fact, his double, and had grown, with his growth, during his long
absence.

Prof. Burkitt points out that this Heavenly Robe represents
the Body Celestial, it is 'our house which is from heaven':

'That which St Paul desired was no fixed "house" or
"habitation" but a Heavenly Form. So here, too, the Robe is no
article of clothing, but a Bright Form. The Syriac word means
The Bright or *The Shining* thing. It is "put off" and "put on"
by the Soul[2].'

Here, then, we have a companion to the belief in the Body of

---

[1] So in Midrash Rabboth:
   'In the Thorah of Rabbi Meir they found it written, Coats of light: these
   are the garments of the first Adam.'
[2] Burkitt, *Early Eastern Christianity*, p. 215.

Light which belonged to Adam before he fell from celestial to terrestrial life. The two ideas, that of the pre-existent soul that has to leave heaven for earth, and that of the unfallen creation of God, whose environment is changed from a coat of light to a coat of skin, are evidently worked out on parallel lines.

Now it is not difficult to recognise the traces of the clothing of the Old Adam and the clothing of the original Man, who is also the New Adam, in the New Testament. We have, for example, the instruction to put off the Old Man, and to put on the New Man, or to put on (it is the language of clothing) the Lord Jesus Christ. But what we want now to examine is whether there are any similar traces in our Odes. Is there any doctrine of a Light-Body or of a Skin-Body? Let us see. For instance, in Ode 25, we have

> 'In me there shall be nothing that is not light : and I was clothed with the covering of Thy Spirit, and I cast away from me *my raiment of skin.*'

Here we have the very figure of the third chapter of Genesis, explained in a spiritual manner of the conversion and regeneration of the Soul.

Something similar to this appears in Ode 21,

> 'I put off darkness and clothed myself with light.'

Very nearly the same idea is involved in Ode 11,

> 'I forsook the folly which is spread over the earth, and I stripped it off and cast it from me : and the Lord renewed me in His raiment (cf. Ps. civ. 2) and possessed me by His light.'

And notice that this re-creating act of God is immediately followed by the statement of Paradise Regained : we are engaged in an allegory of the third chapter of Genesis. I think it will be admitted that the writer (or writers) of the Odes knew the allegorical explanation of the coat of skin with which Adam was clad. If this be conceded, then we must again recognise that we are moving in Jewish circles, for it is very unlikely that, at the early date required for our Odes, a Jewish conceit could have penetrated very far into the Gentile world. The coat of skin' is a significant proof of the Jewish or semi-Jewish author-ship of the Odes[1]. [It appears again in the *Kabbala*, as Mr G. R. S. Mead points out to me. *Zohar* ii. 229 b: 'When Adam was in the Garden of Eden, he was dressed in the celestial garment, which is a Garment of Heavenly Light. But when he was expelled from the Garden of Eden and became subject to the wants of this world, what is written? The Lord God (Elohim) made coats of skins to Adam and his wife and clothed them (Gen. iii. 21), for, prior to this, they had Garments of Light —Light of that Light which was used in the Garden of Eden.' For further allusion to the coats of light see *Sepher Hayyashar* in Migne, *Dict. des Apocryphes*, tom. ii. coll. 1102—1150.]

This allegorical treatment of the particular case in question could not have continued very long in use in the Church, because of the complication with the story of the fig-leaves; if the coat of skin is the human body, what are the fig-leaves? Evidently the allegory will have over-reached itself. It will survive, however, in folk-lore and in Gnosticism.

It may, perhaps, be objected that the interpretation of the coats of skins as equivalent to human bodies might just as well be Gnostic as Judaeo-Christian. For instance, we have quoted above the language of Cassian the Gnostic for this very belief[2]. But we have not only detected the equation of the coat of skin with the human body; we have also found traces of the belief in a coat of light which has been lost when the coat of skin was acquired, and have connected this belief with a various reading, or a Rabbinical conceit, in the text of Gen. iii. 21. So that; while it is quite likely that some early forms of Gnosticism depend directly upon Palestinian teaching, we ought also to allow that the language of our Odes on this subject is very near to the source of the Gnosis, which is very nearly the same thing as saying that it is not Gnostic. We will illustrate this by showing another case of allegorisation of the text of Genesis,

---

[1] For the curious developments of this belief in an original light-body of Adam which are current in Eastern Europe, we may consult Dähnhardt, *Natursagen* ii. 225. The coat of light was held to be of the nature of horn, and this bright integument fell away when Adam and Eve sinned. All that remains of it is the human nails!

[2] We might also have quoted Valentinus, the prince of the Gnostics; for accord-ing to Irenaeus' account of Valentinus' cosmogony, the Demiurge first fashioned the ἄνθρωπος χοικός from some invisible and fluid substance, and then clothed him in the 'coat of skin' which is τὸ αἰσθητὸν σαρκίον (cf. Iren. ed. Mass. p. 27).

which might be claimed as Gnostic, if it were not a recognised fact that the allegorising of these early chapters of Genesis is common to all the early Christian fathers.

In Ode 11 we have a beautiful sketch of the recovery of the lost Paradise, and of the blessedness of those who are planted in that land (being considered as 'trees of righteousness, the planting of the Lord') or who live by the fruit of the trees (being considered as those who have returned to the privileges of the unfallen Adam). Incidentally it is stated that such persons 'have turned from wickedness to God's delights, and have turned back the bitterness of the trees from them, when planted in God's land.'

The metaphor is confused; on the one hand the believers are the trees, on the other hand they are the denizens of Paradise, who will have nothing to do with the bitterness of the trees. Disentangling the similitudes we see that the entry into Paradise goes along with an avoidance of certain bitter trees or products of trees. Can we find out what this means?

The early interpreters of Genesis had to face a Divine injunction to eat of every tree in the Garden, with one single exception of the Tree of Knowledge of Good and Evil. But this injunction raised the question as to whether all the trees, herbs and fruits were fit to eat. What about the bitter herbs? The answer could only be, either that there were no bitter herbs, or else that they were to be avoided as uneatable, being made for some other uses. The author of the Ode to which we refer evidently takes the latter view: there are bitter herbs, but they are to be avoided. He does not think them useless, for nothing is useless in the Paradise of God. Now this doctrine of the avoidance of the bitter herbs had been credited to our Lord Himself, in a conversation between Himself and Salome, which has been preserved for us by Clement of Alexandria from the *Gospel according to the Egyptians.* The passage is strongly Encratite. Salome asks how long death is to rule over men, and receives the answer that it is as long as women bear children. 'Then,' rejoined Salome enquiringly, 'I did well in not having any children?' to which suggestion our Lord replies, 'Eat every herb, but shun the bitter herb.' It is certain that this reply is based upon the language of Genesis, *e.g.* Gen. i. 29 'Behold! I have given you every herb, whose seed is in itself

[Marginal note:] Paradise Regained and the bitter herbs.

on the face of the whole earth and all the trees...to you they
shall be for food': and Gen. ii. 9 'And the Lord God had
brought forth from the ground every tree that was fair to the
sight and pleasant to the taste,' &c. It is clear, then, that the
language of Jesus in the passage cited from the *Gospel accord-
ing to the Egyptians*, refers to the Garden of Eden. What, then,
is meant by shunning the bitter herb? If we examine the
passage in which Clement of Alexandria discusses the meaning
(*Strom.* iii. 9), we shall find that he is opposing a school of
Encratites, who said that the bitter herb was marriage.
Clement, himself, who is Anti-encratite will have none of this:
he challenges the opinion and affirms that marriage is not a sin,
nor is there anything bitter about the rearing or producing of
children. So he rejects the Encratite doctrine. In so doing, he
has shown us that the doctrine existed and that it was a wide-
spread interpretation. What shall we say, then, of the writer of
our eleventh Ode? If he says that the saints restored to the life
of Paradise have nothing to do with the bitter trees, must we not
allow that he, too, is allegorising and that he holds Encratite
views with regard to marriage? Such views were wide-spread
in the early Christian Church, and survived in Gnostic circles, as
in the Old Syrian Church, and amongst the followers of Tatian,
but I do not see that they need to be especially labelled Gnostic,
since they spring quite naturally out of the allegorical treatment
of the first chapters of Genesis, or attached themselves easily to
that particular form of interpretation[1].

This case of the 'bitter herbs' and the previous one of the
'coat of skin,' are the closest points of contact of primitive
teaching with Gnosticism. I do not see that we need to
definitely attach the Gnostic label.

We shall see presently that the writer of the main body of
the Odes does not keep the Sabbath and gives very early
Christian reason for his neglect of that Jewish duty.

We may now go on to discuss the traces of Christian
Scriptures in our book of Odes, and the dogmatic and eccle-
siastical position of the writer or writers involved.

---

[1] We may compare the *Acts of Thomas,* where the King's son and his bride are
persuaded by our Lord to renounce marriage, and 'the care of children, the end of
whom is *bitter* sorrow.' The bride explains to her mother, 'I have not had intercourse
with a husband, the end whereof is *bitter* repentance.'

When we examine the Odes to see how far they are under
Use of the influence of the Scriptures of the Old Testa-
Scriptures. ment, we find the problem is quite different from
that which presents itself in the eighteen Psalms. In these the
use of the Old Testament is patent both in language and in
quotation, as one can see by examining the portions of the
Psalms which are printed in uncial type by Ryle and James, in
order to mark the coincidence of language with the Old Testa-
ment. Moreover certain parts of the prophets, especially the
latter part of Isaiah, have been closely studied and followed:
and it is the recognition of this fact that has suggested to Felix
Perles some of his most attractive emendations through the
supposed original Hebrew[1].

But in the case of the Odes we are at a loss: we cannot tell
what Greek lies behind the Syriac, except in a very few cases:
and this makes linguistic identifications difficult and almost
impossible: nor does the examination of the ideas which the
writer expresses lead to a large harvest of coincidences with the
Canonical Psalter or the Hebrew Prophets. Perhaps this is
natural, in view of the originality of the writer, with whom it
was easier to say inspired things than to report them.

When we turn to the New Testament, the result is equally
surprising: the name of the Gospel is not found, nor the name
of Jesus: direct historical references are limited to those events
which are recorded in the Creed, to which we may perhaps add
an oblique allusion to Christ's power to walk on the waters,
with a possible allusion to the Dove at the Baptism. Not a
single saying of Jesus is directly quoted, though there seem to
be one or two indirect references. For instance Christ's yoke is
spoken of in Ode 42 ('my yoke was over those that love
me') and there is one passage in Ode 22, which looks like a
reflexion from the words 'on this rock I will build my church'
(Matt. xvi. 18)[2]: only in this case if coincidence were more
than accidental, the Ode has the substitution of Kingdom for
Church, which suggests for it priority over the Evangelic
language.

Setting aside for the moment the question of the use of

---

[1] Perles: *Zur Erklärung der Psalmen Salomos.* Berlin, 1902.
[2] *l.c.* 'That the foundation of everything might be thy rock: and on it thou didst
build thy Kingdom.'

Johannine writings, and of the Apocalypse, we find next to
nothing from the Pauline Epistles: there is a sentence in
Ode 3,

> 'The Lord is zealous that those things should be
> known, which by His grace have been given to us,'

which may perhaps be an echo of 1 Cor. ii. 12 'that we may
know the things which are freely given us of God.' We have also
some doubtful references to Rom. viii. 35, 36 in Ode 1 ('I shall
not be separated from Him') and Ode 5 ('If everything should
be shaken, I stand firm') and Ode 28 ('The sword shall not
divide me from Him, nor the scimitar'), and there are occasional
allusions to salvation and justification by Divine Grace. There
are also frequent allusions, which have a Pauline ring, to Christ
as the Head, to whom believers are the members. The figure
is worked out so as to include the souls in Hades, who are
Christ's feet[1].

Frequent allusions to a living crown can be illustrated from
1 Pet. v. 4 and from Jac. i. 12 and Apoc. ii. 10, but no direct
quotations can be established. They may all run back into
a primitive Logion, 'I will give thee a crown of life.'

The chief coincidences with the Apocalypse are in the title of
Ode 3. 11. 'the Living One' (Apoc. i. 17) given to Christ (but this was
Cf. Ode 8. also at the beginning of the book of Sayings of Jesus[2]): in some
24.
of the expressions of victory over spiritual enemies, and the
possession of Paradise and its trees, as well as in the allusion to
an opposing dragon with seven heads, and perhaps to the story of
the Sealed Book. It is doubtful if any of these parallelisms can
be pressed to the point of established quotation: the dragon
with seven heads is, perhaps, the best case for an identification:
but it will be remembered that dragons are a common feature
of apocalyptical machinery in the period to which the Odes
must belong.

It is when we come to the Gospel and Epistles of John
that we find the community of ideas to be the most pronounced.
We have clear statements that Christ is the Word, that He is
before the foundation of the world; that He bestows living

---

[1] As in Ode 42.

[2] *l.c.* 'These are the [wonderful] words which Jesus the Living One spake':
a form of introduction which is imitated in the Coptic Book of Jeu.

water abundantly; that He is the door of everything; that He stands to His people in the relation of Lover to Beloved: that they love Him because He first loved them (for so we may interpret the language of Ode 3: 'I should not have known how to love the Lord, if He had not loved me'), that their love to the Christ makes them His friends (Ode 8). These and similar phrases betray a Johannine atmosphere: but do they betray the use of the Fourth Gospel? The problem is, on a wider scale, something like that which arises in the discussion whether Valentinus the Gnostic used the Fourth Gospel. Hippolytus tells us in his *Refutation of Heresies* (p. 185) that Valentinus taught that 'God the Father was all love, but love is not love where there is no object of love. So the Father begat two emanations, νοῦς and ἀλήθεια¹.' Now is that a case of the Fourth Gospel or not? The serious critic would hesitate to affirm it; yet the language is very like that of our third Ode; and it would probably be wise to hold the judgment in suspense with regard to the use of the Fourth Gospel in the Odes, especially when it is so difficult to trace any other Gospel quotation or incident, or Saying of Jesus. But I think it will be conceded that we are in a Johannine atmosphere.

One coincidence has been detected between the Odes and the Ignatian Epistles, in the allusion to 'talking water'; but there is no need to assume quotation on either side, the language being sufficiently explained by the folk-lore of the time.

The net result of these comparisons is to place the collection of Odes at a very early period in the history of the Christian Church. One or two of them had already been referred to the early part of the second century, on account of the almost canonical use made of them in the *Pistis Sophia*. The main body of the Odes, when studied, takes us in the same direction, only perhaps somewhat further.

We come now to the question of the underlying doctrines which can be traced in the Odes. We have already alluded to Christ's pre-existence[2], to His pre-eminence in the Church[3], and to the spiritual union between Himself and believers[4]. We have also pointed out some refer-

Dogmatic of the Odes.

---

[1] 'Αγάπη γάρ, φησὶν, ἦν ὅλος, ἡ δὲ ἀγάπη οὐκ ἔστιν ἀγάπη, ἐὰν μὴ ᾖ τὸ ἀγαπώμενον.   [2] As in Ode 28, Ode 41, &c.

[3] As in Ode 31, Ode 33, &c.   [4] As in Ode 3, Ode 42, &c.

ences to His yoke, and to the foundation of His Kingdom, and
to His power to walk upon the stormy waters.

One of the strongest expressions with regard to the nature of
Christ will be found in Ode 41, where He is called 'the Son of
the Most High, who appeared in the perfection of His Father,
...the Word that was before-time in Him, the Messiah *or* Christ
who is truly one, and was known before the foundation of the
world.' In the words 'The Christ is truly one,' taken in
connexion with the other statements as to His pre-existence,
we have suggestions of controversy, over a division in the
nature of Christ, of which, perhaps, the earliest known trace is
in the first Epistle of John[1] (πᾶν πνεῦμα ὃ μὴ ὁμολογεῖ τὸν
Ἰησοῦν) where the various reading, λύει for μὴ ὁμολογεῖ, if not
primitive, is certainly very early. This Ode cannot come from
a Docetic, nor can it easily be referred to an Adoptionist
source[2].

An equally pronounced Christology may be detected in
Ode 29 where the writer says,

'I believed in the Lord's Messiah,
And it appeared to me that He is the Lord.'

We must not too hastily assume that all these statements
come from one hand, and we must be prepared to find, along
with variety of authorship (if that can be made out), a variety
also of theological definitions. There are some Odes which are
a little hard of explanation on orthodox lines, because they
appear to use Adoptionist language[3]. But if this suggests
subordination of Christ to the Father, in another Ode it is the
Holy Spirit that is subordinate, for we are told (Ode 24) that
'the Dove fluttered over the Messiah, because He was her
head[4].' Again in the Ode previously quoted (Ode 36) it
appears to follow that the Holy Spirit was the Mother of
Jesus, which we know to have been a feature of Ebionite belief.
These variations suggest that theology had not fixed her land-

---

[1] 1 John iv. 3.

[2] Cf. Novatian, *De Trinitate* 30. Irenaeus (M. 206 *et passim*): 'Non ergo alterum
Filium novit evangelium nisi hunc qui ex Maria est, qui et passus est, sed neque
Christum avolantem ante passionem ab Jesu.'

[3] As in Ode 36.

[4] In later ages this would be known as the heresy of Macedonius, but the language
here is innocent of heretical intention.

marks nor laid down her definitions. On the other hand, it is clear that the Odes do not regard Christ as a mere man, but as a pre-existent being and as the Divine Logos. One Ode has the doctrine of the Trinity under a grotesque form worthy of the Middle Ages. But this Ode we are unwilling to class with the rest of the book.

In regard to the points of early Christian belief which occur in the Odes, it is clear that the Crucifixion is definitely alluded to, less clearly the Resurrection; but what surprises us is the extraordinary emphasis upon the Virgin Birth and the Descent into Hades. The former of these is in a state of evolution beyond the Canonical Gospels : the birth is explained as painless[1], and unexpected : we are on the very verge of the details which occur in the apocryphal Gospels of the Infancy.

The other Article of the Creed, the Descent into Hades, is also treated with picturesque detail, very much as in the Gospel of Nicodemus. Just as in the latter gospel[2] Hades complains of the inward pain which he feels and which intimates an approaching discharge of imprisoned souls, so in Ode 42 we are told that ' Hades saw me and *was miserable* : death *cast me up*, and many along with me.' But the prayer of the Souls in Hades is very fine, and has no vulgar suggestions of Jonah and the Whale about it, such as we find in the byways of Patristic literature.

It will, perhaps, be said that the advanced state of evolution of these two dogmas renders it impossible that the collection should be referred to the end of the first century[3]. There is,

---

[1] Here, at all events, we are in the region of folk-lore; the Chinese legend of the birth and conception of Hou-tsi, the founder of the dynasty of Tchū, runs on the same line. His mother brought him forth as a tender lamb without effort, without pain and without pollution. See amongst the Chinese Classics, the *Shi-King* iii. ii. 1, which has been Englished as follows:

> ' Lo! when her carrying time was done,
> Came like a lamb her first-born son,
> No pains of labour suffered she—
> No hurt, no pain, no injury.'

Cf. *Ev. Ps. Matthaei*, c. 13 'Nulla pollutio sanguinis facta est in nascente, nullus dolor in parturiente.'

[2] Tischendorf, *Evan. Apocrypha*, p. 396 'Contremui perterritus pavore, et omnia officia mea simul mecum conturbata sunt.'

B. H. Cowper, *Apoc. Gospels*, p. 305 'For lo ! I see that all I have ever swallowed are in commotion and my belly is in pain' (Jonah ii. 2); which is taken from the Greek *Descensus*, see Tisch. *l.c.* p. 327.

[3] The Descent into Hades is a first century doctrine. Harnack says of it: 'the notion of a *descensus ad inferna*...commended itself on the ground of Old

however, an alternative suggestion, that the forty-second Ode, for instance, may be a later product : for it has not been demonstrated that all the Odes come from the same hand or time.

The organic life of the Church can hardly be detected in the book of Odes. The Church itself is not mentioned, unless it should be in the reference to a Pure Virgin in Ode 33 who stands and proclaims the invitation of the Gospel. The figure of the Pure Virgin is well known[1] to have been a common one in the first and second centuries, and has influenced the New Testament itself. But the Pure Virgin may equally well be the Divine Wisdom who stands and calls men[2].

Church Order and Discipline.

There is also the implication of corporate unity in the figure of the Head and the members[3] : this may be directly derived from St Paul. Of Church officials there are only, (*a*) the writer of Ode 20 who calls himself a priest of God and defines his priesthood as any mystic might, as the offering to God of the sacrifice of his thought, and (*b*) there are a body of persons engaged in carrying the water of life to the thirsty, who are called Blessed Ministers or Blessed Deacons (Ode 6) : we may compare the language of Perpetua concerning ' Tertius and Pomponius, *blessed deacons* who ministered to us,' who bribed the gaolers and obtained us relief. But the writer of the Odes does not necessarily mean anything so highly evolved as the ministry of the African Church at the beginning of the third century. His ministers have a commission to preach the word and are counted happy in so doing.

Of Sacraments the Odes do not seem to know much[4]. The only directions in which one could look for references to Baptism would be (i) the Living Water, (ii) the allusion to the Seal. Of the former it is unnecessary to speak. It is frankly impossible that the living water which the thirsty are invited in the Scriptures to come and take freely can

Sacraments.

Testament prediction. In the first century, however, it still remained uncertain, lying on the borders of those productions of religious fancy which were not at once able to acquire a right of citizenship in the communities.' *Hist. of Dogma*, i. 202, Eng. tr.

[1] *e.g.* 2 Cor. xi. 2, and cf. Hegesippus in Euseb. *H. E.* iv. 22. In the letter of the Churches of Lyons and Vienna (c. 12) the Virgin Mother is the Church (καὶ ἐνεγίνετο πολλὴ χαρὰ τῇ παρθένῳ μητρί).

[2] Cf. Proverbs viii. 1, 2.   [3] As in Ode 1, Ode 17, &c.

[4] [Unless Diettrich and Bernard should be right that the whole of the hymns are charged with references to Baptism : see preface for details of the argument.]

be any outward affusion: but perhaps something ought to be said of the Seal, because although, in the New Testament, this is a term used of the gift of the Holy Spirit, it is often employed by Patristic writers to denote baptism and the baptized (*e.g.* in the epitaph of Abercius and elsewhere).

In the Odes we have plenty of reference to seals: we have the abysses of Hades sealed up with the Lord's seal in Ode 24: we have the mysterious Letter from Heaven sealed with a magic seal in Ode 23; and we have in Ode 4 a statement of the talismanic power of the Seal of God, which angels as well as men possess and which all creation knows and fears. And in Ode 8 the Lord says He has set His seal upon the faces of His people, just as we have in the Apocalypse (vii. 3, xiv. 1). But in the Apocalypse, as Dr Swete points out, the seal is not sacramental. Perhaps it was a taboo-mark of some Jewish sect.

If there is any scriptural reference in this doctrine of the Seal, it must be sought in Ezekiel ix., and the ink-mark which an angelic scribe is told to set on the righteous[1]. The seal is alluded to in the extant Psalms of Solomon (Ps. Sol. xv. 6) where we are told that 'the sign ($\sigma\eta\mu\epsilon\hat{\iota}o\nu$) of God is upon the righteous for Salvation.' It is, therefore, a pre-Christian conception. Here Perles very naturally compared Ezekiel ix. 6 and supplied the Haggadic explanation from Shabbath 55[a], as follows:

> 'God spake to Gabriel: Go and stamp on the forehead of the righteous a mark of ink, that the destroying angels may have no power over him[2]: and on the forehead of the hypocrites a mark of blood, that the destroying angels may acquire power over them.'

From this talismanic sign (with which the archangels are here entrusted), there was developed, as is well known, the doctrine of the talismanic virtue of the sign of the cross in baptism. But this development (arising out of an interpretation of the use of the letter Tau as the sign in Ezekiel) is, I think, later than what we have in the Odes[3]. There does not seem, therefore, to be any definite allusion to Baptism. We can see

---

[1] In the East it is still common to seal with ink.

[2] Cf. Ode 4. 7, 8 'who is there that shall put on thy grace and be hurt? for thy seal is known.'

[3] We have it in Tert. *Adv. Marc.* iii. 22 where the letter Tau is explained to be 'the very form of the Cross which was foretold to be the sign upon our foreheads.'

the later interpretation very clearly in Lactantius, *Div. Inst.* iv.
27, who says that the gods cannot approach those in whom
they see the heavenly mark, nor hurt those whom the sign as
an impregnable wall protects, which is very like Ode 4. 7, 8.
Perhaps Lactantius has here a reminiscence of the Ode[1].

As to the Eucharist, I can find no allusion whatever : there
are no references to the religious use of bread and wine ; the
writers of the Odes seem to prefer milk and honey ; but these
are not spoken of sacramentally, but mystically and alle-
gorically.

The allegorical use of the terms ' milk and honey ' is natural
enough in view of the Old Testament descriptions of the Land
of Promise : but it should be remembered that there are traces
of a milk-and-honey sacrament in the early Church.   For
example in the Epistle of Barnabas[2], we have a question
raised as to the meaning of the milk and honey in the Old
Testament.   And after some preliminary allegorising to show
that the believers in Jesus are themselves the good land, he
asks, ' Why milk and honey ? '   And the answer is that ' the
young child is first quickened with honey and then with milk.'

Probably this refers in the first instance to a folk-lore custom
in connexion with newly-born children, but it seems to have very
early developed into a Christian sacrament for new converts, who
had been born again into the Kingdom of God[3].

It does not, however, seem that the milk-and-honey passages
in the Odes will bear the sacramental interpretation.   The nine-
teenth Ode, for example, has no suggestion of a recent conversion
about it.   The only one where it seems possible to make
connexion with the new-birth is Ode 8, where the Lord says,
' My own breasts I prepared for them that they might drink my
holy milk and live thereby ' ; this might perhaps, in view of the
previous reference to the ' seal upon the faces,' be interpreted
sacramentally, but it does not seem likely.   The baptismal
sacrament, as we have shown, is not milk but milk and honey.

---

[1] 'Sed quoniam neque accedere ad eos possunt, in quibus coelestem notam
viderint, nec iis nocere, quos signum immortale munierit, tanquam inexpugnabilis
murus.'

[2] c. 6.

[3] Besides Barnabas, we may refer to Tertullian, *De corona*, c. 3 (inde suscepti,
lactis et mellis concordiam praegustamus) : *Adv. Marc.* i. 14 : Clem. Alex. *Paed.* i. 6,
p. 128 : Coptic Canons, ii. 46, &c.

The only allusion to wine is in the account of the Seducer in Ode 38, who lays plots for the elect and wishes, by an intoxicating cup, to rob them of their reason. So far as the enquiry has gone, the Odes are hardly to be quoted in the history of the Sacraments; they ought, therefore, to belong to an early period of evolution in the organic life of the Church.

There is still something to be said with regard to the

The lost Second Ode. missing portions of our MS. The closing portions of the 18 Psalms of Solomon are preserved for us adequately in the Greek, but the lacuna at the beginning of the Odes is serious, and involves the whole of the second Ode, and the beginning of the third Ode.

It has occurred to me that perhaps a sentence from this second Ode may be preserved in Clement of Alexandria. For in his *Protrepticus* (p. 5) we have the following sentence:

ὁ δὲ ἐκ Δαβίδ, καὶ πρὸ αὐτοῦ, ὁ τοῦ Θεοῦ λόγος, λύραν μὲν καὶ κιθάραν, τὰ ἄψυχα ὄργανα, ὑπεριδών, κόσμον δὲ τόνδε, καὶ δὴ καὶ τὸν σμικρὸν κόσμον τὸν ἄνθρωπον, ψυχήν τε καὶ σῶμα αὐτοῦ, ἁγίῳ πνεύματι ἁρμοσάμενος, ψάλλει τῷ Θεῷ διὰ τοῦ πολυφώνου ὀργάνου καὶ προσᾴδει τούτῳ τῷ ὀργάνῳ, τῷ ἀνθρώπῳ,

Σὺ γὰρ εἶ κιθάρα καὶ αὐλὸς καὶ ναὸς ἐμός.

Thus according to Clement the Word of God made music of its own, earlier than David and upon a loftier instrument than his harp and lyre; for its music was produced from the macrocosm of creation and the microcosm of the body and soul of man: to this instrument of many strings[1] it sings and addresses the instrument itself, saying to it:

'' 'Tis thou my harp, and flute and temple art.'

Now this is a quotation from some poetical composition, and we may infer that it is a fragment of an early Psalm or hymn. Accordingly Potter notes on it as follows:

'Christi verba, ut videtur, a sacro hymno citata.'

But if it is a hymn, there are two considerations which suggest that it came from the Odes of Solomon: first, it is one of the features of these Odes (often causing no little perplexity) that the singer makes his Psalm, either wholly or in part, in the

---

[1] [More exactly *notes*: and cf. next page.]

name of Christ : second, the reference to the harp or flute in describing Christ's music, and the representation of the mind of man as an ὄργανον πολύφωνον is thoroughly in the manner of the Odes. Thus in Ode 7 believers go forth to meet the Lord with a harp of many strings [literally, *voices* : = κιθάρα πολύφωνος exactly, as we have it involved in the passage quoted from Clement]. In Ode 14 the writer says :

> 'Open to me the harp of thy Holy Spirit,
>   That with all its notes I may praise Thee,'

and the same spiritual music is in the opening of Ode 6,

> ' As the hand moves over the harp...
>   So speaks in my members the Spirit of the Lord.'

Here it is the Spirit that plays upon the human instrument.

So it is quite possible that Clement's little quotation may be part of the missing matter of our Odes. To which of them shall we refer it ? The first Ode is already identified, the third is almost complete, and it is unlikely that Christ should be the speaker in the opening of the third Ode, when he is not so in the closing portion. So the suggestion arises that the sentence comes from the second Ode.

This is a speculation, and must not be taken too seriously, in view of the insufficiency of the evidence. But it can do no harm to record it, with the necessary *Valeat quantum*. [The observation made above as to the coincidence in language between Clement and the Odes, makes it no longer necessary to speak so diffidently. Harnack passes the matter by too lightly with 'im besten Falle eine blosse Möglichkeit.']

It will, perhaps, be enquired whether the use of the Odes of Solomon by early writers can be detected in cases where there are no introductory formulae or definite allusions. We have just suggested that a fragment of the second Ode may be preserved in an anonymous quotation by Clement of Alexandria. Are there any similar traces to be identified in the early Patristic literature? The difficulty of making such identifications is well known. We had a case in the use of 'talking water' by Ignatius and by the writer of the Odes. Such an expression to us in the present day seems very striking; but a draught from a magical or

The Odes known to Irenaeus.

medical spring is probably a common folk-lore way of obtaining inspiration, and need not imply any dependence of one of the coincident writers upon the other.

Here is a somewhat similar case from Irenaeus, in which the evidence is rather in the direction of recognising a quotation on the part of that writer from the Odes. Irenaeus discusses[1] the question why God made man and why He chose the fathers and why He called the saints. He begins by the doctrine that God, for His part, had no need of man : 'non quasi indigens hominis, plasmavit Adam.' This sentiment of the Divine independence of His works is in our fourth Ode. It is, however, so common an expression in Greek philosophy and theology, that we should pay no attention to its occurrence in Irenaeus, if it were not that it is the key-note of the section and that he returns to it with an added amplification, which is also found in the fourth Ode. For he says that the less God needs man, the more man needs God and *His fellowship* :

> ' in quantum enim Deus nullius indiget, in tantum homo indiget Dei communione.'

Here we have the thought of fellowship with God, as the expression of man's need, which we have in Ode 4 :

> ' *Thou hast given us thy fellowship* :
> It was not that thou wast in need of us,
> but that we were in need of thee.'

A little lower down Irenaeus returns to the same thought : God distributed His prophets over the earth to habituate men to the reception of His Spirit and to fellowship with Himself : 'He Himself was in need of no man : *but on those that needed Him, He bestowed His fellowship.*'

Here we have the same thought, in closely coincident terms ; and since it is the fundamental thought of the chapter, we suggest that Irenaeus may be working from a text, and the text is a verse from the Odes of Solomon. The same sentiments recur in Bk V. c. ii. in the following form : 'Nihil enim illi ante dedimus, neque desiderat aliquid a nobis, quasi indigens: nos autem indigemus *eius quae est ad eum communionis* : et propterea benigne effudit semetipsum ' ; where the last clause may be

---

[1] Lib. IV. c. xxv. (p. 243, Mass.).

compared with what follows in the Ode: 'Distil thy dews upon us and open the rich fountains that pour forth milk and honey.'

There is still, however, something abrupt in the transition from the discussing of the Holy Place and the Holy People to the general question of whether God has any need of man corresponding to the need which man has of God. We may detect the motion of the writer's thought in passing from one subject to the other in the following manner.

From Irenaeus we see that while God has no need of man, man has need of communion with God. The language is, as we have shown, so closely parallel to that of our Ode as almost to amount to a quotation. But at an earlier time than that of Irenaeus the thought of communion with God was not detached from the thought of communion by means of a Holy Place, and by sacrifice offered there.

We get this thought brought out clearly in the prayer of the priests in 2 Macc. xiv. 15:

> 'Thou, O Lord of the universe, *who in thyself hast need of nothing*, wast well pleased *that a sanctuary of thy habitation should be set amongst us*: so now, O Holy Lord of all hallowing, keep undefiled for ever this house that hath been lately cleansed.'

Here the 'sanctuary of the Divine habitation' is an earlier form of the Christian 'communion with God' which we find in Irenaeus. When, therefore, the writer of the Ode, who began by chanting the inalienable sanctity of the Temple, says that God, who did not need us, has given us His fellowship, he is still thinking of the fellowship that is associated with one special holy place. He cannot think that this form of communion is abandoned or made void. The opening verses of the Ode make it clear that this is his key-note. The parallel in the New Testament is in Paul's speech before the Areopagus (Acts xvii. 24, 25), 'God dwelleth not in temples made with hands, neither is worshipped of men's hands, *as though He needed anything.*' Our writer would say, 'He dwells in a Temple, because we need Him.' And as we have pointed out, the situation is for our writer Judaeo-Christian.

At the same time we see clearly that the writer is not really a Jew, though he is in a Judaeo-Christian environ-

The Author does not accept Jewish customs.

ment. We see this in a number of ways, both direct and indirect. First we had his definite statement as to his being of a different race, which must surely mean that he is a proselyte, in the Christian sense, from among the Gentiles to a community of Judaean origin. Then we had his peculiar apologetics, in the person of Christ, for love to the Gentiles. But even more striking is his indirect argument against the necessity of the maintenance of the Sabbath. I have drawn attention to this under Ode 16, by pointing out that the sequence of thought in the words

'He rested from His works:
And created things run in their courses and do their works:
And they know not how to stand and be idle:
And His ⌐heavenly⌐ Hosts are subject to His word'

contain the argument of Justin with Trypho for the non-validity of the Sabbath, on the ground that

'the elements, στοιχεῖα (*or more exactly*, the heavenly bodies[1]), do not idle or keep Sabbath.'

And Justin tells Trypho that he learnt this from the very old man to whom he owed his conversion, who taught him, in reference to the Sabbath and Circumcision, that he should remain as he was born. This is very early teaching on the subject of the leading Jewish practices. It does not necessarily mean the abandonment of the Sabbath by Jews. Our author stands where Justin stood, and both of them employ an argument of the more liberal-minded in the primitive Church. He is no more a Jew than Justin is.

It will be asked whether he argues against circumcision as well as against the Sabbath. This is more difficult to answer. It depends upon the interpretation of the opening sentences of Ode 11. If our alternative translation is correct, the writer refers to the work of Divine Grace which he has experienced as a circumcision of the heart, a figure of speech which is justified by the Old Testament references to Israel as 'uncircumcised in heart and ears[2],' and by the Pauline affirmation that 'we are

---

[1] Gal. iv. 9.
[2] Cf. Deut. x. 16, 'Circumcise your hearts and be not any more stiffnecked.'

the true circumcision,' and that 'he is not a Jew who is one
outwardly, nor is circumcision in the letter, but in the spirit.'
In this sense our writer may be held to affirm that, although not
an Israelite by birth, he is one of the spiritual Israel.   And this
would agree exactly with the other statements to which we have
alluded.

We found no allusions by which we could identify the
Gospels used by the Odists.

But if there are no references of a direct character to the
Gospels, and only scanty allusions to the historical
incidents which make the framework of the Gospels,
there is one indirect reference to an early Apocry-
phal Gospel, which is of the first importance.   We have discussed
under the twenty-fourth Ode the question whether the reference
of the Ode is to the Baptism of Jesus or to some other un-
known incident connected with His crucifixion, and have decided
that the allusion to the fluttering of the Dove over the head of
the Messiah must mean the events at the Baptism, although there
was in the context matter which seemed to suggest the descent
into Hades rather than the Baptism.   The reason for this con-
clusion lies in the coincidence of the expression of the Odist
with the language employed by Justin Martyr in his dialogue
with Trypho (c. 88).   The Syriac of the opening verse is
literally

'The Dove flew upon [*or* over] the Messiah';

and this curious phrase answers exactly to the word which
Justin twice uses in his account of the Baptism.   The repetition
of the word has long since provoked a suggestion on the part of
the critics that we had here a fragment of Justin's actual gospel,
and that it was not one of the canonical Gospels, though Justin
himself refers his account to the Apostles of the Lord.   And
when it was observed that the same peculiar verb turned up
elsewhere in Greek Patristic accounts of the Baptism, a very
strong case was made out for the use of an actual document
of an apocryphal, or, at all events, of a non-canonical character.

When, therefore, we detect the same expression in the Syriac
text of the Odes, the coincidence is so striking that we are
justified in removing the allusions to the Baptism of Jesus from
the matter credited to the canonical Evangelists, and assigning

Trace of an uncanonical Gospel.

it instead to a lost Gospel of a very early date. It will be convenient to collect[1] under one view the cases in which it may reasonably be held that the Greek word ἐπιπτῆναι is used of the Descent of the Dove (Justin Martyr: *Dial.* 88):

ἀναδύντος αὐτοῦ ἀπὸ τοῦ ὕδατος, ὡς περιστερὰν τὸ ἅγιον πνεῦμα ἐπιπτῆναι ἐπ' αὐτὸν ἔγραψαν οἱ ἀπόστολοι αὐτοῦ τούτου τοῦ Χριστοῦ ἡμῶν.

Ibid.:

τὸ πνεῦμα οὖν τὸ ἅγιον καὶ διὰ τοὺς ἀνθρώπους, ὡς προέφην, ἐν εἴδει περιστερᾶς ἐπέπτη αὐτῷ.

Celsus (*v.* Origen *contra Celsum* i. 41):

λουομένῳ, φησί, σοι παρὰ τῷ Ἰωάννῃ [v. l. Ἰορδάνῃ] φάσμα ὄρνιθος ἐξ ἀέρος λέγεις ἐπιπτῆναι.

Origen (*c. Celsum* i. 40):

ἑξῆς δὲ τούτοις ἀπὸ τοῦ κατὰ Ματθαῖον, τάχα δὲ καὶ τῶν λοιπῶν εὐαγγελίων, λαβὼν τὰ περὶ τῆς ἐπιπτάσης τῷ σωτῆρι βαπτιζομένῳ παρὰ τοῦ Ἰωάννου περιστερᾶς διαβάλλειν βούλεται.

Origen (*in Joan.* tom. ii. 11):

ὅτε τῷ σωματικῷ εἴδει ὡσεὶ περιστερὰ ἐφίπταται μετὰ τὸ λοῦτρον αὐτῷ.

Orac. Sib. vii. 64—70:

Ἄ, Συρίη κοίλη, Φοινίκων ὕπατον ἀνδρῶν,
Οἷς ἐπερευγομένη κεῖται Βηρυτιὰς ἅλμη,
Τλήμων, οὐκ ἔγνως τὸν σὸν Θεόν, ὅς ποτ' ἔλουσεν
Ἰορδάνου ἐν ὑδάτεσσι, καὶ ἔπτατο πνεῦμα ἐπ' αὐτῷ.

. . . .

Σάρκ' ἐνδυσάμενος, τάχυς ἔπτατο Πατρὸς ἐς οἴκους.

To the foregoing coincidences from Greek sources, Resch adds a number of suspicious coincidences in Latin:

Tert. *adv. Valent.* c. 27:

'Super hunc itaque Christum *devolasse* tunc in baptismatis sacramento Jesum per effigiem columbae.'

Hilarius *in Ps.* liv. 7:

'Nam et in columbae specie Spiritus in eum *volando* requievit...ut *volando* requiescat.'

[1] See Resch, *Aussercanonische Paralleltexte zu Luc.* p. 15.

Hilarius *in Matt.* ii. 6:

> ' post aquae lavacrum et de caelestibus portis sanctum in nos spiritum *involare*.'

Severi *de ritibus baptismi*, p. 24, ed. Boderianus (Resch, *Agrapha*, p. 363):

> ' Et Spiritus sanctitatis in similitudinem columbae *volans* descendit mansitque super caput filii.'

These references are not of equal value in the determination of the language of a primitive account, but taken together, they certainly make a very strong impression in favour of the belief in an uncanonical account of the Baptism, and it is to that account that the first line of Ode 24 must be referred.

But what are we to say of the Spirit singing over the Messiah? Is this also from the uncanonical source?

We may sum up the investigation as far as it has gone as follows:

There can be no reasonable doubt of the antiquity of the recovered Book of Odes. That which seems to be the latest composition amongst them is attested already by Lactantius in the beginning of the fourth century as having the place in the collection which it occupies in our Manuscript. The portions of the Odes which have been transcribed by the author of the *Pistis Sophia* towards the end of the third century, are evidently taken from a book which was either canonical in the writer's judgment, or not very far removed from canonicity; so that it is quite easy to carry the Odes back into the second century, and those who have studied the extant fragments of them before the recovery of our Manuscript have, in fact, referred them to the earlier part of the second century. Our own investigations have shown that the Odes agree in the extent of their composition with the statistical data for their measurement, preserved in the early Stichometries. We have also shown that they agree in sentiment with the beliefs and practices of the earliest ages of the Church. It came out clearly in the investigation that the writer, while not a Jew, was a member of a community of Christians, who were for the most part of Jewish extraction and beliefs, and the apologetic tone which is displayed, in the Odes, towards the Gentiles, as a part of the Christian Church, is only consistent with the very earliest ages, and with communities like the Palestinian Churches where Judaism was still in evidence and in control. We think, therefore, that it will be admitted on all hands, that the discovery of this collection of Odes and Psalms is not only valuable for the fact that it presents us, for the first time, with the Syriac version of the extant Psalms of Solomon, but that the Syriac text of the Odes of Solomon is in itself a memorial of the first importance for rightly understanding the beliefs and experiences of the Primitive Church.

We have expressed our belief that in part, at least, the collection belongs to the last quarter of the first century ; but if it should be objected that this is too early a date, it cannot be very many years in excess. Even if the writings do not fall within the actual time of the composition of the books of the New Testament, they scarcely fall outside the limits of the same, and we may, therefore, be sure that the Christian Church of to-day has been enriched by the discovery of a literary monument of the highest value. Apart, also, from all critical questions concerned with the little less or little more of a determined date, or with the ' Lo ! here ' or ' Lo ! there ' of an assigned locality, we have in our Odes the language of Christian experience upon the highest levels of the Spiritual Life, and we should have to go far afield to find such expressions of the Joy of the Lord as recur in almost every one of these Spiritual Songs.

We have no means of knowing who it was that in the first instance ascribed them to Solomon, nor have we any clue at present to their actual authorship, but we may be sure that whatever Solomon did, or did not, in the composing of Odes, with which he has been credited to the number of one thousand and five, according to the insistent accuracy of the Jewish Chronicler, we may say of these new-found compositions, that not even Solomon at his very best could have been spiritually arrayed like one of these.

ODE 1. (*Pistis Sophia* 116.)

[1]The Lord is on my head like a crown, and I shall not be without Him[1]. [2]They wove for me a crown of truth, and it caused thy branches to bud in me. [3]For it is not like a withered crown which buddeth not: but thou livest upon my head, and thou hast blossomed upon my head. [4]Thy fruits are full-grown and perfect, they are full of thy salvation.

ODE 1. This Ode is not in our Syriac text, but in the Coptic version of the *Pistis Sophia*, where it is said to be the 19th Ode. I have identified it with the missing first Ode of our collection, on the supposition that in the collection of Solomonic Psalms known to the author of the *Pistis Sophia*, the eighteen Psalms of Solomon stood first, and not, as in the Syriac collection, in the last place. The question is discussed, more at length, under Ode 5. The argument of the Psalm is that God is the crown of the soul, whose supreme experience is the knowledge of His truth. This crown is of the amarant variety; it fadeth not away. On the contrary, it buds and blossoms and is full of immortal fruit. The similitude is not uncommon in the book of Odes to which we have placed this Psalm as an introduction. [Diettrich and Bernard think the reference is to a crown put on the head of newly-baptized persons[2]. We may also compare the crown offered to the worshipper of Mithra on his admission to the rank of *miles*. He sets it aside declaring Mithra to be his only crown[3].]

ODE 2. (*Deest.*)

ODE 3. (*Priora desunt.*)

.... I put on: [2]And his members are with him. And on them do I hang, and He loves me: [3]for I should not have known how to love the Lord, if He had not loved me. [4]For who is able to distinguish love, except the one that is loved? [5]I love the Beloved, and my soul loves Him: [6]and where His rest is, there also am I; [7]and I shall be no stranger, for with the Lord Most High and Merciful there is no grudging. [8]I have been united

---

[1] *Or* it.

[2] Bernard: *J.T.S* for Oct. 1910, p. 7. Diettrich: *Die Reformation* for May 1910, p. 307 n.   [3] Cumont: *Monuments*, i. 318.

⌐to Him⌐¹, for the Lover has found the Beloved, ⁹and because I shall love Him that is the Son, I shall become a son²; ¹⁰for he that is joined to Him that is immortal, will also himself become immortal; ¹¹and he who has pleasure in the Living One³, will become living⁴. ¹²This is the Spirit of the Lord, which doth not lie, which teacheth the sons of men to know His ways. ¹³Be wise and understanding and vigilant. Hallelujah.

ODE 3. This Psalm, of which the first verses have disappeared along with the leaves that contained the first two Psalms, is evidently a Christian product; the author is a mystic with a doctrine, or rather an experience, of union with the Son. With Him his whole nature has become mingled, as water is mixed with wine. In Pauline language, he has been joined to the Lord, and has become one spirit with Him⁵. In Johannine language, because the Beloved lives, he himself lives also⁶. He has, at least in hope and faith, attained immortality through union with the Living One. The name here given to Christ is very ancient, it has been detected by the Revisers of the English New Testament in the Apocalypse ('I am the Living One')⁷, and it is found in the opening sentences of the Sayings of Jesus, recovered in recent years from Egypt: ('these are the words......which Jesus the Living One spake'). [Cf. also Ode 24. 14 where 'Him that liveth' is Christ.]

Other Johannine touches are the doctrine that 'we love Him because He first loved us⁸.' For the Psalmist tells us that 'he should not have known how to love the Lord if the Lord had not loved him.'

It would be a mistake to suppose that we have here any direct quotations or that the language necessarily involves acquaintance with the text of the New Testament. In translating the Syriac, I have not tried to distinguish the two words for love which are used: even if it could be inferred that the Greek had used ἀγαπῶ and φιλῶ, as in the 21st chapter of John's Gospel, it would be a mistake to indicate this in the translation by a subtlety which is now exploded. For the Syriac makes no such distinction, nor need we imagine it in the original Aramaic spoken by Jesus. When the Syriac translators turn back our Lord's words in John xiv. 21, 'He it is that loveth me, and he that loveth me shall be loved of my Father,' although the Greek word is consistently ἀγαπῶ, they use both the available Syriac words, without distinction, and where they do not distinguish we have no call to over-refinement.

---

¹ Mingled with (as water with wine); cf. 1 Cor. vi. 17. ² Or the Son.
³ The MS. has 'in life.' Cf. Apoc. i. 17. ⁴ Or the living One.
⁵ 1 Cor. vi. 17.   ⁶ John xiv. 19.   ⁷ Apoc. i. 17.   ⁸ 1 John iv. 19.

ODE 4.

¹No man, O my God, changeth thy holy place ; ²and it is not [possible] that he should change it and put it in another place : because he hath no power over it : ³for thy sanctuary thou hast designed before thou didst make [other] places : ⁴that which is the elder shall not be altered by those that are younger than itself. ⁵Thou hast given thy heart, O Lord, to thy believers : never wilt thou fail, nor be without fruits : ⁶for one hour of thy Faith is more precious than all days and years. ⁷For who is there that shall put on thy grace, and be hurt ? ⁸For thy seal is known : and thy creatures know it : and thy [heavenly] hosts possess it : and the elect archangels are clad with it. ⁹Thou hast given us thy fellowship : it was not that thou wast in need of us : but that we are in need of thee : ¹⁰distil thy dews upon us and open thy rich fountains that pour forth to us milk and honey : ¹¹for there is no repentance with thee that thou shouldest repent of anything that thou hast promised : ¹²and the end was revealed before thee : for what thou gavest, thou gavest freely : ¹³so that thou mayest not draw them back and take them again : ¹⁴for all was revealed before thee as God, and ordered from the beginning before thee : and thou, O God, hast made all things. Hallelujah.

Ps. lxxxiv. 11.

ODE 4. This Psalm is one of the most important in the whole collection, on account of the historical allusion with which it commences. The reference to an unsuccessful attempt to alter the site of the Sanctuary of the Lord can only be explained by some unknown movement to carry on the Jewish worship outside the desolated and proscribed sanctuary, or by the closing of the Jewish temple at Leontopolis in Egypt, which was, perhaps, itself in the first instance built under the pressure of the situation which resulted in the desecration of the temple at Jerusalem by Antiochus Epiphanes. As the latter explanation leans on fact, rather than on hypothesis, we may accept it provisionally as the real interpretation of our Psalm, which is thus dated soon after A.D. 73 when the temple of Onias was closed and dismantled by the Romans. The writer of the Psalm, if not of Jewish origin is, at least, Jewish in sympathy : he holds the Jewish belief that the Sanctuary at Jerusalem was older than the world in which it stood ; it was, according to Rabbinic teaching, prior to all other created things : thus we find in *Bereshith Rabbah* that 'seven things were created before the world, Thorah, Gehenna, the Garden of Eden, the Throne of Glory, *the Sanctuary*, Repentance and the name of Messiah.'

The proofs of these pre-existent creations can easily be made from the Scriptures: *e.g.* 'the Lord God had planted a garden in Eden *from afore-time*' (Gen. ii. 8)[1], and so on. The matter is discussed with some detail in *Pirqe Aboth* vi. 10 'Five possessions possessed the Holy One, blessed is He, in His world : and these are they : Thorah, one possession ; Heaven and Earth, one possession ; Abraham, one possession : Israel, one possession ; the *Sanctuary, one possession* :...............
...*The Sanctuary*: whence [is it proved]? Because it is written, The place, O Lord, which thou hast made for thee to dwell in, the Sanctuary, O Lord, which thy hands have established (Exod. xv. 17) : and it saith, And He brought them to the border of His sanctuary, even to this mountain, which His right hand had possessed (Ps. lxxviii. 54).' This Rabbinical belief has affected the mind of our Psalmist, who comments upon the fall of the Egyptian temple unsympathetically, and evidently has his heart set amongst the ruins of the Sanctuary at Jerusalem. He does not think the covenant between God and the people of Israel is disannulled ; all God's promises are irrevocable ; His gifts and callings are without repentance on His part. But there are no lamentations on the part of the writer over the ruins of Jerusalem ; the temple which is in his thoughts has not developed a wailing-place. God has sealed His own people with the marks of His ownership. All creation, and both worlds, recognise this seal. And He is able to pour out blessings on His chosen, comparable to the dew of heaven, and the milk and honey or the earth. If we please, we may definitely call it a Judaeo-Christian Psalm : and it might very well have been composed by one of the refugees at Pella. It is not easy to see how it could have been written outside Palestine, nor by a purely Jewish hand.

There are no Scripture references ; perhaps the nearest parallels are Rom. xi. 29 ('the gifts and calling of God are without repentance,' ἀμεταμέλητα), and the adaptation of Ps. lxxxiv. 11 in *v.* 6, where again the temple is in the mind of the writer.

The thought that God does not need us, but we need God, is a common religious expression in this period, and is found constantly in Greek literature. We may compare the *Apology of Aristides*, c. 1, and Irenaeus (ed. Mass. 244) 'ipse quidem nullius indigens : his vero qui indigent eius, suam praebens communionem,' which is very near indeed to the language of our Ode, and may almost be taken as a quotation. The opposite sentiment can be illustrated from Schiller :

> 'Freudlos war der grosse Weltenmeister,
> Fühlte Mangel, darum schuf er Geister,
> Sel'ge Spiegel seiner Seligkeit.'

Clement of Rome, *Ep.* i. *ad Cor.*, c. 52, takes an intermediate position : 'The Lord needs nothing...except our praise.'

---

[1] So Jerome: *a principio.*

ODE 5.

[1]I will give thanks unto thee, O Lord, because I love thee; [2]O most High, thou wilt not forsake me[1], for thou art my hope: [3]freely I have received thy grace, I shall live thereby: [4]my persecutors will come[2] and not see me: [5]a cloud of darkness shall fall ⌜on⌝ their eyes; and an air of thick gloom shall darken them: [6]and they shall have no light to see: that they may not take hold upon me. [7]Let their counsel become thick darkness[3], and what they have cunningly devised, let it return upon their own heads: [8]for they have devised a counsel, and it did not succeed[4]: they have prepared themselves for evil[5], and were found to be empty. [9]For my hope is upon the Lord, and I will not fear, and because the Lord is my salvation[6], I will not fear: [10]and He is as a garland on my head and I shall not be moved; even if everything should be shaken, I stand firm; [11]and if all things visible should perish, I shall not die: because the Lord is with me and I am with Him. Hallelujah.

ODE 5. The interest of this Psalm lies in the fact that at this point we begin to strike the region of coincidences with the Gnostic book, known as the *Pistis Sophia*. The Ode has been used, apparently, in the composition of two Odes or Prophecies of Solomon, quoted respectively by Salome and the Virgin.

Salome recites nearly the whole of the Ode, with some slight variations and expansions: and it is possible that one or two clauses may be missing in the Syriac and may be capable of restoration from the Coptic.

The remaining portion of the Ode before us appears, at first sight, from the parallelism of the first sentence, to be the same as what is given in the *Pistis Sophia* as the recitation of the Virgin from the 19th Ode of Solomon. And this ascription and numbering led Ryle and James astray, to identify the matter in question with the sentences about

---

[1] *Or, as in the Coptic,* do not thou forsake me.

[2] *Or, as in the Coptic,* let my persecutors come.

[3] Copt. weakness.　　　　　　　　[4] *lit.* and it became not to them.

[5] *lit.* evilly, *as in the Coptic,* which expands as follows: *Et vicerunt eos potentes* et quae paraverant malitiose, descenderunt in eos. Cf. the German of Schmidt: ' *Und sie sind besiegt, obwohl sie mächtig sind,* und was sie böswillig (κακῶς) bereitet haben, ist auf sie herabgefallen.'

[6] Copt. quia tu es deus meus, salvator meus.

the Virgin quoted by Lactantius[1], as from the 19th Ode of Solomon. We have, however, shown elsewhere that Lactantius' quotation is really in our 19th Ode, so that Lactantius does not appear in the discussion, having been found in another quarter. And we have suggested that the supposed 19th Ode of the Coptic writer is the first of our collection, and that it followed on the eighteen Psalms of Solomon. The mistake can be traced, by comparing, in the *Pistis Sophia*, the text and the Gnostic comment upon it; it will be found that a wrong Ode has been copied out for the text of the Gnostic comment, in consequence of two Odes, the first and the fifth, having some similar sentences. The difference can be exhibited thus:

Coptic Ode 19
[= our Ode 1]

'The Lord is on my head like a crown, and I shall not be separated from Him: a crown of truth has been woven for me: my branches were planted in me: for they did not bear a crown that was dried up, and without a shoot: but thou livest upon my head: and thou growest upon me: thy fruits are full and perfect: they are filled with thy salvation.'

Syriac Ode 5.

'He is like a crown on my head and I shall not be moved. Even if everything should be shaken, I stand firm: and if all things visible should perish, I shall not die: because the Lord is with me and I am with Him.'

The comment upon the foregoing Coptic Ode follows the text of the Syriac Ode, by an unconscious error of the writer who mistook one hymn for the other.

It is clear, then, that the Coptic nineteenth Ode and the Syriac fifth Ode are two different Odes, as we have explained above. We thus recover the missing first Ode of our collection.

Whether this fifth Ode is Christian or not, does not appear decisively at the first reading. It opens in a rather Jewish strain of praise, accompanied by prayer for the discomfiture of enemies. If there is a definite Christian feature, perhaps it is the garland upon the singer's head, which appears in several other Odes. In the 17th Ode, for example, we get the same figure, and here the theme is the praise of the Messiah for His triumph over Hades. This must, of course, be Christian.

The crown is a crown of life, that is a living crown or garland: and this meaning is carefully brought out in the Coptic Ode, which explains

---

[1] *Psalms of Solomon*, p. 160. '*Ode* ii. [of the Coptic Odes] should be another fragment of that quoted by Lactantius, the 19th Ode. Here alone is a number given. The Virgin, be it noted, is the reciter here, and the Virgin is the subject of Lactantius' quotation.'

that the crown does not wither, but (like Aaron's rod), it buds and bears fruit. We have similar allusions and explanations to the crown of life in the New Testament, as in 1 Pet. v. 4 'a crown of glory, *or* glorious crown, which does not fade away.' The close of the Ode is a noble expression of trust in the Lord, amidst adverse circumstances, which one instinctively compares with the close of the eighth chapter of the Epistle to the Romans. It may be regarded as a Christian composition, on account of its affinity with other Odes that are certainly Christian, as well as on account of its intrinsic spiritual value.

ODE 6.

[1]As the hand[1] moves over the harp, and the strings speak, [2]so speaks in my members the Spirit of the Lord, and I speak by His love. [3]For it destroys what is foreign, and everything that is bitter[2]: [4]for thus it was from the beginning and will be to the end, that nothing should be His adversary, and nothing should stand up against Him. [5]The Lord has multiplied the knowledge of Himself, and is zealous [3]that these things should be known, which by His grace have been given to us[3]. [6]And the praise of His name He gave us[4]: our spirits praise His holy Spirit. [7]For there went forth a stream and became a river great and broad; [8]for it flooded and broke up everything and it brought [water] to the Temple[5]: [9]and the restrainers of the children of men were not able to restrain it, nor the arts of those whose business it is to restrain waters; [10]for it spread over the face of the whole earth, and filled everything: [6]and all the thirsty upon earth were given to drink of it[6]; [11]and thirst was relieved and quenched: for from the Most High the draught was given. [12]Blessed then are the ministers of that draught who are entrusted with that water of His: [13]they have assuaged the dry lips, [7]and the will that had fainted they have raised up; [14]and souls that were near departing they have caught back from death[7]: [15]and limbs that had fallen they straightened and

---

[1] Or *perhaps* plectrum.
[2] Cod. and everything is of the Lord. [3-3] 1 Cor. ii. 12.
[4] *lit.* His praise He gave us to His name.
[5] *i.e.* the temple at Jerusalem. Schmidt: 'wandte sich gegen den Tempel.'
[6-6] Schmidt: es tranken, die sich auf dem trockenen Sande befinden. Cf. Is. xxxv. 1.
[7-7] Schmidt: 'Herzensfreude haben empfangen die Entkräfteten. Sie haben Seelen erfasst, indem sie den Hauch hineinstiessen, dass sie nicht stürben.'

set up : [16]they gave strength for their feebleness[1] and light to their eyes: [17]for everyone knew them in the Lord, and they lived by the water of life[2] for ever. Hallelujah.

ODE 6.   In this Psalm again we are fortunate in having a large part of the Coptic text preserved to us : and, as is common in Coptic texts, some Greek words have been also preserved by it. But this very circumstance has led Ryle and James to a wrong supposition as to the existence of Gnostic elements in the Psalm. They recognize that it is a Christian Psalm but suggest, hesitatingly, that the use of the word ἀπόρροια may stamp it as Gnostic. It is quite unnecessary to pay this little tribute to Gnosticism. Neither here nor anywhere else is there anything definitely Gnostic in the book. And Ryle and James are right in saying, 'we cannot see that there is anything unmistakeably Gnostic in the doctrine[3].' They are also clearly right in saying that what is described in the Psalm is 'the preaching of the Gospel which no human effort can avail to hinder.' We must also recognize a reference to the waters in Ezekiel which go forth from the temple. But there is a suggestive difference in our Psalm from the parable in Ezekiel : in the Syriac text the stream appears to rise elsewhere than in the temple, and part of its function is to water the temple. It is a river deep and broad before it reaches the temple. If this be what is intended, then the restrainers who build dykes to keep waters out or cisterns to keep them in are very likely the Temple officials themselves, who were often hard put to it to hinder the propaganda of the new religion within the limits of the Holy Place.

The writer is exultant in his universalism ; the stream of living water has gone out into all the earth : thirsty souls everywhere have been refreshed by it: dying souls have been revived.

The writer is as universal as St Paul. But he is not so detached from Judaism as not to know that the living water was connected with the temple. Perhaps, then, he is a Judaeo-Christian of an enlightened type. Ryle and James suggest for him a date not later than the second century, and intimate the presence of Johannine phraseology and ideas. We think the date is too late; the Johannine features do not appear to us to be directly due to the Gospel: if such a long composition had been under Johannine influence, it would have betrayed its ancestry more definitely. Neither here nor elsewhere does it seem possible definitely to convict the Psalms of having borrowed from St John. On the other hand there is one expression which

---

[1] Cod. *ex errore* 'for their coming.'   [2] *lit.* by living water.

[3] Harnack, who has missed the meaning of this hymn, called it a Gnostic baptismal hymn (*Hist. of Dogma*, i. 207 note). He admits now that it is not Gnostic, and it is doubtful if it has anything to do with baptism.

recalls a sentence in 1 Cor., where the writer says that God is zealous 'that those things should be known, which have been given us by His grace': this is very like 1 Cor. ii. 12, 'that we may know the things that have been freely given us of God.' Whether the coincidence should be pressed will depend to some extent upon the existence of further and similar echoes of New Testament speech.

Near the close of the Psalm the Greek word παρρησία occurs in the Coptic; but the Syriac 'coming' suggests παρουσία. Παρρησία, as the *Pistis Sophia* shows, is one of the words which the Coptic transliterates: so we must retain it, or else find a Greek word which may be misread either as παρρησία or παρουσία. We have suggested that παράλυσις is the right word. This is confirmed by the preceding clause, 'Members that had fallen they straightened and set up.' Here the Coptic has *erexere* for the two Syriac words which we render by 'straightened and set up.' The Syriac has been translating a compound verb by two simple verbs; and the original was evidently ἀνώρθωσαν. We may now compare Is. xxxv. 3 and Heb. xii. 12; especially note τὰ παραλελυμένα γόνατα ἀνορθώσατε. We now see the meaning of the words which follow, 'they gave strength to their paralysis'; it is a reflexion from ἰσχύσατε, γόνατα παραλελυμένα. The correctness of the reference to Isaiah may be further seen from the following words 'and light to their eyes,' which are a reflexion from 'then shall the eyes of the blind be opened.' It is clear then that the writer is working from Isaiah and not from Hebrews: and in that case the ἀπόρροια of which the *Pistis Sophia* makes so much is the stream of water which, in the prophecy, makes glad the wilderness and the solitary place. We can now explain the variation between the Syriac and Coptic in *v.* 10. The 'dry sand' is the ἔρημος διψῶσα of Is. xxxv. 1, and the Syriac should be 'all upon the thirsty land drank of it.'

[The Ode is translated into English by Barnes in *Expositor* (July 1910). He suggests that we read 'wind' for 'hand' in *v.* 1 as if the harp were an Aeolian harp! Perhaps 'hand' is wrong, as there is the trace of a connecting line before the actually visible Olaph. If it is not 'hand,' I suspect it is 'plectrum.']

ODE 7.

[1]As the impulse of anger against evil, so is the impulse of joy over what is lovely, and brings in of its fruits without restraint: [2]my joy is the Lord and my impulse is toward Him[1]: this path of mine is excellent[2]: [3]for I have a helper, the Lord[3]. [4]He hath caused me to know Himself, without grudging, by His

---

[1] *lit.* my running: cf. Cant. i. 3.　　　　[2] So Schulthess.

[3] B.-L. remove ܟ‌ܝܘ‌ܢ to the end of previous verse.

simplicity: His kindness has [1]humbled His greatness[1]. [5]He became like me, in order that I might receive Him: [6]He was reckoned like myself[2] in order that I might put Him on; [7]and I trembled not when I saw Him: because He was gracious to me: [8]like my nature He became that I might learn Him and like my form, that I might not turn back from Him: [9]the Father of knowledge is the word of knowledge: [10]He who created wisdom is wiser than His works: [11]and He who created me when yet I was not knew what I should do when I came into being: [12]wherefore He pitied me in His abundant grace: and granted me to ask from Him and to receive from His sacrifice[3]: [13]because He it is that is incorrupt, the fulness of the ages and the Father of them[4].

[14]He hath given Him to be seen of them that are His, [15]in order that they may recognize Him that made them: and that they might not suppose that they came of themselves[5]: [16]for knowledge He hath appointed as its way, He hath widened it and extended it; and brought it to all perfection; [17]and set over it the traces of His light, and I walked ⌜therein⌝ from the beginning even to the end. [18]For by Him it was wrought, and He was resting in the Son, and for its salvation He will take hold of everything: [19]and the Most High shall be known in His Saints, to announce to those that have songs of the coming of the Lord; [20]that they may go forth to meet Him, and may sing to Him with joy and with the harp of many tones[6]: [21]the seers shall come before Him and they shall be seen before Him, [22]and they shall praise the Lord for His love: because He is near and beholdeth, [23]and hatred shall be taken from the earth, and along with jealousy it shall be drowned: [24]for ignorance hath been destroyed, because the knowledge of the Lord hath arrived. [25]They who make songs shall sing the grace of the Lord Most High; [26]and they shall bring their songs, and their heart shall be like the day: and like the excellent beauty[7] of

---

[1-1] So Flemming: seine Grösse klein erscheinen lassen.

[2] *lit.* in likeness as myself.

[3] Gk. θυσίας: Nestle conjectures οὐσίας: cf. Clem. *Ep.* ii. *ad Cor.* i. ἠθέλησεν ἐκ τοῦ μὴ ὄντος εἶναι ἡμᾶς: and the verse of the Ode that precedes, 'when I came into being.' Also Ode 8. 16. For an opposite error see Cod. k in Mk. ix. 49.

[4] For the expression 'Father of the Ages,' cf. 1 Clem. *ad Cor.* xxxv. 2, lv. 6, lxi. 2, and Is. xi. 6 (Heb.).

[5] Ps. c. 3.   [6] *lit.* voices.

[7] Gk. μεγαλοπρέπεια as in Ps. lxvii. (lxviii.) 34.

the Lord their pleasant song : [27] and there shall neither be any thing that breathes without knowledge, nor any that is dumb: [28] for He hath given a mouth to His creation, to open the voice of the mouth towards Him, to praise Him : [29] confess ye His power, and show forth His grace. Hallelujah.

ODE 7. In this Psalm the writer dilates joyfully[1] on the theme of the Incarnation ; and the combination of lowliness and wisdom that are involved therein. The condescension of Christ to human form is not only a sympathetic approach to human conditions, it is a divine welcome. He says 'Come unto me' by coming unto us. 'Like my nature He became that I might learn of Him.'

But the incarnate Messiah is still the maker and sustainer of all things, in whom all things consist. The knowledge of this revelation produces praise and expectation, praise for those who sing His advent, expectation for those who look for His triumphant rule among men. All evil is to pass away, and all hate. The saints who sing are already exulting in the new life which He has bestowed upon them[2].

For the argument with which the Ode opens we may compare Lactantius, *de Div. Inst.* iv. 26: 'is, qui humilis advenerat, ut humilibus et infimis opem ferret, et omnibus spem salutis ostenderet, eo genere afficiendus fuit, quo humiles et infimi solent, ne quis esset omnino, qui eum non posset imitari.'

[The difficulty in translating *v.* 3 has been variously met : Flemming translates 'ein Helfer zum Herrn,' Zahn, (in Verhältnis) zum Herrn : Batiffol and Labourt, as intimated, remove the words 'to the Lord' to the end of the previous verse.]

ODE 8.

[1] Open ye, open ye your hearts to the exultation of the Lord: [2] and let your love be multiplied from the heart and even to the lips, [3] to bring forth fruit to the Lord, living ⌜fruit⌝, holy ⌜fruit⌝[3], and to talk with watchfulness in His light. [4] Rise up, and stand erect, ye who sometime were brought low : [5] tell forth ye who were in silence, that your mouth hath been opened. [6] Ye, therefore, that were despised, be henceforth lifted up, because your righteousness hath been exalted. [7] For the right hand of

---

[1] The opening sentence about the 'impulse against evil' may be illustrated from Clem. Alex. *Paed.* i. 8, p. 140 ἕπεται τῷ ἀγαθῷ, ᾗ φύσει ἀγαθός ἐστιν, ἡ μισοπονηρία.

[2] The combination of 'seers' and 'singers' is peculiar, and belongs to a very early period in Church History; it would be best illustrated by the saints in the beginning of Luke's Gospel, who were looking for redemption in Jerusalem, if we could imagine that peculiar religious society of prophets and singers continued and extended.

[3] Ungnad-Stärk, *a holy life.*

the Lord is with you : and He is your helper : [8]and peace was prepared for you, before ever your war was.   [9]Hear the word of truth, and receive the knowledge of the Most High.   [10]Your flesh has not known what I am saying to you : neither have your hearts[1] known what I am showing to you.   [11]Keep my secret[2], ye who are kept by it : [12]keep my faith, ye who are kept by it.   [13]And understand my knowledge, ye who know me in truth.   [14]Love me with affection, ye who love : [15]for I do not turn away my face from them that are mine ; [16]for I know them, and before they came into being I took knowledge of them, and on their faces I set my seal : [17]I fashioned their members : my own breasts I prepared for them that they might drink my holy milk and live thereby.   [18]I took pleasure in them and am not ashamed of them : [19]for my workmanship are they and the strength of my thoughts : [20]who then shall rise up against my handiwork, or who is there that is not subject to them ? [21]I willed and fashioned mind and heart : and they are mine, and by my own right hand I set my elect ones : [22]and my righteousness goeth before them and they shall not be deprived of my name, for it is with them.   [23]Ask, and abound[3] and abide in the love of the Lord, [24]⌐and⌐ ye beloved ones in the Beloved : those who are kept, in Him that liveth : [25]and they that are saved in Him that was saved ; [26]and ye shall be found incorrupt in all ages to the name of your Father.   Hallelujah.

Cf. Is. lxiv. 4.

ODE 8.   This Psalm again is Johannine in many of its ideas and expressions.   But, even when this is conceded, it is difficult to prove a direct dependence on the Fourth Gospel.

The Psalm is, like a number of others, marked by a sudden transition of personality from the Psalmist or Prophet to the Lord Himself : after the writer has addressed those who have been lifted up out of affliction and have found peace after war, he suddenly in prophetic manner, cries out, 'Hear the word of the Lord,' 'Receive the heavenly knowledge,' and then proceeds to speak in the person of the Lord. The same abrupt transitions are found in the canonical Psalter, and they appear to have characterized the Montanist inspirations.   It will be remembered that Montanus describes his own spiritual exaltation in the words : 'Behold ! the man is as a lyre, and I sweep over him as the plectrum.   The man sleeps and I wake.   Behold ! it is the Lord, who

---

[1] The MS. by an error of transcription reads, 'your raiment.'   But perhaps the aiment means the human body ?

[2] *Clem. Hom.* xix. 20; and Clem. Alex. *Strom.* v. 10, apparently from a lost Gospel.

[3] Fl. : Bittet ohne Unterlass.

estranges the souls of men from themselves, and gives men souls.'
The same address by the Lord in the first person is in the utterance of
Maximilla, the Montanist prophetess, who said, 'I am chased as a
wolf from the midst of the flock. I am no wolf; I am word, and spirit,
and power.'

The language of Montanus finds a close parallel in the opening of the
sixth Psalm, where the writer says, 'As the hand [or perhaps plectrum]
moves over the harp, and the strings speak, so speaks in my members the
Spirit of the Lord.' This might easily be claimed as a Montanist utterance,
and I can imagine that on account of these and similar sayings, the whole
Psalter might be claimed as a Montanist product. But the sentiments
are simply Christian, on a high experimental plane; and we must not
forget that one of the chief characteristics of Montanism is its attempt
to perpetuate the life of the primitive Church. Towards the end of the
Psalm the prophet returns abruptly to speech in his own name. There
seems to be some breach of continuity in the discourse, as well
as a change of personality.

I do not know whether the allusion to an actual war, from which the
saints have emerged or escaped, is to be taken literally. If it be a
literal, and not a spiritual reference, the choice will lie between the
Jewish war under Titus or that under Hadrian; in either case we
should be in Judaeo-Christian circles. It is, however, quite possible
that the 'war' and the 'peace' refer only to spiritual experiences.

The injunction in v. 11 to keep the Lord's secret (μυστήριον ἐμὸν)
is frequently quoted in the Fathers. A striking instance will be found
in Lactantius, Div. Instit. vii. 26: 'nos defendere hanc [doctrinam]
publice atque asserere non solemus, Deo jubente, ut quieti ac silentes
arcanum ejus in abdito atque intra nostram conscientiam teneamus...
abscondi enim tegique mysterium quam fidelissime oportet, maxime a nobis,
qui nomen fidei gerimus.' The last sentence is very like the language
of the Ode, 'Keep my secret ye who are kept by it; keep my faith ye
who are kept by it.' These Patristic quotations may be traced ultimately
to a variant translation of Isaiah xxiv. 16, which has crept into some
texts of the LXX from the Hexapla of Origen. But there are a number
of cases where the citation is not directly from Isaiah, but from a saying
of our Lord in an uncanonical Gospel. Thus in Clem. Alex. Strom.
v. 10 we have οὐ γὰρ φθονῶν, φησί, παρήγγειλεν ὁ κύριος ἔν τινι εὐαγγελίῳ·
μυστήριον ἐμὸν ἐμοὶ καὶ τοῖς υἱοῖς τοῦ οἴκου μου. Again in Clem. Hom.
xix. 20 we have, μεμνήμεθα τοῦ κυρίου ἡμῶν καὶ διδασκάλου, ὡς ἐντελλόμενος
εἶπεν ἡμῖν· τὰ μυστήρια ἐμοὶ καὶ τοῖς υἱοῖς μου φυλάξατε. It seems that
the Odist has been working from the same source as Clement of
Alexandria and the Clementine Homilist: and if this be the case, the
uncanonical Gospel of which he makes use is very likely the same which
we shall find quoted in the 24th Ode. [Bernard thinks the reference is
to the disciplina arcani.]

ODE 9.

[1]Open your ears and I will speak to you. Give me your souls that I may also give you my soul, [2]the word of the Lord and His good pleasures, the holy thought which He has devised concerning His Messiah. [3]For in the will of the Lord is your salvation[1], and His thought is everlasting life; and your end is immortality[2]. [4]Be enriched in God the Father, and receive the thought of the Most High. [5]Be strong and be Is. lii. 7. redeemed by His grace. [6]For I announce to you peace, to you Cf. Ps. His saints; [7]that none of those who hear may fall in war, and lxxxv. 9. those again who have known Him may not perish, and that those who receive may not be ashamed. [8]An everlasting crown for ever is Truth. Blessed are they who set it on their heads: [9]a stone of great price is it; and there have been wars on account of the crown. [10]And righteousness hath taken it and hath given it to you. [11]Put on the crown in the true covenant of the Lord. [12]And all those who have conquered shall be written in His book. [13]For their book is victory which is yours. And she (Victory) sees you before her and wills that you shall be saved. Hallelujah.

ODE 9. This Psalm is, from a historical point of view, somewhat colourless. The only definite points are the allusions to the Lord's Messiah, or Christ: and a promise of peace and deliverance from war, which is made to the saints. Of the first of these allusions, we may say that while it makes the Psalm a Messianic one, this does not mean that it is not Christian. The promise of everlasting life which follows must be the holy thought of God concerning the Christ. And this seems to definitely mark out the Psalm as Christian.

What then are we to say of the wars and victory to which the Psalm refers; are they spiritual or are they outward, or a mixture of both? We shall have the same problem before us in other Psalms. From the fact that Victory is personified and writes a book, with which we may compare Apoc. iii. 5 ('He that overcometh shall be clothed in white raiment, and I will not blot out his name from the book of life'), we may perhaps conclude that the Victory spoken of is a spiritual one. This is in harmony with the references to redemption by grace and to the will of Victory that the saints should be saved. These are Christian expressions. On the other hand the promise that none of those who

---

[1] *lit.* life.   [2] *Or,* and without corruption is your perfection.

obey the Lord's word shall fall in war might have been very strikingly illustrated in the case of the Christians who escaped to Pella. But even then the Psalm is a Christian one, and it remains an open question whether outward allusions may not have been coupled with inward victories.

The alternative rendering for the third verse suggests that the Syriac words answer to a Greek sentence, καὶ ἐν ἀφθαρσίᾳ τὸ τέλος ὑμῶν.

ODE 10.

[1]The Lord hath directed my mouth by His word : and He hath opened my heart by His light : and He hath caused to dwell in me His deathless life; [2]and gave me that I might speak the fruit of His peace: [3]to convert the souls of them who are willing to come to Him : and to lead captive a good captivity for freedom. [4]I was strengthened and made mighty and took the world captive ; [5]and it became to me for the praise of the Most High, and of God my Father. [6]And the Gentiles[1] were gathered together who were scattered abroad. [7]And I was unpolluted by my love ⌐for them¬[2], because they confessed me in high places : and the traces of the light were set upon their heart: [8]and they walked in my life and were saved and became my people for ever and ever. Hallelujah.

ODE 10. In this vigorous little Psalm Christ must Himself be accounted the speaker through the mouth of His prophet; unless we should prefer to say that any of the opening sentences are spoken in the Psalmist's own name, and that after them there is an abrupt alteration of personality, such as we have already referred to. It is certain, however, that the one who gathers the peoples together by his love must be the Messiah: ('unto him shall the gathering of the peoples be[3]'). And it can be no psalmist or prophet who declares that the Gentiles became his people for ever and ever. The one who goes forth to lead captivity captive is again the Christ : we have in the New Testament (Eph. iv. 8) the Messianic interpretation of Ps. lxviii. 18, 'He ascended up on high, he led captivity captive'; and the same explanation underlies the Ode before us. The Ode is, therefore, a Christian one : and its soteriology is universal in character. But we are still in the region where apologetic is necessary for the reception of the

---

[1] Christ has accepted the Gentiles.

[2] *i.e.* erasing the plural points, so as not to read 'by my sins.' Barnes suggests the emendation 'by their sins.' Wellhausen: ist natürlich *haubai* zu sprechen, nicht *hubbi*.

[3] Gen. xlix. 10.

Gentiles, and where it does not suffice to quote a verse of the Old Testament and say that such reception was foretold. In our Ode Christ explains that the reception of the Gentiles has not polluted Him. Such language does not belong to the Hellenic world, nor, we think, to the second century. But it is quite natural in a Judaeo-Christian community in Palestine in the first century.

The fact that prophets spoke in the person of God or of Christ was a common observation with the early fathers : a good illustration may be seen in Justin's *Apology*[1], where Justin explains that the opening sentences of Isaiah ('The ox knoweth his owner...but my people doth not consider') are a case of the kind ; and then goes on to explain that the words 'all day long I have stretched out my hands' are to be understood of the prophet speaking in the person of Christ. In the canonical Psalms also the same feature was easily traced, and those who composed the early books of Testimonies against the Jews constantly point out that the real speaker is not the prophet, but One whom he impersonates. It is inevitable that this impersonation should cause difficulties of interpretation, due to the obscurity of personality involved in the different parts of the prophecy or psalm. And we must not be surprised if we sometimes find it hard to tell in the text of our Odes who is to be regarded as the speaker.

ODE 11.

[1]My heart was cloven[2] and its flower appeared ; and grace sprang up in it : and it brought forth fruit to the Lord, [2]for the Most High clave ⌐my heart¬[3] by His Holy Spirit and searched my affection[4] towards Him: and filled me with His love. [3]And His opening[5] of me became my salvation ; and I ran in His way in His peace, even in the way of truth : [4]from the beginning and even to the end I acquired His knowledge : [5]and I was established upon the rock of truth, where He had set me up : [6]and speaking waters[6] touched my lips from the fountain of the Lord plenteously : [7]and I drank and was inebriated with the living water that doth not die ; [8]and my inebriation was not one without knowledge, but I forsook vanity and turned to the Most High my God, [9]and I was enriched by His bounty,

---

[1] 1 *Ap.* 37, 38.   [2] *Or*, circumcised.
[3] *lit.* clave me *or* circumcised me. Cf. Rom. ii. 29.
[4] *lit.* revealed my reins: cf. *Sap. Sol.* i. 6: Ps. vii. 9: Ps. lxii. (lxi.) 2: Apoc. ii. 23.
[5] *Or*, circumcision.
[6] Cf. Ignatius *ad Rom.* 7 ὕδωρ ζῶν καὶ λαλοῦν. Wellhausen : das redende Wasser findet sich bei den Mandäern.

and I forsook the folly which is diffused[1] over the earth; and I stripped it off and cast it from me: [10]and the Lord renewed me in His raiment[2], and possessed me by His light, and from above He gave me rest in incorruption; [11]and I became like the land which blossoms and rejoices in its fruits: [12]and the Lord was like the sun shining on the face of the land; [13]He lightened my eyes, and my face received the dew; and my nostrils[3] enjoyed the pleasant odour of the Lord; [14]and He carried me to His Paradise; where is the abundance of the pleasure of the Lord; [15]and I worshipped the Lord on account of His glory; and I said, Blessed, O Lord, are they who are planted in thy land! and those who have a place in thy Paradise; [16]and they grow by the fruits of thy trees[4]. And they have changed from darkness to light. [17]Behold! all thy servants are fair, who do good works, and turn away from wickedness to the pleasantness that is thine: [18]and they have turned back the bitterness of the trees from them, when they were planted in thy land; [19]and everything became like a relic of thyself, and a memorial for ever of thy faithful works. [20]For there is abundant room in thy Paradise, and nothing is useless[5] therein; [21]but everything is filled with fruit; glory be to thee, O God, the delight of Paradise for ever. Hallelujah.

ODE 11. This lovely Psalm is altogether personal and experimental: the writer describes the visitations of Divine Grace, which he calls the cutting open[6] of his heart, and his establishment upon the rock of eternal truth. He is renewed by these visitations, as if he had been newly clad in light and had already reached the eternal rest. He becomes like a land that drinks in the dew of heaven, and brings forth fruit to God. He finds himself at last in the Paradise of God and amongst the fragrant trees of a new creation. He breaks out into exultant praise of the good things which God has prepared for them that love Him.

There are no Scriptural references in the Psalm that can be claimed as quotations, however closely the language approximates to that of the ancient Scriptures. Perhaps the nearest parallel would be the promise in Apoc. ii. 7, that the one who overcomes, shall eat of the tree of life, which is in the midst of the Paradise of God.

---

[1] *lit.* cast. U.-S.: die auf Erden lagert.
[2] Cp. Ps. civ. 2.   [3] *lit.* my breathing.
[4] Better with Fl.: they grow according to the growth of thy trees.
[5] *Or,* idle = ἀργός. Cf. 2 Pet. i. 8: οὐκ ἀργοὺς οὐδὲ ἀκάρπους.
[6] *perhaps* the circumcising.

ODE 12.

[1]He hath filled me with words of truth; that I may speak the same; [2]and like the flow of waters flows truth from my mouth, and my lips show forth His fruit.   [3]And He has caused Ps. li. 17. His knowledge to abound in me, because the mouth of the Lord is the true Word, and the door of His light; [4]and the Most High hath given it to His worlds, [worlds] which are the interpreters of His own beauty, and the repeaters of His praise, and the confessors of His counsel, and the heralds of His thought, and the chasteners of His servants[1].   [5]For the swiftness of the Word[2] is inexpressible, and like its expression is its swiftness and force; [6]and its course knows no limit. Never doth it fail, but it stands sure and it knows not descent nor the way of it[3].   [7]For as its work is, so is its end: for it is light and the dawning of thought; [8]and by it the worlds[4] talk one to the other; and in the Word there were those that were silent; [9]and from it came love and concord; and they spake one to the other whatever was theirs; and they were penetrated by the Word; [10]and they knew Him who made them, because they were in concord; for the mouth of the Most High spake to them; and His explanation ran by means of it: [11]for the dwelling-place of the Word is man: and its truth is love. [12]Blessed are they who by means thereof have understood everything, and have known the Lord in His truth.   Hallelujah.

ODE 12.   This Psalm rises to a high level of spiritual thought, but for that very reason its language is occasionally obscure.   The writer describes his own inspiration and how his heart and lips become filled with the words of God.   Here, as elsewhere, God's fruit is found in the lips of the faithful, and we are often reminded in these Psalms of the expression which is borrowed in Heb. xiii. 15, from the prophet Hosea, about offering to God the 'fruit of lips that confess to His name.' From the general thought of the words of God, the writer rises to the abstract idea of the Word of God, or Logos, which is the totality of God's revelation and which interpenetrates all things, so that even things that are silent find their speech in it.   But especially this Word, which is both truth and love, finds its dwelling-place in man.   Happy

---

[1] Or, works.

[2] Cf. Sap. Sol. vii. 24.   Philo, De Mut. Nom. 42 κοῦφον γὰρ ὁ λόγος καὶ πτηνὸν φύσει, βέλους θᾶττον φερόμενος καὶ πάντη διάττων.

[3] Or by slight emendations, no man knoweth its length or breadth.

[4] Or possibly, the aeons.

are they that have come to know Him. Here, perhaps, we are nearer
to Gnostic ideas, such as the doctrine of the Word and the Silence,
than in any other part of the Psalter: yet there is nothing that can
fairly be called Gnostic. We are also very close to the doctrine of the
Logos as we have it in John, where the Logos becomes flesh and dwells
amongst us: but it is not the Johannine thought of the Incarnation
that is imitated or reproduced. The dwelling of the Logos with man is
personal and not collective; and we cannot infer from this Psalm a
direct statement of the doctrine of Incarnation, for the writer does not
go beyond Inspiration; but his thought is noble, even if, as we have
said, it is sometimes obscure, at least in a translation.

ODE 13.

[1]Behold! the Lord is°our mirror[1]: open the eyes and see
them in Him: and learn the manner of your face: [2]and tell forth
praise to His spirit: and wipe off the filth from your face: and
love His holiness, and clothe yourselves therewith: [3]and be
without stain at all times before Him. Hallelujah.

ODE 13.   This strange little Psalm is an exhortation to holiness:
we are to behold the Lord in the beauty of His holiness, but we are
also to see ourselves reflected in God as in a mirror; then we shall
behold our natural face in an unexpected glass and know what manner
of men we are: and in that glass we shall cleanse the dirt from off our
faces, and attain to purity. We are reminded of St Paul's statement
that we behold, as in a mirror, the glory of our Lord and are transfigured
into the same image; though here the thought is not as high as in
Corinthians, where holiness is found by the Vision of God rather than
by the scrutiny of ourselves.

We may also in this connexion refer to a remarkable passage which
is found in a tract falsely ascribed to Cyprian, and known as *De
Montibus Sina et Sion*. We are reminded in this passage first that
Christ is the Unspotted Mirror of the Father, as is said of Wisdom in
the book called the Wisdom of Solomon[2]. Hence the Father and
the Son see one another by reflexion. The writer then continues as
follows:

'And even we who believe in Him see Christ in us as in a mirror,
as He Himself instructs and advises us in the Epistle of His disciple

---

[1] Cf. Clem. Alex. *Paed.* i. 9, p. 172 Τὸ ἔσοπτρον τῷ αἰσχρῷ οὐ κακόν, ὅτι δεικνύει
αὐτὸν οἷός ἐστιν. Cf. Jac. i. 24. *Clem. Hom.* xiii. 16 καλῷ ἐσόπτρῳ ὁρᾷ [ἡ σώφρων
γυνὴ] εἰς τὸν Θεὸν ἐμβλέπουσα.

[2] *Sap. Sol.* vii. 26.

John to the people: "See me in yourselves, in the same way as any one of you sees himself in water or in a mirror"; and so he confirmed the saying of Solomon about Himself, that "He is the unspotted mirror of the Father."'

Here we have the doctrine of dual vision in a mirror, as though the mirror saw the observer as well as the observer the mirror; in this way the Father sees Himself in the Son and the Son sees Himself in the Father: and then we are told of something said by John, speaking in the person of Christ, in a lost epistle, that we are to see Christ in ourselves as in a glass. This is something like the doctrine of our Psalm that we are to see ourselves in Christ. If we could really be sure of the correctness of the reference of the supposed Cyprianic tract to St John, we should have more confidence in saying that here also we are in the region of Johannine ideas: but, even in that case, there would seem to be no question of direct quotation from canonical Johannine writings[1].

ODE 14.

[1]As the eyes[2] of a son to his father, so are my eyes, O Lord, at all times towards thee. [2]For with thee are my consolations (*lit.* breasts) and my delight. [3]Turn not away thy mercies from me, O Lord: and take not thy kindness from me. [4]Stretch out to me, O Lord, at all times thy right hand: and be my guide[3] even unto the end, according to thy good pleasure. [5]Let me be well-pleasing[4] before thee, because of thy glory and because of thy name: [6]let me be preserved from evil, and let thy meekness, O Lord, abide with me, and the fruits of thy love. [7]Teach me the Psalms of thy truth, that I may bring forth fruit in thee: [8]and open to me the harp of thy Holy Spirit, that with all its notes I may praise thee, O Lord. [9]And according to the multitude of thy tender mercies, so thou shalt give to me; and hasten to grant our petitions; and thou art able for all our needs. Hallelujah.

---

[1] The passage in Ps.-Cyprian is so curious, that for convenience I transcribe the Latin: *De Mont. Sina et Sion* 13: 'Ita inuenimus ipsum Saluatorem per Salomonem speculum inmaculatum patris esse dictum, eo quod sanctus spiritus Dei filius geminatum se uideat, pater in filio et filius in patre, utrosque se in se uident: ideo speculus inmaculatus. Nam et nos qui illi credimus Christum in nobis tanquam in speculo uidemus, ipso nos instruente et monente in epistula Iohannis discipuli sui ad populum: "ita me in uobis uidete, quomodo quis uestrum se uidet in aquam aut in speculum," et confirmauit Salomonicum dictum de se dicentem, "quis est speculus inmaculatus patris."'

[2] Ps. cxxiii. 2.   [3] Ps. xlviii. 14.

[4] = εὐαρεστεῖν, *walk before God*, as Enoch, Gen. v. 24 etc.; cf. Peshiṭta.

ODE 14. In this Psalm the canonical Psalter is somewhat more closely imitated than is generally the case with our collection. The opening sentences recall Ps. cxxiii. 2, 'As the eyes of servants to the hands of their masters, and as the eyes of a maid to the hand of her mistress, so are our eyes to the Lord our God.' The prayer that the Lord will be 'my guide even to the end,' recalls Ps. xlviii. 14, 'This God is our God for ever and ever: He will be our guide even unto death.' But the Psalm is by no means a cento from the canonical Psalter, even though it does not contain anything that could, at the first reading, be definitely labelled as Christian.

ODE 15.

[1]As the sun is the joy to them that seek for its daybreak[1], so is my joy the Lord; [2]because He is my Sun and His rays have lifted me up[2]; and His light hath dispelled all darkness from my face. [3]In Him I have acquired eyes and have seen His holy day: [4]ears have become mine and I have heard His truth. [5]The thought of knowledge hath been mine, and I have been delighted through Him. [6]The way of error I have left, and have walked towards Him and have received salvation from Him, without grudging. [7]And according to His bounty He hath given to me, and according to His excellent beauty[3] He hath made me. [8]I have put on incorruption through His name: and have put off corruption by His grace. [9]Death hath been destroyed before my face: and Sheol hath been abolished by my word: [10]and there hath gone up deathless life in the Lord's land, [11]and it hath been made known to His faithful ones, and hath been given without stint to all those that trust in Him. Hallelujah.

ODE 15. This beautiful Psalm, like so many others in the collection, opens with a similitude: these openings are characteristic of the book, and betray a single writer. This does not mean that they do not sometimes imitate the opening of the canonical Psalms. In the present case the 130th Psalm seems to have furnished the key-note, viz. the watchers for the morning. It is an experimental Psalm of the first order: the Sun has risen upon the soul of the writer. Eyes, ears and heart have all been opened. Salvation has been realized: the comeliness of the Lord has been put upon him: death has lost its terrors, the grave its power.

[1] Cf. Ps. cxxx. 6.   [2] *Or*, made me rise up.
[3] = Gk. μεγαλοπρέπεια.

There is one passage which is either obscure, incorrect or extravagant where the writer says that 'Sheol has been abolished by my word.' Unless there has been a transition of personality, this seems extravagant, and invites the correction 'has been abolished at His word.' In any case, I think the Psalm is a Christian one, though the positive or dogmatic identifications are not forthcoming, apart from the victory over death and the grave.

ODE 16.

[1]As the work of the husbandman is the ploughshare: and the work of the steersman is the guidance[1] of the ship: [2]so also my work is the Psalm of the Lord : my craft and my occupation are in His praises[2]: [3]because His love hath nourished my heart, and even to my lips His fruits He poured out. [4]For my love is the Lord, and therefore I will sing unto Him: [5]for I am made strong in His praise, and I have faith in Him. [6]I will open my mouth and His spirit will utter in me [7]the glory of the Lord and His beauty ; the work of His hands and the operation of His fingers: [8]the multitude of His mercies and the strength of His word. [9]For the word of the Lord searches out[3] all things, both the invisible and that which reveals His thought ; [10]for the eye sees His works, and the ear hears His thought. [11]He spread out the earth and He settled the waters in the sea : [12]He measured the heavens and fixed the stars : and He established the creation and set it up: [13]and He rested from His works: [14]and created things run in their courses, and do their works: [15]and they know not how to stand and be idle[4] ; and His ⌐heavenly⌐ hosts are subject to His word. [16]The treasure-chamber of the light is the sun, and the treasury of the darkness is the night : [17]and He made the sun for the day that it may be bright, but night brings darkness over the face of the land ; [18]and their alternations one to the other speak[5] the beauty of God : [19]and there is nothing that is without the Lord ; for He was before any thing came into being : [20]and the worlds were made by His word, and by the thought of His heart. Glory and honour to His name. Hallelujah.

Cf. Heb. i. 2.

[1] *lit.* traction. Schulthess suggests 'the mast.' (l. ܚܢܝ̈ܬܐ).

[2] *lit.* in His praises is my craft and in His praises my occupation.

[3] *Or*, searches out: everything, the invisible and the revealed, (is) his thought.

[4] Justin, *Dial.* 22.   [5] Cod. complete; *but read* ܡܡܠܠܝ̈ܢ.

ODE 16. This Psalm is, in its closing sentences, specifically Christian, and it is clearly from the same author as those that have immediately preceded. The theme is the beauty of God's creation; especially the writer considers the heavens which are the works of God's fingers, he contemplates the 'spacious firmament on high' (Ps. xviii.). We frequently catch refrains from the story of Creation. But curiously the writer appears to avoid the mention of the moon: instead of saying that God appointed the sun to rule the day and the moon to rule the night, he says that 'the treasure of the light is the sun, and the treasure of the darkness is—the night': and he tries to work out this broken parallel by a further statement about the offices of the sun and the darkness. It would be, perhaps, too much to assume that he had some reason for neglecting the moon: but the omission is curious: (there is a similar omission in *Sap. Sol.* vii. 18). The Psalm is certainly a beautiful one, especially in its opening verses. These find an appropriate parallel in Clement of Alexandria, who tells us[1]: 'We do not force the horse to plough nor the bull to hunt, but we allure each species of animal to the craft that suits it. So we also invite man to the vision of the open heaven, and to the knowledge of God, because he is of celestial birth......Plough, indeed, if ploughman thou be, but know God while thou ploughest: sail, if thou love to voyage the seas, but make thy appeal to the steersman on high.'

The opening verses of this Ode find also a close parallel to Stoic thought in one of its loftiest expressions; for, according to Epictetus, the praise of God is the greatest of occupations: 'Seeing that most of you are blinded, should there not be some one to fill this place, and sing the hymn to God on behalf of all men?...Were I a nightingale, I should do after the manner of a nightingale. Were I a swan, I should do after the manner of a swan. But now, since I am a reasonable being, *I must sing to God; that is my proper work*: I do it, nor will I desert this my post, as long as it is granted to me to hold it: and unto you I call to join in this self-same hymn' (Epictetus, *Discourses*, i. 16). I am almost tempted to believe that our Odist knew this saying of Epictetus, and had Christianised it. It may well have been a popular religious quotation in the latter part of the first century. Stoicism and Christianity were, as is well known, very near neighbours; and this passage is one of the finest of Epictetus' sayings[2].

On examining the Ode more closely we detect an unmistakeable case of anti-Judaic polemic. The writer after describing the beauty of

---

[1] Clem. Alex. *Protrept.* p. 80.

[2] T. R. Glover (*Conflict of Religions*, p. 165) refers to this saying of Epictetus and remarks that 'Stoicism was never essentially musical. Epictetus announces a hymn to Zeus, but he never starts the tune.' Certainly the language of the Ode is much loftier and more musical than that of Epictetus.

creation and the Lord's rest from His works, goes on to say something which shows that he does not mean to deduce the Jewish Sabbath from the statements in Genesis. 'Created things run in their courses, and *do their works and know not how to stand or be idle.*' Suppose we turn to Justin's *Dialogue with Trypho*, c. 22, where Justin is arguing with Trypho for the non-necessity of circumcision and the Sabbath: 'I will declare to you and to those who may wish to become proselytes,' says Justin, 'a divine word which I heard from the old man to whom I owe my conversion. He said, "you observe that the heavenly bodies *do not idle nor keep sabbath*[1]. Remain, therefore, as you were born, do not keep sabbath nor practise circumcision."'

It is clear, then, that the 16th Ode means to say that the Sabbath is not kept by the Heavenly bodies; and as it goes on to say 'and the [Heavenly] hosts are subject to His word,' it follows that God is regulating the motions of the worlds on the Sabbath days as well as on the week-days: a point which Justin expressly makes in c. 29, 'God undertakes the regulation of the world on this day, exactly as on other days[2].'

The writer then is a Christian of the type of Justin Martyr, who accepts the Gospel without the obligation of the Law, and makes a quiet intimation of the position which he takes towards the stricter Judaism. But we notice, further, that the argument which underlies his verse is older than Justin Martyr; it is contained in the reply of the ancient Christian whom Justin consulted on the question of sabbath and circumcision; he calls it a Divine Word or Oracle (θεῖον λόγον). It may, then, have come from some early Christian handbook; but, whether this be the case or not, it is a dictum of the first century; for the very old man who talked with Justin was not inventing a solution for immediate perplexities, but giving him a rule which prevailed in the Church to which he belonged.

So it seems clear that the Ode is really Christian, and that its Christianity is of a very early type, to judge from the arguments involved in it.

ODE 17.

[1] I was crowned by my God: my crown is living: [2] and I was justified in my Lord: my incorruptible salvation is He. [3] I was loosed from vanity, and I was not condemned: [4] the choking bonds were cut off by her[3] hands: I received the face

---

[1] *l.c.* τὰ στοιχεῖα οὐκ ἀργεῖ οὐδὲ σαββατίζει.

[2] ὁ θεὸς τὴν αὐτὴν διοίκησιν τοῦ κόσμου ὁμοίως καὶ ἐν ταύτῃ τῇ ἡμέρᾳ πεποίητα καθάπερ ἐν ταῖς ἄλλαις ἁπάσαις.

[3] *Query* his?

and the fashion of a new person: and I walked in it and was saved; [5]and the thought of truth led me on.   And I walked after it and did not wander: [6]and all that have seen me were amazed: and I was regarded by them as a strange person: [7]and He who knew and brought me up is the Most High in all His perfection.   And He glorified me by His kindness, and raised my thought to the height of ⌜His⌝ truth.   [8]And from thence He gave me the way of His precepts[1] and I opened the doors that were closed, [9]and brake in pieces the bars of iron; but my iron melted and dissolved before me; [10]nothing appeared closed to me: because I was the door of everything. [11]And I went over all my bondmen to loose them; that I might not leave any man bound or binding: [12]and I imparted my knowledge without grudging: and my prayer was in my love: [13]and I sowed my fruits in hearts, and transformed them into myself: and they received my blessing and lived; [14]and they were gathered to me and were saved; because they were to me as my own members and I was their head.   Glory to thee our head, the Lord Messiah.   Hallelujah.

ODE 17.   This Psalm is one that we alluded to above in connexion with 'the crown of life' that has been put upon the writer's head. That it is a Christian Psalm is evident: the Messiah or Christ is definitely referred to, and he is spoken of as being to believers in the relation of the head to the members.   But we have again in this Psalm the peculiar change of personality: this time it comes so imperceptibly that we might be tempted to doubt the reality of the transition, if it were not for the abruptness of the return from it at the close of the Psalm.   The breaking of the bars of iron must surely refer to the Messiah[2]: it need not be an allusion to the descent into Hades[3]; for the problem of liberation of souls is stated in general terms: all men are to be free; there is to be no more one that binds and one that is bound. The transformation of believers into Christ's nature is also referred to; 'I transformed them into myself......they became my own members.'

ODE 18.

[1]My heart was lifted up in the love of the Most High and was enlarged: that I might praise Him for His[4] name's sake.

---

[1] *lit.* steps.

[2] So Zahn: Wer anders sollte das sein als Jesus der Messias?

[3] Batiffol: Avec M. Harris, avec M. Harnack aussi, et contre M. Gunkel, je crois que ces vv. ne parlent pas de la descente du Christ aux enfers.

[4] *Cod.* my.

[2]My members were strengthened that they might not fall from His strength. [3]Sicknesses removed from my body, and it stood to the Lord by His will. For His Kingdom is true. [4]O Lord, for the sake of them that are deficient do not remove thy word from me! [5]Neither for the sake of their works do thou restrain from me thy perfection! [6]Let not the luminary be conquered Cf.Joh.i.5 by the darkness; nor let truth flee away from falsehood. [7]Thou wilt appoint me to victory; our Salvation is thy right hand[1]. And thou wilt receive men from all quarters, [8]and thou wilt preserve whosoever is held in evils: [9]Thou art my God. [2]Falsehood and death[2] are not in thy mouth: [10]for thy will is perfection; and vanity thou knowest not, [11]nor does it know thee. [12]And error thou knowest not, [13]neither does it know thee. [14]And ignorance appeared like a blind man[3]; and like the foam of the sea, [15]and they supposed of that vain thing that it was something great; [16]and they too came in likeness of it and became vain; and those have understood who have known and meditated; [17]and they have not been corrupt in their imagination; for such were in the mind of the Lord; [18]and they mocked at them that were walking in error; [19]and they spake truth from the inspiration which the Most High breathed into them; Praise and great comeliness[4] to His name. Hallelujah.

ODE 18. The writer of this Psalm speaks as a prophet, who has known the Divine visitation, and has felt its effect both on mind and body, in the dispelling of error and the healing of disease. He prays for a continuance of the heavenly gift for the sake of the needy people to whom he gives his message. He has evidently been regarded by them as a light and foolish person, whose talk is like the foam on the wave of the sea. But there are others who are inspired like himself, and who mock at the unbelievers for their stupidity and ignorance. We catch the echo of some serious controversy upon religious matters, but the subject of the dispute is unknown. There are no definitely Christian features in the Psalm.

[1] Or, To Victory may thy right hand bring our Salvation.

[2-2] Perhaps Falsehood and the like.

[3] Or by a slight change, And I appeared like a blind man without knowledge. Or better, like chaff, reading ܟܚܩܐ (so Schulthess). Cf. Ode 29. 10.

[4] Gk. μεγαλοπρέπεια.

ODE 19.

[1]A cup of milk was offered to me: and I drank it in the sweetness of the delight of the Lord. [2]The Son is the cup, and He who was milked is the Father: [3]and the Holy Spirit milked Him: because His breasts were full, and it was necessary for Him that His milk should be sufficiently released; [4]and the Holy Spirit opened His[1] bosom and mingled the milk from the two breasts of the Father; and gave the mixture to the world without their knowing: [5]and they who receive in its fulness are the ones on the right hand. [6][The Spirit][2] opened the womb of the Virgin and she received conception and brought forth; and the Virgin became a Mother with many mercies; [7]and she travailed and brought forth a Son, without incurring pain; [8]and because she was not sufficiently prepared[3], and she had not sought a midwife, (for He brought her to bear), she brought forth, as if she were a man[4], of her own will[5]; [9]and she brought Him forth openly, and acquired Him with great dignity, [10]and loved Him in His swaddling clothes[6], and guarded Him kindly, and showed Him in Majesty.   Hallelujah.

ODE 19.   Fantastic as this Psalm is, it might at first sight have been discarded as being out of harmony with the lofty spiritual tone of the rest of the collection.   But it happens to be attested by Lactantius, and in the MSS. of his *Divine Institutes* we have not only a quotation from the Psalm in regard to the painless delivery of the Blessed Virgin, but we have also the number of the Psalm given, either as 19 or 20.   So it was found in the collection known to Lactantius.

The harshness of the opening figure with regard to the bosom of the Father does not necessarily detach it from the rest of the collection; for we have had already allusion to the breasts of God.   Thus in Psalm 8, the Lord is represented as saying: 'My own breasts I prepared for them that they might drink my holy milk and live thereby.' The eighth and the nineteenth of our Psalms appear therefore to be connected together by a common authorship.   For the figure of the breasts of God in the literature of the early Church we may refer to Clement of Alexandria who, in the *Paedagogus* (lib. i. c. 6, p. 124), has

---

[1] MS. her bosom.

[2] Lact. *Div. Instit.* iv. 12; *Epit. Div. Instit.* c. 44.   The original Greek was perhaps ἐνεκολπίσθη (= Aram. חבק).   Flemming: er umarmte (?)

[3] *Perhaps*: and because there was not (pain) she was sufficient.

[4] Batiffol: as it were a man: *reading* ὡς ἄνθρωπον for ὡς ἄνθρωπος.

[5] Batiffol: by the will [of God]: cf. Joh. i. 13 ἐκ θελήματος.

[6] *Reading* ⲕⲑⲁⲓⲁⲥ for ⲕⲓⲟⲓⲁⲥ.

a long discussion of the milk with which Christ's babes are nourished. Our nourishment, he says, is the Divine Word, it is '*the milk of the Father*, by which only the babes are fed.' Through the Word 'we have believed in God, to whose care-allaying breast we have fled.' And again (p. 125) 'to the babes, who seek for the Word, the breasts of the Father's kindness supply the milk' (τοῖς ζητοῦσι νηπίοις τὸν Λόγον αἱ πατρικαὶ τῆς φιλανθρωπίας θηλαὶ χορηγοῦσι τὸ γάλα). So Clement comes very near to the figurative language of the Ode, without its crudity of expression. The harshness of the figures employed and the tritheistic character of the theology may be paralleled in writers of the middle ages, whose repute in the Church is very wide. For is it not St Bernard who expounds the Evangelic statement that the beloved disciple leaned on Jesus' breast in the words 'hausit de sinu Unigeniti quod de paterno hauserat ille'? but if John imbibed from the breast of the Only-begotten what He had imbibed in like manner from the Father, we can only say that a very lofty theology is presented in a very harsh metaphor; but we cannot dismiss St Bernard as unworthy of further notice. And if it comes to tritheism, with which all the Christian Ages are more or less discoloured, where shall we find it more pronounced than in John Tauler's great sermon on the coming of the Bridegroom, where God the Father presides over the nuptials of Christ and the Church, and where the Holy Spirit acts as cup-bearer at the feast: a representation which is not so very remote from what we have in our Psalm, when wine has been substituted for milk. But I am afraid the matter is past apologetic. Further than this, we must admit that it is in many ways perplexing: the doctrine seems too highly evolved to allow us to reckon the Psalm to the same period of production as the rest of the book. When the writer speaks of milk from the two breasts of God, he evidently means the two covenants, or testaments. But that exegesis implies that the writer is no Marcionite rejecting an old covenant in the interests of a new, or else he wishes us to understand that he is no Jew, clinging to an old covenant to the neglect of the new covenant. And he seems to imply that the Christians whom he represents are distinguished from some other body of believers by being on the right hand of Christ. Is it the Jews from whom he wishes to be distinguished or is it the Marcionites? The Ode must be, at the earliest, a product of the second century. It is conceivable that the allusion to the Cup of Milk may cover an early Milk-Eucharist. Wine is nowhere mentioned in the religious language of our Psalter.

Turn in the next place to the account of the Virgin Birth, which follows the parable of the cup of milk, and can almost be detached as a separate composition. It certainly presents the miraculous conception and birth in a form which has already undergone considerable development: that the birth was painless was a very early corollary to the statement that it was supernatural; in the commentary of Ephrem on the Gospel there was a statement that 'it was indecent that she who had been a habitation of the Spirit should bring forth with pains and curses[1]'; and this must have been a very early reflection upon the statement of the Virgin Birth. But our writer goes much further than that: he dispenses with the usual aids to child-birth, and introduces details for which we find parallels in the Apocryphal Gospels of the Infancy. And it is frankly impossible that the doctrine of the Miraculous Birth should have become so highly evolved in the first century. So that the doubts raised by the first part of the Psalm are reinforced by a study of its latter half. As far then as this Psalm is concerned, it seems as if we must refer it to a later date than the majority of those which we have been discussing. We detected something like polemical tendency in the first half of the composition, as if the writer turned aside to rebuke either Jews or Marcionites: if we might assume tendency in the latter half, it must be directed against persons who did not believe in the Virgin Birth. Palestine and especially trans-Jordanic Palestine would furnish opponents of all the classes mentioned; so that, if we should be obliged to depress the date to the second century, we have no reason to remove the composition to another locality than that which has already been suggested.

ODE 20.

[1]I am a priest of the Lord, and to Him I do priestly service: and to Him I offer the sacrifice of His thought. [2]For His thought is not like ⌜the thought of⌝ the world nor ⌜the thought of⌝ the flesh, nor like them that serve carnally. [3]The sacrifice of the Lord is righteousness, and purity of heart and lips. [4]Present your reins before Him blamelessly: and let not thy heart do violence to heart, nor thy soul to soul. [5]Thou shalt not acquire a stranger by ⌜the price of thy silver⌝[2], neither shalt thou seek to devour thy neighbour[3], [6]neither shalt thou deprive him of the covering of his nakedness[4]. [7]But put on the grace of the Lord without stint; and come into His Paradise and make thee a garland from its tree, [8]and put it on thy head and be glad; and recline on His rest, and glory shall go before thee, [9]and thou shalt receive of His kindness and of His grace; and thou shalt be flourishing[5] in truth in the praise of His holiness. Praise and honour be to His name. Hallelujah.

[1] J. R. Harris, *Ephrem on the Gospel*, p. 31.
[2] *Literally*, by the blood of thy soul. I correct the Syriac, which is faulty, and has repeated 'thy soul' from the previous verse.
[3] Cf. Exod. xxii. 24.   [4] Exod. xxii. 26.   [5] *lit.* fat.

ODE 20. This Psalm is a mixture of ethics and of mysticism, of the golden rule and of the tree of life. The writer, whether Jew or Christian, is wholly detached from external ritual; he calls himself a priest of God, but explains that this means the thinking of God's thought, and that the sacrifice he offers is the pure heart and life. He might be an Essene, one of that strange company who did not frequent the temple because they had purer sacrifices of their own. He drops a few ethical maxims, such as we find in the Pentateuch, protests against the owning of slaves (another Essene tenet) and against taking the neighbour's garment in pledge. Then he leaves morals and is away in search of the honey-dew and milk of Paradise. There glory waits the soul that enters into the Divine rest.

It is a beautiful Psalm, but one could not say of it, taken by itself, that it was necessarily Christian; though its affinities are with Psalms that are definitely Christian. For the sacrifices which the good man offers to God we may compare Lactantius, *Div. Instit.* vi. 25 'Donum est integritas animi; sacrificium, laus et hymnus: si enim Deus non videtur, ergo iis rebus coli debet, quae non videntur. Nulla igitur alia religio est vera, nisi quae virtute et justitia constat.'

In Clem. Alex. *Strom.* v. 11 the sacrifice is an ascetic life.

ODE 21.

[1]My arms I lifted up to the Most High, even to the grace of the Lord : because He had cast off my bonds from me : and my Helper had lifted me up to His grace and to His salvation : [2]and I put off darkness and clothed myself with light, [3]and my soul acquired a body[1] free from sorrow or affliction or pains. [4]And increasingly helpful to me was the thought of the Lord, and His fellowship in incorruption : [5]and I was lifted up in His light; and I served before Him, [6]and I became near to Him, praising and confessing Him; [7]my heart ran over and was found in my mouth: and it arose upon my lips; and the exultation of the Lord increased on my face, and His praise likewise. Hallelujah.

ODE 21. This Psalm is short, and somewhat obscure. The reason for this lies in the fact that the writer is assuming a mystical explanation of the 'coats of skin' in the third chapter of Genesis, which are held to represent the ordinary human body which has replaced a body originally clad in light. See Ode 25 where the same idea of the acquisition of a Light-Body, and of its freedom from pain is more definitely expressed. It is impossible to decide definitely from the reading of the

---

[1] *lit.* there became members to my soul, etc.

Psalm whether it is Christian or Jewish: if the writer was a Christian, he was a very joyous Christian; if he was a Jew, he knew the salvation of Israel that comes out of Zion, and had the dew of Heaven upon his vineyard.

ODE 22.

[1]He who brought me down from on high, also brought me up from the regions below; [2]and He who gathers together the things that are betwixt is He also who cast me down: [3]He who scattered my enemies and my adversaries: [4]He who gave me authority over bonds that I might loose them; [5]He that overthrew by my hands the dragon with seven heads[1]: and thou hast set me over his roots that I might destroy his seed. [6]Thou wast there and didst help me, and in every place thy name was a rampart to me[2]. [7]Thy right hand destroyed his wicked poison[3]; and thy hand levelled the way for those who believe in thee: [8]and thou didst choose them from the graves and didst separate them from the dead. [9]Thou didst take dead bones and didst cover them with bodies; [10]they were motionless, and thou didst give ⌜them⌝ energy for life. [11]Thy way was without corruption, and thy face; thou didst bring[4] thy world to corruption: that everything might be dissolved[5], and then renewed, [12]and that the foundation for everything might be thy rock[6]: and on it thou didst build thy Kingdom; and it became the dwelling-place of the saints. Hallelujah.

ODE 22. In this Psalm we seem to be nearer to the known Psalter of Solomon than elsewhere. There is a pointed reference to a dragon with seven heads whose seed is to be destroyed, and whose wicked poison has found its antidote in the Divine power. We think at once of the description of Pompey as the great dragon in the second of the published Psalms of Solomon. But dragons generally are difficult to identify. Who, for instance, is the dragon in Ps. lxxiii. (lxxiv.) 14 whose heads are broken? Is it Tiamat the Babylonian cosmic monster or the Leviathan whom the faithful are to eat in the last day, or is it a real person? In Ezekiel xxix. 3 it is Pharaoh of Egypt that is called the great dragon in the midst of the waters, but it might not be so easy to say which Pharaoh: any political monster may be a beast or a dragon:

---

[1] Cf. Apoc. xii. 3: and *Pistis Sophia*: see Introd. pp. 61—63.
[2] *Reading* ܟܣܝ with the Coptic, so Diettrich and others.
[3] Copt. the poison of the slanderer.
[4] Following a correction of Flemming.
[5] Cf. 2 Pet. iii. 11.   [6] Cf. Matt. xvi. 18.

so in the present case we have to hunt around among the fallen gods to find him. There has evidently been a great slaughter of Jews for the writer uses the imagery of the Valley of Dry Bones in Ezekiel, in order to show that God can raise up His people from the gates of death : the ruin of all things becomes the occasion for a new Kingdom founded upon the rock.

The Psalm is one of those which are transferred to the pages of the *Pistis Sophia* where it is recited by Matthew from an Ode of Solomon. It is suggested by Ryle and James that the opening sentences are of a Gnostic character, from the allusion to things above and things below and things between. But the whole tenor of our Psalms is foreign to Gnosticism, and I do not see any reason to introduce it as a factor in the interpretation. If the Psalm is really the expression of some person triumphing over a fallen tyrant, or of Israel personified in such a situation, we have to search the political crises for such a time of trial and recovery. It is not easy to find the solution. The Hadrianic wars are too late, and they were followed by no recovery on the part of the Jews in Palestine. Antiochus Epiphanes is too early, in every respect. The next cases to examine are those of Pompey and Titus. Pompey is already known as the dragon, and the destruction of the dragon is historical. Titus on the other hand is a triumphant dragon without a subsequent collapse : nor does there seem to be in his case a sufficient recovery of Judaism to justify the triumphant language of the Odist. The statement that God levelled the way for those who believe in Him seems to imply a return from exile, in greater or less degree; but this also is not easy to justify from a historical point of view. [Bernard thinks the dragon is to be explained by Patristic gnosis of the defeat of the devil in the waters of Baptism, as in Cyril *Cat.* iii. 11 and the Baptismal rituals. I add to Dr Bernard's references one from a MS. of Moses Bar Kepha on Baptism, in my own collection : 'Our Lord was baptized that he might trample on the head of the spiritual dragon that lurked in the water etc.' The passage has been borrowed by Bar Salibi, *Comm. in Matt.* p. 98. See Preface to this edition.]

ODE 23.

¹Joy is of the saints! and who shall put it on, but they alone? ²Grace is of the elect! and who shall receive it except those who trust in it from the beginning? ³Love is of the elect! And who shall put it on except those who have possessed it from the beginning? ⁴Walk ye in the knowledge of the Most High without grudging : to His exultation and to the perfection of His knowledge. ⁵And His thought was like a

letter; His will descended from on high, and it was sent like an arrow which is violently shot from the bow: [6]and many hands rushed to the letter to seize it and to take and read it: [7]and it escaped their fingers and they were affrighted at it and at the seal that was upon it. [8]Because it was not permitted to them to loose its seal: for the power that was over the seal was greater than they. [9]But those who saw it went after the letter that they might know where it would alight, and who should read it and who should hear it. [10]But a wheel received it and came over it: [11]and there was with it a sign of the Kingdom and of the Government: [12]and everything which tried to move the wheel it mowed and cut down: [13]and it gathered the multitude of adversaries, and bridged[1] the rivers and crossed over and rooted up many forests and made a broad path. [14]The head went down to the feet, for down to the feet ran the wheel, and that which was a sign upon it. [15]The letter was one of command, for there were included[2] in it all districts; [16]and there was seen at its [?] head, the head which was revealed, even the Son of Truth from the Most High Father, [17]and He inherited and took possession of everything. And the thought of the many was brought to nought, [18]and all the apostates hasted and fled away. And those who persecuted and were enraged became extinct.

[19]And the letter was a great volume[3], which was wholly written by the finger of God: [20]and the name of the Father was on it, and of the Son and of the Holy Spirit, to rule for ever and ever. Hallelujah.

ODE 23. This is the most difficult of all the Psalms in the collection, and I have almost despaired of being able to explain it. It describes the descent from heaven of a sealed document, with a message from God in it. The description is something like that of the little sealed book in the Apocalypse, which no one can open, except the triumphant Lamb[4]. If the allusion in the Apocalypse is to some previous document which the author has incorporated, perhaps the same thing may be true here. Some book may have been published, claiming Divine Authority. What can it have been? A Gospel? An Apocalypse? It appeared suddenly, unexpectedly, and met with opposition rather than with universal acceptance. It came from the head and it went down to the feet. If we may use the language of a later Psalm in which the saints

---

[1] *lit.* covered.   [2] *lit.* gathered.   [3] *Or* tablet.

[4] Another parallel would be the letter sent from the home-land in Bardesanes' *Hymn of the Soul* in the Acts of Thomas.

in Hades are called the feet of Christ, we should say that the mysterious little book conveyed a message to those below from one above, and that it interpreted the region below to include the invisible world. Was the little book then a 'Descensus ad Inferos'? It is impossible to decide with certainty. It contained some pronounced statement concerning the Trinity, for we are expressly told that it had the name of Father, Son and Holy Ghost upon it. When any one writes in cipher, about a document which itself appears to have been written in cipher, for that is the natural meaning of a sealed book, we ought not to be surprised if it is not quite obvious, two thousand years later, what the writer meant or to what he was referring.

ODE 24.

[1]The Dove fluttered over the Messiah, because He was her head; and she sang over Him and her voice was heard: [2]and the inhabitants were afraid and the sojourners were moved: [3]the birds dropped their wings, and all creeping things died in their holes: and the abysses were opened which had been hidden; and they cried to the Lord like women in travail: [4]and no food was given to them, [1]because it did not belong to them[1]; [5][2]and they sealed up the abysses with the seal of the Lord[2]. [3]And they perished, in the thought, those that had existed from ancient times[3]; [6]for they were corrupt from the beginning; and the end of their corruption was life[4]: [7]and every one of them that was imperfect perished: for it was not possible to give ⌐them⌐ a word that they might remain: [8]and the Lord destroyed the imaginations of all them that had not the truth with them. [9]For they who in their hearts were lifted up were deficient in wisdom, and so they were rejected, because the truth was not with them. [10]For the Lord disclosed His way, and spread abroad His grace: and those who understood it[5], know His holiness. Hallelujah.

[1-1] *Or perhaps*, because that which was non-existent belonged to them.

[2-2] U.-S.: und es versanken die Abgründe in der Versenkung des Herrn.

[3-3] Fl.: und es gingen zugrunde durch diesen Gedanken sie, die vorher existiert hatten.

U.-S.: und es gingen durch jenen Gedanken die zugrunde, die vor alters gewesen waren.

[4] *Or*, was the life of all; and whatever of them, etc.   [5] sc. the way.

ODE 24. The Psalm opens with a reference to the Baptism of the Lord, when the Holy Spirit descended in the form of a Dove on the head of the Messiah. The occasion was one of great dread to all created things, man and beast and creeping things shared the terror. The abysses, personified as living creatures, cried out in pain. They were sealed up and ended, as belonging to the order of non-existent things. Men also whose hearts were proud were rejected, when the way of the Lord was revealed and His holiness known.

In this Psalm with its reference to the abysses, and the things which are not and are brought to nought, we seem to be nearer to the world of Gnostic ideas: but it would be difficult to say that any of the catch-words or peculiar terms of Gnosticism are here. If we are right in referring the Psalm to the Baptism of the Lord, we are only furnishing one more proof of the extraordinary prominence given to that event in the early Church, for which it was the beginning of the Gospel: and we need not be surprised that the event should be treated in many ways, both theological and hymnological.

If it is not the Baptism that is alluded to, it must be the Crucifixion, and in that case we must assume an unknown incident connected with the Crucifixion, comparable with the appearance of the Dove at the Baptism. In that case the plaint of the abysses is another allusion to the descent into Hades.

But there is a special reason why I feel sure that the Baptism must be the incident to which reference is made: I think we can say that a written Gospel has here been employed, but not a Canonical Gospel. It will be remembered that Justin Martyr in his *Dialogue with Trypho*, c. 88, takes his account of the Baptism from a source which is either uncanonical: or, if canonical, is interpolated. When Jesus went down into the water, a fire was kindled in the Jordan, and when He came up from the water, the Holy Spirit, like a dove, *fluttered upon Him* (ἐπι-πτῆναι ἐπ᾽ αὐτὸν ὡς περιστερὰν τὸ ἅγιον πνεῦμα): and Justin says expressly that this was recorded by the Apostles of our Christ (ἔγραψαν οἱ ἀπόστολοι αὐτοῦ τούτου τοῦ Χριστοῦ ἡμῶν). This 'fluttering down' of the dove is very near indeed to the language of our Ode. Its ultimate origin is probably to be found in the language of Gen. i. 3.

It is well known that the account of the Baptism by Justin has been the centre of serious controversy, on account of the apocryphal expansions of the narrative, especially the reference to the Fire which appeared at the Jordan: and it has been argued, reasonably enough, that Justin cannot have used our Canonical Gospels, or at least must have used an uncanonical Gospel with them. The same difficulty turns up in the descent of the Dove, for the word ἐπιπτῆναι, which recurs in Justin, must come from the written source which the author is using. A reference to Resch, *Aussercanonische Parallele zu Luc.* p. 15, will show the wide diffusion of the account from which Justin is working[1]. The word ἐπιπτῆναι can be traced in Celsus and in Origen and in the seventh book of Sibyllines, as well as in a number of Latin authors. The inference, therefore, is that a very early written Gospel is responsible for the detail : and it is this early Gospel that has been employed by the writer of the Ode. We conclude, then, that the reference is to the Baptism and that it is taken from a lost primitive Gospel. [If the Dove sang the words ' Thou art my beloved Son,' the Holy Spirit must be regarded as the mother of Jesus as in the Gospel according to the Hebrews. The same belief is involved in Ode 36.]

There is, however, a possible suggestion that the Psalm may refer to the Descent into Hades, and to the Baptism, as events happening in close connexion. I mean that it is not out of the region of reasonable criticism to suggest that in the earliest times the Baptism of Christ was the occasion of His triumph over Hades. We find suspicious hints of this in the *Descensus ad Inferos.* Thus in c. xx[2] we have a statement made by Seth concerning his father Adam that he will receive the oil of healing from Paradise in the last days : 'veniet enim amantissimus dei filius de caelis in mundum, et baptizabitur a Johanne in Jordane flumine, et *tunc* recipiet pater tuus Adam de hoc oleo misericordiae et omnes credentes in eum.'

And in c. xxi we find Jesus talking to John the Baptist concerning his Descent into Hades : 'Ego Johannes vocem patris de caelo super eum intonantem audivi et proclamantem, Hic est filius meus dilectus, in quo mihi bene complacuit. *Ego ab eo responsum accepi quia ipse descensurus esset ad inferos.'*

Here are two curious references connecting the Baptism and the Descent into Hades. And the question arises whether this 24th Ode may not look in the same direction. The evidence is, of course, inadequate, but the statement of the case may perhaps lead to the discovery of fresh evidence in the same direction.

ODE 25.

[1] I was rescued from my bonds and unto thee, my God, I fled : [2] for thou art the right hand of my Salvation and my helper. [3] Thou hast restrained those that rise up against me, [4] and I shall see him[3] no more : because thy face was with me, which saved me by thy grace. [5] But I was despised and rejected in the eyes of many : and I was in their eyes like lead[4],

---

[1] See Introd. pp. 84, 85.

[2] Tischendorf, *Ev. Apoc.* p. 425.   [3] *l.* them.

[4] Cf. *Sap. Sol.* ii. 16 εἰς κίβδηλον ἐλογίσθημεν αὐτῷ.

[6]and strength was mine from thyself and help. [7]Thou didst set me a lamp[1] at my right hand and at my left: and in me there shall be nothing that is not bright[2]: [8]and I was clothed with the covering of thy Spirit, and thou didst remove from me my raiment of skin[3]; [9]for thy right hand lifted me up and removed sickness from me: [10]and I became mighty in the truth, and holy by thy righteousness; and all my adversaries were afraid of me; [11]and I became admirable by the name of the Lord, and was justified by His gentleness, and His rest is for ever and ever. Hallelujah.

ODE 25. In this Psalm we are back again in the region of personal experience, and there is no allusion to any definite historical event. The writer, whether Christian or Jew, has been brought out of spiritual bondage into liberty: he has had to face contempt and scorn, but the Lord has filled him with brightness and covered him with beauty, and given him health of mind and body: his enemies have turned back, and his portion is with the justified saints of the Most High. It is possible that this Psalm may be meant to express the experience of the Messiah, emerging from His conflicts into victory: in that case it need not be the Christian conception of the Messiah, but it might conceivably be such a human representation as we find in the Psalms of the Pharisees (*e.g.* Ps. 17, which is our Ps. 60). But our collection, as to its first block of Psalms, is certainly of a later period than the Pharisee Psalms, so we ought to hesitate before ascribing the same Messianic ideas to the two parts of the hymnal. For the allusion to the 'coat of skin,' see Introd. pp. 66—70, and cf. Ode 21.

ODE 26.

[1]I poured out praise to the Lord, for I am His: [2]and I will speak His holy song, for my heart is with Him. [3]For His harp is in my hands, and the Odes of His rest shall not be silent. [4]I will cry unto Him from my whole heart: I will praise and exalt Him with all my members. [5]For from the east and even to the west is His praise: [6]and from the south and even to the north is the confession of Him: [7]and from the top of the hills to their utmost bound is His perfection. [8]Who can write the Psalms of the Lord, or who read them? [9]or who can train his

---

[1] Ps. cxxxii. 17.   [2] *lit.* light.

[3] Cp. Clem. Alex. *Paed.* i. 6, p. 117 τῆς κακίας ἐκδυσάμενοι τὸν χιτῶνα and Gen. iii. 21.

soul for life, that his soul may be saved, [10] or who can rest on the Most High, so that with His mouth he may speak? [11] Who is able to interpret the wonders of the Lord? [12] For he who could interpret would be dissolved and would become that which is interpreted[1]. [13] For it suffices to know and to rest[2]: for in rest the singers stand, [14] like a river which has an abundant fountain, and flows to the help of them that seek it[3]. Hallelujah.

ODE 26. This beautiful song of praise recounts the goodness and greatness of the Lord. All within the writer magnifies the great Name, but all within is insufficient to tell out what waits to be told. His praise is widespread to the utmost bound of earth and beyond the bound of the everlasting hills. The creature cannot express God's praise perfectly; if he could, he would be no longer a creature: he would be the Word, and not the interpreter of the Word. So it suffices to know and to rest, while at our feet the river of grace rolls on, an unchanging flood:

Labitur et labetur in omne volubilis aevum.

It is impossible to say whether the Psalm, as detached from the rest of the collection, is Jewish or Christian.

ODE 27.

[1] I stretched out my hands and sanctified my Lord[4]: [2] for the extension of my hands is His sign: [3] and my expansion is the upright tree (*or* cross).

ODE 27. This tiny Psalm is Christian, and is based upon the early Christian fondness for finding the Cross everywhere in the outward world: in the handle of the labourer's plough, in the mast and yards of the seaman's ship; and in the human body, when the man stands erect in the act of prayer with outstretched arms. There can, therefore, be no doubt that this is a Christian Psalm, and the figurative language which it employs is characteristic of the second century and not unknown in the first century. Justin Martyr, for example, sees the

---

[1] Cf. Lactantius, *Div. Inst.* praef.: 'there would be no difference between God and man, if human thought could reach to the counsels and arrangements of that eternal Majesty.'

[2] Cf. Clem. Alex. *Paed.* i. 6 (p. 115) ὥστε ἡ μὲν γνῶσις ἐν τῷ φωτίσματι· τὸ δὲ πέρας τῆς γνώσεως, ἡ ἀνάπαυσις.

[3] Cf. Lactantius, *Div. Inst.* iv. 30 'Si quis aquam vitae cupiat haurire, non ad detritos lacus deferatur, qui non habent venam, sed uberrimum Dei noverit fontem, quo irrigatus perenni luce potiatur.'

[4] U.-S.: und heiligte [sie] meinem Herrn.

Cross, in the outspread arms of Moses in the battle against Amalek ; but so does Barnabas also : and the same thought is involved in the conclusion of the Teaching of the Apostles, where an outspread cross in the sky is one of the signs of the Advent and answers to the Sign of the Son of Man in Matthew. So it is very likely that the figure in our Psalm is one of the oldest forms of Christian symbolic teaching. We shall find it used again in the 42nd Psalm which may, therefore, be by the same hand as the present one : otherwise it would be an imitation of it.

Those who care to have a Gnostic example of the use of this wide-spread Christian figure, will find one in Schmidt, *Unbekanntes altgnostisches Werk* (l.c. p. 336) : 'Die Haare seines Gesichtes sind die Zahl der äusseren Welten, und die Ausbreitung seiner Hände ist die Offenbarung des Kreuzes.'

ODE 28.

[1]As the wings of doves over their nestlings ; and the mouth of their nestlings towards their mouths, [2]so also are the wings of the Spirit over my heart : [3]my heart is delighted and exults : like the babe who exults[1] in the womb of his mother[2] : [4]I believed ; therefore I was at rest ; for faithful is He in whom I have believed : [5]He has richly blessed me and my head is with Him : and the sword shall not divide me from Him, nor the scimitar ; [6]for I am ready before destruction comes : and I have been set on His immortal[3] pinions : [7]and immortal life has come forth and given me to drink[4], and from that life is the spirit within me, and it cannot die, for it lives. [8]They who saw me marvelled at me, because I was persecuted, and they supposed that I was swallowed up : for I seemed to them as one of the lost ; [9]and my oppression became my salvation ; and I was their reprobation because there was no zeal in me[5] ; [10]because I did good to every man I was hated, [11]and they came round me like mad dogs[6], who ignorantly attack their masters, [12]for their thought is corrupt and their understanding perverted. [13]But I was carrying water in my right hand[7], and their bitterness[8] I

---

[1] *Or*, leaps.   [2] Cf. Luke i. 41.

[3] *lit.* pinions without corruption.

[4] Reading ＿＿＿＿. Fl.: has kissed me. So U.-S.

[5] *Perhaps* because I was not a Zealot.   [6] Ps. xxii. 16.

[7] *Query* ⌐that I might put out their flame.¬

[8] As water is plural, Fl. would refer the bitterness to it ; but Zahn says : 'das pluralische Suffix an dem Worte Bitterkeit ist selbstverständlich nicht mit Fl. auf das Wasser zu beziehen.'

endured by my sweetness; [14] and I did not perish, for I was not their brother nor was my birth like theirs, [15] and they sought for my death and did not find it : for I was older than the memorial of them ; [16] and vainly did they make attack upon me[1] and those who, without reward, came after me[2] : [17] they sought to destroy the memorial of him who was before them : [18] for the thought of the Most High cannot be anticipated : and His heart is superior to all wisdom. Hallelujah.

ODE 28. This exquisite Psalm has the music in it of the 'Quis separabit?' of Romans viii. Nor sword nor scimitar divide the believer from the Lord. In some respects the Psalm appears to be Messianic in a Christian sense, for the writer concludes his exulting strain over enemies who had come round him like mad dogs and had left him for dead, with the remark that it was not possible for them to blot out the memory of one who existed before them, and who was of a different birth from theirs. He also speaks of their attacks as having been directed against his followers as well as himself. Perhaps, then, the writer is speaking, in these verses, as if in the person of Christ.

ODE 29.

[1] The Lord is my hope : in Him I shall not be confounded. [2] For according to His praise He made me, and according to His goodness even so He gave unto me : [3] and according to His mercies He exalted me : and according to His excellent beauty He set me on high : [4] and brought me up out of the depths of Sheol : and from the mouth of death He drew me : [5] and thou didst lay my enemies low, and He justified me by His grace. [6] For I believed in the Lord's Messiah[3] : and it appeared to me that He is the Lord ; [7] and He showed him[4] His sign : and He led me by His light, and gave me the rod of His power ; [8] that I might subdue the imaginations of the peoples ; and the power of the men of might to bring them low : [9] to make war by His word, and to take victory by His power. [10] And the Lord overthrew my enemy by His word ; and he became like the stubble which the wind carries away ; [11] and I gave praise to the Most High because He exalted ⌜me⌝ His servant and the son of His handmaid. Hallelujah.

---

[1] *The margin suggests,* slaughtering me: *i.e.* reading ܢܡܚܣܘ for the marginal ܢܡܚܣܘ (cast lots).

[2] *Or,* who came after me. To no purpose they sought, etc.

[3] *Or,* Christ.　　　　　　　　[4] *Query* me?

ODE 29. Some one wrote this Psalm, who was a follower of the Christ and had recognised Him to be the Lord. Out of great conflicts he had been brought into the place of victory: his enemies had become like the straw before the wind: he has passed through deep distresses, which he speaks of figuratively as the pains of Sheol and the gates of death. But for the reference to the Lordship of the Messiah and to faith in Him, we might have imagined this Psalm to belong to the ancient Psalter: we shall be justified in regarding it as a Judaeo-Christian composition.

ODE 30.

[1]Fill ye waters for yourselves from the living fountain of the Lord, for it is opened to you: [2]and come all ye thirsty, and take the draught; and rest by the fountain of the Lord. [3]For fair it is and pure and gives rest to the soul. Much more pleasant are its waters than honey; [4]and the honeycomb of bees is not to be compared with it. [5]For it flows forth from the lips of the Lord and from the heart of the Lord is its name. [6]And it came infinitely and invisibly: and until it was set[1] in the midst they did not know it: [7]blessed are they who have drunk therefrom and have found rest thereby. Hallelujah.

ODE 30. The Psalm is an invitation to the thirsty, somewhat in the manner of Isaiah lv. The water of life, which here is explained to be the teaching of the Lord, is flowing from an open fountain, whose waters, to use the language of the 19th Psalm in the canonical Psalter, are 'sweeter than honey and the honeycomb.' The Ode is not so far removed from Old Testament thought and expression that we can positively call it a Christian composition. The writer is fond of the similitude of honey and the honeycomb: we find it, for instance, again in our fortieth Ode, where we have it for the opening similitude:

'Like the honey that drops from the comb of the bees......so is my hope on thee, O God.'

But this Psalm, also, appears, at first sight, to be destitute of specific Christian colouring.

The fountain, however, whose waters come without limit, and invisibly, corresponds to the unexpected appearance of Christ and Christ's teaching in the world, when there stood in the midst One whom they knew not.

---

[1] *lit.* given.

ODE 31.

[1]The abysses were dissolved before the Lord : and darkness was destroyed by His appearance: [2]error went astray and perished at His hand : [1]and folly found no path to walk in[1], and was submerged by the truth of the Lord. [3]He opened His mouth and spake grace and joy : and He spake a new song of praise to His name : [4]and He lifted up His voice to the Most High, and offered to Him the sons that were with Him[2]. [5]And His face was justified, for thus His holy Father had given to Him. [6]Come forth, ye that have been afflicted and receive joy, and possess your souls by His grace ; and take to you immortal life. [7]And they made me a debtor when I rose up, me who had not been a debtor[3]: and they divided my spoil, though nothing was due to them. [8]But I endured and held my peace and was silent[4], as if not moved by them. [9]But I stood unshaken like a firm rock which is beaten by the waves and endures. [10]And I bore their bitterness for humility's sake : [11]in order that I might redeem my people, and inherit it, and that I might not make void my promises to the fathers[5], to whom I promised the salvation of their seed. Hallelujah.

ODE 31. The Psalm is Messianic, and records how the Christ fulfilled the promises which, in a pre-existent state, He had made to the fathers. He has closed the abysses and banished error and vanity. With a new song in His mouth, He appears before God with the children whom God has given Him. His similitude is the rock against which the waves had beaten in vain. It stands firm, whether the waves advance or retire. Here Christian speech comes near to the language of the Stoics. One thinks of Marcus Aurelius, and his advice to 'be like the promontory against which the waves continually break, but it stands firm and tames the fury of the water around it[6].' One thinks also of Ignatius, and his advice 'to stand steady like the beaten anvil[7].' For the opening sentences about the destroying of the abysses, we must compare the language of the 24th Psalm of our collection, where the abysses cry out in pain at the time of the Baptism of the Lord. These Psalms are by the same Christian hand.

[1-1] *lit.* and folly, there was given her no path.
[2] *lit.* in His hands. Cf. Is. viii. 18; Heb. ii. 13.
[3] 2 Cor. v. 21. Perhaps we should translate 'a criminal.'
[4] 1 Pet. ii. 23.   [5] Rom. xv. 8; Luke i. 55.
[6] *Medit.* iv. 49.   [7] *ad Polyc.* 3.

ODE 32.

[1]To the blessed there is joy from their hearts, and light from
Him that dwells in them : [2]and words from the Truth, who was
self-originate[1] : for He is strengthened by the holy power of
the Most High : and He is unperturbed for ever and ever.
Hallelujah.

ODE 32.   Joy, Light, Inspiration, Strength and Calmness belong to
the believer through Him that dwells within.

ODE 33.

[1]Again Grace ran and forsook corruption, and came down in
Him to bring it to nought ; [2]and He destroyed perdition from
before Him, and devastated all its order ; [3]and He stood on
a lofty summit[2] and uttered His voice from one end of the
earth to the other : [4]and drew to Him all those who obeyed
Him ; and there did not appear as it were an evil person, [5]but
there stood a perfect virgin[3] who was proclaiming and calling
and saying, [6]O ye sons of men[4], return ye, and ye daughters of
men, come ye : [7]and forsake the ways of that corruption and
draw near unto me, and I will enter into you, and will bring
you forth from perdition, [8]and make you wise in the ways of
truth : that you be not destroyed nor perish : [9]hear ye me and
be redeemed.   For the grace of God I am telling among you :
and by my means you shall be redeemed and become blessed.
[10]I am your judge ; and they who have put me on shall not be
injured : but they shall possess the new world that is incorrupt :
[11]my chosen ones walk in me, and my ways I will make known
to them that seek me, and I will make them trust in my name.
Hallelujah.

ODE 33.   Apparently this Psalm is Messianic, though Christ is not
named.   He must be the one that rises from the dead and sends forth
his triumphant voice to the ends of the earth.   A virgin also stands and
proclaims, who must be either the Divine Wisdom (the language is

---

[1] Gk. αὐτοφυής, as in the oracular reply to the enquiry as to the Divine Nature,
αὐτοφυής, ἀδίδακτος, ἀμήτωρ, ἀστυφέλικτος.   See Lact. *De Div. Inst.* i. 7.
[2] Prov. viii. 2.   [3] Prov. viii. 1.   [4] Prov. viii. 4.

very like that of the eighth chapter of Proverbs) or the Church[1]. She promises salvation by Divine Grace and immortality in a new world to those that walk in her ways.

ODE 34.

[1]No way is hard where there is a simple heart. [2]Nor is there any wound where the thoughts are upright : [3]nor is there any storm in the depth of the illuminated thought : [4]where one is surrounded on every side by beauty, there is nothing that is divided. [5]The likeness of what is below is that which is above; for everything is above : what is below is nothing but the imagination of those that are without knowledge. [6]Grace has been revealed for your salvation.   Believe and live and be saved. Hallelujah.

ODE 34.   All the hard things are easy, where the soul itself is right: no storms invade the hidden place of communion with God.   Evil itself becomes unreal, and that which is beneath exists not before that which is above.

ODE 35.

[1]The dew of the Lord in quietness He distilled upon me : [2]and the cloud of peace He caused to rise over my head, which guarded me continually ; [3]it was to me for salvation : everything was shaken and they were affrighted ; [4]and there came forth from them a smoke and a judgment; and I was keeping quiet in the order of the Lord : [5]more than shelter was He to me, and more than foundation.   [6]And I was carried like a child by his mother : [2]and He gave me milk, the dew of the Lord[2] : [7]and I grew great by His bounty, and rested in His perfection, [8]and I spread out my hands in the lifting up of my soul : and I was made right with the Most High, and I was redeemed with Him. Hallelujah.

ODE 35.   The dew lies on the branch of the man that sings this Psalm : Divine Peace guards him like a sheltering cloud.   The Lord is his sure defence in the day of evil.   Mother's arms are his place and mother's milk his portion.   ' No cradled child more softly lies than I : Come soon, eternity.'

---

[1] Or Prov. i. 20.   Cf. Clem. Alex. Paed. i. 6 (p. 123) μία δὲ μόνη γίνεται μήτηρ Παρθένος· 'Εκκλησίαν ἐμοὶ φίλον αὐτὴν καλεῖν.   See also Introd. p. 77.

[2-2] Or, and the dew of the Lord gave me milk.   U.-S.

ODE 36.

¹I rested on the Spirit of the Lord: and ⌜the Spirit⌝ raised me on high: ²and made me stand on my feet in the height of the Lord, before His perfection and His glory, while I was praising ⌜Him⌝ by the composition of His songs. ³⌜The Spirit⌝ brought me forth before the face of the Lord: and, although a son of man, I was named the Illuminate, the Son of God: ⁴while I praised amongst the praising ones, and great was I amongst the mighty ones. ⁵For according to the greatness of the Most High, so He made me: and like His own newness He renewed me; and He anointed me from His own perfection: ⁶and I became one of His neighbours; and my mouth was opened, like a cloud of dew; ⁷and my heart poured out as it were a gushing stream of righteousness, ⁸and ¹my access ⌜to Him⌝¹ was in peace; and I was established by the spirit of His government. Hallelujah.

ODE 36. This is a perplexing Psalm, from a theological point of view. It is almost impossible to determine whether the Psalmist is speaking in his own name, or in that of the Messiah; or whether it is an alternation of one with the other. It seems almost a necessity, when the Holy Spirit is spoken of as a Mother, that the offspring should be the Son of God: and that such was the theology of certain early believers we know from the fragment of the Ebionite Gospel, in which Christ speaks of being taken by the hair of His head by His mother, the Holy Spirit, and carried to Mount Tabor. If this be the right interpretation, then the Illuminated Son of God is Christ. But the latter part of the Psalm seems to be in too low a strain for this interpretation: to be one of those who are near to God is certainly not orthodox theology, though it may conceivably be Adoptionist: and the heart that pours out righteousness and makes its offering in peace seems rather to be the language that describes one of the pious in Israel.

ODE 37.

¹I stretched out my hands to my Lord: and to the Most High I raised my voice: ²and I spake with the lips of my heart; and He heard me, when my voice reached Him²: ³His answer came to me, and gave me the fruits of my labours; ⁴and it gave me rest by the grace of the Lord. Hallelujah.

¹⁻¹ *Or perhaps*, my offering.   ² *lit.* fell to Him.

ODE 37. A colourless Psalm, something like one of the shorter and more elementary Psalms of the Hebrew Psalter. The writer has cried to God: his prayer has been heard: his heart has appealed, and an answer has come. His work has been followed by Divine blessing.

ODE 38.

¹I went up to the light of truth as if into a chariot: ²and the Truth took me and led me: and carried me across pits and gulleys; and from the rocks and the waves it preserved me: ³and it became to me a haven of Salvation : and set me on the arms of immortal life: ⁴and it went with me and made me rest, and suffered me not to wander, because it was the Truth ; ⁵and I ran no risk, because I walked with Him ; ⁶and I did not make an error in anything because I obeyed the Truth. ⁷For Error flees away from it, and meets it not : but the Truth proceeds in the right path, and ⁸whatever I did not know, it made clear to me, all the poisons of error, and the plagues of death which they think to be sweetness: ⁹and I saw the destroyer of destruction, when the bride who is corrupted is adorned ; and the bridegroom who corrupts and is corrupted ; ¹⁰and I asked the Truth, ' Who are these ?'; and He said to me, This is the deceiver and the error: 2 Joh. 7 ¹¹and they are alike in the beloved and in his bride : and they lead astray and corrupt the ⌐whole¬ world : ¹²and they invite many to the banquet, ¹³and give them to drink of the wine of their intoxication, and remove¹ their wisdom and knowledge, and ⌐so they¬ make them without intelligence ; ¹⁴and then they leave them ; and then these go about like madmen corrupting : seeing that they are without heart, nor do they seek for it. ¹⁵And I was made wise so as not to fall into the hands of the deceiver ; and I congratulated myself because the Truth went with me, ¹⁶and I was established and lived and was redeemed, ¹⁷and my foundations were laid on the hand of the Lord : because He established me. ¹⁸For He set the root and watered it and fixed it and blessed it ; and its fruits are for ever. ¹⁹It struck deep and sprung up and spread out, and was full and enlarged ; ²⁰and the Lord alone was glorified in His planting and in His husbandry : by His care and by the blessing of His lips, ²¹by the beautiful planting of His right hand² : and by the

---

¹ *lit.* they vomit up. ² Is. lx. 21.

discovery[1] of His planting, and by the thought of His mind. Hallelujah.

ODE 38. The Psalm opens with a beautiful description of the power of the truth over those that surrender to it. Truth becomes to them guidance in all difficult and rough and dangerous places. But the Psalm is not merely a Psalm of the Truth, it is a Psalm concerning Truth and Error. They appear to stand like Christ and Antichrist. We are tempted to believe that the writer had at one time been brought face to face with some special outbreak of erroneous teaching, one of the many Antichrists of the first century. There are some things which suggest Simon Magus and his Helena, who went about to mislead the faithful. It is, however, useless to try and define the situation more closely. Whatever form the attractions of Truth and Error took to the Psalmist, he tells us that he escaped the Circean blandishments, and sailed past the Sirens. His foundations were in the holy mountain; his growth was in God and of God. God planted, God watered, God gave the increase. The Father was the husbandman.

ODE 39.

[1]Great rivers are the power of the Lord[2]: [2]and they carry headlong those who despise Him: and entangle their paths: [3]and they sweep away their fords, and catch their bodies and destroy their lives. [4]For they are more swift than lightning and more rapid, and those who cross them in faith are not moved; [5]and those who walk on them without blemish shall not be afraid. [6]For the sign in them is the Lord; and the sign is the way of those who cross in the name of the Lord; [7]put on, therefore, the name of the Most High, and know Him: and you shall cross without danger, for the rivers will be subject to you. [8]The Lord has bridged them by His word; and He walked and crossed them on foot[3]: [9]and His footsteps stand ⌜firm⌝ on the water, and are not injured; they are as firm as a tree that is truly set up. [10]And the waves were lifted up on this side and on that, but the footsteps of our Lord Messiah stand firm and are not obliterated and are not defaced. [11]And a way has been appointed for those who cross after Him and for those who adhere to[4] the course of faith in Him and worship His name[5]. Hallelujah.

---

[1] *Or perhaps*, reading ⲣⲁⲟⲩⲙⲁⲝ with Schulthess, 'by the splendour of His planting.'

[2] Is. xliii. 2.   [3] Matt. xiv. 25.

[4] I follow the correction of Flemming.   [5] Cf. Matt. xiv. 28.

ODE 39. When I first read this Psalm I thought that we had another historical landmark, in the allusion to some great accident connected with the sudden rise of one of the great Oriental rivers. But upon reflection, I have come to the conclusion that the writer is speaking of disasters generally, under the natural figure of a rising and rushing river. In such times of flood the unbelievers find no footing and are swept away : believers on the other hand walk the waters like their Lord and with their Lord. Perhaps there is a reference to Isaiah xliii. 2, 'When thou passest through the waters I will be with thee.' The same promise appears to be quoted in Psalms of Solomon vi. 5, 'When he passeth through rivers, yea, through the surge of the sea, he is not affrighted.' Their feet stand firm where His feet had stood unmoved. Here the background of the teaching is the account of our Lord's walking on the sea of Galilee. The reference is valuable[1], for we have hardly any other allusion to events recorded in the Gospel, beyond the Birth, Baptism and Crucifixion, to which we have already referred. The paucity of parallels to the New Testament in the new Psalter should be one of the strongest reasons for believing that, as regards the major part of the collection, we are dealing with very early material.

ODE 40.

[1]As the honey distils from the comb of the bees, [2]and the milk flows from the woman that loves her children[2]; [3]so also is my hope on Thee, my God. [4]As the fountain gushes out its water, [5]so my heart gushes out the praise of the Lord and my lips utter praise to Him, and my tongue His psalms. [6]And my face exults with His gladness, and my spirit exults in His love, and my soul shines in Him : [7]and reverence confides in Him ; and redemption in Him stands assured : [8]and His inheritance[3] is immortal life, and those who participate in it are incorrupt. Hallelujah.

ODE 40. One may say of the writer in the language of St Bernard: 'Inebriabuntur ab ubertate domus tuae et torrente voluptatis tuae potabis eos (Ps. xxxv. 9). O quanta amoris vis! quanta in spiritu libertatis fiducia.' Praise flows out of his life and from his lips as honey drops from the comb or milk from the breast. God's gladness

---

[1] Moreover, if Peter's walking on the sea is involved in the reference of the Odist, it is not Mark's gospel that is being quoted, nor any of the canonical four except Matthew.

[2] Cf. Clem. Alex. *Paed.* i. 6 (p. 119) φιλοστόργοις πηγάζουσα μαστοῖς.

[3] Following the emendation of Charles.

makes his face without to shine, and his soul within to be radiant. If mortality is not quite swallowed up of life, it is irradiated by it. There is assurance of faith and the confident hope of immortality.

ODE 41.

[1]All the Lord's children will praise Him, and will collect the truth of His faith. [2]And His children shall be known to Him. Therefore we will sing in His love : [3]we live in the Lord by His grace : and life we receive in His Messiah : [4]for a great day has shined upon us : and marvellous is He who has given us of His glory. [5]Let us, therefore, all of us unite together in the name of the Lord, and let us honour Him in His goodness, [6]and let our faces shine in His light : and let our hearts meditate in His love by night and by day. [7]Let us exult with the joy of the Lord. [8]All those will be astonished that see me. For from another race am I : [9]for the Father of truth remembered me : He who possessed me from the beginning : [10]for His bounty begat me, and the thought of His heart : [11]and His Word is with us in all our way ; [12]the Saviour who makes alive and does not reject our souls : [13]the man who was humbled, and exalted by His own righteousness, [14]the Son of the Most High appeared in the perfection of His Father ; [15]and light dawned from the Word that was beforetime in Him ; [16]the Messiah is truly one[1] ; and He was known before the foundation of the world, [17]that He might save souls for ever by the truth of His name : a new song ⌜arises⌝ from those who love Him.   Hallelujah.

ODE 41. This Psalm, again, is Messianic, but certainly not in the prophetic sense. The writer knows that the Son of God is come. The glorious day of which prophets spoke has dawned : the dayspring from on high has become the noontide glory. Christ who was humbled is now exalted ; the Word, who existed before the foundation of the world, has appeared. The language finds its nearest parallel in the Johannine theology.

It is not, at first sight, quite clear what the writer means by being sprung from another race[2]. Is it that he is of Gentile origin and persuaded to dwell in the tents of Shem ? That would agree well with the general Palestinian origin of the Psalms. In that case he has become

---

[1] Cf. Ign. ad Magn. 7 εἶς ἐστιν 'Ιησοῦς Χριστός.
[2] But see Introd. p. 66.

sufficiently Hebraized to sing Zion's songs in a Zionite manner: and to praise God night and day, where a Gentile would naturally have done it by day and night.

ODE 42.

[1] I stretched out my hands and approached my Lord : [2] for the stretching of my hands is His sign: [3] my expansion is the outspread tree which was set up on the way of the Righteous One[1]. [4] And I[2] became of no account to those who did not take hold of me ; and I shall be with those who love me.   [5] All my persecutors are dead ; and they sought after me who hoped in me, because I was alive : [6] and I rose up and am with them ; and I will speak by their mouths. [7] For they have despised those who persecuted them ; [8] and I lifted up over them the yoke of my love ; [9] like the arm of the bridegroom over the bride, [10] so was my yoke[3] over those that know me : [11] and as the couch that is spread in the house of the ⌐bridegroom and bride⌐[4], [12] so is my love over those that believe in me.   [13] And I was not rejected though I was reckoned to be so.   [14] I did not perish, though they devised ⌐it⌐ against me.   [15] Sheol saw me and was made miserable : [16] death cast me up and many along with me. [17] I[5] had gall and bitterness[6], and I went down with him to the utmost of his[7] depth : [18] and the feet and the head he let go, for they were not able to endure my face : [19] and I made a congregation of living men amongst his dead men, and I spake with them by living lips : [20] because my word shall not be void : [21] and those who had died ran towards me : and they cried and said, Son of God, have pity on us, and do with us according to thy kindness, [22] and bring us out from the bonds of darkness: and open to us the door by which we shall come out to thee.   [23] For we see that our death has not touched thee. [24] Let us also be redeemed with thee: for thou art our

---

[1] Zahn thinks the text of this verse has been altered, and suggests ܐܟܪܘܬܗ ܥܠܝܗ ܐܬܬܣܝܡ, 'on which the Beloved was hanged.'

[2] Christ speaks.

[3] Matt. xi. 29.   [4-4] *lit.* bridegrooms.   [5] *Cod.* He.

[6] Cf. *Descensus ad Inferos* 4 'They crucified him, and gave him gall and vinegar to drink. Be ready, therefore, to hold him firmly when he cometh.' Flemming objects to the correction which I have made in the text, and says we should render 'I was gall and bitterness to him.' So U.-S.   Probably this is the right sense of the passage : but I am not quite satisfied.   [7] *or* its : sc. Sheol's.

Redeemer. [25] And I heard their voice; and my name I sealed upon their heads: [26] for they are free men and they are mine. Hallelujah.

ODE 42. This Psalm concludes the collection of Odes ascribed to Solomon: what follows is the extant book of Solomonic Psalms. The collection up to the present point is marked in each case with a final Hallelujah. The remaining Psalms, with one accidental exception, are not marked this way. So we may add the editorial remark at the end of this Psalm, that 'the Odes of Solomon, the Son of David, are ended.'

The concluding Psalm is Christian and Messianic: its main theme is the descent of Christ into Hades in order to liberate the imprisoned souls of the fathers: and it should be read along with the extant apocryphal books that deal with this subject.

Almost the whole of the Psalm is *ex ore Christi*: the writer begins, as in the short 29th Ode, with the statement that his lifted hands make the figure of the Cross of the Righteous One. But he soon diverges into the harrowing of hell. The imprisoned souls cry out for release to Him over whom death, which binds them, has no power. A congregation of saints is gathered in the place of the dead. They become Christ's free men. Incidentally an expression is used of their relation to the Lord which appears to be employed elsewhere: they are called, not the members, but the feet of the Lord. Hades disgorges both the head and the feet: the head is, of course, Christ; and the feet are the saints of old time[1]. [For *v.* 18 we may compare *Acta Thomae* c. 156 οὗ τὴν θέαν οὐκ ἤνεγκαν οἱ τοῦ θανάτου ἄρχοντες.]

The Psalm is too highly evolved, in its imaginary treatment of the Descent into Hell, to be reckoned as belonging to the same period as the main body of the collection. Still it cannot be very much later, for its mystical language is in close agreement with many of the most beautiful of the Psalms before us: and the union of Christ with the Church, under the figure of the Bridegroom and the Bride, is expressed with great beauty. Incidentally the textual critic will find something suggestive for his New Testament apparatus. The writer speaks of 'the couch that is spread in the house of the bridegrooms,' marking the plural by dots in the usual Syriac manner: it is evident that he means 'in the house of the bridegroom and the bride.' Perhaps, then, the curious Western reading of Matt. xxv. 1, 'went out to meet the bridegroom and the bride,' may be due to a more accurate interpretation of an Aramaic original than what we find in the received and edited texts.

---

[1] Cf. Ode 23.

PSALM 43 = PSALMS OF SOLOMON I.

[1]I cried unto the Lord, when I was in affliction at my end ; and to God when sinners set upon me : [2]for suddenly there was heard before me the sound of war : for He will hear me, because I am filled with righteousness : [3]and I reckoned in my heart that I was filled with righteousness : in the day that I became rich and was with the multitude of my children. [4]Their wealth, however, has been given to the whole earth : and their glory as far as the ends of the earth. [5]They were lifted up as high as the stars : and they said, [6]speaking without knowledge.... [7]For their sins were in secret, and I knew them not : [8]and their wickedness exceeded that of the nations that had been before them : and they defiled the sanctuary of the Lord with pollution.

PSALM 44 = PSALMS OF SOLOMON 2.

[1]In the insolence of the sinful man, he cast down with battering rams[1] the strong walls and thou didst not restrain him. [2]And the Gentile foreigners went up on thy altar, and were trampling on it with their shoes in their insolence. [3]For the children of Jerusalem had polluted the Holy House of the Lord : and they were profaning the offerings [2]to God[2] with wickedness. [4]Wherefore He said, Remove them, cast them away from me. And He did not establish with them the beauty of His glory : [5]it was rejected before the Lord : and they were utterly torn in pieces. [6]Her sons and her daughters were in bitter captivity : and on their neck was put the sealed yoke of the Gentiles : [7]according to their sins, so He dealt with them : for He suffered them to pass into the hand of him that was stronger than they : [8]for He turned away His face from His mercy : young men and old men

---

[1] *lit.* great beams.   [2-2] *lit.* of God.

and their children together: [9]because they also had worked evil together, that they might not hearken unto me: [10]and the heaven was mightily angered, and the earth rejected them: [11]because none in the earth had done therein like their doings: [12]and that the earth may know all thy righteous judgments, O God. [13]They set up the sons of Jerusalem for mockery within her, in the place of harlots; and every one that transgressed[1], was transgressing as if before the sun: while they made sport in their villainies, as they were used to do. [14]In the face of the sun they made a show of their villainies. And the daughters of Jerusalem were polluted according to thy judgments; [15]for they had polluted themselves in lustful intercourse. My belly and my bowels are pained over these things. [16]But I will justify thee, O Lord, in the uprightness of my heart; because in thy judgments is thy righteousness, O God. [17]For thou dost reward sinful men according to their deeds: and according to their wicked and bitter sins. [18]Thou didst disclose their sins, in order that thy· judgment might be known: [19]and Thou didst blot out their remembrance from the earth. God is a judge and righteous, and accepteth no man's person. [20]For the Gentiles reproached Jerusalem, in their wickedness, and her beauty was cut off from the throne of His[2] glory. [21]And she was covered with sackcloth instead of beauteous raiment: and there was a rope on her head instead of a crown. [22]She cast off from her the dazzling[3] glory which God had put upon her: [23]and in contempt her beauty was cast away on the ground. [24]And I beheld and I besought the face of the Lord, and I said: Enough! Thou hast made thy hand heavy, O Lord, upon Israel, by the bringing in of the Gentiles: [25]for they have mocked and not pitied, in anger; [26]and in reproach they are consumed, unless thou, O Lord, shalt restrain them in thy wrath. [27]For it was not in zeal that they did ⌐this⌐, but in the lust of the soul: [28]that they might pour out their wrath upon us in plundering us. But thou, O Lord, delay not to recompense them upon their own heads: [29]to cast down the pride of the dragon to contempt. [30]And I delayed not until the Lord showed me his insolence smitten on the mountains of Egypt: and despised more than him that is least on land and on sea: [31]and his body coming on the waves in much contempt, and none to bury

---

[1] _Or_, passed by.   [2] Gk. her.   [3] Gk. her diadem of glory.

⌐him⌐. ³²Because He had rejected him with scorn, for he did
not consider that he is a man. And the end he did not regard.
³³For he said ; I will be lord of land and sea : and he knew not
that the Lord is God, great and mighty and powerful, ³⁴and He
is King over Heaven and over Earth : and He judges kingdoms
and princes, ³⁵He who raiseth me up in glory and layeth low[1]
the proud in contempt, not temporal but eternal ; because they
knew Him ⌐not⌐.

³⁶And now, behold, ye great ones of the earth, the judgment
of the Lord, for He is a righteous King, and judges what is under
the whole heaven. ³⁷Bless ye the Lord, ye who fear the Lord
reverently : for the mercies of the Lord are on them that fear
Him with judgment, ³⁸to separate between the righteous and the
sinful, and to reward the sinful for ever according to their deeds :
³⁹and to be gracious to the righteous after their oppression
by sinners : and to reward the sinful for what he has done that
is right : ⁴⁰because the Lord is kind to those that call upon Him
in patience, to do according to His mercy to His saints : so as
to stand before Him at all times in strength. ⁴¹Blessed is the
Lord for ever by His servants.

PSALM 45 = PSALMS OF SOLOMON 3.

¹Why sleepest thou, my soul, and dost not bless the Lord ?
²Sing a new song to God and keep vigil in His watch. For a
psalm is good ⌐to sing⌐ to God out of a good heart. ³The
righteous will ever make mention of the Lord : in confession and
in righteousness are the judgments of the Lord. ⁴The righteous
will never neglect[2], when he is chastened by the Lord : because
his will is always before the Lord. ⁵The righteous stumbles and
justifies God : he falls and I wait[3] what the Lord will do to him.
⁶And he looks to see from whence his salvation comes. ⁷The
stability of the righteous is from God their Saviour : for in the
house of the righteous there does not lodge sin upon sin :
⁸because He always visits the house of the righteous to remove
the sins of his transgressions. ⁹And He delivers his soul, in
whatever he has sinned without knowledge, by fasting and by
humiliation : ¹⁰and the Lord purifies every holy man and his house.

---

[1] Gk. κοιμίζων and so Syr.
[2] = Gk. ὀλιγωρήσει : cf. Prov. iii. 11 ; Heb. xii. 5.   [3] Read, 'and he waits.'

[11]But the sinner stumbleth and curseth his own life, and the day in which he was born: and the birth-pangs of his mother; [12]and he adds sin upon sin to his life: [13]he falls, and because his fall is grievous, he rises not again: for the destruction of the sinner is for ever: [14]and He will not remember him when He visits the righteous: [15]this is the portion of sinners for ever. [16]But those who fear the Lord shall rise to eternal life: and their life shall be in the light of the Lord, and he will not fail any more. [Hallelujah[1].]

PSALM 46 (47) = PSALMS OF SOLOMON 4.

[1]Why sittest thou, O wicked man, in the congregation of the righteous: and thy heart is far removed from God; and by thy wickedness thou provokest to anger the God of Israel, [2]exceedingly by thy words, and exceedingly by thy ⌐outward⌐ signs, more than all men? He who is severe in his words in his condemnation of sinners in judgment, [3]and his hand is the first to be on him, as though ⌐he acted⌐ in zeal: and he is guilty himself of all kinds of sinful crimes: [4]his eyes are upon every woman immodestly: and his tongue lies when he answers with oaths. [5]In the night and in the darkness, as if he were not seen; by his eyes he talketh with every woman in the cunning of wickedness: [6]and he is quick to go into every house with joy, as if he had no wickedness. [7]God shall remove those who judge with respect of persons: but He lives with the upright, in the corruption of his body and in the poverty of his life. [8]God will disclose the deeds of those who are men-pleasers: in scorn and derision are his works: [9]and let the saints justify the judgment of their God, when the wicked shall be removed from before the righteous: [10]the accepter of persons who talks law with guile, [11]and his eyes are on a house, quietly like a serpent, to dispel the wisdom of each one by words of villainy: [12]his words are with an evil intent, with a view to the working of the lust of the wicked: [13]and he does not remove until he has scattered in bereavement, and has desolated the house because of his sinful lust. [14]And he supposes in his words that there is none that sees and judges: [15]and he is filled with this sinfulness; and his

---

[1] This is an addition by the scribe, under the influence of the Odes of Solomon, which he has been copying.

eyes are on another house to devastate it with words of prodi-
gality: and his soul is, like Sheol, never satisfied. [16]For all
these things, let ⌐his portion⌐¹, O Lord, be before thee in
dishonour; let his going out be with groans and his coming in
with curses: [17]in pains, and in poverty and in destitution, O
Lord, let his life be: let his sleep be in anguish and his waking
in vexation: [18]let sleep be removed from his eyelids by night:
let him fall from every work of his hands in dishonour; [19]and
let him enter his house empty-handed: and let his house be
destitute of everything that can satisfy his soul: [20]and from
his offspring let not one draw near unto him: [21]let the flesh of
the hypocrites be scattered by wild beasts; and the bones of
the wicked be before the sun in dishonour: [22]let the ravens pick
out the eyes of those who are men-pleasers: [23]because they
have laid waste many houses of men in dishonour: and have
scattered them in lust: [24]and they remembered not God; nor
feared God in all these things; [25]and they provoked God,
and He was angered to destroy them from the earth; because
with crafty intent they had played the hypocrite with innocent
souls. [26]Blessed are they that fear the Lord in their innocency:
[27]and the Lord will save them from all the cunning and wicked
men; and He will redeem us from every stumbling-block of the
wicked. [28]May God destroy all them that work fraud with
pride[2]: for a strong judge is the Lord our God in righteousness;
[29]let thy mercy, O Lord, be upon all them that love thee.

PSALM 47 (48) = PSALMS OF SOLOMON 5.

[1]O Lord my God, I will praise thy name with exultation,
amongst those that know thy righteous judgments. [2]For thou
art gracious and merciful, and the place of refuge of the poor.
[3]When I cry unto thee, be not thou silent unto me. [4]For one
does not take spoil from the strong man: [5]or who shall take
aught from what thou hast made, unless thou give it him?
[6]Because he is man, and his portion is before thee in the
balance: and he shall not add aught to better it apart from thy
judgment, O God. [7]In our afflictions we call thee to our help:
and thou hast not turned away our petition: for thou art our
God. [8]Delay not thou thy hand from us: lest we be strengthened

---

¹ Syr. let him. ² *lit.* excess.

to sin: [9]and turn not away thy face from us, lest we remove
away from thee : but to thee we will come : [10]for if I should
be hungry, O Lord, unto thee will I cry, O God: and thou
wilt bestow.   [11]For the fowl and the fish thou dost feed.
When thou givest rain in the desert to cause the grass to
spring up, [12]to prepare food in the wilderness for every living
thing, and if they shall be hungry, unto thee will they lift
up their faces : [13]kings and rulers and peoples thou dost
provide for, O God: and the hope of the poor and the
miserable, who is it except thyself, O Lord? [14]and thou wilt
answer him, because thou art kind and gentle : and his soul shall
be satisfied when thou openest thy hand in mercy.   [15]For the
kindness of a man is with parsimony ; to-day and to-morrow ;
and if it should be that he repeats his gift and does not grumble,
ᴦwell !ᴎ that is a wonder !   [16]But thy bounty is plenteous in
kindness and in wealth ; and there is no expectation towards
thee that He will be sparing in gifts[1].   [17]For over all the earth is
thy mercy, O Lord, in kindness.   [18]Blessed is the man whom the
Lord shall remember in poverty : for that a man should exceed
his measure means that he will sin.   [19]Sufficient is a low estate
with righteousness[2]: [20]for those that fear the Lord are pleased
with good things : and thy grace is on Israel in thy Kingdom:
[21]blessed be the glory of the Lord, for He is our King.

PSALM 48 (49) = PSALMS OF SOLOMON 6.

[1]Blessed is the man whose heart is prepared to call upon the
name of the Lord : [2]and when he shall' remember the name of
the Lord, he will be saved.   [3]His ways are directed from before
the Lord : and the works of his hands are preserved by his God:
[4]and ᴦinᴎ the evil vision of the night his soul shall not be moved.
because he is His : [5]and his soul shall not be affrighted in the
passing through the rivers, and in the tumult of the seas.   [6]For
he rose from his sleep and praised the name of the Lord, [7]and
in the quiet of his heart he sang psalms to the name of the
Lord : and he made request from the face of the Lord con-
cerning all his house : [8]and the Lord hears the prayer of every

---

[1] The Gk. οὗ ἐστιν ἐπί σε has been misread οὐκ ἐστιν τέ.

[2] The Syriac has omitted a sentence of the Greek by a common transcriptional
error.   Add ᴦand herein is the blessing of the Lord that a man be satisfied in
righteousnessᴎ.

one that is in His fear, and every petition of the soul that trusts in Him ; and the Lord fulfils it. [9] Blessed is he who doeth mercy upon them that love Him in truth.

PSALM 49 (50) = PSALMS OF SOLOMON 7.

[1] Remove not thy tabernacle from us, O Lord, lest those rise up against us who hate us without a cause : [2] for thou hast put them away, O God, that their foot may not tread the inheritance of thy sanctuary. [3] Thou in thy good pleasure chasten me and deliver us not over to the Gentiles. [4] For if thou shouldest send death, it is thou who givest it command against us ; [5] for thou art the Merciful One, and wilt not be angry so as to consume us utterly. [6] For because of thy Name that encamps amongst us, mercies shall be upon us : and the Gentiles shall not be able to prevail against us, [7] for thou art our strength : and we will call upon thee and thou wilt answer us : [8] for thou wilt be gracious to the seed of Israel, for ever, and thou wilt not forget him[1] : [9] thou wilt establish us in the time of thy help, to show favour to the house of Jacob, in the day that is prepared for them.

PSALM 50 (51) = PSALMS OF SOLOMON 8.

[1] Distress and the sound of war mine ears have heard, the sound of the trumpet, and the noise of slaughter and destruction : [2] the sound of much people like a mighty and frequent wind : like the tempest of fire which comes over the wilderness. [3] And I said to my heart : Where will he judge him ? [4] I heard a sound in Jerusalem, the Holy City ; [5] the bonds of my loins were loosed at the report[2] : and my knees trembled, [6] and my bones were moved like flax. [7] And I said, They will make straight their paths in righteousness and I remembered the judgments of the Lord, from the creation of the heaven and the earth : and I justified God in all His judgments from the beginning[3]. [8] But God laid bare their sins before the sun : and to all the earth was made known the righteous judgments of the Lord. [9] For in

---

[1] The Syriac has dropped the sentence : 'and we are under thy yoke for ever, and under the scourge of thy chastening.'

[2] Gk. *adds*: and my heart was afraid.   [3] *lit.* from eternity.

secret places of the earth were they doing evil; ¹⁰the son had connexion with the mother and the father with the daughter: ¹¹and all of them committed adultery with their neighbours' wives: and they made solemn covenants amongst themselves concerning these things: ¹²they were plundering the House of God's Holiness, as if there was none to inherit and to deliver. ¹³And they were treading His sanctuary in all their pollutions, and in the time¹ of their separation they polluted the sacrifices, as common meat: ¹⁴and they left no sins which they did not commit, and even worse than the Gentiles. ¹⁵For this cause God mingled for them a spirit of error, and caused them to drink a living cup for drunkenness: ¹⁶He brought him from the other side of the world, the one that afflicts grievously: ¹⁷and he decrees war against Jerusalem and against her land: ¹⁸and the judges of the land met him with joy: and they said to him: Thy path shall be ordered, come, enter in peace. ¹⁹They levelled the lofty paths² for his entering: they opened the doors against Jerusalem: and they crowned the walls. ²⁰And he entered like a father into the house of his children, in peace: and he set his feet ⌐there¬ in great firmness: ²¹and they took possession of the towers and the walls of Jerusalem. ²²For God brought him in assurance against their error: ²³and they destroyed their princes because he was cunning in counsel: and they poured out the blood of the dwellers in Jerusalem like the water of uncleanness: ²⁴and he carried off their sons and daughters, who had been ⌐born¬ in pollution, ²⁵and had wrought their pollution even as also their fathers had done. ²⁶And Jerusalem defiled even those things that were consecrated to the name of God: ²⁷and God was justified in His judgments upon the nations of the earth, ²⁸and the saints of God were as innocent lambs in their midst. ²⁹God is to be praised who judges all the earth in His righteousness. ³⁰Behold, O God, thou hast shown us ⌐thy judgments¬³ in thy righteousness, ³¹and our eyes have seen thy judgments, O God: and we have justified thy name that is honoured for ever.

³²For thou art a God of righteousness: who judgest Israel with chastening. ³³Turn thy mercy towards us and be gracious to us: ³⁴and gather the dispersion of Israel, in mercy

---

¹ *lit.* blood.　　　² *lit.* paths of elevation.　　　³ Cod. om.

and in kindness : [35]for thy faithfulness is with us : and we are stiff-necked, and thou art our chastener : [36]do not desert us, O our God ! lest the Gentiles should swallow us up, as though there were none to deliver : [37]and thou art our God from the beginning, and upon thee is our hope, O Lord : [38]and we will not depart from thee, for thy judgments are good ; [39]upon us and upon our children is thy good will for ever, O Lord God, our Saviour, and we shall not be shaken again, for ever. [40]The Lord is to be praised for His judgments by the mouth of His saints : [41]and blessed is Israel from the Lord for evermore.

PSALM 51 (52) = PSALMS OF SOLOMON 9.

[1]When Israel went forth into captivity to a strange land, because they departed from the Lord their Saviour : [2]then were they cast out from the inheritance that God gave them : amongst all the Gentiles was the dispersion of Israel, according to the word of God, [3]that thou mightest be justified, O God, in thy righteousness over our wickedness : [4]for thou art a just Judge over all the peoples of the earth. [5]For there will not be hidden from thy knowledge any one who doeth wickedness : [6]and the righteousness of thy upright ones, O Lord, is before thee. And where shall a man be hidden from thy knowledge, O God ? [7]For we work by free-will and the choice of our own souls to do either good or evil by the work of our hands : [8]and in thy righteousness thou dost visit the children of men. [9]For he who does righteousness lays up a treasure of life with the Lord : and he who does wickedness incurs judgment upon his soul in perdition.

[10]For His judgments are in righteousness upon every man and his house. [11]For with whom wilt thou deal graciously, O God, unless with them that call upon the Lord ? [12]For he purifies the sins of the soul by confession, [13]because shame is on us and our faces because of all these things. [14]For to whom will He remit sins except to those that have sinned ? [15]For the righteous thou dost bless, and dost not reprove them for any of their sins; for thy grace is on those that have sinned when they have repented. [16]And, now, thou art our God : and we are thy people whom thou hast loved : behold and have mercy, O God of Israel; for thine are we : remove not thy compassions

from us, lest the Gentiles should set upon us : [17]for thou hast
chosen the seed of Abraham rather than all the Gentiles, [18]and
thou hast put on us thy Name, O Lord : and thou wilt not
remove for ever.   [19]Thou didst surely covenant with our fathers
concerning us : and we hope in thee, in the repentance of our
souls.   [20]The mercies over the house of Israel are of the Lord,
now and evermore.

PSALM 52 (53) = PSALMS OF SOLOMON 10.

[1]Blessed is the man whom God remembers with reproof :
and He has restrained him from the way of evil by stripes: so as
to be purified from his sin, that he may not abound ⌜therein⌝.
[2]For he who prepares his loins for beating shall also be purified :
for He is good to those that receive His chastening.   [3]For the
way of the righteous is straight, and His chastisement does not
turn it aside.   [4]For the face[1] of the Lord is upon them that
love Him in truth, and the Lord will remember His servants in
mercy.   [5]For the testimony is in the law of the everlasting
covenant : the testimony of the Lord is in the ways of the
children of men, by ⌜His⌝ visitations.   [6]Righteous and upright
is our God in all His judgments : and Israel will praise the name
of the Lord with joy.   [7]And the saints shall give thanks in
the congregation of the people : and on the poor the Lord will
have mercy, in the gladness of Israel.   [8]For God is kind and
merciful for ever : and the congregations of Israel shall praise
the name of the Lord : [9]for of the Lord is the salvation upon the
house of Israel, unto the everlasting kingdom[2].

PSALM 53 (54) = PSALMS OF SOLOMON 11.

[1]Blow ye ⌜the trumpet⌝ in Zion, the certain trumpet of the
saints : [2]proclaim in Jerusalem the voice of the heralds, because
God is merciful to Israel in His visitation.   [3]Stand up on high[3],
Jerusalem, and behold thy children, who are all being gathered
from the East and the West by the Lord : [4]and from the North
they come to the joy of their God : and from the far-away
islands God gathereth them.   [5]Lofty mountains has He humbled
and made plain before them ; and the hills fled away before their

---

[1] Gk. mercy (ἔλεος).   [2] Gk. gladness, εὐφροσύνην.
[3] Baruch v. 5—8.

entrance : [6]the cedar[1] gave shelter to them as they passed by : and every tree of sweet odour God made to breathe[2] upon them : [7]in order that Israel might pass by in the visitation of the glory of their God. [8]O Jerusalem, put on the garments of thy glory ; and make ready thy robe of holiness. For God speaks good things to Israel, now and ever. [9]May the Lord do what He hath spoken concerning Israel : and concerning Jerusalem : may the Lord raise up Israel in the name of His glory. May the mercies of the Lord be upon Israel, now and evermore.

PSALM 54 (55) = PSALMS OF SOLOMON 12.

[1]O Lord, save my soul from the perverse and wicked man and from the whispering and transgressing tongue, that speaks lies and deceit. [2]For in the response of his words is the tongue of the transgressor[3] : for he shows like one whose deeds are fair, and kindles fire among the people. [3]For his sojourning is to fill[4] (set fire to) houses by his lying talk : for the trees of his delight he will cut down with the flame [5]of his tongue[5] that does lawlessly. [4]He has destroyed the houses of the transgressors by war : and the slandering[6] lips God has removed from the innocent, the lips of transgressors : and the bones of the slanderer shall be scattered far from those who fear the Lord. [5]By flaming fire He will destroy the slanderous tongue from among the upright, and their houses. [6]And the Lord shall preserve[7] the soul of the righteous who hateth them that are evil : and the Lord shall establish the man that makes peace in the house of the Lord. [7]Of the Lord is salvation upon Israel His servant for ever : [8]and the sinners shall perish together from before the face of the Lord : and the saints of the Lord shall inherit the promises of the Lord.

PSALM 55 (56) = PSALMS OF SOLOMON 13.

[1]The right hand of the Lord has covered us : the right hand of the Lord has spared us : [2]and the arm of the Lord has saved

---

[1] Gk. οἱ δρυμοί, the groves.
[2] Gk. ἀνέτειλεν, caused to rise. Corr. the Syriac to ܡܢܚ (Schulthess).
[3] The Greek of this passage is obscure.
[4] The translator read ἐμπλῆσαι for ἐμπρῆσαι.
[5-5] Cod. om.   [6] *lit.* whispering.
[7] *Better* : 'and may the Lord preserve' as in Gk. : and so in following clauses.

me from the spear that goes through and from famine and the pestilence of sinners. ³Evil beasts ran upon them: and with their teeth were tearing their flesh; and with their jaw-teeth¹ were breaking their bones. But us the Lord has delivered from all these things. ⁴But the wicked man was troubled on account of his transgression: lest he should be broken along with the evil men. ⁵Because dread is the fall of the wicked: but the righteous not one of these things shall touch. ⁶For one cannot compare the chastening of the righteous who have ⌐sinned¬ ignorantly with the overthrow of evil men who sin ²knowingly. ⁷For the righteous is chastened² so that the sinner will not exult over him. ⁸For the righteous He will admonish as His beloved son³; and his chastening is like that of the first-born: ⁹for the Righteous One will spare His saints, and their transgressions He will blot out by His chastisement. For the life of the righteous is for ever. ¹⁰But sinners shall be cast into perdition: and their memorial shall no more be found. ¹¹But upon the saints shall be the mercy of the Lord. He will cherish all them that fear Him.

PSALM 56 (57) = PSALMS OF SOLOMON 14.

¹The Lord is faithful to them that love Him in truth: even to them that abide His chastening: to them who walk in righteousness in His commandments: He has given us the Law for our life: ²and the saints of the Lord shall live thereby for ever. The Paradise of the Lord, the trees of life, are His saints: ³and the planting of them is sure for ever; nor shall they be rooted up all the days of the heaven. For the portion of the Lord and His inheritance is Israel. ⁴Not so are the sinners and evil men, those who have loved a day in the participation of sin: for in the brevity of wickedness is their lust; ⁵and they did not remember God; that the ways of the children of men are open before Him continually: and the secrets⁴ of the heart He knoweth before they come to pass: ⁶therefore their inheritance is Sheol, and Perdition and Darkness: and in the day of mercy upon the righteous they shall not be found. ⁷For the saints of the Lord shall inherit life in delight.

¹ *Or* molars: rendering the Greek μύλαι literally, as Wellhausen has observed: it should have been ܐܟܪ̈ܐ.

²⁻² Or perhaps: For the righteous is chastened secretly. (See Ryle and James, ad loc.)

³ Corr. 'He will cause the righteous to inherit Him.'   ⁴ *lit.* secret places.

PSALM 57 (58) = PSALMS OF SOLOMON 15.

[1]In my affliction I called on the name of the Lord, and for my help I called on the God of Jacob: and I was delivered, [2]because thou, O God, art the hope and the refuge of the poor. [3]For who that is strong will praise thee in truth? [4]and what is the strength of a man, except that he should praise thy name? [5]A new song with the voice in the delight of the heart: the fruit of the lips with the instrument attuned to the tongue: the firstfruit of the lips from a heart that is holy and just. [6]He that doeth these things shall never be moved by evil: the flame of fire and the anger of sinners shall not touch them, [7]when it goeth forth against the sinners from before the Most High to root up all the roots of sinners: [8]because the sign of the Lord is upon the righteous for their salvation: death and the spear and famine shall remove from the righteous; [9]for they shall flee from them, as death flees from life: but they shall pursue after the wicked and catch them: and those who do evil shall not escape from the judgment of the Lord: for they will get before them like skilled warriors: [10]for the sign of destruction is upon their faces. [11]And the inheritance of sinners is Perdition and Darkness: and their iniquity shall pursue them down to the lower hell. [12]And their inheritance shall not be found by their children: [13]for their sins shall lay waste the houses of sinners: and sinners shall perish for ever in the day of the Lord's judgment: [14]when God visits the earth with His judgment. [15]And upon those who fear the Lord there shall be mercy therein; and they shall live in the compassion of our God: and sinners shall perish unto eternity[1].

PSALM 58 (59) = PSALMS OF SOLOMON 16.

[1]When my soul declined a little from the Lord, I had almost been in the lapses of the sleep of destruction; and when I was far away from the Lord, [2]my soul had almost been poured out to death, hard by the gates of Sheol along with the sinners: [3]and when my soul declined from the God of Israel, unless the Lord had helped me by His mercy which is for ever—! [4]He

---

[1] *lit.* the time of eternity.

pricked me, like the spur of the horse, according to His watchfulness: my Saviour and Helper at all times is He: He saved me: ⁵I will praise thee, O God, because thou hast helped me with thy salvation : and hast not reckoned me with sinners for destruction. ⁶Withdraw not thy mercy from me, O God: and let not the remembrance of thee remove from my heart until I die : ⁷save me, O Lord, from the wicked sinful woman, and from every wicked woman who sets traps for the simple : ⁸and let not the beauty of a wicked woman lead me astray, nor any sin that is, ⁹and establish the work of my hands before thee : and preserve my walk in the remembrance of thee. ¹⁰My tongue and my lips in words of truth do thou establish: anger and unreasonable passion do thou remove from me : ¹¹grumbling and little-mindedness in affliction do thou remove from me : for if I shall sin when thou hast chastened me, it is for repentance : ¹²but by thy good-will establish my soul : and when thou shalt strengthen my soul, whatever has been given shall be sufficient for me : ¹³for if thou strengthenest me not, who can endure thy chastening in poverty ? ¹⁴for a soul shall be reproved[1] in his flesh and by the affliction of poverty : ¹⁵and when a righteous man shall endure these things, mercy shall be upon him from the Lord.

PSALM 59 (60) = PSALMS OF SOLOMON 17.

¹O Lord, thou art our King, now and for ever: for in thee, O God, our soul shall glory.   ²And what is the life of man upon the earth? for according to his time, so also is his hope. ³But we hope on God our Saviour: for the stronghold of our God is for ever according to mercy: ⁴and the Kingdom of our God is over the Gentiles for ever with judgment.   ⁵Thou, O Lord, didst choose David for king over Israel : and thou didst swear to him concerning his seed, that their kingdom should not be removed from before thee.   ⁶But for our sins sinners rose up against us : and they set upon us, and removed me far away: they to whom thou gavest no command have taken by violence, ⁷and have not glorified thy honourable name with praises : and they have set up a kingdom instead of that which was their pride. ⁸They laid waste the throne of David in exultation of their change[2]. But thou wilt overthrow them, and wilt remove their

---

[1] Or (see note to text) : thou wilt reprove.
[2] Reading ἀλλάγματος.

seed from the earth : [9]even when there shall rise up against them a man that was a stranger to our race. [10]According to their sins, thou wilt reward them, O God : and it shall befall them according to their works. [11]And thou wilt not have mercy upon them, O God. Command their seed, and do not leave a single one of them. [12]The Lord is faithful in all His judgments which He has done upon the earth. [13]The wicked man[1] has devastated our land, so that there is none to dwell therein. They have destroyed both young and old and their children together. [14]In the splendour of his wrath he sent them away to the West, and the princes of the land to mockery without sparing. [15]In his foreign way the enemy exults, and his heart is alien from our God. [16]And Jerusalem did all things[2] according as the Gentiles did in their cities to their gods. [17]And the children of the covenant took hold of them in the midst of the mingled Gentiles : and there was none amongst them that did mercy and truth in Jerusalem. [18]They that love the assemblies of the saints fled away from them : and they flew like sparrows who fly from their nests : [19]and they were wandering in the wilderness, in order to save their soul from evil: and precious in their eyes was the sojourning with them of any soul that was saved from them. [20]Over all the earth they were scattered by the wicked. Therefore were the heavens restrained that they should not send down rain upon the earth, [21]and the everlasting fountains were restrained, both the abysses, and from the lofty mountains : because there was none among them who did righteousness and judgment; from their ruler to the lowest of them they were sinning in everything. [22]The king was in transgression, and the judge in wrath, and the people in sin. [23]Behold, O Lord, and raise up to them their king, the Son of David, according to the time which thou seest, O God : and let Him reign over Israel thy servant, [24]and strengthen Him with power that He may humble the sinful rulers : [25]and may purify Jerusalem from the Gentiles who trample her down to destruction, [26]so as to destroy the wicked from my inheritance : and to break their pride like a potter's vessel : to break with a rod of iron all their firmness : [27]to destroy the sinful Gentiles with the word of His mouth : at His rebuke the Gentiles shall flee from before His face : and to confute sinners by the word of their

---

[1] Gk. ἄνομος, not ἄνεμος.   [2] Gk. = ὅσα ἐποίησεν Ἱερουσαλήμ.

heart : [28]that He may gather together a holy people that shall exult in righteousness : and may judge the tribes of the people whom the Lord His God sanctified : [29]and He shall not any more suffer sin to lodge amongst them ; and no more shall dwell amongst them the man that knoweth evil. [30]For He knoweth them that they are all the children of God, and He shall divide them according to their tribes upon the earth : [31]and the sojourner and the foreigner shall not dwell with them : for He will judge the Gentiles and the peoples in the wisdom of His righteousness : [32]and He shall possess a people from among the Gentiles : and they shall serve Him under His yoke : and they shall praise the Lord openly over all the earth : [33]and He shall purify Jerusalem in holiness, as it was of old time : [34]that the Gentiles may come from the ends of the earth to behold His glory : bringing her sons with them as an honourable gift ; those who were scattered from her, [35]and to see the glory of the Lord wherewith He hath glorified her: and He the righteous king, taught of God, is over them : [36]and there is no wicked person in His days amongst them, because they are all righteous, and their king is the Lord Messiah : [37]for He will not trust on horse nor on his rider ; nor on the bow : nor shall He multiply to himself gold and silver for war: nor shall He rely on a multitude in the day of war : [38]for the Lord ——.

(Caetera desunt.)

For EU product safety concerns, contact us at Calle de José Abascal, 56–1°,
28003 Madrid, Spain or eugpsr@cambridge.org.

www.ingramcontent.com/pod-product-compliance
Ingram Content Group UK Ltd.
Pitfield, Milton Keynes, MK11 3LW, UK
UKHW040620240426
470322UK00010B/227

ܐܡܝܢܬܐ
ܘܒܝܫܬܐ
ܕܝܠܦܘ ܀

ODE 1.

[=*Pistis Sophia* 116 (tr. Schmidt): *Texte u. Untersuch.* Bd. VII. pp. 37, 38.]

[Dominus super caput meum sicut corona, neque ero absque eo. Plexerunt mihi coronam veritatis, et ramos tuos in me germinare fecit. Nam non similis est coronae aridae quae non germinat; sed vivis super caput meum. Et germinasti super caput meum: fructus tui pleni et perfecti sunt, pleni salute tua.]

ODE 2.

Deest.

ODE 3.

Priora desunt.

*   *   *   *   *   *   *   *

ܡܠܒܫ ܐܢܐ. ܘܗܕܡ̈ܘܗܝ[a] 2 ܠܘܬܗ ܐܝܬ ܐܢܘܢ̱ ܘܒܗܘܢ ܬܠܐ
ܐܢܐ ܘܪܚܡ ܠܝ. 3 ܠܐ ܓܝܪ ܝܕܥ ܗܘܝܬ ܠܡܪܚܡ ܠܡܪܝܐ.
ܐܠܘ ܗܘ ܠܐ ܪܚܡ ܗܘܐ ܠܝ. 4 ܡܢܘ ܡܫܟܚ ܠܡܦܪܫ ܪܚܡܬܐ.
ܐܠܐ ܗܘ ܕܡܬܪܚܡ. 5 ܡܚܒ ܐܢܐ ܠܚܒܝܒܐ ܘܪܚܡܐ ܠܗ
ܢܦܫܝ. 6 ܘܐܝܟܐ ܕܢܝܚܗ ܐܦ ܐܢܐ ܐܝܬܝ. 7 ܘܠܐ ܐܗܘܐ
ܢܘܟܪܝܐ. ܡܛܠ ܕܠܝܬ ܚܣܡܐ ܠܘܬ ܡܪܝܐ ܡܪܝܡܐ.
ܘܡܪܚܡܢܐ. 8 ܐܬܚܠܛܬ ܡܛܠ ܕܐܫܟܚ ܪܚܡܐ ܠܗܘ
ܪܚܡܐ. 9 ܡܛܠ ܕܐܪܚܡ ܠܗܘ ܒܪܐ. ܕܒܪܐ ܐܗܘܐ. 10 ܗܘ ܓܝܪ
ܕܡܬܢܩܦ ܠܗܘ ܕܠܐ ܡܐܬ. ܐܦ ܗܘ ܕܠܐ ܡܝܘܬܐ ܢܗܘܐ.
11 ܘܗܘ ܕܒܚܝܐ[b] ܡܨܛܒܐ[c]. ܚܝܐ ܢܗܘܐ. 12 ܗܢܐ ܗܝ ܪܘܚܗ
ܕܡܪܝܐ ܕܠܐ ܕܓܠܘܬܐ. ܕܡܠܦܐ ܠܒܢܝ̈ܢܫܐ ܕܢܕܥܘܢ̱
ܐܘܪܚܬܗ. 13 ܐܬܚܟܡܘ ܘܕܥܘ ܘܐܬܬܥܝܪܘ. ܗܠܠܘܝܐ.

[a] Cod. prima manu ܘܗܕܡ̈ܘܗܝ, sed ipse correxit. [b] Cod. ܕܒܚ̈ܝܐ

[c] = εὐδόκησεν (cf. Matt. iii. 17).

ODE 4.

1 ܠܐ ܐܢܫ [a]ܡܫܚܠܦ ܐܬܪܟ ܩܕܝܫܐ ܐܠܗܝ. 2 ܘܠܐ ܕܢܫܚܠܦܝܘܗܝ
ܘܢܣܝܡܝܘܗܝ ܒܐܬܪܐ ܐܚܪܢܐ. ܡܛܠ ܕܠܝܬ ܥܠܘܗܝ ܫܘܠܛܢܐ.
3 ܩܘܕܫܟ ܓܝܪ ܐܬܪܫܡܬ ܡܢ ܩܕܡ ܕܬܥܒܕ ܐܬܪ̈ܘܬܐ. 4 ܥܬܝܩܐ
ܠܐ ܢܫܬܚܠܦ. ܡܢ ܗܢܘܢ ܕܒܨܝܪܝܢ ܡܢܗ. 5 ܝܗܒܬ ܠܒܟ ܡܪܝܐ
ܠܡܗܝܡ̈ܢܝܟ. ܠܐ ܡܬܘܡ ܬܒܛܠ. ܘܠܐ ܬܗܘܐ ܕܠܐ ܦܐܪ̈ܐ.
6 ܫܥܐ ܓܝܪ ܚܕܐ ܕܗܝܡܢܘܬܟ ܡܝܬܪܐ ܡܢ ܟܠܗܘܢ
ܝܘ̈ܡܬܐ ܘܫܢ̈ܝܐ. 7 ܡܢܘ ܓܝܪ ܢܠܒܫ ܛܝܒܘܬܟ. ܘܢܬܛܠܡ.
8 ܡܛܠ ܕܚܬܡܟ ⌜ܝܕܝܥ⌝ ܗܘ. [b]ܘܝܕ̈ܥܢ ܠܗ ܒܪ̈ܝܬܟ. ܘܚܝܠ̈ܘܬܟ
⌜⌝[c]ܐܚܝܕܝܢ ܠܗ. ܘܐܦ ܡܠܐ̈ܟܐ ܓܒܝ̈ܐ ܠܒܝܫܝܢ ⌜ܗܘܘ⌝ ܠܗ. 9 ܝܗܒܬ
ܠܢ ܫܘܬܦܘܬܟ. ܠܐ ܗܘܐ ܕܣܢܝܩ ܐܢܬ ܡܢܢ. ܐܠܐ ܚܢܢ ܣܢܝܩܝܢ
ܠܟ. 10 ܪ̈ܣܣ ܥܠܝܢ ܪ̈ܣܝܣܝܟ. ܘܦܬܚ ܡܒ̈ܘܥܝܟ ܚܠ̈ܝܬܐ
ܕܡܪ̈ܕܝܢ ܠܢ ܚܠܒܐ ܘܕܒܫܐ. 11 ܠܝܬ ܓܝܪ ܬܘܬܐ ܠܘܬܟ.
ܕܬܬܘܐ ܥܠ ܡܕܡ ܕܐܫܬܘܕܝܬ. 12 ܘܚܪܬܐ ܓܠܝܐ ܗܘܬ ܠܟ.
ܘܝܗܒܬ ܓܝܪ ܕܝܗܒܬ ܡܓܢ ܝܗܒܬ. 13 ܕܠܐ ܡܫܩܠ [d]ܬܬܘܒ ܘܬܣܒ[d]
ܐܢܝܢ. 14 ܟܠ ܡܕܡ ܓܝܪ ܐܝܟ ܐܠܗܐ ܓܠܝܐ ܗܘܐ ܠܟ.
ܘܡܬܩܢ ܗܘܐ ܡܢ ܒܪܝܫܝܬ ܩܕܡܝܟ. ܘܐܢܬ ܡܪܝܐ ܥܒܕܬ
ܟܠ. ܗܠܠܘܝܐ.

[a] Perhaps ܡܫܟܚ ܕܢܫܚܠܦ [b] Cod. ܘܡܕ̈ܥܢ

[c] Charles suggests ܚܕܝܢ, 'thy hosts rejoice therein'; but the MS. is torn at the edge, and there was certainly another letter.

[d–d] Probably a double translation (? ὑποστείλῃς).

ODE 5 [= *Pistis Sophia*, pp. 113—117].

1 [a]ܡܘܕܐ ܐܢܐ[a] ܠܟ ܡܪܝܐ. ܡܛܠ ܕܪܚܡ ܐܢܐ ܠܟ. 2 ܡܪܝܡܐ
ܠܐ ܬܫܒܘܩܝܢܝ ܡܛܠ ܕܣܒܪܝ ܐܢܬ ܗܘ. 3 [b]ܡܓܢ ܢܣܒܬ[b]

[a–a] = ἐξομολογήσομαι. [b–b] = δωρεὰν ἔλαβον· cf. Matt. x. 9.

Ode 5, v. 1. The Coptic has 'for thou art my God,' instead of last clause.

[Syriac text, verses 4–12]

ODE 6 [= *Pistis Sophia*, pp. 131—135].

[Syriac text, verses 1–7]

a—a Perhaps ܕܩܘܪܒ̈ܐ (Schulthess) but I follow the MS.
b Cod. ܕܒܝܪܐ   c Cod. ܐܬܟܣܘ

Ode 5, v. 8. The Coptic expands the second clause thus: 'et vicerunt eos potentes, et quae paraverant malitiose, descenderunt in eos.'

ܪܒܐ ܘܦܬܝܐ. 8 ܫܛܦ ܓܝܪ ܠܟܠܡܕܡ ܘܬܒܪ ܘܐܝܬܝ ܠܗܝܟܠܐ.
9 ܘܠܐ ܐܫܟܚܘ ܠܡܟܠܝܘܗܝ ܟ̈ܠܝܢܐ ܕܒ̈ܢܝ ܐܢܫܐ. ܘܐܦ ܠܐ
ܐܘܡܢ̈ܘܬܗܘܢ ܕܗܢܘܢ ܕܟܠܝܢ ܡ̈ܝܐ. 10 ܐܬܬ ܓܝܪ ܥܠ ܟܠ ܐܦ̈ܝ
ܟܠܗ̇ ܚܘܪܒܐ. ܘܡܠܐ ܟܠܡܕܡ. ܘܐܫܬܝܘ ܟܠܗܘܢ [d]ܨܗ̈ܝܐ
ܕܥܠ ܚܘܪܒܐ.[d] 11 ܘܨܗܝܐ ܐܫܬܪܝ ܘܕܥܟ. ܡܢ ܡܪܘܡܐ ܓܝܪ
ܐܬܝܗܒ ܡܫܩܝܬܐ. 12 ܛܘܒܝܗܘܢ ܗܟܝܠ ܠܡܫܡܫܢܘܗܝ، ܕܗܘ
ܡܫܩܝܬܐ. ܗܢܘܢ ܕܐܬܗܝܡܢܘ ܡ̈ܝܘܗܝ، 13 ܐܢܝܚܘ ܣܦ̈ܘܬܐ
ܡ̈ܝܒܫܬܐ. ܘܨܒܝܢܐ ܕܡܫܪܐ، ܗܘܐ ܐܩܝܡܘܗ. 14 ܘܢܦܫܬܐ ܕܩܪ̈ܝܒܢ
ܗܘ، ܠܡܦܩ ܡܢ ܡܘܬܐ ܐܚܕܘ ܐܢܝܢ. 15 ܘܗܕ̈ܡܐ ܕܢܦܠܝܢ ܗܘܘ
[e]ܬܪܝܨܘ ܘܐܩܝܡܘܢ.[e] 16 ܝܗܒܘ [f]ܚܝܠܐ[f] ܠܡܐܬܝܬܗܘܢ ܘܢܘܗܪܐ

[d–d] Read ܕܥܠ ܚܘܪܒܐ ܨܗܝܐ (ἐπὶ ἐρήμῳ διψώσῃ Is. xxxv. 1) and cf. Copt. infra.

[e–e] Double translation of ἀνώρθωσαν (cf. Heb. xii. 12).

[f–f] = ἴσχυσαν (Is. xxxv. 3).

Ode 6, v. 8. I should suggest an emendation to the Syriac, ܐܫܬܝ for ܐܝܬܝ, but it is not borne out by the Coptic, which has in the Targum 'et duxit eos super templum,' and in the text 'et conversa est super templum.' 'Duxit' would answer to the Syriac ܐܝܬܝ, but an object to the verb is wanting. Probably the missing word is ܡ̈ܝܐ.

v. 9. The Coptic text suggests that a line has dropped in the Syriac: the comment has 'haud potuerunt capere eam [loca] clausa neque loca aedificata,' and the text has 'non potuerunt eum capere in locis munitis et aedificatis.'

v. 10. There seems to be a slight displacement in the Syriac; for the Coptic Targum has 'biberunt versantes in arena arida,' and the text has 'biberunt qui habitabant in arena arida.'

v. 13. The Coptic shows some variation: the comment has 'acceperunt vigorem in me hi qui sunt soluti,' and the text has 'accipiebant gaudium cordis, qui soluti erant.'

v. 16. The Syriac has παρουσία where the Coptic has παρρησία. Neither Greek word makes very easy reading. Perhaps the Greek was παρέσει αὐτῶν or παραλύσει αὐτῶν, in which case we translate 'they received strength for their paralysed state and light for their [darkened] eyes.' Cf. Is. xxxv. 3, 5.

[Syriac text, two lines, verse 17]

ODE 7.

[Syriac text of Ode 7, verses 1–16, with superscript letters a, b, c, d, e, f, g and verse numbers 1–16]

a–a = ἀκωλύτως.

b–b Apparently an attempt to translate βοηθὸν γὰρ ἔχω τὸν Κύριον.

c–c = ἀφθόνως.   d Sic cod.

e θυσία, for which Nestle proposes to read οὐσία.

f–f = ἄφθαρτος and cf. Rom. i. 23 [Syriac]

g–g = τοῖς ἰδίοις αὐτοῦ as in Joh. i. 11.

Ode 6, v. 17. The Syriac 'lived by,' answers to the Coptic 'were saved by': the Greek being ἐσώθησαν or ἐσώζοντο διὰ τοῦ ὕδατος τῆς ζωῆς.

[Syriac text, verses 17–29]

h–h = κιθάρα πολύφωνος.　　　i–i = μεγαλοπρέπεια.

ODE 8.

[Syriac text, verses 1–7]

ܕܡܪܝܐ ܥܡܟܘܢ ܗܝ. ܘܗܘ ܗܘܐ ܠܟܘܢ ܡܥܕܪܢܐ.
8 ܘܐܬܛܝܒ ܠܟܘܢ ܫܠܡܐ. ܩܕܡ ܥܕܡ ܕܢܗܘܐ ܩܪܒܟܘܢ:
9 ܫܡܥܘ ܡܠܬܐ ܕܫܪܪܐ. ܘܩܒܠܘ ܝܕܥܬܗ ܕܡܪܝܡܐ. 10 ܠܐ
ܢܕܥ ܒܣܪܟܘܢ ܡܕܡ ܕܐܡܪ ܐܢܐ ܠܟܘܢ: ܐܦ. ܠܐ [a]ܠܒܘܬܟܘܢ
ܡܕܡ ܕܡܚܘܐ ܐܢܐ ܠܟܘܢ: 11 ܛܪܘ ܐܪ̈ܙܝ، ܗܢܘܢ ܕܡܬܢܛܪܝܢ
ܒܗ. 12 ܛܪܘ ܗܝܡܢܘܬܝ، ܗܢܘܢ ܕܡܬܢܛܪܝܢ ܒܗ̇. 13 ܘܕܥܘ
ܝܕܥܬܝ، ܗܢܘܢ ܕܒܫܪܪܐ ܝܕܥܝܢ ܠܝ. 14 ܘܪܚܡܘܢܝ ܒܚܘܒܐ
ܐܝܠܝܢ ܕܪܚܡܝܢ. 15 ܠܐ ܓܝܪ ܡܗܦܟ ܐܢܐ ܐ̈ܦܝ ܡܢ ܕܝܠܝ.
16 ܡܛܠ ܕܝܕܥ ܐܢܐ ܠܗܘܢ: ܘܩܕܡ ܥܕܡ ܕܠܐ ܢܗܘܘܢ:
ܐܣܬܟܠܬ ܐܢܘܢ: ܘܦܪ̈ܨܘܦܝܗܘܢ ܐܢܐ ܚܬܡܬ ܐܢܘܢ: 17 ܐܢܐ
ܐܬܩܢܬ ܗܕ̈ܡܝܗܘܢ: ܘܬܕ̈ܝܐ ܕܝܠܝ ܛܒܥܬ ܠܗܘܢ: ܕܢܝܢܩܘܢ
ܚܠܒܐ ܩܕܝܫܐ ܕܝܠܝ ܕܢܐܚܘܢ ܒܗ. 18 ܐܨܛܒܝܬ[b] ܒܗܘܢ
ܘܠܐ ܒܗܬܬ ܐܢܐ ܒܗܘܢ: 19 ܕܝܠܝ ܓܝܪ ܥܒ̈ܕܐ ܐܝܬܝܗܘܢ
ܘܚܝܠܐ ܕܡܚܫܒܬܝ، 20 ܡܢܘ ܗܟܝܠ ܢܩܘܡ ܠܘܩܒܠ ܥܒ̈ܕܝ، ܐܘ ܡܢܘ
ܕܠܐ ܡܫܬܥܒܕ ܠܗܘܢ: 21 ܐܢܐ ܡܕܥܐ ܘܠܒܐ ܨܒܝܬ ܘܓܒܠܬ.
ܘܕܝܠܝ ܐܝܬܝܗܘܢ: ܘܡܢ ܝܡܝܢܐ ܕܝܠܝ ܣܡܬ ܠܓܒ̈ܝܝ. 22 [c]ܘܐܪܠܐ
ܩܕܡܝܗܘܢ ܙܕܝܩܘܬܝ، ܘܠܐ ܢܬܦܪܫܘܢ ܡܢ ܫܡܝ. ܡܛܠ
ܕܥܡܗܘܢ ܗܘ̣. 23 ܒܥܘ ܘ[d]ܐܣܓܘ ܘܗܘܘ ܒܪܚܡܬܗ ܕܡܪܝܐ.
24 ܘܚܒ̈ܝܒܐ ܒܚܒܝܒܐ. ܘܗܢܘܢ ܕܢܛܝܪܝܢ ܒܗܘ ܕܚܝ. 25 ܘܦܪ̈ܘܩܐ
ܒܗܘ ܕܐܬܦܪܩܘ. 26 ܘܕܠܐ ܚܒܠܐ ܬܫܬܟܚܘܢ ܒܟܠܗܘܢ
ܥܠܡ̈ܐ. ܠܫܡܗ ܕܐܒܘܟܘܢ: ܗܠܠܘܝܐ.

[a] Cod. ex errore ܠܒܘܫܟܘܢ; unless 'clothing' should mean the human body, the 'coat of skin.'

[b] = εὐδόκησα as in Matt. iii. 17.

[c] Sic cod.

[d] Cod. ܐܣܝܘ

ODE 9.

ܐܪ̈ܢ ܐܘܬܒ ܗܘ̈ܝ ... [1]

... [2]

... [3]

... [4]

... [5]

... [6]

... [7]

... [8]

... [9]

... [10] ... [11]

... [12]

... [13]

a—a = εὐαγγελίζω γὰρ ὑμῖν εἰρήνην· cf. Is. lii. 7. b Sic cod.

ODE 10.

... [1]

... [2]

... [3]

... [4]

... [5]

... [6] ... [7]

ܐܬܦܠܓܬ ᵃܒܣܘ̈ܦܝ. ܡܛܠ ܕܐܘܕܝܘ ܠܝ ܒܡܪ̈ܘܡܐ. ܘܐܬܬܣ̈ܝܡܘ
ܥܩ̈ܒܬܐ ܕܢܘܗܪܐ ܥܠ ܠܒܗܘܢ. ⁸ܘܗܠܟܘ ܒܚ̈ܝܝ ܘܐܬܦܪܩܘ
ܘܗܘܘ ܥܡܝ ܠܥܠܡܥܠܡܝܢ. ܗܠܠܘܝܐ.

ᵃ Read ܒܣܘܦܝ

ODE 11.

¹ܐܬܓܙܪ ܠܒܝ ܘܐܬܚܙܝ، ܗܦܥܗ. ܘܢܒܥ ܒܗ ܛܝܒܘܬܐ. ܘܥܒܕ
ܦܐܪ̈ܐ ܠܡܪܝܐ. ²ܓܙܪܢܝ ܓܝܪ ܥܠܝܐ ܒܪܘܚܗ ܩܕܝܫܐ.
ܘܓܠܐ ܠܘܬܗ ܟܘ̈ܠܝܬܝ. ܘܡܠܢܝ ܡܢ ܚܘܒܗ. ³ܘܗܘܬ ܠܝ
ܓܙܘܪܬܗ ܠܦܘܪܩܢܐ. ܘܪܗܛܬ ܒܐܘܪܚܐ ܒܫܠܡܗ. ܒܐܘܪܚܐ
ܕܫܪܪܐ. ⁴ܡܢ ܪܫܝܬܐ ܘܥܕܡܐ ܠܚܪܬܐ ܢܣܒܬ ܝܕܥܬܗ.
⁵ܘܐܫܬܪܪܬ ܥܠ ܟܐܦܐ ܕܫܪܪܐ. ܐܝܟܐ ܕܗܘ ܐܩܝܡܢܝ.
⁶ܘܡ̈ܝܐ ܡܡܠ̈ܠܐ ܩܪܒܘ ܠܣܦܘ̈ܬܝ، ܡܢ ܡܒܘܥܗ ܕܡܪܝܐ ܕܠܐ
ܚܣܡ. ⁷ܘܐܫܬܝܬ ܘܪܘܝܬ ܡܢ ܡ̈ܝܐ ܚ̈ܝܐ ܕܠܐ ܡ̈ܝܬܝܢ.
⁸ܘܪܘܝܬ، ܠܐ ܗܘܬ ܕܠܐ ܝܕܥܬܐ. ܐܠܐ ܫܒܩܬ ܣܪܝܩܘܬܐ.
ܘܐܬܦܢܝܬ ܠܘܬ ܡܪܝܐ ܐܠܗܝ، ⁹ܘܐܬܥܬܪܬ ܒܡܘܗܒܬܗ.
ܘܫܒܩܬ ܠܫܛܝܘܬܐ ܫܕܝܐ ܥܠ ܐܪܥܐ. ܘܫܠܚܬܗ̇ ܘܫܕܝܬܗ̇.
ܡܢܝ. ¹⁰ܘܡܪܝܐ ܚܕܬܢܝ ܒܠܒܘܫܗ ᵃܘܩܢܢܝ ܒܢܘܗܪܗ. ܘܡܢ
ܠܥܠ ܐܢܝܚܢܝ ܕܠܐ ܚܒܠ. ¹¹ܘܗܘܝܬ ܐܝܟ ܐܪܥܐ ܕܫܘܫܚܐ
ܘܪܘܙܐ ܒܦܐܪ̈ܝܗ̇. ¹²ܘܡܪܝܐ ܐܝܟ ܫܡܫܐ ܥܠ ܐܦ̈ܝܗ̇
ܕܐܪܥܐ. ¹³ܥܝ̈ܢܝ ܐܢܗܪ. ܘܦܪܨܘܦܝ ܩܒܠ ܛܠܐ. ܘܐܬܒܣܡܬ
ܢܫܡܬܝ، ܒܪܝܚܐ ܒܣܝܡܐ ܕܡܪܝܐ. ¹⁴ܘܐܘܒܠܢܝ ܠܦܪܕܝܣܗ.
ܐܝܟܐ ܕܥܘܬܪܐ ܕܒܘܣܡܗ ܕܡܪܝܐ. ¹⁵ܘܣܓܕܬ ܠܡܪܝܐ
ܡܛܠ ܫܘܒܚܗ. ܘܐܡܪܬ ܕܛܘܒܝܗܘܢ ܡܪܝܐ ܠܐܝܠܝܢ
ܕܢܨܝܒܝܢ ܒܐܪܥܟ. ܘܗܘܝܢ ܕܐܝܬ ܠܗܘܢ ܐܬܪܐ ܒܦܪܕܝܣܟ.

ᵃ We should probably read ܘܬܩܢܢܝ

16ܘܢܦܫܝܢ ܒܡܘܒܠܘܬܐ ܕܐܝܠܢܝܟ. ܘܥܒܪܘ ܡܢ ܚܫܘܟܐ ܠܢܘܗܪܐ.
17ܗܐ ܟܠܗܘܢ ܦܠܚܝܟ ܫܦܝܪܝܢ. ܕܥܒܕܝܢ ܥܒ̈ܕܐ ܛܒ̈ܐ. ܘܗܦܟܝܢ
ܡܢ ܒܝܫܘܬܐ ܠܒܣܝܡܘܬܐ ܕܝܠܟ. 18ܘܐܗܦܟܘ ܡܪܝܪܐ ܕܐܝܠܢ̈ܐ
ܡܢܗܘܢ ܟܕ ܐܬܢܨܒܘ ܒܐܪܥܐ ܕܝܠܟ. 19ܘܗܘܐ ܟܠܡܕܡ
ܐܝܟ ܫܪܟܐ ܕܝܠܟ. ܘܥܘܗܕܢܐ ܕܠܥܠܡ ܕܥܒ̈ܕܝܟ ܡܗܝܡ̈ܢܐ.
20ܣܓܝ ܗܘ ܓܝܪ ܐܬܪܐ ܒܦܪܕܝܣܟ. ܘܠܝܬ ܒܗ ܡܕܡ ܕܒܛܝܠ.
b21ܐܠܐ ܟܠܡܕܡ ܡܠܐ ܦܐܪ̈ܐ. ܫܘܒܚܐ ܠܟ ܐܠܗܐ ܒܣܘܡܐ
ܕܦܪܕܝܣܐ ܕܠܥܠܡ. ܗܠܠܘܝܐ.

[b] Sic cod.

ODE 12.

1ܡܠܢܝ ܦܬܓܡ̈ܐ ܕܫܪܪܐ. ܡܛܠ ܕܐܡܠܠ ܠܗ. 2ܘܐܝܟ ܪܕܝܐ
ܕܡ̈ܝܐ ܪܕܐ ܫܪܪܐ ܡܢ ܦܘܡܝ ܘܣܦܘܬ̈ܝ ܚ̈ܘܝ ܦܐܪ̈ܘܗܝ.
3ܘܐܣܓܝ ܒܝ ܝܕܥܬܗ ܡܛܠ ܕܦܘܡܗ ܕܡܪܝܐ ܦܬܓܡܐ ܗ̇ܘ
ܫܪܪܐ. ܘܬܪܥܐ ܕܢܘܗܪܗ. 4ܘܝܗܒܗ ܡܪܝܡܐ ܠܥܠܡ̈ܘܗܝ.
ܡܬܪ̈ܓܡܢܐ ܕܫܘܦܪܐ ܕܝܠܗ. ܘܡܬ̈ܢܝܢܐ ܕܬܫܒܘܚܬܗ.
ܘܡܘ̈ܕܝܢܐ ܕܡܚܫܒܬܗ. ܘܡܟܪ̈ܙܢܐ ܕܬܪܥܝܬܗ. ܘܡܪ̈ܕܝܢܐ
ܕܥܒ̈ܕܘܗܝ. 5ܘܩܠܝܠܘܬܗ ܓܝܪ ܕ[a]ܦܬܓܡܐ ܕܠܐ ܡܬܡܠܠܐ ܐܝܬܝܗ̇.
ܘܐܝܟ ܬܚܘܝܬܗ̇ ܗܟܢܐ ܐܦ ܩܠܝܠܘܬܗ̇ ܘܚܪܝܦܘܬܗ̇. 6ܘܪܕܗ̇ ܠܐ
ܣܘܟܐ ܐܝܬܘܗ̇ ܠܗ̇. ܘܠܐ ܡܡܬܘܡ ܢܦܠ ܐܠܐ ܡܩܘܡ
ܗ̇ܘ ܩܐܡ. ܘܠܐ ܝܕܥ [b]ܡܚܬܬܗ̇ ܐܦܠܐ ܐܘܪܚܗ̇. 7ܐܝܟ ܥܒܕܗ̇
ܗܟܢܐ [c]ܣܘܟܗ̇. ܢܘܗܪܐ ܓܝܪ ܘܕܢܚܗ̇ ܕܡܚܫܒܬܐ
ܐܝܬܘܗ̇. 8ܘܥܠܡ̈ܐ ܒܗ ܡܠܠܘ ܚܕ ܠܚܕ. ܘܗܘܘ [a]ܒܡܠܬܐ
ܗܢܘܢ ܕܫܬܝܩܝܢ ܗܘܘ. 9ܘܡܢܗ̇ ܗܘܬ ܪܚܡܘܬܐ ܘܫܘܝܘܬܐ.

[a] Apparently the Ode has two different renderings of λόγος.
[b] Sic cod. but read ܡܚܬܗ̇
[c] It would be better to read ܣܘܟܝܗ̇

ܘܡܠܠܘ ܚܕ ܠܘܬ ܚܕ ܡܕܡ ܕܐܝܬ ܗܘܐ ܠܗܘܢ܆ ܘܐܙܕܥܙܥܘ[d]
ܡܢ ܦܬܓܡܐ. [10] ܘܝܕܥܘ ܠܗܘ ܕܥܒܕ ܐܢܘܢ܆ ܒܕ ܗܘܘ
ܒܫܘܝܘܬܐ. ܡܛܠ ܕܡܠܠ ܠܗܘܢ ܦܘܡܗ ܕܡܪܝܡܐ. ܘܪܗܛܬ
ܒܐܝܕܗ ܡܦܫܩܢܘܬܗ. [11] ܡܥܡܪܐ ܓܝܪ ܕܦܬܓܡܐ ܒܪ ܐܢܫܐ
ܗܘ. ܘܫܪܪܗ ܚܘܒܐ ܗܘ. [12] ܛܘܒܝܗܘܢ ܠܐܝܠܝܢ ܕܒܝܕ ܗܢܐ
ܐܣܬܟܠܘ ܟܠ ܡܕܡ. ܘܝܕܥܘ ܠܡܪܝܐ ܒܫܪܪܗ. ܗܠܠܘܝܐ.

[d] Cod. add. in marg.

ODE 13.

[1] ܗܐ ܡܚܙܝܬܢ ܡܪܝܐ ܗܘ. ܦܬܚܘ ܥܝܢ̈ܝܐ ܘܚܙܘ ܐܢܝܢ ܒܗ.
ܘܝܠܦܘ ܐܝܟܢܐ ܐܦ̈ܝܟܘܢ܆ [2] ܘܐܡܪܘ ܬܫܒ̈ܘܚܬܐ
ܠܪܘܚܗ. ܘܫܘܘ ܨܒܬܐ ܡܢ ܐܦ̈ܝܟܘܢ܆ ܘܪܚܡܘ ܩܕܝܫܘܬܗ
ܘܠܒܫܘܗ̇. [3] ܘܬܗܘܘܢ [a]ܕܠܐ ܡܘܡܐ[a] ܒܟܠܙܒܢ ܠܘܬܗ.
ܗܠܠܘܝܐ.

a—a = ἄμωμοι.

ODE 14.

[1] ܐܝܟ ܥܝ̈ܢܘܗܝ ܕܒܪܐ ܠܐܒܘܗܝ. ܗܟܢܐ ܥܝ̈ܢܝ ܡܪܝܐ
ܒܟܠܙܒܢ ܠܘܬܟ ܐܝܬܝܗܝܢ. [2] ܡܛܠ ܕܠܘܬܟ ܐܢܘܢ ܬܕ̈ܝ.
ܘܒܘܣܡܝ. [3] ܠܐ ܬܥܒܪ ܚܢ̈ܢܝܟ ܡܢܝ ܡܪܝܐ. ܘܠܐ ܬܫܩܘܠ
ܡܢܝ ܒܣܝܡܘܬܟ. [4] ܐܘܫܛ ܠܝ ܡܪܝ، ܒܟܠܙܒܢ ܝܡܝܢܟ. ܘܡܕܒܪܢܐ
ܗܘܝ ܠܝ. ܥܕܡܐ ܠܫܘܠܡܐ ܥܠ ܨܒܝܢܟ. [5] ܐܫܦܪ ܩܕܡܝܟ
ܡܛܠ ܬܫܒܘܚܬܟ ܘܡܛܠ ܫܡܟ. [6] ܐܬܦܪܩ ܡܢ ܒܝܫܐ.
ܘܢܝܚܘܬܟ ܡܪܝܐ ܬܩܘܐ ܠܘܬܝ، ܘܦܐܪ̈ܘܗܝ، ܕܚܘܒܟ. [7] ܐܠܦܝܢܝ
ܙܡܝܪ̈ܬܐ ܕܫܪܪܟ. ܕܐܥܒܕ ܒܟ ܦܐܪ̈ܐ. [8] ܘܩܝܬܪܐ ܕܪܘܚܟ

ܩܕܝܫܐ ܦܬܘܚ ܠܝ. ܕܒܟܠ ܩܠܝܢ ܐܫܒܚܟ ܡܪܝܐ. 9ܘܐܝܟ
ܣܘܓܐܐ ܕܪ̈ܚܡܝܟ ܗܟܢܐ ܬܬܠ ܠܝ. ܘܣܪܗܒ ܠܡܬܠ ܫܐ̈ܠܬܢ
ܘܐܝܬܝܟ ܗܘ ܡܣܦܩ ܠܟܠܗܝܢ ܣܘܢ̈ܩܢܬܢ ܗܠܠܘܝܐ.

ODE 15.

1ܐܝܟܢܐ ܕܫܡܫܐ ܚܕܘܬܐ ܗܘ̇ ܠܐܝܠܝܢ ܕܒܥܝܢ ܝܘܡܗ.
ܗܟܢܐ ܚܕܘܬܝ ܡܪܝܐ ܗܘ̇. 2ܡܛܠ ܕܗܘܝܘ ܫܡܫܝ ܘܙܠܝ̈ܩܘܗܝ
ܐܩܝܡܘܢܝ. ܘܢܘܗܪܗ ܫܪܐ ܟܠ ܚܫܘܟܐ ܡܢ ܐܦ̈ܝ. 3ܥܝܢ̈ܐ
ܩܢܝܬ ܒܗ ܘܚܙܝܬ ܠܝܘܡܗ ܩܕܝܫܐ. 4ܐܕܢ̈ܐ ܗܘ̈ܝ ܠܝ
ܘܫܡܥܬ ܠܫܪܪܗ. 5ܗܘܬ ܠܝ ܡܕܥܬܐ ܕܝܕܥܬܐ. ܘܐܬܦܢܩܬ
ܒܐܝܕܗ. 6ܐܘܪܚܐ ܕܛܥܝܘܬܐ ܫܒܩܬ. ܘܐܙܠܬ ܠܘܬܗ ܘܢܣܒܬ
ܦܘܪܩܢܐ ܡܢܗ ܕܠܐ ܚܣܡܐ. 7ܘܐܝܟ ܡܘܗܒܬܗ ܝܗ̇ܒ
ܠܝ. ܘܐܝܟ [a]ܪܒܘܬ ܫܘܦܪܗ[a] ܥܒܕܢܝ. 8ܠܒܫܬ ܠܐ ܚܒܠܐ
ܒܝܕ ܫܡܗ. ܘܫܠܚܬ ܠܚܒܠܐ ܒܛܝܒܘܬܗ. 9[b]ܡܝܘܬܘܬܐ ܐܬܚܒܠ
ܡܢ ܩܕܡ ܦܪܨܘܦܝ. ܘܫܝܘܠ ܐܬܒܛܠܬ ܒܡܠܬܝ. 10ܘܣܠܩ ܒܐܪܥܗ
ܕܡܪܝܐ [c]ܚ̈ܝܐ ܕܠܐ ܡܘܬܐ[c]. 11ܘܐܬܝܕܥܘ ܠܡܗܝܡ̈ܢܘܗܝ.
ܘܐܬܝܗܒܘ ܕܠܐ ܚܘܣܪܢܐ ܠܟܠܗܘܢ ܐܝܠܝܢ ܕܬܟܝܠܝܢ ܥܠܘܗܝ.
ܗܠܠܘܝܐ.

a—a = *μεγαλοπρέπεια.* b = *τὸ θνητόν.* c—c = *ζωὴ ἀθάνατος.*

ODE 16.

1ܐܝܟܢܐ ܕܥܒܕܗ ܕܐܟܪܐ ܦܕܢܐ ܗܝ̇. ܘܥܒܕܗ ܕܩܘܒܪܢܝܛܐ
ܓܪܪܗ̇[a] ܕܐܠܦܐ. 2ܗܟܢܐ ܐܦ ܥܒܕܝ ܡܙܡܘܪܐ ܗܘ̇ ܕܡܪܝܐ
ܒܬܫܒ̈ܘܚܬܗ. ܐܘܡܢܘܬܝ ܘܦܘܠܚܢܝ ܒܬܫܒ̈ܘܚܬܗ ܐܝܬ. 3ܡܛܠ
ܕܚܘܒܗ ܬܪܣܝ ܠܠܒܝ ܘܥܕܡܐ ܠܣܦܘ̈ܬܝ ܢܦܩܐ ܗܘܐ ܦܐܪ̈ܘܗܝ.

[a] Schulthess emends to ܕܒܪܗ̇

4ܣܘܥܪܢ ܓܝܪ ܡܪܝܐ ܗܘ. ܡܡܠܠܢܐ ܐܡܪܢ ܠܗ. 5ܡܚܒܝܠ ܐܢܐ
ܓܝܪ ܒܬܫܒܘܚܬܗ. ܘܡܫܡܫܘܬܐ ܐܝܬ ܠܝ ܒܗ. 6ܐܬܦܬܚ ܦܘܡܝ
ܘܬܬܡܠܠ ܒܗ ܪܘܚܗ. 7ܬܫܒܘܚܬܗ ܕܡܪܝܐ ܘܐܝܩܪܗ. ܒܥܒܕܐ
ܕܐܝ̈ܕܘܗܝ، ܘܦܘܠܚܢܐ ܕܨܒ̈ܥܬܗ. 8ܠܣܘܓܐܐ ܕܪ̈ܚܡܘܗܝ،
ܘܠܚܘܣܢܐ ܕܡܠܬܗ. 9ܡܠܬܗ ܓܝܪ ܕܡܪܝܐ ܒܨܝܐ ܡܕܡ
ܕܠܐ ܡܬܚܙܝܐ ܘܓܠܝܐ ܡܚܫܒܬܗ. 10ܚܙܝܐ ܓܝܪ ܥܝܢܐ
ܥܒ̈ܕܘܗܝ، ܘܐܕܢܐ ܫܡܥܐ ܠܡܚܫܒܬܗ. 11ܗܘ ܐܦܫܬ، ܠܐܪܥܐ
ܘܐܬܒ ܡ̈ܝܐ ܒܝܡܐ. 12ܡܬܚ ܫܡܝܐ ܘܐܬܩܢ ܟܘ̈ܟܒܐ.
ܘܐܬܩܢ ܠܒܪܝܬܐ ܘܐܩܝܡܗ̇. 13ܘܐܬܬܢܝܚ ܗܘ ܡܢ ܥܒ̈ܕܘܗܝ.
14ܘܒܪ̈ܝܬܐ ܒܪ̈ܗܛܝܗܘܢ ܪ̈ܗܛܝܢ. ܘܥܒ̈ܕܝܗܘܢ ܥܒ̈ܕܝܢ. 15ܘܠܐ
ܝܕܥܝܢ ܠܡܩܡ ܘܠܡܒܛܠ. ܘܚܝ̈ܠܘܬܗ ܡܫܬܥܒ̈ܕܝܢ ܠܡܠܬܗ.
16ܣܝܡܬܐ ܕܢܘܗܪܐ ܫܡܫܐ ܗܘ. ܣܝܡܬܐ ܕܚܫܘܟܐ ܠܠܝܐ
ܗܘ. 17ܥܒܕ ܕܝܢ ܫܡܫܐ ܠܐܝܡܡܐ ܕܢܗܘܐ ܢܗܝܪ. ܠܠܝܐ ܕܝܢ
ܠܚܫܘܟܐ ܠܠܝܐ ܥܠ ܐܦ̈ܘܗ̇ ܕܐܪܥܐ. 18ܘܫܘܚܠܦܗܘܢ ܕܚܕ
ܡܢ ܚܕ ܡܫܡܠܝܢ ܫܘܦܪܗ ܕܐܠܗܐ. 19ܘܠܝܬ ܡܕܡ ܕܠܒܪ ܡܢ
ܡܪܝܐ. ܡܛܠ ܕܗܘ ܐܝܬܘܗܝ، ܗܘܐ ܡܢ ܩܕܡ ܕܟܠ ܢܗܘܐ.
20ܘܥܠܡ̈ܐ ܒܡܠܬܗ ܗܘܘ. ܘܒܡܚܫܒܬܐ ܕܠܒܗ. ܬܫܒܘܚܬܐ
ܘܐܝܩܪܐ ܠܫܡܗ. ܗܠܠܘܝܐ.

ODE 17.

1ܐܬܥܛܪܬ ܕܝܢ ܒܐܠܗܝ. ܟܠܝܠܝ ܚܝܐ ܗܘ. 2ܘܐܙܕܕܩܬ ܒܡܪܝ.
ܦܘܪܩܢܝ ܕܝܢ ܕܠܐ ܚܒܠܐ ܗܘ. 3ܐܫܬܪܝܬ ܠܝ ܡܢ ܣܪ̈ܝܩܘܬܐ
ܘܠܐ ܐܝܬܝ، ܡܚܝܒܐ. 4ܚܢ̈ܩܝ ܐܬܦܣܩܘ ܒܐܝ̈ܕܘܗܝ. ܐܦ̈ܐ
ܘܕܡܘܬܐ ܕܦܪ̈ܨܘܦܐ ܚܕܬܐ ܢܣܒܬ. ܘܗܠܟܬ ܒܗ ܘܐܬܦܪܩܬ.
5ܘܡܚܫܒܬܐ ܕܫܪܪܐ ܕܒܪܬܢܝ. ܘܐܙܠܬ ܒܬܪܗ̇ ܘܠܐ ܛܥܝܬ.

[6]ܘܟܠ ܕܚܙܐܘܢܝ ܐܬܕܡܪܘ. ܘܐܝܟ ܢܘܟܪܝܐ ܐܬܚܫܒܬ ܠܗܘܢ܂
[7]ܘܗܘ ܕܝܕܥ ܗܘܐ [a] ܘܪܒܢܝ ܡܪܝܡܐ ܒܟܠܗ ܫܘܡܠܝܗ. ܘܫܒܚܢܝ
ܒܒܣܝܡܘܬܗ. ܘܐܪܝܡ ܠܡܕܥܝ ܕܫܪܪܐ ܡܢܗ. [8]ܘܡܢ ܬܡܢ
ܝܗܒ ܠܝ ܐܘܪܚܐ ܕܡܠܟܘܗܝ ܘܦܬܚܬ ܬܪ̈ܥܐ ܕܐܚܝܕܝܢ ܗܘܘ.
[9]ܘܬܒܪܬ ܡܘܫ̈ܠܐ ܕܦܪܙܠܐ. ܦܪܙܠܐ ܕܝܢ [b]ܕܝܠܝ ܫܚܢ[b]. ܘܐܬܦܫܪ
ܩܕܡܝ. [10]ܘܠܐ ܡܕܡ ܐܬܚܙܝ ܠܝ ܟܕ ܐܚܝܕ. ܡܛܠ ܕܦܬܚܐ
ܕܟܠܡܕܡ ܐܢܐ ܐܝܬܝ ܗܘܝܬ. [11]ܘܐܙܠܬ ܗܘܝܬ ܥܠ ܟܠܗܘܢ
[c]ܐܣܝܪ̈ܝ ܠܡܫܪܝܘ ܐܢܘܢ. ܕܠܐ ܐܫܒܘܩ ܠܐܢܫ ܟܕ ܐܣܝܪ
ܘܐܣܘܪ. [12]ܘܝܗܒܬ ܝܕܥܬܝ ܕܠܐ ܚܣܡ. ܘܒܥܘܬܝ ܒܚܘܒܐ
ܕܝܠܝ. [13]ܘܙܪܥܬ ܒܠܒ̈ܘܬܐ ܦܐܪ̈ܝ. ܘܫܚܠܦܬ ܐܢܘܢ ܒܝ. ܘܩܒܠܘ
ܒܘܪܟܬܐ ܕܝܠܝ ܘܚܝܘ. [14]ܘܐܬܟܢܫܘ ܠܘܬܝ ܘܐܬܦܪܩܘ. ܡܛܠ
ܕܗܘܘ ܠܝ ܗܕ̈ܡܐ ܘܐܢܐ ܪܫܗܘܢ. [15]ܫܘܒܚܐ ܠܟ ܪܫܢ
ܡܪܢ ܡܫܝܚܐ. ܗܠܠܘܝܐ.

[a] B.-L. suggest that ܠܝ should be added.
[b—b] Something wrong here: perhaps ܕܠܗ ܘܪܬܚ
[c] Marg. ܐܚܝܕ̈ܝ . ܢܣ i.e. one copy reads ܐܚܝܕ̈ܝ instead of ܐܣܝܪ̈ܝ

ODE 18.

[1]ܐܬܬܪܝܡ ܠܒܝ ܒܚܘܒܗ ܕܡܪܝܡܐ ܘܐܬܬܪ. ܕܐܫܒܚܝܘܗܝ
ܒܫܡܗ. [2]ܐܬܚܝܠܘ ܗܕ̈ܡܝ ܐܝܟ ܕܠܐ ܢܦܠܘܢ ܡܢ ܚܝܠܗ.
[3]ܟܘܪ̈ܗܢܐ ܐܬܪܚܩܘ ܡܢ ܦܓܪܝ. ܘܩܡ ܠܡܪܝܐ ܒܨܒܝܢܗ. ܡܛܠ
ܕܫܪܝܪܐ ܗܝ ܡܠܟܘܬܗ. [4]ܡܪܝܐ ܕܠܡܐ ܡܛܠ ܐܝܠܝܢ ܕܚܣܝܪܝܢ
ܬܫܕܐ ܡܢܟ ܡܠܬܟ. [5]ܐܦܠܐ ܡܛܠ ܥܒ̈ܕܝܗܘܢ. ܬܟܠܐ
ܡܢ ܛܒܘܬܟ. [6]ܠܐ ܢܙܕܟܐ ܢܘܗܪܐ ܡܢ ܚܫܘܟܐ. ܐܦ ܠܐ
[a]ܢܥܪܘܩ ܫܪܪܐ ܡܢ ܕܓܠܘܬܐ. [7]ܠܙܟܘܬܐ ܬܣܝܡ ܝܡܝܢܟ. ܦܘܪܩܢ ܡܚܝܠܝܢ.
ܘܬܩܒܠ ܡܢ ܟܠ ܐܬܪ. [8]ܘܬܛܪ [b]ܠܟܠ ܡܢ[b] ܕܒܒܝܫܬܐ ܐܚܝܕ.

[a] Cod. ܢܥܘܪܩ [b—b] Cod. ܡܢ ܠܟܠ

⁹ܐܢܬ ܐܠܗܝ܆ ܕܓܠܘܬܐ ܘܡܘܬܐ ܠܝܬ ܒܦܘܡܟ. ¹⁰ܐܠܐ
ܐܝܬܘܗܝ܆ ܫܘܡܠܝܐ ܨܒܝܢܟ. ܘܣܪܝܩܘܬܐ ܠܐ ܝܕܥ ܐܢܬ.
¹¹ܡܛܠ ܕܐܦܠܐ ⌜ܗܘ⌝ ܝܕܥܐ ܠܟ. ¹²ܘܠܐ ܝܕܥ ܐܢܬ ܠܛܥܝܘܬܐ.
¹³ܐܠܐ ܡܛܠ ܕܐܦ ܠܐ ܗܘ ܝܕܥܐ ܠܟ. ¹⁴ܘܐܬܚܫܒܬ ܐܝܟ
ܒܘܪܐ ܠܐ ܝܕܥܬܐ. ܘܐܝܟ ܣܪܝܩܘܬܗ ܕܡܟܐ. ¹⁵ܘܣܓ̈ܪܘ ܚܠܬܗ̇
ܣܪܝܩܐ ܕܝܪܒܐ ܗ̇ܝ܆ ¹⁶ܘܐܬܘ ܐܦ ܗܘܘ ܐܝܟ ܕܡܘܬܗ̇
ܘܐܬܚܡܪܘ. ܘܝܕܥܘ ܐܝܠܝܢ ܕܝܕܥܝܢ ܘܐܬܚܫܒܘ ¹⁷ܘܠܐ ܐܬܛܢܦܘ
ܒܡܚܫܒܬܗܘܢ܆ ܡܛܠ ܕܗܘܘ ܒܪܥܝܢܗ ܕܡܪܝܐ. ¹⁸ܘܓܚܟܘ
ܥܠ ܐܝܠܝܢ ܕܡܗܠܟܝܢ ܗܘܘ ܒܛܥܝܘܬܐ. ¹⁹ܘܗܘܘ ܕܝܢ ܡܠܠܘ
ܫܪܪܐ ܡܢ ܢܦܚܐ ܕܢܦܚ ܒܗܘܢ ܡܪܝܡܐ. ܬܫܒܘܚܬܐ ܘܪܒܘܬ
ܐܝܩܪܬܐ ܠܫܡܗ. ܗܠܠܘܝܐ.

ODE 19.

¹ܟܣܐ ܕܚܠܒܐ ܐܬܩܪܒ ܠܝ. ܘܐܫܬܝܬܗ ܒܚܠܝܘܬܐ
ܕܒܣܝܡܘܬܗ ܕܡܪܝܐ. ²ܒܪܐ ܟܣܐ ܐܝܬܘܗܝ܆ ܘܗ̇ܘ ܕܐܬܚܠܒ
ܐܒܐ. ³ܘܚܠܒܬܗ ܪܘܚܐ ܕܩܘܕܫܐ. ܡܛܠ ܕܬܕ̈ܘܗܝ܆ ܐܬܡܠܝܘ.
ᵃܘܠܗ ܡܬܒܥܐ ܗܘܐ ܕܡܫܬܦܥܐܝܬ ܢܫܬܕܪܐ ܚܠܒܗ. ⁴ܦܬܚܬ
ܥܘܒܗ̇ ܪܘܚܐ ܕܩܘܕܫܐ ܘܡܙܓܬ ܚܠܒܐ ܕܬܪܝܢ ܬܕ̈ܘܗܝ
ܕܐܒܐ. ܘܝܗܒܬ ܚܘܠܛܢܐ ܠܥܠܡܐ ܟܕ ܠܐ ܝܕܥܝܢ. ⁵ܘܗܠܝܢ
ܕܢܣܒܝܢ ܒܫܘܡܠܝܗ̇ ܐܝܠܝܢ ܕܒܝܡܝܢܐ. ᵇ⁶ܓܦܬ ܟܪܣܗ̇ ܕܒܬܘܠܬܐ
ܘܩܒܠܬ ܒܛܢܐ ܘܝܠܕܬ. ܘܗܘܬ ܐܡܐ ܒܬܘܠܬܐ ܒܪ̈ܚܡܐ
ܣܓ̈ܝܐܐ. ⁷ܘܚܒܠܬ ܘܝܠܕܬ ܒܪܐ ܕܠܐ ܟܐܒ ܠܗ̇. ⁸ܘܡܛܠ

ᵃ Cod. ܘܠܐ. Diettrich and Flemming retain the MS. reading.

ᵇ Barnes suggests ܟܪܗܬ, which might answer to the 'infirmatus est' of Lactantius: but query, as the passage would still be unintelligible. Batiffol-Labourt suggest an original ἐπέπτη. Cf. Gen. i. 2: in which case we should have to add ܥܠ before ܟܪܣܗ̇.

ܕܠܐ ܗܘܐ ܡܣܥܘܪܢܝܬܐ ܗܘܬ. ܘܠܐ ܒܥܬ ܚܝܠܐ ܡܛܠ
ܕܐܝܠܝܗ̇. ܐܝܟ ܓܒܪܐ ܝܠܕܬ ܒܨܒܝܢܐ. ⁹ܘܝܠܕܬ ܒܬܘܚܝܬܐ.
ܘܩܢܬ ܒܐܘܚܕܢܐ ܣܓܝܐܐ. ¹⁰ܘܐܚܒܬ ܒܦܘܪܩܢܘܬܐ.ᶜ ܘܢܛܪܬ
ܒܒܣܝܡܘܬܐ. ܘܚܘܝܬ ܒܪܒܘܬܐ. ܗܠܠܘܝܐ.

[c] Cod. ܒܦܘܪܩܢܐ

ODE 20.

¹ܟܗܢܐ ܕܡܪܝܐ ܐܢܐ. ܘܠܗ ܗܘ ܡܟܗܢ ܐܢܐ. ܘܠܗ
ܡܩܪܒ ܐܢܐ ܩܘܪܒܢܐ ܕܡܚܫܒܬܗ. ²ܠܐ ܗܘܬ ܓܝܪ ܐܝܟ
ܥܠܡܐ. ܐܦܠܐ ܐܝܟ ܒܣܪܐ ܡܚܫܒܬܗ. ܐܦܠܐ ܐܝܟ ܗܢܘܢ
ܕܦܠܚܝܢ ܒܣܪܢܐܝܬ. ³ܩܘܪܒܢܗ ܕܡܪܝܐ ܙܕܝܩܘܬܐ ܗ̄ܝ.
ܘܕܟܝܘܬܐ ܕܠܒܐ ܘܕܣܦ̈ܘܬܐ. ⁴ܩܪܒ ܟܘ̈ܠܝܬܟ ܕܠܐ ܡܘܡܐ.
ܘܪ̈ܚܡܝܟ ܠܐ ܢܐܠܨܘܢ ܪ̈ܚܡܐ. ܘܢܦܫܟ ܠܐ ܬܐܠܘܨ
ܢܦܫܐ. ⁵ܠܐ ܬܩܢܐ ܢܘܟܪܝܐ ᵃܒܕܡܝܐ ܕܢܦܫܟᵃ. ܘܐܦܠܐ
ܬܒܥܐ ܠܓܝܒܠ ܠܚܒܪܟ. ⁶ܘܐܦܠܐ ܬܫܪܘܩܝܘܗܝ، ܠܬܟܣܝܬܐ
ܕܦܘܪܣܢܗ. ⁷ܠܒܫ ܕܝܢ ܒܛܝܒܘܬܗ ܕܡܪܝܐ ܕܠܐ ܚܣܡܐ.
ܘܬܐ ܠܦܪܕܝܣܐ ܘܥܒܕ ܠܟ ܟܠܝܠܐ ܡܢ ܐܝܠܢܗ. ⁸ܘܣܝܡ ܥܠ
ܪܫܟ ܘܐܬܒܣܡ. ܘܐܣܬܡܟ ܥܠ ܢܝܚܘܬܗ ܘܬܗܘܐ
ܡܕܡܝܢ ܬܫܒܘܚܬܐ. ⁹ܘܬܩܒܠ ܡܢ ܒܣܝܡܘܬܗ ܘܡܢ
ܒܛܝܒܘܬܗ. ܘܬܗܕܪ ܒܪܝܪܐ ܠܬܫܒܘܚܬܐ ܕܩܕܝܫܘܬܗ.
ܬܫܒܘܚܬܐ ܘܐܝܩܪܐ ܠܫܡܗ. ܗܠܠܘܝܐ.

[a—a] The MS. has ܕܡܟܐ ܕܢܦܫܟ, which is clearly corrupt: but ܢܦܫܟ is repeated by an eye-error from the previous line, and the correction of ܕܡܟܐ to ܕܡܝܐ is obvious and easy.

ODE 21.

1 ܐܝ̈ܕܝ ܐܪܝܡܬ ܠܪܘܡܐ. ܠܚܢܢܗ ܕܡܪܝܐ ܡܛܠ ܕܐܣܘܪ̈ܝ
ܫܪܐ ܡܢܝ. ܘܐܪܝܡܢܝ ܡܥܕܪܢܝ ܠܚܢܢܗ ܘܠܦܘܪܩܢܗ. 2 ܘܫܠܚܬ
ܚܫܘܟܐ ܘܠܒܫܬ ܢܘܗܪܐ. 3 ܘܗܘܘ ܠܝ ܗܕ̈ܡܐ ܠܘܬ ܢܦܫܝ.
ܕܒ ܠܝܬ[a] ܒܗܘܢ ܟܐܒܐ. ܐܦܠܐ ܐܘܠܨܢܐ ܐܦܠܐ
ܚ̈ܫܐ. 4 ܘܬܪܥܝܬ ܡܥܕܪܢܝܬܐ ܗܘܬ ܠܝ ܡܫܘܬܦܘܬܗ ܕܡܪܝܐ.
ܘܫܘܬܦܘܬܗ ܕܠܐ ܚܒܠܐ. 5 ܘܐܬܬܪܝܡܬ ܒܢܘܗܪܐ ܘܥܒܪܬ
ܩܕܡ ܐܦ̈ܘܗܝ. 6 ܘܗܘܝܬ ܩܪܝܒ ܐܢܐ ܠܗ ܟܕ ܡܫܒܚ ܐܢܐ
ܘܡܘܕܐ ܐܢܐ ܠܗ. 7 ܐܪܒܝ ܠܒܝ ܘܐܫܬܟܚ ܒܦܘܡܝ. ܘܕܢܚ
ܥܠ ܣܦ̈ܘܬܝ. ܘܪܒ ܥܠ ܐܦ̈ܝ ܕܘܨܗ ܕܡܪܝܐ. ܘܫܘܒܚܬܗ.
ܗܠܠܝܐ.

[a] Cod. ܐܝܬ

ODE 22 [= *Pistis Sophia*, pp. 154—160].

1 ܗܘ ܕܡܚܬ ܠܝ ܡܢ ܪܘܡܐ ܘܡܣܩ ܠܝ ܡܢ ܬܚܬܝ̈ܬܐ.
2 ܘܗܘ ܕܡܟܢܫ ܡܨܥ̈ܝܬܐ ܘܪܡܐ[a] ܠܝ. 3 ܗܘ ܕܒܕܪ ܠܒܥܠܕܒ̈ܒܝ
ܘܒܥ̈ܠܝ ܕܝܢܝ. 4 ܗܘ ܕܝܗܒ ܠܝ ܫܘܠܛܢܐ ܕܐܣܘܪ̈ܐ ܐܝܟܢ
ܕܐܫܪܐ ܐܢܘܢ. 5 ܗܘ ܕܣܚܦ ܒܐܝ̈ܕܝ ܠܬܢܝܢܐ ܕܫܒܥܐ
ܪ̈ܝܫܘܗܝ. ܘܐܘܩܡܬܢܝ ܥܠ ܥܩ̈ܪܘܗܝ ܕܐܘܒܕ ܙܪܥܗ. 6 ܐܢܬ
ܗܘܝܬ ܬܡܢ ܘܥܕܪܬܢܝ. ܘܒܟܠ ܐܬܪ ܫܡܟ ܒܪܝܟ ܗܘܐ
ܠܝ. 7 ܚܒܠܬ ܝܡܝܢܟ [b]ܠܡܪܬܗ ܒܝܫܬܐ.[b] ܘܐܫܘܝܬ ܐܘܪܚܟ
ܐܘܪܚܐ ܠܗܠܝܢ ܕܡܗܝܡܢܝܢ ܒܟ. 8 [c]ܘܓܒܝܬ ܐܢܘܢ ܡܢ
ܩܒܪ̈ܐ. ܘܦܪܫܬ ܐܢܘܢ ܡܢ ܡܝ̈ܬܐ. 9 ܢܣܒܬ ܓܪ̈ܡܐ

[a] l. ܘܪܕܐ. Cf. Copt. *et docuit me*.
[b—b] Copt. *venenum hujus qui dicit* [*malum*]. [c] Copt. *liberasti*.

Ode 22. In v. 6 the Coptic 'in omni loco circumdedit me nomen tuum' requires, as Schulthess points out, that we should emend ܒܪܝܟ to ܟܪܝܟ. So too Diettrich.

ODE 23.

[Syriac text, verses 1–10]

Ode 22, v. 12. Here the Coptic texts have gone astray, under the influence of the Gnosticism in the mind of the writer, who brings in the 'light' from the story of Pistis Sophia. The text of Schwartze is 'et uti lumen sit duplicatum iis omnibus'; and the Gnostic Targum is 'ut tuum lumen sit in iis omnibus.' But Petermann notes that for 'duplicatum' we should read 'fundamentum.' This brings the text nearer to the Syriac, which may be taken as correct in these concluding sentences. The Coptic 'opulentiam' for the Syriac 'kingdom' is an error which Schmidt has corrected in his German translation.

(Syriac text, verses 11–20)

---

^a Barnes suggests ܐܕܐ, as if ܪܥܝ were repeated from the previous word.

ODE 24.

(Syriac text, verses 1–5)

---

^a = ἐπέπτη, cf. Gen. i. 3 (ܝܘܢܐ)   ^b Cod. ܐܬܚܙܝܘ

^c Cod. ܐܢ ut videtur.

ܕܐܝܬܝܗܘܢ ܗܘܘ ܡܢ ܠܩܘܕܡ. 6 ܘܥܡܠܘ ܓܝܪ ܡܢ ܒܪܫܝܬ.
ܘܫܘܠܡܐ ܕܥܡܠܗܘܢ ܐܝܬܘܗܝ ܗܘܐ ܚܝ̈ܐ. 7 ܘܐܒ̣ܕ ܡܢܗܘܢ
ܟܠ[d] ܕܚܣܝܪ ܗܘܐ. ܡܛܠ ܕܠܝܬ ܗܘܐ ܠܡܬܠ ܦܬܓܡܐ
ܐܝܟ ܕܢܩܘܘܢ܀. 8 ܘܡܪܝܐ ܡܚܫܒ̈ܬܐ ܐܘܒܕ. ܕܟܠܗܘܢ
ܐܝܠܝܢ ܕܠܝܬ ܠܘܬܗܘܢ ܫܪܪܐ. 9 ܚܣܪܘ ܓܝܪ ܡܢ ܚܟܡܬܐ
ܗܢܘܢ ܕܡܬܬܪܝܡܝܢ ܗܘܘ ܒܠܒܗܘܢ ܘܐܣܬܠܝܘ. ܡܛܠ
ܕܠܝܬ ܗܘܐ ܠܘܬܗܘܢ ܫܪܪܐ. 10 ܡܛܠ ܕܡܪܝܐ ܚܘܝ ܐܘܪܚܗ.
ܘܐܦܬܝ ܛܝܒܘܬܗ. ܘܗܢܘܢ ܕܐܫܬܘܕܥܘܗ̇. ܝ̇ܕܥܝܢ ܩܕܝܫܘܬܗ.
ܗܠܠܘܝܐ.

[d] Cod. ܕܟܠ

ODE 25 [= *Pistis Sophia*, pp. 148—153].

1 ܐܬܦܨܝܬ ܡܢ ܐܣܘܪ̈ܝ. ܘܠܘܬܟ ܥܪܩܬ ܐܠܗܝ. 2 ܡܛܠ
ܕܗܘ̇ܝܬ ܝܡܝܢܐ ܕܦܘܪܩܢܐ ܘܡܥܕܪܢܐ ܕܝܠܝ. 3 ܟܠܝܬ ܠܐܝܠܝܢ
ܕܩܝܡܝܢ ܠܘܩܒܠܝ. 4 ܘܬܘܒ ܠܐ ܐ̇ܚܝܘܗܝ. ܡܛܠ ܕܦܪ̈ܨܘܦܟ
ܥܡܝ ܗܘܐ ܗ̇ܘ ܕܦ̣ܪܩ ܗܘܐ ܠܝ ܒܛܝܒܘܬܟ. 5 ܐܬܒܣܪܬ
ܕܝܢ ܘܐܣܬܠܝܬ ܒܥܝ̈ܢܝ ܣܓ̈ܝܐܐ. ܘܗܘܝܬ ܒܥܝ̈ܢܝܗܘܢ ܐܝܟ
ܐܒܪܐ. 6 ܘܗܘܝܬ ܠܝ ܚܝܠܐ ܡܢ ܠܘܬܟ. ܘܡܥܕܪܢܐ. 7 ܫܪܓܐ
ܣܡܬ ܠܝ ܡܢ ܝܡܝܢܐ ܘܡܢ ܣܡܠܐ. ܘܠܐ ܢܗܘܐ ܒܝ ܡܕܡ
ܕܠܐ ܢܗܝܪܐ. 8 ܘܐܬܟܣܝܬ ܒܬܟܣܝܬܐ ܕܪܘܚܟ. ܘܐܪܚܩܬ
ܡܢܝ ܠܒ̈ܘܫܐ ܕܡܫ̈ܟܐ. 9 ܡܛܠ ܕܝܡܝܢܟ ܐܪܝܡܬܢܝ. ܘܐܥܒܪܬ
ܟܘܪܗܢܐ ܡܢܝ. 10 ܘܗܘܝܬ ܚܝܠܬܢܐ ܒܫܪܪܐ ܘܩܕܝܫܐ ܒܙܕܝܩܘܬܟ.

Ode 25, v. 7. B.-L. read ܕܠܐ for ܘܠܐ

v. 8. Copt. 'et texisti me sub umbra gratiae tuae et superavi vestimenta pellicea.'

ܘܕܚܝܠܗ ܡܢܝ ܟܠܗܘܢ ܕܠܘܩܒܠܝ. 11ܘܗܘܝܬ [a]ܕܡܫܝܚܐ ܒܫܡܗ
ܕܡܪܝܐ. 12ܘܐܙܕܕܩܬ ܒܡܫܝܢܘܬܗ ܘܢܝܚܗ ܠܥܠܡܥܠܡܝܢ ܗܘ.
ܗܠܠܘܝܐ.

[a] Cod. ܕܡܪܝܐ

ODE 26.

1[a]ܐܢܒܥܬ ܬܫܒܘܚܬܐ ܠܡܪܝܐ ܡܛܠ ܕܕܝܠܗ ܐܢܐ. 2ܘܐܡܠܠ
ܙܡܪܬܐ ܩܕܝܫܬܐ ܕܝܠܗ. ܡܛܠ ܕܠܒܝ ܠܘܬܗ ܗܘ. 3ܟܢܪܗ
ܓܝܪ ܒܐܝܕܝ. ܘܠܐ ܢܫܠܝܢ ܙܡܪ̈ܬܐ ܕܢܝܚܗ. 4ܐܩܥܐ ܠܘܬܗ
ܡܢ ܟܠܗ ܠܒܝ. ܐܫܒܚ ܘܐܪܘܡܡܝܘܗܝ، ܡܢ ܟܠܗܘܢ ܗܕܡܝ.
5ܡܢ ܡܕܢܚܐ ܓܝܪ ܘܥܕܡܐ ܠܡܥܪܒܐ ܬܫܒܘܚܬܐ ܕܝܠܗ ܗܝ.
6ܘܡܢ ܬܝܡܢܐ ܘܥܕܡܐ ܠܓܪܒܝܐ ܕܝܠܗ ܗܝ، ܬܘܕܝܬܐ. 7ܘܡܢ
ܪܝܫܐ ܕܪ̈ܘܡܐ ܘܥܕܡܐ ܠܣܘܦܗܘܢ ܥܒܕܘܗܝ ܕܝܠܗ ܗܝ.
8ܡܢܘ ܕܟܬܒ ܙܡܪ̈ܬܗ ܕܡܪܝܐ. ܐܘ ܡܢܘ ܕܩܪܐ ܠܗܝܢ.
9ܐܘ ܡܢܘ ܕܪܕܐ ܢܦܫܗ ܠܚܝ̈ܐ. ܕܬܬܦܪܩ ܢܦܫܗ. 10ܐܘ ܡܢܘ
ܕܡܬܬܢܝܚ ܥܠ ܡܪܝܡܐ. ܕܢܡܠܠ ܡܢ ܦܘܡܗ. 11ܡܢܘ ܡܫܟܚ
ܕܢܦܫܘܩ ܬܕܡܪ̈ܬܗ ܕܡܪܝܐ. 12ܡܛܠ ܓܝܪ ܗܘ ܕܡܬܦܫܩ
ܢܫܬܪܐ. ܘܢܗܘܐ ܗܘ ܕܡܬܦܫܩ. 13ܣܦܩ ܓܝܪ ܠܡܕܥ
ܘܠܡܬܬܢܝܚܘ. ܡܙܡܪ̈ܢܐ ܓܝܪ ܩܝܡܝܢ ܒܫܝܢܐ. 14ܐܝܟ ܢܗܪܐ
ܕܐܝܬ ܠܗ ܡܒܘܥܐ ܣܓܝܐܐ. ܘܪܕܐ ܠܡܥܕܪܢܐ ܕܐܝܠܝܢ ܕܒܥܝܢ
ܠܗ. ܗܠܠܘܝܐ.

[a] Charles suggests ܐܒܥ (I will pour), which is an improvement.

ODE 27.

1ܦܫܛܬ ܐܝܕܝ، ܘܩܕܫܬ ܠܡܪܝ. 2ܡܛܠ ܕܦܫܝܛܘܬܐ ܕܐܝܕܝ، ܐܬܗ
ܗܝ. 3ܘܦܫܝܛܘܬܝ، ܩܝܣܐ ܕܬܪܝܨ. ܗܠܠܘܝܐ.

Ode 25, v. 10. Copt. 'remoti sunt.' l. ܐܬܪܚܩܘ
v. 11. Copt. om.

ODE 28.

¹ܐܝܟ [a]ܓ̈ܦܐ ܕܝܘ̈ܢܐ [b]ܥܠ ܦܪ̈ܘܓܝܗܘܢ[b]. ܘܦܘܡܐ ܕܦܪ̈ܘܓܝܗܘܢ
ܠܘܬ ܦܘ̈ܡܝܗܘܢ. ²ܗܟܢܐ ܐܦ ܓ̈ܦܐ ܕܪܘܚܐ ܥܠ ܠܒܝ. ³ܡܬܒܣܡ
ܠܒܝ ܘܕܐܨ. ܐܝܟ ܥܘܠܐ ܕܕܐܨ ܒܟܪܣܐ ܕܐܡܗ. ⁴ܗܝܡܢܬ.
ܡܛܠ ܗܢܐ ܐܬܬܢܝܚܬ. ܡܛܠ ܕܡܗܝܡܢ ܗܘ ܗܘ ܕܗܝܡܢܬ
ܒܗ. ⁵ܡܒܪܟܘ ܒܪܟܢܝ. ܘܪܫܝ ܠܘܬܗ ܗܘ. ܘܚܪܒܐ ܠܐ ܬܦܠܓܢܝ
ܡܢܗ. ܐܦ ܠܐ ܣܦܣܝܪܐ. ⁶ܡܛܠ [c]ܕܛܝܒܬ ܡܢ ܩܕܡ ܕܢܗܘܐ
ܐܒܕܢܐ. ܘܐܬܬܣܝܡܬ ܒܟܢ̈ܦܘܗܝ ܕܠܐ ܚܒܠܐ. ⁷ܘܢܦܫܘ
ܚܝ̈ܐ ܕܠܐ ܡܘܬܐ ܘܢܫܩܘܢܝ. ܘܡܢܗܘܢ ܐܝܬܝܗ̇ ܪܘܚܐ ܒܝ.
ܘܠܐ ܡܡܝܬܐ ܠܡܡܬ. ܡܛܠ ܕܚܝܐ ܗܝ. ⁸ܐܬܕܡܪܘ ܐܝܠܝܢ
ܕܚܙܘ ܗܘܘ ܠܝ. ܡܛܠ ܕܐܬܪܕܦܬ. ܘܣܓܝܘ ܕܐܬܓܠܝܬ ܠܝ.
ܡܛܠ ܕܐܬܚܫܒܬ ܠܗܘܢ ܐܝܟ ܚܕ ܡܢ ܐܒ̈ܕܢܐ. ⁹ܘܛܠܘܡܝܐ
ܕܝܠܝ. ܦܘܪܩܢܐ ܗܘܐ ܠܝ. ܘܡܣܠܐܝܬܗܘܢ ܕܝܢ ܗܘܝܬ.
ܡܛܠ ܕܛܢܢܐ ܠܝܬ ܗܘܐ ܒܝ. ¹⁰ܡܛܠ ܕܠܟܠܢܫ ܥܒܕ ܗܘܝܬ
ܛܒܬܐ ܐܣܬܢܝܬ. ¹¹ܘܚܕܪܘܢܝ ܐܝܟ ܟܠ̈ܒܐ ܦܩܪ̈ܐ. ܗܢܘܢ
ܕܒܠܐ ܝܕܥܬܐ ܐܙܠܝܢ ܥܠ ܡܪ̈ܝܗܘܢ. ¹²ܡܛܠ ܕܡܣܟܠܐ ܗܝ,
ܬܪܥܝܬܗܘܢ. ܘܡܚܒܠܐ ܪ̈ܥܝܢܝܗܘܢ. ¹³ܐܢܐ ܕܝܢ ܡܝ̈ܐ ܐܚܝܕ.
ܗܘܝܬ ܒܝܡܝܢܝ. ܘܠܡܪܝܪܘܬܗܘܢ ܣܝܒܪܬ ܒܚܠܝܘܬܝ. ¹⁴ܘܠܐ
ܐܒܕܬ ܡܛܠ ܕܠܐ ܗܘܝܬ ܐܚܘܗܘܢ. ܐܦ ܠܐ ܒܢܝ ܝܠܕܘܬܝ,
ܐܝܟܘܬܗܘܢ. ¹⁵ܘܒܥܘ ܡܘܬܝ, ܘܠܐ ܐܫܟܚܘ. ܡܛܠ ܕܩܕܝܡ
ܗܘܝܬ ܡܢ ܕܥܘܗܕܢܗܘܢ. ¹⁶ܘܣܪܝܩܐܝܬ [d]ܢܚܬܘ ܗܘܘ ܥܠܝ.
¹⁷ܘܐܝܠܝܢ ܕܡܢ ܒܬܪܝ, ܗܘܘ ܡܛܠܝ. ܕܥܘܕܪܢܐ ܕܗܘ̇ ܕܡܢ
ܩܕܡܝܗܘܢ ܒܥܘ ܠܡܥܒܕܘ. ¹⁸ܡܛܠ ܕܠܐ ܡܬܡܕܡܝܢܐ ܬܪܥܝܬܗ
ܕܡܪܝܡܐ. ܘܠܒܗ ܡܥܠܐ ܗܘ ܡܢ ܟܠ ܚܟܡܬܐ. ܗܠܠܘܝܐ.

[a] Sic cod.: as Flemming suspected.

[b—b] = ἐπὶ τῇ ἑαυτῶν νοσσιᾷ· cf. Luke xiii. 34.

[c] Schulthess suggests ܕܐܬܛܝܒܬ

[d] Marg. ܢܚܫܝܢ

ODE 29.

¹ܡܪܝܐ ܗܘ ܣܒܪܝ، ܠܐ ܐܬܒܗܬ ܒܗ. ²ܐܝܟ ܬܫܒܘܚܬܗ ܓܝܪ
ܥܒܕܢܝ. ܘܐܝܟ ܛܝܒܘܬܗ ܗܟܢܐ ܐܦ ܝܗܒ ܠܝ. ³ܘܐܝܟ
ܪ̈ܚܡܘܗܝ ܐܪܝܡܢܝ. ܘܐܝܟ ܪܒܘܬ ܫܘܦܪܗ ܪܘܡܪܡܢܝ. ⁴ܘܐܣܩܢܝ
ܡܢ ܥܘܡܩܝ̈ܗ ܕܫܝܘܠ. ܘܡܢ ܦܘܡܗ ܕܡܘܬܐ ܢܓܕܢܝ.
⁵ܘܡܟܟܬ ܠܒܥܠܕܒ̈ܒܝ ܘܙܕܩܢܝ ܒܛܝܒܘܬܗ. ⁶ܗܝܡܢܬ ܓܝܪ
ܒܡܫܝܚܗ ܕܡܪܝܐ. ܘܐܬܚܙܝ ܠܝ ܕܗܘܝܘ ܡܪܝܐ. ⁷ܘܚܘܝ ᵃܠܗ
ܐܬܘܗܝᵃ ܘܕܒܪܢܝ ܒܢܘܗܪܗ. ܘܝܗܒ ܠܝ ܫܒܛܐ ܕܚܝܠܬܢܘܬܗ.
⁸ܕܐܫܥܒܕ ܡܚܫ̈ܒܬܐ ܕܥܡܡ̈ܐ. ܘܡܥܒܕܐ ܕܓܢܒܪ̈ܐ ܠܡܡܟܟܘ.
⁹ܠܡܥܒܕ ܩܪܒܐ ܒܡܠܬܗ. ܘܙܟܘܬܐ ܠܡܥܒܕ ܒܚܝܠܗ. ¹⁰ܘܐܪܡܝܗ
ܠܒܥܠܕܒܒܝ ܡܪܝܐ ܒܡܠܬܗ. ܘܗܘܐ ܐܝܟ ܚܘܪܐ ܕܥܠܥܠܐ
ܠܗ ܪܘܚܐ. ¹¹ܘܝܗܒܬ ܬܫܒܘܚܬܐ ܠܡܪܝܡܐ. ܡܛܠ ܕܐܘܪܒܗ
ܠܥܒܕܗ ܘܠܒܪ ܐܡܬܗ. ܗܠܠܘܝܐ.

a—a We should perhaps read ܠ ܐܬܐ

ODE 30.

¹ܡܠܘ ܠܟܘܢ ܡ̈ܝܐ ܡܢ ܡܒܘܥܐ ܚܝܐ ܕܡܪܝܐ. ܡܛܠ
ܕܐܬܦܬܚ ܠܟܘܢ. ²ܘܬܘ ܟܠܟܘܢ ܨ̈ܗܝܐ ܘܣܒܘ ܡܫܬܝܐ.
ܘܐܬܬܢܝܚܘ ܥܠ ܡܒܘܥܗ ܕܡܪܝܐ. ³ܡܛܠ ܕܫܦܝܪ ܗܘ ܘܢܩܕ
ܘܡܢܝܚ ܠܢܦܫܐ. ܡܢ ܕܒܫܐ ܓܝܪ ܚܠܐ ܒܣܝܡܝܢ ܡ̈ܝܘܗܝ.
⁴ܘܟܘܪܬܐ ܕܕܒܘܪ̈ܝܬܐ ܠܐ ܡܬܦܚܡܐ ܠܗ. ⁵ܡܛܠ ܕܡܢ
ܣܦܘܬܗ ܕܡܪܝܐ ܢܦܩ. ܘܡܢ ܠܒܗ ܕܡܪܝܐ ܫܡܗ. ⁶ܘܐܬܐ ܟܕ
ܠܐ ܡܬܬܚܡ ܘܠܐ ܡܬܚܙܝܐ. ܘܥܕܡܐ ܕܐܬܝܗܒ ܒܡܨܥܬܐ
ܠܐ ܝܕܥܘܗܝ. ⁷ܛܘܒܝܗܘܢ ܠܐܝܠܝܢ ܕܐܫܬܝܘ ܡܢܗ ܘܐܬܬܢܝܚܘ
ܒܗ. ܗܠܠܘܝܐ.

ODE 31.

¹ܐܬܦܫܪܘ ܡܢ ܩܕܡ ܡܪܝܐ ܬܗ̈ܘܡܐ. ܘܐܬܚܒܠ ܚܫܘܟܐ ܡܢ
ܚܙܘܗ. ²ܛܥܝܬ ܛܥܝܘܬܐ ܘܐܒܕܬ ܡܢܗ. [a]ܘܫܝܛܘܬܐ ܡܣܒܬܗ̇
ܠܐ ܡܠܟܬܐ ܘܛܒܥܬ ܡܢ ܥܘܕܪܗ ܕܡܪܝܐ. ³ܦܘܡܗ ܦܬܚ
ܘܡܠܠ ܛܝܒܘܬܐ ܘܚܕܘܬܐ. ܘܡܠܠ ܬܫܒܘܚܬܐ ܚܕܬܐ ܠܫܡܗ.
⁴ܘܐܪܝܡ ܩܠܗ ܠܘܬ ܡܪܝܡܐ ܘܩܪܒ ܠܗ ܒܢ̈ܝܐ ܗܢܘܢ
ܕܒܐܝ̈ܕܘܗܝ، ܗܘܘ. ⁵ܘܐܙܕܕܩ ܦܪ̈ܨܘܦܗ. ܡܛܠ ܕܗܟܢܐ ܝܗܒ.
ܠܗ ܐܒܘܗܝ، ܩܕܝܫܐ. ⁶ܦܘܩܘ ܗܘܝܢ ܕܐܬܐܠܨܘ ܘܩܒܠܘ
ܚܕܘܬܐ. ܘܐܪܬܘ ܢܦܫܟܘܢ ܒܛܝܒܘܬܐ ܘܣܒܘ ܠܟܘܢ ܚܝ̈ܐ
ܕܠܐ ܡܘܬܐ. ⁷ܘܚܝܒܘܢܝ ܟܕ ܩܡܬ. ܠܗ̇ܘ ܕܠܐ ܐܝܬܝ، ܗ̇ܘܝܬ
ܡܚܝܒܐ. ܘܦܠܓܘ ܒܙܬܝ، ܟܕ ܡܕܡ ܠܐ ܡܬܚܝܒ ܠܗܘܢ.
⁸ܐܢܐ ܕܝܢ ܣܝܒܪܬ ܘܫܬܩܬ ܘܫܠܝܬ. ܐܝܟ ܕܠܐ ܐܬܬܙܝܥ
ܡܢܗܘܢ. ⁹ܐܠܐ ܩܡܬ ܕܠܐ ܙܘܥܬܐ ܐܝܟ ܟܐܦܐ ܫܪܝܪܬܐ. ܗ̇ܝ،
ܕܡܬܢܓܕܐ ܡܢ ܓ̈ܠܠܐ ܘܡܣܝܒܪܐ. ¹⁰ܘܣܝܒܪܬ ܡܪܝܪܘܬܗܘܢ
ܡܛܠ ܡܟܝܟܘܬܐ. ¹¹ܡܛܠ ܕܐܦܪܘܩ ܠܥܡܝ. ܘܐܝܪܬܝܘܗܝ، ܘܕܠܐ
ܐ̇ܩܝܡ ܠܫܘܘܕ̈ܝܐ ܕܠܘܬ ܐܒܗ̈ܬܐ. ܗܘܝܢ ܕܐܫܬܘܕܝܬ
ܠܦܘܪܩܢܐ ܕܙܪܥܗܘܢ ܗܠܠܘܝܐ

[a] Sic cod.

ODE 32.

¹ܠܛܘ̈ܒܢܐ ܚܕܘܬܐ ܡܢ ܠܒܗܘܢ. ܘܢܘܗܪܐ ܡܢ ܗ̇ܘ ܕܥܡܪ
ܒܗܘܢ. ²ܘܦܬ⌜ܓܡ̈ܐ⌝ ܡܢ ܫܪܪܐ ܗ̇ܘ ܕܗܘܐ ܡܢ ܢܦܫܗ. ܡܛܠ
ܕܐܬܥܫܢ ܒܚܝܠܗ ܩܕܝܫܐ ܕܪܘܡܐ. ܘܗܘ̣ ܕܠܐ ܙܘܥܐ ܗ̇ܘ
ܠܥܠܡ ܠܥܠܡܝܢ. ܗܠܠܘܝܐ.

ODE 33.

¹ܪܗܛܬ ܕܝܢ ܬܘܒ ܛܝܒܘܬܐ ܘܫܒܩܬ ܠܡܚܒܠܐ. ܘܢܚܬܬ ܒܗ
ܐܝܟ ܕܬܒܛܠܝܘܗܝ. ²ܘܐܘܒܕ ܠܐܘܒܕܢܐ ܡܢ ܩܕܡܘܗܝ. ܘܚܒܠ
ܟܠܗ ܬܩܘܢܬܗ. ³ܘܩܡ ܥܠ ܪܝܫܐ ܪܘܡܐ ܘܝܗܒ ܩܠܗ ܡܢ ܣܘܦܝܗ̇
ܕܐܪܥܐ. ܘܥܕܡܐ ܠܣܘ̈ܦܝܗ̇. ⁴ܘܢܓܕ ܠܘܬܗ ܠܟܠ ܐܝܠܝܢ
ܕܐܫܬܡܥܘ ܠܗ. ܘܠܐ ܐܬܚܙܝ ܐܝܟ ܒܝܫܐ. ⁵ܐܠܐ ܩܡܬ
ܒܬܘܠܬܐ ܓܡܝܪܬܐ. ܕܡܟܪܙܐ ܘܩܪܝܐ ܘܐܡܪܐ. ⁶ܒܢܝ̈ ܐܢܫܐ
ܐܬܦܢܘ. ܘܒܢ̈ܬܗܘܢ ܬܐܝ̈ܢ[a]. ⁷ܘܫܒܘܩܘ ܐܘܪܚܬܗ ܕܚܒܠܐ
ܗܢܐ ܘܐܬܩܪܒܘ ܠܝ. ܘܐܥܘܠ ܒܟܘܢ܆ ܘܐܦܩܟܘܢ ܡܢ
ܐܒܕܢܐ. ⁸ܘܐܚܟܡܟܘܢ ܒܐܘܪܚܬܐ ܕܫܪܪܐ. ܠܐ ܬܬܚܒܠܘܢ
ܐܦ ܠܐ ܬܐܒܕܘܢ. ⁹ܫܡܥܘܢܝ ܘܐܬܦܪܩܘ. ܛܝܒܘܬܗ ܓܝܪ
ܕܐܠܗܐ ܡܡܠܠܐ ܐܢܐ ܒܟܘܢ܆ ܘܒܐܝܕܝ̈ ܬܬܦܪܩܘܢ ܘܬܗܘܘܢ
ܛܘܒܢܐ. ¹⁰ܕܝܢܟܘܢ ܐܢܐ ܐܝܬܝ. ܘܗܢܘܢ ܕܠܒܫܘܢܝ ܠܐ
ܢܬܛܠܡܘܢ܆ ܐܠܐ ܢܩܢܘܢ ܠܥܠܡܐ ܚܕܬܐ ܠܐ[b] ܚܒܠܐ.
¹¹ܓܒܝ̈ܝ ܗܠܟܘ ܒܝ ܘܐܘܪܚܬܝ, ܐܟܪܙ ܠܗܘܢ ܕܒܥܝܢ ܠܝ.
ܘܐܬܟܠ ܐܢܘܢ ܒܫܡܝ. ܗܠܠܘܝܐ.

[a] Sic cod.: as Fl. suspected.
[b] Fl. suggests ܕܠܐ. I follow the MS.

ODE 34.

¹ܠܝܬ ܐܘܪܚܐ ܥܫܝܢܬܐ ܐܝܟܐ ܕܠܒܐ ܦܫܝܛܐ. ²ܐܦ ܠܐ
ܡܚܘܬܐ ܒܡܚܫ̈ܒܬܐ ܬܪ̈ܝܨܬܐ. ³ܐܦ ܠܐ ܥܠܥܠܐ ܒܥܘܡܩܗ̇
ܕܡܚܫܒܬܐ ܢܗܝܪܬܐ. ⁴ܐܝܟܐ ܕܒܪܝܢ ܡܢ ܟܠ ܐܬܪ ܫܦܝܪܐ.
ܠܝܬ ܒܗ ܡܕܡ ܕܦܠܝܓ. ܕܡܘܬܗ ܕܗܘ ܕܠܬܚܬ. ⁵ܗܘܝܘ ܗܘ
ܕܠܥܠ. ܟܠܡܕܡ ܓܝܪ ܠܥܠ ܗܘ. ܠܬܚܬ ܠܝܬ ܡܕܡ ܐܠܐ
ܡܣܬܒܪ ܠܐܝܠܝܢ ܕܝܕܥܬܐ ܠܝܬ ܒܗܘܢ܆ ⁶ܛܝܒܘܬܐ ܐܬܓܠܝܬ
ܠܦܘܪܩܢܟܘܢ܆ ܗܝܡܢܘ ܘܚܘܘ ܘܐܬܦܪܩܘ. ܗܠܠܘܝܐ.

ODE 35.

[1]ܪܣܣܘܗܝ ܕܡܪܝܐ ܒܢܝܚܘܬܐ ܐܛܠ ܥܠܝ. [2]ܘܥܢܢܐ ܕܫܠܡܐ ܐܩܝܡ
ܠܥܠ ܡܢ ܪܫܝ. ܕܗܘܬ ܡܛܪܬܐ ܠܝ ܒܟܠ ܙܒܢ. [3]ܘܦܘܪܩܢܐ ܗܘܬ
ܠܝ. ܐܬܬܙܝܥܘ ܟܠ ܘܐܬܕܗܠܘ. [4]ܘܢܦܩ ܡܢܗܘܢ ܬܢܢܐ [a]ܘܕܝܢܐ.
ܘܐܢܐ ܫܠܐ ܗܘܝܬ ܒܬܓܡܗ ܕܡܪܝܐ. [5]ܘܝܬܝܪ ܡܢ ܛܠܠܐ
ܗܘܐ ܠܝ ܘܝܬܝܪ ܡܢ ܫܘܬܐܣܬܐ. [6]ܘܐܝܟ ܛܠܝܐ ܡܢ ܐܡܗ
ܡܬܛܥܢ ܗܘܝܬ. ܘܝܗܒ ܠܝ ܚܠܒܐ ܛܠܗ ܕܡܪܝܐ. [7]ܘܐܬܪܒܝܬ
ܒܡܘܗܒܬܗ ܘܐܬܢܝܚܬ ܒܫܘܡܠܝܗ. [8]ܘܦܫܛܬ ܐܝܕ̈ܝ ܒܣܘܠܩܗ̇
ܕܢܦܫܝ. ܘܐܬܬܪܝܨܬ ܠܘܬ ܡܪܝܡܐ. ܘܐܬܦܪܩܬ ܠܘܬܗ. ܗܠܠܘܝܐ.

[a] Gunkel suggests ܘܪܝܚܐ

ODE 36.

[1]ܐܬܬܢܝܚܬ ܥܠ ܪܘܚܗ ܕܡܪܝܐ. ܘܐܪܝܡܬܢܝ ܠܡܪܘܡܐ.
[2]ܘܐܘܩܡܬܢܝ ܥܠ ܪ̈ܓܠܝ ܒܪܘܡܗ ܕܡܪܝܐ. ܩܕܡ ܫܘܡܠܝܗ
ܘܬܫܒܘܚܬܗ ܟܕ ܡܫܒܚ ܐܢܐ ܒܬܘܩܢܐ ܕܙܡܝ̈ܪܬܗ. [3]ܝܠܕܬܢܝ
ܩܕܡ ܐܦ̈ܘܗܝ ܕܡܪܝܐ. ܘܟܕ ܒܪ ܐܢܫܐ ܐܢܐ ܗܘܝܬ. ܐܬܩܪܝܬ
ܢܘܗܪܐ ܒܪܗ ܕܐܠܗܐ. [4]ܟܕ ܡܫܒܚ ܐܢܐ ܒܡܫܒ̈ܚܢܐ. ܘܪܒ
ܐܢܐ ܒܪܘܪ̈ܒܢܐ. [5]ܐܝܟ ܪܒܘܬܗ ܓܒܠܢܝ ܕܡܪܝܡܐ. ܘܐܝܟ ܚܕܬܘܬܗ
ܚܕܬܢܝ. ܘܐܝܟ ܢܘܗܪܗ ܢܗܪܢܝ. ܘܡܫܚܢܝ ܡܢ ܡܫܡܠܝܘܬܗ.
[6]ܘܗܘܝܬ ܚܕ ܡܢ ܩܪ̈ܝܒܘܗܝ. ܘܐܬܦܬܚ ܦܘܡܝ ܐܝܟ ܥܢܢܐ
ܕܛܠܠܐ. [7]ܘܠܒܝ ܐܒܥ ܐܝܟ ܡܒܘܥܐ ܕܙܕܝܩܘܬܐ. [8]ܘܗܘܐ
ܩܘܪܒܝ ܒܫܠܡܐ ܘܐܬܫܪܪܬ ܒܪܘܚܐ ܕܡܕܒܪܢܘܬܗ. ܗܠܠܘܝܐ.

ODE 37.

[1]ܦܫܛܬ ܐܝܕ̈ܝ ܠܘܬ ܡܪܝ. ܘܠܘܬ ܡܪܝܡܐ ܐܪܝܡܬ ܩܠܝ.
[2]ܘܡܡܠܠܬ ܒܣܦ̈ܘܬܗ ܕܠܒܝ. ܘܫܡܥܢܝ ܟܕ ܢܦܠ ܩܠܝ ܠܘܬܗ.
[3]ܦܬܓܡܗ ܐܬܐ ܠܘܬܝ. ܕܢܬܠ ܠܝ ܦܐܪ̈ܐ ܕܥܡܠܝ. [4]ܘܝܗܒ
ܠܝ ܢܝܚܐ ܒܛܝܒܘܬܗ ܕܡܪܝܐ. ܗܠܠܘܝܐ.

ODE 38.

[1]ܣܠܩܬ ܠܢܘܗܪܐ ܕܫܪܪܐ ܐܝܟ ܕܠܡܪܟܒܬܐ. [2]ܘܕܒܪܢܝ ܫܪܪܐ
ܘܐܝܬܝܢܝ. [a]ܘܐܥܒܪܢܝ ܦܚܬܐ ܘܫܩܝܦܐ. ܘܡܢ ܫܘܥܐ ܘ̈ܓܠܠܐ
ܦܨܝܢܝ. [3]ܘܗܘܐ ܠܝ ܠܡܚܣܢܐ ܕܦܘܪܩܢܐ. ܘܣܡܢܝ ܥܠ ܐ̈ܕܪܥܐ
ܕܚ̈ܝܐ ܕܠܐ ܡܘܬܐ. [4]ܘܐܙܠ ܥܡܝ ܘܐܢܝܚܢܝ ܘܠܐ ܫܒܩܢܝ
ܕܐܛܥܐ ܡܛܠ ܕܫܪܪܐ ܐܝܬܘܗܝ ܗܘܐ ܗܘ. [5]ܘܠܐ ܗܘܐ ܠܝ
ܣܘܪܘܚܐ ܕܥܡܗ ܡܛܠ ܕܗܠܟܬ ܥܡܗ. [6]ܘܠܐ ܛܥܝܬ ܒܡܕܡ
ܡܛܠ ܕܐܫܬܡܥܬ ܠܗ. ܛܘܥܝܐ ܓܝܪ ܥܪܩܐ ܗܘܬ ܡܢܗ. ܘܠܐ
ܐܪܥܐ ܗܘܬ ܠܗ. [7]ܫܪܪܐ ܕܝܢ ܐܙܠ ܗܘܐ ܒܐܘܪܚܐ ܬܪܝܨܬܐ.
[8]ܘܟܠܡܕܡ ܕܠܐ ܝܕܥ ܗܘܝܬ ܡܚܘܐ ܗܘܐ ܠܝ ܠܟܠܗܘܢ
ܣܡ̈ܡܢܐ ܕܛܘܥܝܘܬܐ ܘܠܡ̈ܚܘܬܐ ܗܢܘܢ ܕܡܬܚܫܒܝܢ [b]ܕܒܣܝܡܘܬܐ ܗܘ
ܕܡܘܬܐ. [9]ܘܠܡܚܒܠܢܘܬܐ ܕܚܒܠܐ ܚܙܝܬ ܗܘܬ ܟܕ ܡܬܛܝܒܐ ܟܠܬܐ
ܟܠܬܐ ܕܡܚܒܠܐ ܘܚܬܢܐ ܕܡܚܒܠ ܘܡܬܚܒܠ. [10]ܘܫܐܠܬ
ܠܫܪܪܐ ܕܡܢ ܐܢܘܢ ܗܠܝܢ ܘܐܡܪ ܠܝ ܗܢܘ ܡܛܥܝܢܐ ܘܛܘܥܝܘܬܐ.
[11]ܘܡܬܕܡܝܢ ܒܚܒܝܒܐ ܘܒܟܠܬܗ. ܘܡܛܥܝܢ ܠܥܠܡܐ ܘܡܚܒܠܝܢ
ܠܗ. [12]ܘܩܪܝܢ ܠܣ̈ܓܝܐܐ ܠܡܫܬܘܬܐ. [13]ܘܝܗܒܝܢ ܠܗܘܢ
ܕܢܫܬܘܢ ܚܡܪܐ ܕܙܢܝܘܬܗܘܢ ܘܡܬܬܝܒܝܢ ܚܟܡܬܗܘܢ
ܘܡܕ̈ܥܝܗܘܢ. ܘܥܒܕܝܢ ܠܗܘܢ ܕܠܐ ܪܥܝܢܐ. [14]ܘܗܝܕܝܢ ܫܒܩܝܢ
ܠܗܘܢ. ܘܗܢܘܢ ܕܝܢ ܗܘܘ ܡܬܦܪܥܝܢ ܒܗ [c]ܘܦܩܪܝܢ ܘܡܚܒܠܝܢ. ܟܕ
ܠܝܬ ܒܗܘܢ ܠܒܐ. ܐܦ ܠܐ ܒܥܝܢ ܠܗ. [15]ܘܐܬܚܟܡܬ
ܐܢܐ ܕܠܐ ܐܦܠ ܒܐܝ̈ܕܝ ܡܛܥܝܢܐ. ܘܚܕܝܬ ܠܢܦܫܝ ܡܛܠ ܕܐܙܠ
ܗܘܐ ܥܡܝ ܫܪܪܐ. [16]ܘܐܫܬܪܪܬ ܘܚܝܬ ܘܐܬܦܪܩܬ.

[a] Sic cod.

[b] An obscure passage: the MS. appears to have ܕܒܣܝܡܘܬܐ which might be resolved into ܕܒܣܝܡܘܬܐ (fear: so Fl.) or into ܕܒܣܝܡܘܬܐ (sweetness: so U.-S.).

[c] Cod. ܦܩܪܝܢ (the emendation is Nestle's).

17 ܘܐܬܬܩܢܬ ܫܬܐܣܘ̈ܗܝ ܥܠ ܐܝܕܗ ܕܡܪܝܐ. ܡܛܠ ܕܗܘ
ܢܨܒܗ. 18 ܗܘ ܓܝܪ ܫܪܫ ܢܨܒܐ. ܘܐܫܩܝܗ ܘܐܬܩܢܗ ܘܒܪܟܗ.
ܘܦܐܪ̈ܘܗܝ, ܠܥܠܡ ܗ̇ܘܘܢ. 19 ܥܡܩ ܘܐܣܩ ܘܦܫܛ,. ܘܡܠܐ
ܘܐܬܪܘܪܒ. 20 ܘܐܫܬܒܚ ܡܪܝܐ ܒܠܚܘܕܘܗܝ, ܒܢܨܒܬܗ
ܘܒܦܘܠܚܢܗ. ܒܢܛܘܪܘܬܗ ܘܒܡܒܪܟܢܘܬܐ ܕܣܦ̈ܘܬܗ. 21 ܒܢܨܒܬܐ
ܫܦܝܪܬܐ ܕܝܡܝܢܗ. ܘܒܡܫܟܚܢܘܬܐ ܕܢܨܒܬܗ. ܘܒܡܚܫܒܬܐ
ܕܪܥܝܢܗ. ܗܠܠܘܝܐ.

ODE 39.

1 ܢܗܪ̈ܘܬܐ ܚܝ̈ܠܬܢܐ ܚܝܠܗ ܕܡܪܝܐ. 2 ܘܠܐܝܠܝܢ ܕܡܒܣܪܝܢ ܠܗ̇,
ܡܚܬܝܢ ܒܬܪ ܪܫܗܘܢ. ܘܡܥܪܩܠܝܢ ܗܠܟܬܗܘܢ. 3 ܘܡܚܣܪܝܢ
ܡܥܒܪ̈ܬܗܘܢ. ܘܚܛܦܝܢ ܦܓܪ̈ܝܗܘܢ. ܘܡܚܒܠܝܢ ܢܦ̈ܫܬܗܘܢ.
4 ܚܪܝܦܝܢ ܐܢܘܢ ܓܝܪ ܡܢ ܒܪ̈ܩܐ ܘܩܠܝܠܝܢ. ܘܗܢܘܢ ܕܥܒܪܝܢ
ܠܗܘܢ ܒܗܝܡܢܘܬܐ ܠܐ ܢܬܬܙܝܥܘܢ. 5 ܘܗܢܘܢ ܕܡܗܠܟܝܢ
ܒܗܘܢ ܕܠܐ ܡܘܡܐ ܠܐ ܢܬܕܠܚܘܢ. ܡܛܠ ܕܐܬ̈ܐ ܒܗܘܢ
ܡܪܝܐ ܗܘ. 6 ܘܐܬ̈ܐ ܗܘܝܐ ܐܘܪܚܐ ܕܗܢܘܢ ܕܥܒܪܝܢ ܒܫܡܗ
ܕܡܪܝܐ. 7 ܠܒܫܘ ܗܟܝܠ ܫܡܗ ܕܡܪܝܡܐ ܘܕܥܘܗܝ,. ܘܬܥܒܪܘܢ
ܕܠܐ ܩܝܢܕܘܢܘܣ. ܟܕ ܢܗܘܘܢ ܢܗܪ̈ܘܬܐ ܡܫܬܡܥܝܢ ܠܟܘܢ.
8 ܓܫܪ ܐܢܘܢ ܡܪܝܐ ܒܡܠܬܗ. ܘܗܠܟ ܘܥܒܪ ܐܢܘܢ ܡܢ
ܪ̇ܓܠ. 9 ܘܥܩܒ̈ܬܗ ܩܝ̈ܡܢ ܥܠ ܡ̈ܝܐ. ܘܠܐ ܐܬܚܒ̈ܠ. ܐܠܐ
ܐܝܬܝܗܝܢ ܐܝܟ ܩܝܣܐ ܕܩܒܝܥ ܒܫܪܪܐ. 10 ܘܡܟܐ ܘܡܟܐ
ܡܬܬܪܝܡܝܢ ܗܘܘ ܓ̈ܠܠܐ. ܘܥܩ̈ܒܬܗ ܕܝܢ ܕܡܪܢ ܡܫܝܚܐ
ܩܝ̈ܡܢ ܐܝܢ. ܘܠܐ ܡܬܥܛܝܢ ܐܦܠܐ ܡܬܚ̈ܒܠܢ. 11 ܘܐܬܬܣܝܡܬ
ܐܘܪܚܐ ܠܐܝܠܝܢ ܕܥܒܪܝܢ ܒܬܪܗ. ܘܠܗܢܘܢ ܕܢ̈ܩܦܝܢ ܠܗܠܟܬܐ
ܕܗܝܡܢܘܬܗ ܘܡܣܓܕܝܢ ܠܫܡܗ. ܗܠܠܘܝܐ.

ODE 40.

[1]ܐܝܟ ܕܢܒܥ ܕܒܫܐ ܡܢ ܟܘܪܬܐ ܕܕܒܘܪܬܐ. [2]ܘܪܕܐ ܚܠܒܐ
ܡܢ ܐܢܬܬܐ ܪܚܡܬ ܒ̈ܢܝܗ̇. [3]ܗܟܢܐ ܐܦ ܣܒܪܝ ܠܘܬܟ ܗܘ
ܐܠܗܝ. [4]ܐܝܟ ܕܢܒܥܐ ܡܒܘܥܐ ܡ̈ܝܘܗܝ. [5]ܗܟܢܐ ܢܒܥ ܠܒܝ
ܬܫܒܘܚܬܗ ܕܡܪܝܐ ܘܣܦܘ̈ܬܝ ܡܦܩ̈ܢ ܠܗ ܬܫܒܘܚܬܐ. ܘܠܫܢܝ
ܡܚ̈ܠܝܬܗ. [6]ܘܪܘܙܘ ܐܦ̈ܝ ܒܕܝܨܘܬܗ. ܘܕܝܨܐ ܪܘܚܝ ܒܚܘܒܗ. ܘܢܦܫܝ
ܢܗܪܐ ܒܗ. [7]ܘܕܚܝܠܐ ܒܗ ܢܬܬܟܠ. ܘܦܘܪܩܢܐ ܒܗ ܢܬܬܪܪ.
[8]ܘܝܘܪܬܢܗ[a] ܐܝܬܝܗܘܢ ܚ̈ܝܐ ܕܠܐ ܡܘܬܐ. ܘܡܩ̈ܒܠܢܝܗܘܢ
ܕܠܐ ܚܒܠܐ. ܗܠܠܘܝܐ.

[a] Cod. ܘܝܘܪܬܗ: the emendation is by Charles.

ODE 41.

[1]ܢܫܒܚܘܢ ܠܡܪܝܐ ܟܠܗܘܢ ܝ̈ܠܘܕܘܗܝ. ܘܢܩܒܠܘܢ ܫܪܪܐ
ܕܗܝܡܢܘܬܗ. [2]ܘܢܬܝܕܥܘܢ ܠܒ̈ܢܘܗܝ. ܡܛܠ ܗܢܐ ܢܙܡܪ
ܒܚܘܒܗ. [3]ܚܝܝܢ ܒܡܪܝܐ ܒܛܝܒܘܬܗ. ܘܚ̈ܝܐ ܡܩܒܠܝܢܢ
ܒܡܫܝܚܗ. [4]ܝܘܡܐ ܓܝܪ ܪܒܐ ܐܢܗܪ ܠܢ. ܘܬܡܝܗ ܗܘ ܕܝܗܒ
ܠܢ ܡܢ ܫܘܒܚܗ. [5]ܢܬܚܫܒ ܗܟܝܠ ܟܠܢ ܐܟܚܕܐ ܥܠ ܫܡܗ
ܕܡܪܝܐ. ܘܢܝܩܪܝܘܗܝ ܒܛܝܒܘܬܗ. [6]ܘܢܢܗܪ̈ܢ ܐܦ̈ܝܢ ܒܢܘܗܪܗ.
ܘܢܬܗܓܐ ܠܒ̈ܘܬܢ ܒܚܘܒܗ ܒܠܠܝܐ ܘܒܐܝܡܡܐ. [7]ܢܕܘܨ
ܡܢ ܕܝܨܗ ܕܡܪܝܐ. [8]ܢܬܕܡܪܘܢ ܟܠܗܘܢ ܐܝܠܝܢ ܕܚܙܝܢ ܠܝ. ܡܛܠ
ܕܡܢ ܓܢܣܐ ܐܚܪܢܐ ܐܢܐ. [9]ܐܒܐ ܓܝܪ ܕܫܪܪܐ ܐܬܕܟܪܢܝ.
ܗܘ ܕܩܢܢܝ ܡܢ ܒܪܫܝܬ. [10]ܥܘܬܪܗ ܓܝܪ ܝܠܕܢܝ ܘܡܚܫܒܬܗ
ܕܠܒܗ. [11]ܘܡܠܬܗ ܥܡܢ ܒܟܠܗ̇ ܐܘܪܚܢ. [12]ܦܪܘܩܐ ܕܡܚܝܐ
ܘܠܐ ܡܗܡܠܐ ܢܦܫܬܗ. [13]ܓܒܪܐ ܕܐܬܡܟܟ. ܘܐܬܬܪܝܡ
ܒܙܕܝܩܘܬܐ ܕܝܠܗ. [14]ܒܪܗ ܕܡܪܝܡܐ ܐܬܚܙܝ ܒܫܘܡܠܝܐ
ܕܐܒܘܗܝ. [15]ܘܢܘܗܪܐ ܕܢܚ ܡܢ ܡܠܬܐ ܗܝ، ܕܡܢ ܩܕܝܡ ܒܗ ܗܘܬ.
[16]ܡܫܝܚܐ ܒܫܪܪܐ ܚܕ ܗܘ. ܘܐܬܝܕܥ ܡܢ ܩܕܡ ܬܪܡܝܬܗ ܕܥܠܡܐ
[17]ܕܢܚܐ ܢܦܫ̈ܬܐ ܠܥܠܡ ܒܫܪܪܐ ܕܫܡܗ. ܬܫܒܘܚܬܐ ܚܕܬܐ ܡܢ
ܐܝܠܝܢ ܕܡܚܒܝܢ ܠܗ. ܗܠܠܘܝܐ.

ODE 42.

[1]ܦܫܛܬ ܐܝܕܝ ܘܐܬܩܪܒܬ ܠܘܬ ܡܪܝ. [2]ܡܛܠ ܕܦܫܝܛܘܬܐ ܕܐܝܕܝ
ܐܬܐ ܗܝ. [3]ܦܫܝܛܘܬܝ ܗܘܐ ܩܝܣܐ ܦܫܝܛܐ ܕܐܬܬܠܝ ܥܠ ܐܘܪܚܗ
ܕܬܪܝܨܐ. [4]ܘܗܘܝܬ ܕܠܐ ܚܫܚܬ ܠܐܝܠܝܢ ܕܠܐ ܐܚܕܝܢ ܗܘܘ
ܠܝ. ܘܐܗܘܐ ܠܘܬ ܐܝܠܝܢ ܕܪܚܡܝܢ ܠܝ. [5]ܡܝܬܘ ܟܠܗܘܢ ܪܕܘܦܝ
ܘܒܥܘܢܝ ܐܝܠܝܢ ܕܣܒܪܘ ܥܠܝ ܡܛܠ ܕܚܝ ܐܢܐ. [6]ܘܩܡܬ ܠܝ
ܘܐܝܬܝ ܥܡܗܘܢ. ܘܐܡܠܠ ܒܦܘܡܗܘܢ. [7]ܐܣܠܝܘ ܓܝܪ ܠܐܝܠܝܢ
ܕܪܕܦܝܢ ܠܗܘܢ. [8]ܘܐܪܡܝܬ ܥܠܝܗܘܢ ܢܝܪܗ ܕܚܘܒܝ. [9]ܐܝܟ
ܢܝܪܗ ܕܚܬܢܐ ܥܠ ܟܠܬܐ. [10]ܗܟܢܐ ܢܝܪܝ ܥܠ ܐܝܠܝܢ ܕܡܗܝܡܢܝܢ ܒܝ.
[11]ܘܐܝܟ ܓܢܘܢܐ ܕܡܫܬܘܬܐ ܒܒܝܬ ܚܬܢܐ. [12]ܗܟܢܐ ܚܘܒܝ ܥܠ
ܐܝܠܝܢ ܕܡܗܝܡܢܝܢ ܒܝ. [13]ܠܐ ܐܣܬܠܝܬ ܐܝܟ ܕܐܬܚܫܒܬ. [14]ܘܠܐ
ܐܒܕܬ ܐܝܟ ܪܢܘ ܥܠܝ. [15]ܫܝܘܠ ܚܙܬܢܝ ܘܐܬܕܘܝܬ. [16]ܘܡܘܬܐ
ܐܦܠܛܢܝ ܘܠܣܓܝܐܐ ܥܡܝ. [17]ܚܠܐ ܘܡܪܪܬܐ ܗܘܝܬ ܠܗ. ܘܢܚܬܬ
ܥܡܗ ܥܕܡܐ ܕܐܝܟ ܗܘܐ ܥܘܡܩܗ. [18]ܘܪܓܠܐ ܘܪܫܐ
ܐܪܦܝ. ܡܛܠ ܕܠܐ ܐܫܟܚܘ ܠܡܣܝܒܪܘ ܦܪܨܘܦܝ. [19]ܘܥܒܕܬ
ܟܢܘܫܬܐ ܕܚܝܐ ܒܡܝܬܘܗܝ. ܘܡܠܠܬ ܥܡܗܘܢ ܒܣܦܘܬܐ
ܚܝܬܐ. [20]ܡܛܠ ܕܠܐ ܢܗܘܐ ܣܦܝܠ ܡܠܬܝ. [21]ܘܪܗܛܘ ܠܘܬܝ،
ܗܢܘܢ ܕܡܝܬܘ. ܘܩܥܘ ܘܐܡܪܘ ܚܘܣ ܥܠܝܢ ܒܪܗ ܕܐܠܗܐ. ܘܥܒܕ
ܥܡܢ ܐܝܟ ܒܣܝܡܘܬܟ. [22]ܘܐܦܩܢ ܡܢ ܐܣܘܪܐ ܕܚܫܘܟܐ.
ܘܦܬܚ ܠܢ ܬܪܥܐ ܕܒܗ ܢܦܘܩ ܠܘܬܟ. [23]ܚܙܝܢ ܓܝܪ ܕܠܐ
ܡܬܩܪܒ ܠܢ ܡܘܬܟ. [24]ܦܪܘܩ ܐܦ ܚܢܢ ܥܡܟ. ܡܛܠ ܕܐܢܬ
ܗܘ ܦܪܘܩܢ. [25]ܐܢܐ ܕܝܢ ܫܡܥܬ ܩܠܗܘܢ. ܘܪܫܡܬ[a] ܥܠ ܪܫܗܘܢ
ܫܡܝ. [26]ܡܛܠ ܕܒܢܝ ܚܐܪܐ ܐܢܘܢ ܘܕܝܠܝ ܐܝܬܝܗܘܢ. ܗܠܠܘܝܐ

[a] Cod., ut videtur, ܫܡܥܬ, probably under the influence of the preceding ܫܡܥܬ.

PSALM I (=Psalm 43 of MS.).

[1] ܩܥܝܬ ܠܘܬ ܡܪܝܐ. ܟܕ ܐܬܐܠܨܬ ܒܐܘܠܨܢܝ܆ ܘܠܘܬ ܐܠܗܐ
ܟܕ ܣܡܟܘ ܥܠܝ ܚܛܝ̈ܐ. [2] ܡܢ ܫܠܝܐ ܓܝܪ ܐܫܬܡܥ ܩܕܡܝ ܩܠܐ
ܕܩܪܒܐ. ܢܥܢܝܢܝ ܓܝܪ ܡܛܠ ܕܐܬܡܠܝܬ ܙܕܝܩܘܬܐ. [3] ܘܐܬܚܫܒܬ
ܒܠܒܝ [a]ܡܛܠ ܕܐܬܡܠܝܬ ܙܕܝܩܘܬܐ. ܟܕ ܥܬܪܬ ܘܗܘܝܬ
ܒܣܘܓܐܐ ܕܒܢ̈ܝܐ. [4] ܥܘܬܪܗܘܢ ܓܝܪ ܐܬܦܪܣ ܠܟܠܗ ܐܪܥܐ.
ܘܬܫܒܘܚܬܗܘܢ܆ ܥܕܡܐ [b]ܠܣܘܦ̈ܝܗ ܕܐܪܥܐ. [5] ܐܬܬܪܝܡܘ
ܥܕܡܐ ܠܟܘ̈ܟܒܐ. ܘܐܡܪܘ [c] ܕܠܐ ܝܕܥܘ.[d] [7] ܚܛܗ̈ܝܗܘܢ ܓܝܪ
ܒܟܣܝܐ ܗܘܘ. ܐܢܐ ܠܐ ܝܕܥ ܗܘܝܬ. [8][e] ܘܥܘܠܗܘܢ ܝܬܝܪ ܡܢ
ܥܡ̈ܡܐ ܕܩܕܡܝܗܘܢ܆ ܘܛܢܦܘ ܠܩܘܕܫܗ ܕܡܪܝܐ ܒܛܢܦܘܬܐ܀

[a] ܡܛܠ is superfluous, being repeated from the previous clause.

[b] Reading ἐσχάτων for ἐσχάτου.

[c] Here the Syriac has dropped a sentence, corresponding to the Greek οὐ μὴ πέσωσιν, [6]καὶ ἐξύβρισαν ἐν τοῖς ἀγαθοῖς αὐτῶν.

[d] The Greek here has the difficult, if not unintelligible καὶ οὐκ ἤνεγκαν: the Syriac appears to have read this as καὶ οὐκ ἔγνωκαν. We should perhaps correct ܕܠܐ ܝܕܥܘ to ܘܠܐ ܝܕܥܘ

[e] Cod. *ex errore* ܘܒܗܘܢ

PSALM 2 (=Psalm 44).

[1] ܒܫܘܒܗܪܗ ܕܚܛܝܐ ܐܪܡܝ[a] ܒܒܪܐܕܐ ܫܘܪ̈ܐ ܚܣܝ̈ܢܐ ܘܠܐ
ܟܠܝܬ. [2] ܘܣܠܩܘ ܥܠ ܡܕܒܚܟ ܥܡ̈ܡܐ ܢܘܟܪ̈ܝܐ ܘܕܝܫܝܢ ܗܘܘ
ܒܡܣܐܢ̈ܝܗܘܢ ܒܫܘܒܗܪܬܐ. [3] ܡܛܠ ܕܒܢ̈ܝ ܐܘܪܫܠܡ ܘܐܛܢܦܘ [b]ܒܝܬ

[a] i.e. κατέβαλε. For ܒܒܪܐܕܐ *read* ܒܒܪ̈ܕܐ, *with great beams*; and cf. *Acts of Thomas*, pp. ܩܟܕ, ܩܟܗ

[b–b] τὰ ἅγια = the Sanctuary.

ܡܩܕܫܗ[b] ܕܡܪܝܐ. ܘܡܣܠܐܝܢ ܗܘܘ ܩܘܪܒܢܘܗܝ ܕܐܠܗܐ.
ܒܡܣܠܝܘܬܐ. 4ܡܛܠ ܗܢܐ ܐܡܪ. ܕܐܪܚܩܘܗ[c] ܫܕܘ ܐܢܘܢ[c] ܡܢܝ.
5ܘܠܐ[d] ܐܬܛܝܒ ܒܗܘܢ ܫܘܦܪܐ ܕܫܘܒܚܘܬܗ. ܐܬܫܝܛ ܩܕܡ
ܡܪܝܐ. ܘܐܨܛܥܪܘ[e] ܥܕܡܐ ܠܚܪܬܐ. 6ܒܢܝܗ̇ ܘܒܢܬܗ̇ ܒܫܒܝܐ
ܡܪܝܪܐ. ܘܩܕܠܗܘܢ ܚܬܝܡ ܥܠܘܗܝ. ܢܝܫܐ ܣܝܡܐ ܕܥܡܡܐ.
7ܘܐܝܟ ܣܘܥܪܢܗܘܢ ܗܟܢܐ ܥܒܕ ܠܗܘܢ܆ ܡܛܠ ܕܐܪܦܝ ܐܢܘܢ
ܒܐܝܕܝܐ ܗܘ ܕܚܣܝܢ ܡܢܗܘܢ܆ 8ܐܗܦܟ ܠܒܪ ܐܦܘܗܝ ܡܢ
ܪ̈ܚܡܘܗܝ. ܛܠܝܐ ܘܣ̈ܒܐ ܘܒܢܝܗܘܢ ܐܟܚܕܐ. 9ܡܛܠ ܕܚܛܝܬܐ
ܒܒܢܘ ܐܦ ܗܢܘܢ ܐܟܚܕܐ[f] ܕܠܐ ܢܫܡܥܘܢ. 10ܘܐܬܚܣܡܬ
ܫܡܝܐ ܙܪܘܬܬ. ܘܐܪܥܐ ܐܬܛܠܝܬ ܐܢܘܢ܆ 11ܡܛܠ ܕܠܐ ܥܒܕ
ܥܠ ܒܪ ܐܢܫ ܥܠܝܗ̇ ܐܝܟ ܕܥܒܕܘ. 12ܘܬܕܥܢ ܐܪܥܐ ܟܠܗܘܢ
ܕܝ̈ܢܝܟ ܙܕܝ̈ܩܐ ܐܠܗܐ. ܐܩܝܡܘ ܠܒܢܝܗ̇ ܕܐܘܪܫܠܡ ܒܡܘܣܒܐ
ܒܓܘܗ̇. ܣܠܩ ܙܢܝܘܬܐ. 13ܘܟܠ ܡܢ ܕܥܒܪ ܗܘܐ. ܥܒܪ ܗܘܐ
ܐܝܟ ܕܠܘܬ ܙܢܝܬܐ. 14ܟܕ ܡܟܥܣܝܢ ܗܘܘ ܒܡܣܠܝܘܬܗܘܢ܆
ܐܝܟ ܕܐܦ ܗܢܘܢ ܥܒܕܝܢ ܗܘܘ. ܠܘܩܒܠ ܫܡܫܐ ܦܪܣܘ
ܒܡܣܠܝܘܬܗܘܢ܆ ܘܒܢܬܗ̇ ܕܐܘܪܫܠܡ ܐܬܛܡ̈ܐܝ ܐܝܟ ܕܣܢܝܢ.
15ܣܠܩ ܕܗܘܝܢ ܠܥܡ̈ܡܐ، ܢܦܫܗܘܢ ܒܣܘܠܛܢܐ ܕܙܢܝܘܬܐ. ܒܪܫ
ܘܪܘ̈ܫܡܐ ܟܬܝ̈ܒܝܢ ܥܠ ܗܠܝܢ. 16ܐܢܐ ܕܝܢ ܐܘܕܝܟ ܡܪܝܐ.
ܒܬܪܝܨܘܬܗ ܕܠܒܐ. ܡܛܠ ܕܒܕܝ̈ܢܝܟ ܙܕܝܩܘܬܟ ܐܠܗܐ. 17ܡܛܠ

c—c A double translation to express *ἀπορίψατε...μακράν*.

d Here the division of the sentences follows the Greek MS.: *οὐκ εὐόδωκεν αὐτοῖς τὸ κάλλος τῆς δόξης αὐτοῦ· ἐξουθενώθη ἐνώπιον τοῦ θεοῦ.* For the emendation (Hilgenfeld's) of the passage (*οὐκ εὐδοκῶ ἐν αὐτοῖς· τὸ κάλλος τῆς δόξης αὐτοῦ* [so Syr., not *αὐτῆς*]) see Gebhardt in loc. The Syriac ܐܬܛܝܒ appears to be a rough translation of *εὐόδωκεν*.

e *Read* ܘܐܨܛܥܪ (Wellhausen) to agree with the Greek *ἠτιμώθη*.

f The Syriac has twice ܐܟܚܕܐ for *εἰσάπαξ*, the Greek word which is found in Daniel as the rendering of כחדה: *εἰσάπαξ* must mean 'together,' and the Syriac must have very nearly restored the original word employed by the Psalmist.

ܘ̈ܩܪܒܐ ܐܠܨ ܠܗܘܢ ܀ ܐܝܟ ܐܠܨ ܠܗܘܢ ܀ ܐܝܟ ܐܠܗܐ ... ܟܣܐ ܘܣܝܦܐ ܀

¹⁸ ܟܠܗܘܢ ܀

¹⁹ ... ²⁰ ...

ᵍ ... ᵏ²³ ... ²⁴ ...

²⁵ ... ˡ ... ²⁶ ...

²⁷ ... ᵐ²⁸ ...

ⁿ²⁹ ... ³⁰ ...

ᵒ ... ᵖ ... ³¹ ...

³² ...

ᵍ We should restore ܟܪܣܘܡ which answers to the Greek καταπατήσει.

ʰ Cod. ܫܘܒܚܗ ⁱ⁻ⁱ Gk. μίτραν δόξης.

ᵏ Cod. *ut videtur* ܩܝܡܐܘ. ˡ Syr. om. μετὰ μηνίσεως καί.

ᵐ l. ܐܫܘܕ (Well.) to agree with Greek ἐκχέαι.

ⁿ This answers to the unintelligible Greek τοῦ εἰπεῖν, which Geiger explained as a misunderstanding of לדבר in the sense of לְדַבֵּר (to destroy); and which Wellhausen explained by taking לאמר as a late Hebrew form for לְהָמִיר = לְהָמִיר. Cf. Hos. iv. 7. ᵒ κύριος for θεός.

ᵖ The Syriac evidently had ὀρέων, and not as Hilgenfeld suggested ὁρίων.

ܐܬܪܒ. 33ܐܡܪ ܠܒܪ ܕܐܢܐ ܐܗܘܐ ܡܪܗ̇ ܕܐܪܥܐ ܘܕܝܡܐ.
ܘܠܐ ܝܕܥ ܕܡܪܝܐ ܗܘ̇ ܐܠܗܐ. ܪܒܐ ܘܚܝܠܬܢܐ ܘܫܠܝܛܢܐ.
34ܘܗܘܝܘ ܡܠܟܐ ܥܠ ܫܡܝܐ ܘܥܠ ܐܪܥܐ. ܘܕܐܢ ܡܠܟܘ̈ܬܐ
ܘܪ̈ܘܪܒܢܐ. 35ܗܘ ܕܡܩܝܡ ܠܝ ܠܬܫܒܘܚܬܐ. ܘܡܕܡܟ[q] ܠܫܒܗܪ̈ܢܐ
ܠܐ [r]ܒܥܒܕܢܐ ܐܠܐ ܠܥܠܡ ܒܝܩܪܐ. ܡܛܠ [s]ܕ⌜ܠܐ⌝ ܝܕܥܘܗܝ,[s].
36ܘܗܫܐ ܚܙܘ ܪ̈ܘܪܒܢܘܗܝ ܕܐܪܥܐ ܕܝܢܗ ܕܡܪܝܐ. ܡܛܠ ܕܡܠܟܐ
ܗܘ̇ ܕܪܒܐ. ܘܕܐܢ ܠܡܠܟܘܬܐ ܡܢ ܟܠܗ̇ ܫܡܝܐ. 37ܒܪܟܘ ܠܡܪܝܐ
ܗܢܘܢ ܕܕܚܠܝܢ ܡܢ ܡܪܝܐ [t]ܒܐܣܟܡܐ. ܡܛܠ ܕܪ̈ܚܡܘܗܝ,
ܕܡܪܝܐ ܥܠ ܕܚ̈ܠܘܗܝ, ܒܕܝܢܐ. 38ܠܡܦܪܫ ܒܝܢܬ ܙܕ̈ܝܩܐ ܘܚ̈ܛܝܐ.
ܠܡܦܪܥ ܠܚ̈ܛܝܐ ܠܥܠܡܐ ܐܝܟ ܥܒ̈ܕܝܗܘܢ. 39ܘܠܡܚܣ ܠܙܕ̈ܝܩܐ
ܡܢ ܡܘܟܟܐ ܕܚ̈ܛܝܐ. ܘܠܡܦܪܥ ܠܚ̈ܛܝܐ ܚܠܦ ܕܥܒܕ [u]ܠܙܕܝܩܐ.
40ܡܛܠ ܕܒܣܝܡ ܗܘ ܡܪܝܐ ܠܐܝܠܝܢ ܕܩܪܝܢ ܠܗ ܒܡܣܝܒܪܢܘܬܐ.
ܠܡܥܒܕ ܐܝܟ ܪ̈ܚܡܘܗܝ, ܠܚ̈ܣܝܘܗܝ., ܠܡܩܡ ܩܕܡܘܗܝ, ܒܟܠ ܙܒܢ
ܒܚܘܣܢܐ. 41ܒܪܝܟ ܗܘ ܡܪܝܐ ܠܥܠܡ ܡܢ ܥܒ̈ܕܘܗܝ ⁘

[q] The Syriac corresponds exactly to the Greek *κοιμίζων*. In spite of Ryle and James' advocacy of this difficult word, I think it must be a translator's blunder. The Syriac itself suggests the emendation ܕܡܡܟܟ (and lowers the proud).

[r] This looks like a corruption of ܠܐܒܕܢܐ (= *εἰς ἀπώλειαν*): but with the added ܐܠܐ it makes good sense.

[s—s] Cod. ܡܛܠ ܕܝܕܥܘܗܝ.

[t] Gk. *ἐν ἐπιστήμῃ* (read as *ἐπὶ σχήματι*?).

[u] The translator has misunderstood or misread the Greek.

PSALM 3 (= Ps. 45).

1ܠܡܢܐ ܕܡܟܬ, ܢܦܫ, ܘܠܐ ܡܒܪܟܬ, ܠܡܪܝܐ. 2ܬܫܒܘܚܬܐ
ܚܕܬܐ [a] ܠܐܠܗܐ. ܙܡܪܝ, ܘܐܬܬܥܝܪܝ, ܒܥܝܪܘܬܗ. ܡܛܠ

[a] The translator or scribe has dropped the words *ψάλατε* [*τῷ θεῷ*] *τῷ αἰνετῷ*.

(Syriac text, verses 3–16)

³ ܘܒܝܐܪ̈ܐ ܘܓ ܐܠܗܐ ܐܠܗܐ ܡܢ ܠܟܠ ܐܠܗܐ ܨܠ. ܕܗܘ̈ܝܢ ܚܠܦܝ

⁴ ...

⁵ ...

⁶ ...

⁷ ...

⁸ ...

⁹ ...

¹⁰ ...

¹¹ ...

¹² ...

¹³ ...

¹⁴ ...

¹⁵ ...

¹⁶ ...

b–b ἀποβλέπω for ἀποβλέπει.   c κύριος for θεός.
d An addition by the transcriber, due to reminiscence from the Odes.

PSALM 4 (= Ps. 47ᵃ).

¹ ...

b ...

² ...

a Either the numeration has gone wrong, or a Psalm 46 has been dropped. The Greek shows that the former must be the correct explanation.

b A marginal note says that one copy reads ܪܚܘܣ

ܗܘ ܕܩܕܡܐ ܒܡܠܘܗܝ، ܠܡܚܝܒܘ ܠܚܛܝܐ ܒܕܝܢܐ. 3ܘܐܝܕܗ
ܠܘܩܕܡ ܥܠܘܗܝ، ܐܝܟ ܕܒܛܢܢܐ. ܘܗ݁ܘ ܡܚܝܒ ܒܣܘܓܐܐ
ܕܙܢܝܘܬܐ ܕܚܛܝܐ. 4ܥܝ̈ܢܘܗܝ، ܥܠ ܟܠ ܐܢܬܬܐ ܕܠܐ
ܦܘܪܫܢܐ. ܘܠܫܢܗ ܕܓܠ ܒܡܘ̈ܗܒܐ ܕܡܘܡܬܐ. 5ܒܠܠܝܐ ܘܒܚܫܘܟܐ
ܐܝܟ ܕܠܐ ܡܬܚܙܝܐ ܒܥܝ̈ܢܘܗܝ، ܡܡܠܠ ܥܡ ܟܠ ܐܢܬܬܐ ܒܪܡܙܬܐ
ܕܒܝܫܬܐ 6ܘܥܠܠ ܠܡܥܠ ܒܟܠ ܒܝܬܐ ܒܚܕܘܬܐ. ܐܝܟ ܗܘ
ܕܠܝܬ ܒܗ ܒܝܫܬܐ. 7ܐܘܒܕ ܐܠܗܐ ܠܐܝܠܝܢ ܕܒܡܣܒ ܒܐܦ̈ܐ
ܕܝܢܝܢ. [c]ܚܝܐ ܕܝܢ ܥܡ ܬܪ̈ܝܨܐ ܒܚܘܒܠܐ ܕܦܪܨܘܦܗ [d]ܘܒܡܣܡܣܢܘܬܐ
ܕܫܝܢܘܗܝ، [e] 8ܢܓܠܐ ܐܠܗܐ ܥܒ̈ܕܘܗܝ ܕܐܝܠܝܢ ܕܡܫܦܪܝܢ ܠܒܢܝ̈ܢܫܐ.
ܒܓܘܚܟܐ ܘܒܒܘܙܚܐ ܥܒ̈ܕܘܗܝ، 9ܘܢܙܕܕܩܘܢ [f]ܚܣ̈ܝܐ ܕܝܢܗ
ܕܐܠܗܗܘܢ܆ ܟܕ ܢܬܬܪܝܡܘܢ ܚܛ̈ܝܐ ܡܢ ܩܕܡ ܙܕܝܩܐ. 10ܢܥܒܕ
ܒܐܦ̈ܐ ܕܡܡܠܠ ܢܡܘܣܐ ܒܢܟܠܐ. 11ܘܥܝ̈ܢܘܗܝ، ܥܠ ܒܝܬܐ[g]
ܒܫܠܝܘܬܐ ܐܝܟ ܚܘܝܐ. ܠܡܫܪܐ ܚܟܡܬܐ ܕܚܕ ܚܕ ܒܡ̈ܠܐ
ܕܒܠܘܬܐ. 12ܦܬܓܡ̈ܘܗܝ، ܒܣܘܥܪܢܐ ܒܝܫܐ ܐܬܝܗܘܢ܆
ܠܡܫܠܡܢܐ ܕܪܓܬܐ ܕܥܘܠܐ. ܘܠܐ ܦܪܩ 13ܥܕܡܐ [h]ܕܒܕܪ
ܒܝܬܡܘܬܐ. ܘܐܚܪܒ ܒܝܬܐ ܡܛܠ ܪܓܬܐ ܕܥܘܠܐ. 14ܘܐܬܚܫܒ
ܒܡ̈ܠܐ ܕܠܝܬ ܡܢܘ ܕܚܙܐ ܘܕܐܢ. 15ܘܐܬܡܠܝ ܒܗܕܐ ܒܥܘܠܐ.
ܘܥܝ̈ܢܘܗܝ، ܥܠ ܒܝܬܐ ܐܚܪܢܐ ܠܡܚܪܒܘܬܗ ܒܡ̈ܠܐ ܕܦܪܣܘܬܐ
ܘܠܐ ܡܬܡܠܝܐ ܢܦܫܗ ܐܝܟ ܫܝܘܠ. 16ܒܗܠܝܢ ܟܠܗܝܢ ܬܗܘܐ
[i]⌜ܡܢܬܗ⌝ ܡܪܝܐ ܒܨܥܪܐ ܡܢ ܩܕܡܝܟ. ܡܦܩܗ ܒܬܢܚ̈ܬܐ ܘܡܥܠܗ
ܒܠܘܛܬܐ. 17ܒܟܐ̈ܒܐ ܘܒܡܣܟܢܘܬܐ ܘܒܐܘܠܨܢܐ ܚܝ̈ܘܗܝ، ܡܪܝܐ
ܢܗܘܘܢ܆ ܫܢܬܗ ܒܥܩ̈ܬܐ ܘܥܝܪܘܬܗ ܒܟܐ̈ܒܐ. 18ܘܬܬܪܝܡ ܫܢܬܐ

[c] Gk. ἐν ὑποκρίσει ζῶντας μετὰ ὁσίων.

[d] Sic cod. but read ܘܒܡܣܒܢܘܬܐ

[e] The Gk. which has omitted κρίνοντας carried back the next words to the previous sentence and left the sentence ἐν πενίᾳ κτέ. without a head.

[f] Cod. ܚܣ̈ܝܐ

[g] Gk. adds ἀνδρός.

[h] Gk. ἐνίκησεν σκορπίσαι.

[i] Cod. om.

ܡܢ ܝܕ̈ܥܘܗܝ ܟܠܠܐ. ܢܦܠ ܡܢ ܟܠ ܚܒܪܐ ܕܐܒ̈ܗܘܗܝ ܒܨܥܪܐ.
19 ܘܚܪ ܦܪ̈ܣܝܗܘܢ[k] ܐܒ̈ܗܘܗܝ، ܢܚܘܠ ܠܒܝܬܗ. ܘܢܣܘܐ ܣܚܝܪ ܒܝܬܗ
ܡܢ ܟܠ ܡܕܡ. ܕܡܣܬܒܥܐ ܢܦܫܐ. 20 ܘܡܢ ܠܒܪܗ [l]ܠܐ ܢܫ ܢܩܝܡܘܢܗܝ.
21 ܢܬܒܕܪ ܡܢ ܚܝܘܬܐ ܒܣܪܐ ܕܢܣ̈ܒܝ ܒܐ̈ܦܐ. ܘܓܪ̈ܡܐ
ܕܥܘ̈ܠܐ ܩܕܡ ܫܡܫܐ ܒܓܠܝܐ. 22 ܢܣܚܘܢ ܥܘܪ̈ܒܐ [ܥܝ̈ܢܐ[m]]
ܕܐܝܠܝܢ ܕܢܦܩܘܢ ܠܒܢܝ̈ܢܫܐ. 23 ܡܛܠ ܕܐܚܪܒܘ ܒ̈ܬܐ ܣܓܝ̈ܐܐ
ܕܐܢܫܐ ܒܨܥܪܐ. ܘܒܕܪܘܗܝ ܒܪܓܬܐ. 24 ܘܠܐ ܐܬܕܟܪܘ
ܠܐܠܗܐ. ܘܠܐ ܕܚܠܘ ܡܢ ܐܠܗܐ ܒܗܠܝܢ ܟܠܗܝܢ. 25 ܘܐܪܓܙܘ
ܠܐܠܗܐ. ܘܐܬܚܡܬ ܕܢܘܒܕ ܐܢܘܢ ܡܢ ܐܪܥܐ. ܡܛܠ ܕܠܢܦ̈ܫܬܐ
ܬܡܝ̈ܡܬܐ ܒܡܫܥܒܕܘܬܐ ܗܦܝܟܘܬܐ ܢܣܒܘ ܒܐܦ̈ܝܗܘܢ.
26 ܛܘܒܝܗܘܢ ܠܐܝܠܝܢ ܕܕܚܠܝܢ ܡܢ ܡܪܝܐ ܒܬܡܝܡܘܬܗܘܢ.
27 ܘܡܪܝܐ ܢܦܪܘܩ ܐܢܘܢ ܡܢ ܓܒܪ̈ܐ ܢܟܠܬܢ̈ܐ ܘܥܘ̈ܠܐ.
ܘܢܦܪܘܩ ܡܢ ܟܠ ܡܟܫܘܠܐ ܕܥܘ̈ܠܐ. 28 ܐܘܒܕ ܐܠܗܐ ܠܟܠ ܕܥܒܕܝܢ
ܛܠܘܡܝܐ ܒܫܬܝܪܘܬܐ. ܡܛܠ ܕܕܝܢܐ ܥܫܝܢܐ ܡܪܝܐ ܗܘ
ܐܠܗܢ ܒܙܕܝܩܘܬܐ. 29 ܢܗܘܘܢ ܡܪܝܐ ܪ̈ܚܡܝܟ ܥܠ ܟܠܗܘܢ
ܐܝܠܝܢ ܕܡܚܒܝܢ ܠܟ.

[k] Cod. *ex errore* ܡܚܣܢ.

[l] Cod. om. ܠܐ. The translation is a free paraphrase of *ἐν μονώσει ἀτεκνίας τὸ γῆρας αὐτοῦ εἰς ἀνάληψιν.*

[m] Accidentally omitted in passing from one page to the next.

PSALM 5 (= Ps. 48).

1 ܡܪܝܐ ܐܠܗܝ، ܐܫܒܚ ܫܡܟ ܒܚܕܘܬܐ. ܒܝܢܬ ܐܝܠܝܢ ܕܝܕܥܝܢ
ܕܝ̈ܢܝܟ ܙܕܝܩ̈ܐ. 2 ܡܛܠ ܕܐܢܬ ܒܣܝܡ ܘܡܪܚܡܢ. ܘܒܟ ܓܘܣܗ
ܕܡܣܟܢܐ. 3 ܟܕ ܐܓܥܐ ܠܘܬܟ ܠܐ ܬܫܬܘܩ ܡܢܝ. 4 ܡܛܠ ܕܠܐ
ܢܣܒ ܓܒܪ ܒܙܬܐ ܡܢ ܓܒܪܐ ܚܝܠܬܢܐ. 5 ܘܐܢ ܡܢܘ

ܢܣܒ ܓܝܪ ܥܠ ܡܢܐ ܕܒܙܬ. ܐܠܐ ܐܢ ܐܢܬ ܬܬܠ ܠܗ. 6 ܡܛܠ
ܕܒܪ ܐܢܫܐ ܘܡܢܬܗ ܠܘܬܟ ܗܝ܆ ܒܡܬܩܠܬܐ. ܘܠܐ ܢܘܣܦ
ܠܡܬܝܬܪܘ ܠܒܪ ܡܢ ܕܨܒܝܢܟ. ܐܠܗܐ. 7 ܒܐܘܠܨܢܢ ܩܥܝܢܢ ܠܟ ܠܡܥܕܪܢ.
ܘܐܢܬ ܠܐ ܐܗܦܟܬ ܒܥܘܬܢ: ܡܛܠ ܕܐܢܬ ܗܘ ܐܠܗܢ: [a]8 ܠܐ
ܬܬܘܚܪ[a] ܐܝܕܟ ܡܢܢ. [b]ܕܠܐ ܢܬܥܨܐ ܕܢܚܛܐ[b]. 9 ܘܠܐ [c]ܬܗܦܟ
ܐܦܝܟ ܡܢܢ. ܕܠܐ ܢܦܫ ܡܢܟ. ܐܠܐ ܠܘܬܟ ܢܐܬܐ. 10 ܐܢ
ܓܝܪ ܐܟܦܢ ܡܣܟܢܐ ܠܘܬܟ ܐܩܪܐ ܐܠܗܐ ܘܐܢܬ ܬܬܠ.
11 ܠܦܪܚܬܐ ܓܝܪ ܘܠܢܘ̈ܢܐ ܐܢܬ ܡܬܪܣܐ ܐܢܬ. ܟܕ ܬܬܠ
ܡܛܪܐ ܒܡܕܒܪܐ ܠܡܪܥܝܬܐ ܕܥܣܒܐ. ܠܡܛܝܒܘ ܡܐܟܘܠܬܐ
ܒܡܕܒܪܐ ܠܟܠ ܚܝܘܬܐ. 12 ܘܐܢ ܢܟܦܘܢ ܠܘܬܟ ܢܪܝܡܘܢ
ܐܦܝܗܘܢ: 13 ܠܡ̈ܠܟܐ ܘܠܪ̈ܘܪܒܢܐ ܘܠܥܡ̈ܡܐ ܐܢܬ ܗܘ ܡܬܪܣܐ
ܐܠܗܐ. ܘܣܒܪܗ ܕܡܣܟܢܐ ܘܕܒܨܝܪܐ[d]. ܡܢܘ. ܐܠܐ ܐܢ ܐܢܬ
ܡܪܝܐ. 14 ܘܬܫܒܘܚܬܗ܆ ܡܛܠ ܕܐܢܬ ܗܘ ܒܣܝܡܐ ܘܢܝܚܐ.
ܘܬܣܒܥ ܢܦܫܗ ܟܕ ܬܦܬܚ ܠܗ ܐܝܕܝܟ ܒܪ̈ܚܡܐ. 15 [e]ܚܣܝܟܘܬܗ
ܛܒܘ ܕܒܪ ܐܢܫܐ. ܒܚܘܣܟܐ ܗ̇ܝ. ܝܘܡܢ ܘܡܚܪ. ܘܐܢ ܗܘ
ܕܬܢܝܢܐ ܠܡܬܠ ܘܠܐ ܪܛܢ. ܘܗܢܐ ܬܕܡܘܪܬܐ ܗܘ̇[e]. 16 ܡܘܗܒܬܟ
ܕܝܢ ܕܥܠܝܟ ܡܣܓܝܐܐ ܒܛܝܒܘܬܐ ܘܒܒܥܘܬܐ[f]. ܘܠܝܬ[g] ܡܣܒܪܐ

a—a i.e. *μὴ βραδύνῃς*, the Greek is *μὴ βαρύνῃς* (= ܠܐ ܬܘܩܪ).

b—b A paraphrase for *ἵνα μὴ δι' ἀνάγκην ἁμάρτωμεν*.

c The Syriac here varies from the Greek (*καὶ ἐὰν μὴ ἐπιστρέψῃς ἡμᾶς, οὐκ ἀφεξόμεθα*), whether by conjecture or by the tradition of a better text. It stands for *καὶ μὴ ἀποστρέψῃς ἀφ' ἡμῶν, ἵνα μὴ ἀφεξώμεθα ἀπὸ σοῦ*.

d Gk. *πένητος*. Cf. Matt. v. 45.

e—e A passage of some difficulty. The Syriac supports Ryle and James in their emendation [*σήμερον καὶ*] *αὔριον*. And it certainly reads *φειδῷ*. But the emendation is unnecessary: Gebhardt's text is right or nearly so: *ἐν φειδοῖ καὶ ἡ αὔριον*: omit *ἡ*, and translate: 'Human kindness is scant and of to-morrow: and if a man repeats a kindness without grumbling, why! 'tis a marvel.'

f Sic cod. *Lege* ܘܒܥܘܬܪܐ (= Gk. *πλούσιον*).

g Misreading Gk. *οὗ* as *οὐ*.

ܕܠܘܬܟ ܕܢܣܒܘܢ ܒܡܣܒܪܢܘܬܐ. [17] ܟܠ ܕܠܗ ܐܘܪܚܐ ܒܪ ܡܢ ܕܡܣܟܢ
ܡܪܝܐ ܒܛܝܒܘܬܐ. [18] ܛܝܒܘܬܗ، ܠܒܪܢܫܐ ܕܢܬܪܒܘܢܗ،
[h]ܡܪܝܐ [i]ܒܡܣܬܦܩܢܘܬܐ. [19] ܕܡܣܬܦܩ ܗܘ ܒܪ ܢܬܬܪ ܒܪܢܫܐ
ܕܚܛܐ ܠܗ. [20] ܣܦܘܩܐ [k]ܡܣܬܦܩܢܘܬܐ ܒܙܕܝܩܘܬܐ.[l] [21] ܐܬܒܣܡܘ
ܒܢܝ ܕܚ̈ܠܘܗܝ، ܕܡܪܝܐ ܒܛ̈ܒܬܐ ܘܛܝܒܘܬܟ ܥܠ ܐܝܣܪܐܝܠ
ܒܡܠܟܘܬܟ. [22] ܡܒܪܟܐ ܗ̇ܝ، ܬܫܒܘܚܬܗ ܕܡܪܝܐ ܡܛܠ ܕܗܘܝܘ
ܡܠܟܢ.

[h] Gk. *θεός*.

[i] Gk. *συμμετρίᾳ αὐταρκείας*.

[k] Gk. *τὸ μέτριον*.

[l] Syr. omits by ὁμοιοτέλευτον the words *καὶ ἐν τούτῳ ἡ εὐλογία τοῦ κυρίου εἰς πλησμονὴν ἐν δικαιοσύνῃ*.

PSALM 6 (= Ps. 49).

[1] ܛܘܒܘܗܝ، ܠܓܒܪܐ ܕܡܛܝܒ ܠܒܗ ܠܡܩܪܐ ܒܫܡܗ ܕܡܪܝܐ.
[2] ܘܟܕ ܡܬܕܟܪ ܫܡܗ ܕܡܪܝܐ ܢܬܦܪܩ. [3] ܘܐܘܪ̈ܚܬܗ ܡܬܬܪ̈ܨܢ ܡܢ
ܩܕܡ ܡܪܝܐ. ܘܡܬܢܛܪܝܢ ܥܒ̈ܕܐ ܕܐܝ̈ܕܘܗܝ، ܡܢ ܐܠܗܗ. [a4] ܘܚܙܘܬܗ
ܒܝܫܬܐ ܕܚܠܡܐ ܠܐ ܬܬܙܝܥ. ܡܛܠ ܕܕܚܠܗ ܗ̣ܘ. ܘܒܥܒܪܗ[a]
[b5] ܒܥܒܪܐ ܕܢܗܪ̈ܘܬܐ. ܘܒܙܘܥܙܥܐ ܕܝܡ̈ܡܐ ܠܐ ܬܬܪܗܒ. [6] ܩܡ
ܡܢ ܫܢܬܗ ܘܒܪܟ ܠܫܡܗ ܕܡܪܝܐ. [7] ܘܒܫܝܢܘܬܐ ܕܠܒܗ ܙܡܪ
ܠܫܡܗ [c]ܕܡܪܝܐ. ܘܒܥܐ ܡܢ ܩܕܡ ܐܦ̈ܘܗܝ ܕܡܪܝܐ ܥܠ ܟܠܗ
ܒܝܬܗ. [8] ܘܡܪܝܐ ܫܡܥ ܨܠܘܬܗ ܕܟܠ ܕܒܕܚܠܬܗ ܗ̣ܘ[d]. ܘܟܠ
[e]ܫܐܠܬܐ ܕܢܦܫܐ ܕܡܣܒܪܐ ܒܗ. ܘܡܫܡܠܐ ܡܪܝܐ. [9] ܒܪܝܟ
ܗ̣ܘ ܕܥܒܕ ܪ̈ܚܡܐ. ܥܠ ܐܝܠܝܢ ܕܡܚܒܝܢ [f]ܠܗ ܒܫܪܪܐ.

[a–a] The text is in confusion: we should read ܒܝܫܬܐ, and add ܢܦܫܗ after ܬܬܙܝܥ. The words ܡܛܠ ܕܕܚܠܗ ܗ̣ܘ are missing in the Greek.

[b] Cod. ܒܥܒܕܐ

[c] Gk. *τοῦ θεοῦ αὐτοῦ*.

[d] Gk. adds *θεοῦ*.

[e] Cod. *ex errore* ܫܐܬܠܐ

[f] Cod. *ex errore* repeats ܠܗ in passing from one page to the next.

PSALM 7 (=Ps. 50).

¹ܠܐ ܬܪܚܩ ܡܫܪܝܢܟ ܡܢܢ ܐܠܗܐ. ܕܕܠܡܐ ܢܩܘܡܘܢ ܥܠܝܢ
ܐܝܠܝܢ ᵃܕܣܢܐܘܢ ܡܓܢ. ²ܡܛܠ ܕܕܚܩܬ ܐܢܘܢ ܐܠܗܐ. ܕܠܐ
ܬܕܘܫ ܪ̈ܓܠܗܘܢ ܝܪܬܘܬܐ ܕܩܘܕܫܟ. ³ܐܢܬ ܒܪܚܡܝܟ ܪ̈ܕܝ
ܘܠܐ ܬܫܠܛܝܢ ܠܥܡ̈ܡܐ. ⁴ܐܢ ܓܝܪ ܬܫܕܪ ܡܘܬܐ. ܐܢܬ ᵇܦܩܘܕ
ܠܗ ܥܠܝܢ. ܡܛܠ ܕܐܢܬ ܗܘ ܡܪܚܡܢܐ ܘܠܐ ܬܪܓܙ ܐܝܟ
ܕܠܡܓܡܪܘܬܢ. ⁵ܡܛܠ ܫܡܟ ܓܝܪ ܕܫܪܐ ܒܝܢܬܢ ܢܚܘܘܢ
ܥܠܝܢ ܪ̈ܚܡܐ. ⁶ܘܠܐ ܢܥܫܢܘܢ ܥܡ̈ܡܐ ܠܡܬܦܪܥܘ ܥܠܝܢ.
ܡܛܠ ܕܐܢܬ ܗ̣ܘ ᶜܡܥܕܪܢ. ⁷ܘܡܐ ܢܩܪܐ ܠܘܬܟ ܘܐܢܬ ܬܥܢܝܢ.
⁸ܡܛܠ ܕܐܢܬ ܬܚܘܣ ܥܠ ܫܪܒܗ ܕܐܝܣܪܝܠ ܠܥܠܡ ܘܠܐ ܬܫܒܩܝܘܗܝ.ᵈ
⁹ᵉܐܬܬܩܢ ܒܝܘܡܐ ܕܡܥܕܪܢܟ ܠܡܪܚܡ ܥܠ ܒܝܬܗ ܕܝܥܩܘܒ ܠܝܘܡܐ
ܗ̇ܘ ܕܡܠܟܬ ܠܗܘܢ.

ᵃ Cod. ܕܣܢܐܘܢ

ᵇ Cod. *ex errore* ܦܩܘܕ, cf. Gk. σὺ ἐντελῇ αὐτῷ περὶ ἡμῶν.

ᶜ Gk. ὑπερασπιστής.

ᵈ The Syriac has dropped the following sentence: καὶ ἡμεῖς ὑπὸ ζυγόν σου [εἰς] τὸν αἰῶνα καὶ μάστιγα παιδείας σου.

ᵉ Cod. ܐܬܬܩܢ

PSALM 8 (=Ps. 51).

¹ܐܘܠܨܢܐ ܘܩܠܐ ܕܩܪܒܐ ܫܡ̈ܥܬ ܐܕܢ̈ܝ. ܩܠܐ ᵃܕܫܝܦܘܪܐ ܘܪܓܫܐ
ܕܩܛܠܐ ܘܐܒܕܢܐ. ²ܩܠܐ ܕܥܡܐ ܣܓܝܐܐ ܐܝܟ ܪܘܚܐ
ܥܫܝܢܬܐ ܘܣܓܝܐܬܐ. ܐܝܟ ܥܠܥܠܐ ܕܢܘܪܐ ܕܐܬܝܐ ܥܠ
ܡܕܒܪܐ. ³ܘܐܡܪܬ ܠܠܒܝ. ܕܐܝܟܐ ܒܗ ܕܝܢ ܠܗ. ⁴ܩܠܐ
ܫܡܥܬ ܒܐܘܪܫܠܡ ܡܕܝܢܬܐ ܕܩܘܕܫܐ. ⁵ܘܐܬܬܒܪ̈ܝ، ܚܨ̈ܝ، ܣܪܝ
ܡܢ ܫܡܥܬܐ. ܘܟܘܪ̈ܗܝ ܬ̈ܠܝᵇ ⁶ܘܐܬܬܕܟܪܬ ܒܥܘܬܗ ܠܡ̈ܕܝܢ ܐܝܟ ܟܠܝܬܐ.
⁷ܘܐܡܪܬ ܢܬܪܨܘܢ ܐܘܪ̈ܚܬܗܘܢ ܒܙܕܝܩܘܬܐ. ܘܐܬܕܟܪܬ
ܕܝܢ̈ܘܗܝ ᶜܕܡܪܝܐ. ܕܡܢ ܟܕ ܐܬܒܪܝܘ ܫܡܝܐ ܘܐܪܥܐ. ܘܙܕܩܬ

ᵃ Cod. ܕܫܘܦܪܐ   ᵇ Syr. om. ἐφοβήθη ἡ καρδία μου.   ᶜ Gk. θεοῦ.

ܠܐܠܗܐ ܒܟܠܗܘܢ ܕܝ̈ܢܘܗܝ، ܕܡܢ ܥܠܡ. [8]ܓܠܐ ܕܝܢ ܐܠܗܐ
[d]ܠܚܛܗ̈ܝܗܘܢ ܩܕܡ ܫܡܫܐ. ܘܐܬܝܕܥ ܠܟܠܗ̇ ܐܪܥܐ ܕܝ̈ܢܘܗܝ،
ܕܡܪܝܐ ܙܕ̈ܝܩܐ. [9]ܒܡ̈ܛܫܝܬܐ ܬܚܝܬ ܕܐܪܥܐ ܡܣܟܠܝܢ ܗܘܘ[e]
[10]ܒܪܐ ܥܡ ܐܡܗ. ܘܐܒܐ ܥܡ ܒܪܬܗ. ܡܬܚܠܛܝܢ ܗܘܘ.
[11]ܘܟܠܗܘܢ ܓܝ̈ܪܝܢ ܗܘܘ ܢܫ̈ܐ ܕܚܒܪ̈ܝܗܘܢ܇ ܘܐܩܝܡܘ ܒܝܢܬܗܘܢ
ܩܝ̈ܡܐ [f] ܥܠ ܗܠܝܢ. [12]ܒܝܬ ܡܩܕܫܗ ܕܐܠܗܐ ܓܝܣܝܢ ܗܘܘ.
ܐܝܟ ܗܘ̇ ܕܠܝܬ ܕܝܪܬ ܘܦܪܘܩ. [13]ܘܕܝܫܝܢ ܗܘܘ [g]ܡܕܒܚܗ ܒܟܠܗ̇
ܛܡܐܘܬܗܘܢ܇ ܘܒܕܡܐ ܕܡܣܘܒܬܐ ܛܡܐܘ ܕܒ̈ܚܐ ܐܝܟ ܒܣܪܐ
ܛܡܐܐ. [14]ܘܠܐ ܫܒܩܘ ܚܛܝܬܐ ܕܠܐ ܥܒܕܘ ܘܐܘܬܪܘ ܡܢ ܥܡ̈ܡܐ.
[15]ܡܛܠ ܗܢܐ ܡܙܓ ܠܗܘܢ ܐܠܗܐ ܪܘܚܐ ܕܛܘܥܝܘܬܐ. ܘܐܫܩܝ
ܐܢܘܢ ܟܣܐ [h]ܚܡܪܐ ܠܪܘܝܘܬܐ. [16]ܐܝܬܝ، ܠܗܘ̇ ܕܡܢ ܚܪ̈ܬܗ̇
ܕܐܪܥܐ ܕܡܚܐ ܥܫܝܢܐܝܬ. [17]ܘܕܢ ܩܪܒܐ܆ ܥܠ ܐܘܪܫܠܡ ܘܥܠ
ܐܪܥܗ̇. [18]ܘܐܪܥܘܗܝ، ܪ̈ܝܫܢܝܗ̇ ܕܐܪܥܐ ܒܚܕܘܬܐ. ܘܐܡܪܘ ܠܗ.
[i]ܬܬܩܒܠ ܐܘܪܚܟ. ܬܐ ܥܘܠ ܒܫܠܡܐ. [19]ܘܫܘܝܘ ܐܘܪ̈ܚܬܐ
ܕܪ̈ܘܡܐ ܠܡܥܠܢܗ. ܦܬܚܘ ܬܪ̈ܥܐ ܥܠ ܐܘܪܫܠܡ ܘܟܠܠܘ
ܫܘܪ̈ܝܗ̇. [20]ܘܥܠ ܐܝܟ ܐܒܐ ܠܒܝܬܐ ܕܒܢ̈ܘܗܝ، ܒܫܠܡܐ.
ܘܐܩܝܡ ܪ̈ܓܠܘܗܝ، ܒܫܪܪܐ ܣܓܝܐܐ. [21]ܘܐܚܕ ܡܓ̈ܕܠܝܗ̇
ܘܫܘܪ̈ܝܗ̇ ܕܐܘܪܫܠܡ. [22]ܡܛܠ ܕܐܠܗܐ [k]ܐܝܬܝܗ̇ ܒܬܘܟܠܢܐ ܥܠ
ܛܘܥܝܘܬܗܘܢ܇ [23]ܘܐܘܒܕ ܪ̈ܝܫܢܝܗܘܢ [l]ܡܛܠ ܕܚܟܝܡ
ܒܡܠܟܐ.[l] ܘܐܫܕ ܕܡܐ ܕܥܡܘܪ̈ܝܗ̇ ܕܐܘܪܫܠܡ ܐܝܟ ܡܝ̈ܐ
ܕܣܘܚܬܐ. [24]ܘܐܘܒܠ ܒܢ̈ܝܗܘܢ ܘܒܢ̈ܬܗܘܢ ܗܢܘܢ ܕܗܘܘ
ܒܡܘܠܕܘܬܐ. [m][25]ܘܥܒܕܘ ܠܛܡܐܘܬܗܘܢ ܐܝܟ ܕܐܦ ܐܒ̈ܗܝܗܘܢ.

[d] Cod. *ex errore* ܒܚܛܗ̈ܝܗܘܢ. [e] Gk. adds *ἐν παροργισμῷ*.
[f] Gk. adds *μετὰ ὅρκου*. [g] Gk. *τὸ θυσιαστήριον κυρίου*.
[h] Gk. *οἴνου ἀκράτου*. [i] Gk. *ἐπευκτή*. [k] Cod. ܐܝܬܝܗܝ
[l–l] Gk. *καὶ πάντα σοφὸν ἐν βουλῇ*. This requires that we correct ܡܛܠ to ܘܟܠ.
[m] Cod. ܘܥܒܕ

[n]26ܘܛܢܦܬ ܐܘܪܫܠܡ ܐܦ ܠܩܘܕܫܝܢ ܕܡܬܩܕܫܝܢ ܗܘܘ ܠܫܡܗ
ܕܐܠܗܐ. 27ܘܐܙܕܕܩ ܐܠܗܐ ܒܕܝ̈ܢܘܗܝ، ܒܥܡ̈ܡܐ ܕܐܪܥܐ.
28ܘܚ̈ܣܝܕܘܗܝ، ܕܐܠܗܐ ܐܝܟ ܐܡܪ̈ܐ ܬܡܝܡܬܐ ܒܝܢܬܗܘܢ܀
29ܡܫܒܚ ܗܘ ܐܠܗܐ ܕܕܐܢ ܠܟܠܗ̇ ܐܪܥܐ ܒܙܕܝܩܘܬܗ.
30ܗܐ ܚܙܝܬ ܐܠܗܐ ܚܘܝܬܢ [o]ܒܙܕܝܩܘܬܟ. 31ܘܥܝ̈ܢܝܢ، ܚܙ̈ܝܢ ܕܝ̈ܢܝܟ.
ܐܠܗܐ. ܘܙܕܩܢ ܫܡܟ ܡܝܩܪܐ ܠܥܠܡܝܢ. 32ܡܛܠ ܕܐܢܬ ܗܘ
ܐܠܗܐ ܕܙܕܝܩܘܬܐ. ܕܕܐܢ ܐܢܬ ܠܐܝܣܪܝܠ ܒܡܪܕܘܬܐ.
33ܐܗܦܟ ܥܠܝܢ ܪ̈ܚܡܝܟ ܘܚܘܢܝܢ. 34ܘܟܢܫ ܒܕܪܘܗ ܕܐܝܣܪܝܠ.
ܒܪ̈ܚܡܐ ܘܒܛܝܒܘܬܐ. 35ܡܛܠ ܕܗܝܡܢܘܬܟ ܥܡܢ. ܘܚܢܢ ܡܩܫܝܢ
ܩ̈ܕܠܝܢ. ܘܐܢܬ ܪܕܘܝܢ ܐܢܬ. 36ܠܐ ܬܗܡܐ ܡܢܢ ܐܠܗܢ܀
ܕܕܠܡܐ ܢܒܠܥܘܢ ܥܡ̈ܡܐ ܐܝܟ ܕܠܝܬ ܕܦܪܘܩ. 37ܘܐܢܬ ܐܠܗܢ
ܐܢܬ ܡܢ ܒܪܫܝܬ. ܘܥܠܝܟ ܗܘ ܣܒܪܢ ܡܪܝܐ. 38ܘܡܢܢ ܠܐ
ܢܣܘܓ ܡܢܟ. ܡܛܠ ܕܛ̈ܒܝܢ ܐܢܘܢ ܕܝ̈ܢܝܟ 39ܥܠܝܢ ܘܥܠ ܒܢ̈ܝܢ.
ܨܒܝܢ ܠܥܠܡ ܡܪܝܐ ܐܠܗܐ ܦܪܘܩܢ. ܘܬܘܒ ܠܐ ܢܬܬܙܝܥ
ܠܥܠܡ. 40ܡܫܒܚ ܗܘ ܡܪܝܐ ܒܕܝ̈ܢܘܗܝ، ܒܦܘܡܐ ܕܚ̈ܣܝܕܘܗܝ.
41ܘܒܪܝܟ ܗܘ ܐܝܣܪܝܠ ܡܢ ܡܪܝܐ ܠܥܠܡ.

[n] Gk. ἐμίαναν, (not as in Cod. R ἐμίανεν).

[o] Cod. om. τὸ κρίμα σου.

PSALM 9 (= Ps. 52).

1ܟܕ ܢܦܩ ܐܝܣܪܝܠ ܒܫܒܝܐ ܠܐܪܥܐ ܢܘܟܪܝܬܐ. ܟܕ ܐܪܫܥܘ
ܡܢ ܡܪܝܐ ܦܪܘܩܗܘܢ܀ 2ܐܫܬܕܝܘ ܡܢ ܝܪܬܘܬܐ ܗ̇ܝ، ܕܝܗܒ
ܠܗܘܢ [a]ܐܠܗܐ. ܒܟܠܗܘܢ ܥܡ̈ܡܐ ܗܘܐ ܒܕܪܘܗ ܕܐܝܣܪܝܠ.
ܐܝܟ ܡܠܬܗ ܕܐܠܗܐ. 3ܡܛܠ ܕܬܙܕܕܩ ܐܠܗܐ ܒܙܕܝܩܘܬܟ.
ܒܥܘܠ ܕܥܠܡ. 4ܡܛܠ ܕܐܢܬ ܗܘ ܕܝܢܐ ܙܕܝܩܐ. ܥܠ ܟܠܗܘܢ

[a] Gk. κύριος.

ܒܥ̈ܡܡܐ ܕܐܪܥܐ. 5ܡܛܠ ܕܠܐ ܡܬܛܫܝܐ ܓܝܪ ܡܢ ܝܕܥܬܟ
ܟܠ ܡܢ ܕܥܒܕ ܥܘܠܐ. 6ܘܙܕܝܩܘܬܐ ܕܝܢ ܕܚܣ̈ܝܕܝܟ ܡܪܝܐ
ܩܕܡܝܟ. ܘܠܐܝܟܐ ܢܬܛܫܐ ܒܪܢܫܐ ܡܢ ܝܕܥܬܟ ܐܠܗܐ.
7ܥܒ̈ܕܝܢ ܓܝܪ ܒܚܐܪܘܬܐ ܘܒܫܘܠܛܢܘܬܐ ܕܢܦܫܢ ܠܡܥܒܕ ܟܐܢܘܬܐ
ܘܒܝܫܘܬܐ. ܒܥܒ̈ܕܐ ܕܐܝ̈ܕܝܢ. 8ܘܒܙܕܝܩܘܬܟ ܣܥܪ ܐܢܬ
ܠܒܢ̈ܝܢܫܐ. 9ܗܘ ܓܝܪ ܕܥܒܕ ܙܕܝܩܘܬܐ. ܣܝܡܬܐ ܕܚ̈ܝܐ ܣܐܡ
ܠܗ ܠܘܬ ܡܪܝܐ. ܘܗܘ ܕܥܒܕ ܥܘܠܐ ܗܘ ܚܐܒ ܕܝܢܐ ܕܢܦܫܗ
ܒܐܒܕܢܐ. 10ܕܝ̈ܢܘܗܝ[b] ܓܝܪ ܒܙܕܝܩܘܬܐ ܥܠ ܟܠ ܒܪܢܫ ܘܒܝܬܗ.
11ܠܡܢܘ ܓܝܪ ܢܛܐܒ ܐܠܗܐ. ܐܠܐ ܐܢ ܠܗܘܢ ܕܩܪܝܢ
ܠܡܪܝܐ. 12ܡܕܟܐ ܓܝܪ ܚܛܗ̈ܝܗ ܕܢܦܫܐ ܒܡܘܕܝܢܘܬܐ[c]. 13ܡܛܠ
ܕܒܗܬܬܐ ܗ̇ܝ ܠܢ ܘܠܐܦ̈ܝܢ ܥܠ ܟܠܗܘܢ ܗܠܝܢ. 14ܠܡܢܘ ܓܝܪ
ܢܫܒܘܩ ܚܛ̈ܗܐ. ܐܠܐ ܐܢ ܠܗܠܝܢ ܕܚܛܘ. 15ܠܙܕܝ̈ܩܐ ܓܝܪ
ܡܒܪܟ ܘܠܐ [d]ܡܟܣ ܐܢܬ ܠܗܘܢ ܥܠ ܡܕܡ ܕܚܛܘ. [e]ܒܛܝܒܘܬܟ
ܓܝܪ ܥܠ ܐܝܠܝܢ ܕܚܛܘ ܡܟܐ ܕܬܒܘ ܐܬܪܚܡܬ. 16ܘܗܫܐ ܐܢܬ
ܗܘ ܐܠܗܢ ܘܚܢܢ ܥܡܟ ܗܘ ܕܐܚܒܬ. ܚܘܪ ܘܪܚܡ ܐܠܗܗ
ܕܐܝܣܪܐܝܠ. ܡܛܠ ܕܕܝܠܟ ܚܢܢ. ܠܐ ܬܪܚܩ ܪ̈ܚܡܝܟ ܡܢܢ. ܕܠܐ
ܢܩܦܘܢ ܥܠܝܢ [f]ܒܥܡ̈ܡܐ. 17ܡܛܠ ܕܐܢܬ ܓܒܝܬ ܠܙܪܥܗ
ܕܐܒܪܗܡ. ܝܬܝܪ ܡܢ ܟܠܗܘܢ ܥܡ̈ܡܐ. 18ܘܣܡܬ ܥܠܝܢ ܫܡܟ
ܡܪܝܐ. ܘܠܐ [g]ܬܫܠܐ ܒܕܘܡܐ ܠܥܠܡ. 19ܒܢܡܘܣܐ ܐܩܝܡܬ
ܠܐܒܗ̈ܬܢ ܥܠܝܢ. ܘܚܢܢ ܡܣܒܪܝܢ ܒܟ. ܒܬܝܒܘܬܗ ܕܢܦܫܢ.
20ܕܡܪܝܐ ܐܢܘܢ ܪ̈ܚܡܐ ܥܠ ܒܝܬܐ ܕܐܝܣܪܐܝܠ [h]ܗܫܐ
ܘܠܥܠܡ.

[b] Gk. adds κυρίου.
[c] Gk. adds ἐν ἐξαγορίαις.
[d] Gk. εὐθυνεῖς.
[e] Gk. χρηστότης.
[f] Gk. om.
[g] i.e. οὐ καταπαύσεις, as in Cod. R.
[h] Gk. εἰς τὸν αἰῶνα καὶ ἔτι = Heb. לעלם ועד.

PSALM 10 (= Ps. 53).

[1] ܛܘܒܘܗܝ ܠܓܒܪܐ ܕܐܬܕܟܪܗ ܐܠܗܐ ܒܡܟܣܢܘܬܐ[a]. ܘܟܠܝܗܝ[b]
ܡܢ ܐܘܪܚܐ ܕܒܝܫܬܐ. ܒܡ̈ܚܘܬܐ. ܠܡܬܕܟܝܘ ܡܢ ܚܛܝܬܗ ܕܠܐ
ܬܣܓܐ. [2] ܗܘ̇ ܓܝܪ ܕܡܛܝܒ ܚܨܗ ܠܡ̈ܚܘܬܐ ܐܦ ܢܬܕܟܐ.
ܛܒ ܗܘ̣ ܓܝܪ[c] ܠܟܐܢܐ ܕܡܣܝܒܪܝܢ ܡܪܕܘܬܐ. [3] ܬܬܪܝܨܐ ܗ̇ܝ ܓܝܪ
ܐܘܪܚܗ ܕܙܕܝܩܐ. ܘܠܐ ܡܥܩܠܐ ܠܗ ܡܪܕܘܬܗ. [4] ܚܣܝܬܗ[d]
ܓܝܪ ܕܡܪܝܐ ܥܠ ܗ̇ܢܘܢ ܕܪܚܡܝܢ ܠܗ ܒܫܪܪܐ. ܘܢܬܕܟܪ
ܡܪܝܐ ܠܥܒ̈ܕܘܗܝ ܒܚ̈ܢܢܐ. [5] ܣܗܕܘܬܐ ܓܝܪ ܒܢܡܘܣܐ
ܕܩܝܡܐ ܕܠܥܠܡ. ܣܗܕܘܬܗ ܕܡܪܝܐ ܒܐܘܪ̈ܚܬܐ ܕܒ̈ܢܝ ܐܢܫܐ
ܒܣܘܥܪܢܐ. [6] ܙܕܝܩܐ ܗ̣ܘ ܘܬܪܝܨ [e]ܐܠܗܢ ܒܟܠܗܘܢ ܕܝ̈ܢܘܗܝ[f].
ܘܐܝܣܪܐܝܠ ܢܫܒܚ ܠܫܡܗ ܕܡܪܝܐ ܒܚܕܘܬܐ. [7] ܘܚܣ̈ܝܐ ܢܘܕܘܢ
ܒܟܢܘܫܬܐ ܕܥܡܐ. ܘܥܠ ܡܣܟ̈ܢܐ ܢܚܘܣ ܡܪܝܐ[g] ܒܒܘܣܡܗ
ܕܐܝܣܪܐܝܠ. [8] ܡܛܠ ܕܒܣܝܡ ܗ̣ܘ ܘܡܪܚܡܢ ܐܠܗܐ ܠܥܠܡ.
ܘܟܢܘ̈ܫܬܐ ܕܐܝܣܪܐܝܠ ܢܫܒ̈ܚܢ ܠܫܡܗ ܕܡܪܝܐ. [9] ܕܡܪܝܐ ܗ̣ܘ ܓܝܪ
ܦܘܪܩܢܐ ܥܠ ܒܝܬܐ ܕܐܝܣܪܐܝܠ. ܠܡܠܟܘܬܐ[h] ܕܠܥܠܡ.

[a] Cod. ܒܡܟܣܘܬܐ. Gk. *ἐν ἐλεγμῷ*.

[b] l. *ἐκωλύθη* as suggested by Fritzsche, for *ἐκυκλώθη* of the MSS.

[c] Gk. adds *ὁ κύριος*.

[d] Gk. *τὸ ἔλεος* (= ܚܣܗ, cf. 14^{6}).

[e] Gk. *ὁ κύριος ἡμῶν*.

[f] Gk. *ἐν κρίμασιν αὐτοῦ* and adds *εἰς τὸν αἰῶνα*.

[g] Gk. *ὁ θεός*.

[h] Perhaps we should read ܒܠܟܘܬܐ answering to the Gk. *σωφροσύνην*.

PSALM 11 (= Ps. 54).

[1] ܩܪܘ ܒܨܗܝܘܢ ܒܩܪܢܐ ܕܢܝܫܘܬܐ[a] ܕܩܕ̈ܝܫܐ. [2] ܐܟܪܙܘ ܒܐܘܪܫܠܡ
ܩܠܐ ܕܡܣܒܪܢܐ. ܡܛܠ ܕܪܚܡ ܐܠܗܐ ܥܠ ܐܝܣܪܐܝܠ ܒܣܘܥܪܢܗ.
[3] ܩܘܡܝ ܐܘܪܫܠܡ ܒܪܘܡܐ ܘܚܙܝ ܠܒ̈ܢܝܟܝ ܕܡܢ ܡܕܢܚܐ ܘܡܢ

[a] Gk. *σημασίας*.

ܡܚܪܒܐ ܡܚܒܫܝܢ [b]ܟܠܗܘܢ ܐܝܟ ܡܪܥܝܐ. [4]ܘܐܝܟ ܠܒܪ̈ܬܐ ܢܘܪܐ ܐܬܝܢ
ܠܡܪܥܝܬܗ ܕܐܠܗܗܘܢ. ܘܐܝܟ ܠܒܪ̈ܬܐ ܪ̈ܚܡܬܐ ܟܢܫ ܐܢܘܢ
ܐܠܗܐ. [5]ܛܘܪ̈ܐ ܪ̈ܡܐ ܡܟܟ ܘܫܘܝ ܠܗܘܢ܆ [6]ܘܪ̈ܡܬܐ ܥܪ̈ܩ
ܡܢ ܡܥܠܝܗܘܢ܆ [c][7]ܐܪ̈ܙܐ ܛܠܠ ܥܠܝܗܘܢ ܟܕ ܥܒܪܝܢ ܗܘܘ. ܘܟܠ
ܩܝܣܐ ܕܪܝܚܐ ܒܣܝܡܐ [d]ܐܪܝܚ ܠܗܘܢ ܐܠܗܐ. ܡܛܠ
ܕܢܥܒܪ ܝܣܪܐܝܠ. ܒܣܘܥܪܢܐ ܕܬܫܒܘܚܬܗ ܕܐܠܗܗܘܢ܆
[8]ܐܬܠܒܫܝ ܐܘܪܫܠܡ ܡܐܢ̈ܐ ܕܬܫܒܘܚܬܟܝ. ܘܛܝܒܝ ܐܣܛܠܐ
ܕܩܘܕܫܟܝ. ܡܛܠ ܕܐܠܗܐ ܡܠܠ ܛܒ̈ܬܐ ܠܝܣܪܐܝܠ [e]ܗܫܐ
ܘܠܥܠܡ[e]. [9]ܢܥܒܕ ܡܪܝܐ ܡܕܡ ܕܡܠܠ ܥܠ ܝܣܪܐܝܠ. ܘܥܠ
ܐܘܪܫܠܡ. ܢܩܝܡ ܡܪܝܐ ܠܝܣܪܐܝܠ. ܒܫܡܗ ܕܬܫܒܘܚܬܗ.
ܪ̈ܚܡܘܗܝ، ܕܡܪܝܐ ܥܠ ܝܣܪܐܝܠ [f]ܗܫܐ ܘܠܥܠܡ[f].

[b] Gk. εἰσάπαξ (= Heb. כחדה). [c] Gk. οἱ δρύμοι.
[d] Gk. ἀνέτειλεν (= Syr. ܐܕܢܚ ?).
[e—e] Gk. εἰς τὸν αἰῶνα καὶ ἔτι = Heb. לעלם ועד ut supra.
[f—f] Gk. as in note [e—e].

PSALM 12 (= Ps. 55).

[1]ܡܪܝܐ ܦܨܝܗ̇ ܠܢܦܫܝ ܡܢ ܓܒܪܐ ܗܦܝܟܐ ܘܒܝܫܐ. ܘܡܢ
ܠܫܢܐ ܡܠܫܢܢܐ. ܘܡܢ ܓܒܪ ܢܚܘܫܐ. ܕܡܠܠ ܕܓܠܬܐ ܘܢܟܠܐ.
[2]ܒܗܘܦܟܐ ܓܒܪ ܕܡ̈ܠܐ. ܐܘܪܚܬܗ، ܠܥܝܢܗ ܕܓܒܪܐ ܓܒܪ ܢܚܘܫܐ.
ܡܫܘܚܐ ܓܒܪ ܕܐܝܟ ܗܘ ܕܙܪܥ ܟܪܒ. ܘܡܫܘܚ ܢܘܪܐ ܒܥܡܐ[a].
[3]ܡܟܒܪܘܗ̇ ܓܒܪ [b]ܠܡܡܠܝܘ ܒ̈ܬܐ ܒܡܡܠܠܐ ܕܓܠܬܐ. [c]ܡܦܠ

[a] The Syriac translator has had difficulty, as every one else, with this passage: but it seems clear that he had a text very near to the Gk. ὥσπερ ἐν λαῷ πῦρ ἀνάπτον καλλόνην αὐτοῦ. It seems natural to correct this to ὥσπερ ἐν ἅλῳ πῦρ ἀνάπτον καλάμην with the Copenhagen MS. But the Syr. is clear for λαῷ, and it suggests καλλόνην αὐτοῦ by the clause which it prefixes (ܕܙܪܥ).
[b] i.e. ἐμπλῆσαι (H) for ἐμπρῆσαι (RJLC). [c] Gk. ἐκκόψαι.

[Syriac text, four lines]

d—d Gk. ἐν φλογὶ παρανόμου?   e Gk. συγχέαι.   f Cod. ܟܚܐܒܡܘ

g Gk. adds ἐν ἀπορίᾳ.   h Gk. omits.   i Gk. ἡσύχιον.   k Gk. omits.

PSALM 13 (= Ps. 56).

[Syriac text, several lines]

a Cod. ܘܗܘ

b i.e. Gk. ἀσεβής as in Codd. and not εὐσεβής as Wellhausen conjectured.

c Perhaps for ܪܕܒܘ (= Gk. συμπαραλημφθῇ).   d Cod. ܪܒܡܕܬܕ

e = Gk. ἐν περιστολῇ?   f Syr. begins verse here.   g Gk. νουθετήσει,

ܓܝܪ ܕܙܕܝܩܐ. ܐܝܟ ܕܠܒܪܗ ܪܚܡܐ. ܘܡܪܕܘܬܗ ܐܝܟ
ܕܒܘܟܪܐ. [9]ܡܛܠ ܕܚܣ ܗܘ [h]ܕܙܕܝܩܐ ܥܠ ܚܣܝ̈ܕܘܗܝ، ܘܡܥܒܪ ܣܟܠܘܬܗܘܢ
ܢܛܠܐ ܒܡܪܕܘܬܐ. ܚܝ̈ܝܗܘܢ ܓܝܪ ܕܙܕܝ̈ܩܐ ܠܥܠܡ ܐܢܘܢ:
[10]ܚܛܝ̈ܐ ܕܝܢ ܢܬܬܪܝܡܘܢ ܠܐܒܕܢܐ. ܘܠܐ ܢܫܬܟܚ ܬܘܒ
ܕܘܟܪܢܗܘܢ: [11]ܥܠ ܚܣܝ̈ܕܐ ܕܝܢ ܢܗܘܘܢ ܪ̈ܚܡܘܗܝ ܕܡܪܝܐ.
ܥܠ ܟܠܗܘܢ ܕܕ̈ܚܠܘܗܝ، ܚܢܢܗ.

[h] Gk. ὁ κύριος.

PSALM 14 (= Ps. 57).

[1]ܡܗܝܡܢ ܡܪܝܐ ܠܐܝܠܝܢ ܕܡܚܒܝܢ ܠܗ ܒܫܪܪܐ. ܠܗܘܢ
ܕܡܣܝܒܪܝܢ ܡܪܕܘܬܗ. ܠܗܘܢ ܕܡܗܠܟܝܢ ܒܙܕܝܩܘܬܐ
ܒܦܘ̈ܩܕܢܘܗܝ، ܒܢܡܘܣܐ ܗܘ ܕܦܩܕ ܠܢ ܠܚܝ̈ܝܢ. [2]ܘܚܣܝ̈ܕܘܗܝ، ܕܡܪܝܐ
ܢܐܚܘܢ ܒܗ ܠܥܠܡ. ܦܪܕܝܣܗ ܕܡܪܝܐ ܐܝ̈ܠܢܐ ܕܚܝ̈ܐ.
ܕܐܝܬܝܗܘܢ ܚܣܝ̈ܕܘܗܝ، [3]ܘܢܨܒܬܗܘܢ [a]ܡܫܪܪܐ ܠܥܠܡ. ܘܠܐ
ܢܬܥܩܪܘܢ ܟܠܗܘܢ ܝܘܡ̈ܬܐ ܕܫܡܝܐ. ܡܛܠ ܕܡܢܬܗ ܕܡܪܝܐ
ܘܝܪܬܘܬܗ ܐܝܣܪܐܝܠ. [4]ܘܠܐ ܗܟܢܐ ܚܛܝ̈ܐ ܘܥܘ̈ܠܐ. ܗ̇ܢܘܢ
ܕܐܚܒܘ ܝܘܡܐ ܒܫܘܬܦܘܬܐ ܕܚܛܗܐ. ܒܙܥܘܪܘܬܗ ܕܚܒܪ
ܕܒܫܬܐ ܪܓܬܗܘܢ: [5]ܘܠܐ ܐܬܕܟܪܘ ܠܐܠܗܐ. ܕܐܘܪܚܬܗܘܢ
ܕܒܢ̈ܝ ܐܢܫܐ ܓ̈ܠܝܢ ܐܢܝܢ ܩܕܡܘܗܝ، ܒܟܠܙܒܢ. ܘܬܘ̈ܢܝܐ ܕܠܒܐ
ܝܕܥ ܡܢ ܩܕܡ ܕܢܗܘܘܢ: [6]ܡܛܠ ܗܢܐ ܝܪܬܘܬܗܘܢ ܫܝܘܠ
ܘܐܒܕܢܐ ܘܚܫܘܟܐ. ܘܒܝܘܡܐ ܕܚܢܢܐ ܕܙܕܝ̈ܩܐ ܠܐ
ܢܫܬܟܚܘܢ: [7]ܚܣܝ̈ܕܘܗܝ، ܓܝܪ ܕܡܪܝܐ ܢܐܪܬܘܢ ܚܝ̈ܐ
ܒܚܕܘܬܐ.

[a] Gk. ἐρριζωμένη, which seems to stand for ܡܫܪܪܐ.

PSALM 15 (= Ps. 58).

[1]ܒܐܘܠܨܢܝ ܩܪܝܬ ܫܡܗ ܕܡܪܝܐ. ܘܠܥܘܕܪܢܝ ܣܒܪܬ ܠܐܠܗܗ
ܕܝܥܩܘܒ. ܘܐܬܦܪܩܬ[2] ܡܛܠ ܕܣܒܪܐ ܘܒܝܬ ܓܘܣܐ ܕܡܣ̈ܟܢܐ
ܐܢܬ ܗ̣ܘ ܐܠܗܐ. [3]ܡܢܘ ܓܝܪ ܕܡܫܟܚ [a]ܢܘܕܐ ܠܟ ܒܫܪܪܐ[a].
[4]ܘܡܢܘ ܚܝܠܗ ܕܒܪܐܢܫܐ. ܐܠܐ ܕܢܘܕܐ ܠܫܡܟ. [5]ܙܡܝܪܬܐ
ܚܕܬܐ ܒܩܠܐ ܒܒܘܣܡܐ ܕܠܒܐ. ܦܐܪܐ ܕܣܦܘ̈ܬܐ ܒܡܐܢܐ
ܕܡܬܩܢ ܠܠܫܢܐ. ̈ܕܒܚܬܐ ܕܣܦܘ̈ܬܐ ܡܢ ܠܒܐ ܚܣܝܐ ܘܙܕܝܩܐ.
[6]ܟܠ ܕܥܒܕ ܗܠܝܢ ܠܐ ܢܬܬܙܝܥ ܠܥܠܡ ܡܢ ܒܝܫܐ. ܕܫܠܗܒܝܬܐ
ܕܢܘܪܐ ܘܪܘܓܙܐ ܕܥܘ̈ܠܐ ܠܐ ܢܬܩܪܒ ܠܗܘܢ܆ [7]ܐܡܬܝ، ܕܢܦܩ
ܥܠ ܚܛ̈ܝܐ ܡܢ ܩܕܡ [b]ܡܪܝܐ ܠܡܚܡܪ ܟܠܗܘܢ [c]ܫܪܫܝ̈ܗܘܢ
ܕܚܛ̈ܝܐ. [8]ܡܛܠ ܕܐܬܘܬܗ ܓܝܪ [d]ܕܡܪܝܐ ܥܠ ܙܕ̈ܝܩܐ ܠܦܘܪܫܢܐ.
ܡܘܬܐ ܓܝܪ ܘܪܘܡܚܐ ܘܟܦܢܐ ܡܢ ܙܕ̈ܝܩܐ ܢܥܪܩܘܢ. [9]ܢܪܕܦܘܢ
ܓܝܪ ܡܢܗܘܢ܆ ܐܝܟ ܕܪܕܦ [e]ܡܘܬܐ ܡܢ [f]ܣܢ̈ܐ. ܢܪܕܦܘܢ
ܕܝܢ ܒܬܪ ܚܛ̈ܝܐ ܘܢܕܪܟܘܢ ܐܢܘܢ܆ ܘܐܝܠܝܢ ܕܥܒܕܝܢ ܥܘܠܐ
ܠܐ ܢܥܪܩܘܢ܆ ܡܢ ܕܝܢܗ ܕܡܪܝܐ. ܐܝܟ ܢܩ̈ܕܒ ܓܝܪ ܩܘܪܒܐ
ܢܬܕܪܟܘܢ ܐܢܘܢ܆ [10]ܡܛܠ ܕܐܬܘܬܐ ܕܐܒܕܢܐ ܥܠ ܐܦ̈ܝܗܘܢ܆
[11]ܘܝܪܬܘܬܗܘܢ ܕܚܛ̈ܝܐ ܐܒܕܢܐ ܘܚܫܘܟܐ. ܘܥܘܠܗܘܢ
ܢܪܕܦܘܢ ܐܢܘܢ ܒܕܡܐ ܠܫܝܘܠ ܬܚܬܝܬܐ. [12]ܘܝܪܬܘܬܗܘܢ
ܠܐ ܢܫܬܟܚ ܠܒܢ̈ܝܗܘܢ܆ [13]ܚܛܗ̈ܝܗܘܢ ܓܝܪ ܢܚܪܒܘܢ ܒܬ̈ܐ
ܕܚܛ̈ܝܐ. ܘܢܐܒܕܘܢ ܚܛ̈ܝܐ ܒܝܘܡܐ ܕܕܝܢܗ ܕܡܪܝܐ ܠܥܠܡ.
[14]ܐܡܬܝ، ܕܢܦܩܕ ܐܠܗܐ ܐܪܥܐ ܒܕܝܢܗ. [15]ܘܥܠ ܐܝܠܝܢ ܕܕܚܠܝܢ
ܡܢ ܡܪܝܐ ܢܗܘܘܢ ܪ̈ܚܡܐ ܒܗ̇. ܘܢܐܚܘܢ ܒܡܪܚܡܢܘܬܗ
[g]ܕܐܠܗܘܢ܆ ܘܚܛ̈ܝܐ ܢܐܒܕܘܢ ܠܙܒܢܐ ܕܠܥܠܡ.

a—a Gk. *εἰ μὴ ἐξομολογήσασθαι σοὶ ἐν ἀληθείᾳ.*

b Gk. *κυρίου.* c Gk. *ὑπόστασιν*, cf. Ps. xvii. 26. d Gk. *θεοῦ.*

e Perhaps ܡܘܬܢܐ, i.e. Gk. *λοιμός*. The MSS. have [*ἀπὸ*] *λιμοῦ* which Gebhardt emended to *ἀπὸ πολέμου*.

f Probably an error for ܟܦ̈ܢܐ. g Gk. *τοῦ θεοῦ αὐτῶν.*

PSALM 16 (= Ps. 59)[a].

[b] 1 ܟܕ ܐܬܡܟܟܬ ܢܦܫܝ ܩܠܝܠ ܡܢ ܡܪܝܐ. ܟܕ ܩܠܝܠ ܫܘܐ ܗܘܬ
ܒܫܢ̈ܬܐ ܕܢܝܡܬܐ ܕܚܛܝܐ. 2 ܘܟܕ ܐܪܚܩܬ ܡܢ ܡܪܝܐ. ܟܕ
ܩܠܝܠ ܡܬܐܫܕܐ ܗܘܬ ܢܦܫܝ ܠܡܘܬܐ. ܥܠ ܩܪܝܒ. ܬܪ̈ܥܐ
ܕܫܝܘܠ ܥܡ ܚܛܝܐ. 3 ܘܟܕ ܐܬܦܪܕܬ ܢܦܫܝ ܡܢ [c]ܐܠܗܐ ܕܐܝܣܪܐܝܠ.
ܐܠܘ ܠܐ ܡܪܝܐ ܥܕܪܢܝ ܒܪ̈ܚܡܘܗܝ ܕܠܥܠܡ. 4 ܕܩܪܒܢܝ ܐܝܟ
ܣܘܣܝܐ ܕܡܣܩܝܐ ܠܡܘܬܗ. ܦܪܩܢܝ ܘܡܥܕܪܢܝ ܒܟܠ ܙܒܢ ܗܘ.
[d]ܐܚܝܢ. 5 ܐܘܕܐ ܠܟ ܐܠܗܐ. ܡܛܠ ܕܥܕܪܬܢܝ ܒܦܘܪܩܢܝ. ܘܠܐ
ܚܫܒܬܢܝ [e]ܥܡ ܚܛܝ̈ܐ ܠܐܒܕܢܐ. 6 [f]ܠܐ ܬܪܚܩ ܪ̈ܚܡܝܟ [g]ܡܢܝ
ܐܠܗܐ[g]. ܘܠܐ ܢܕܟܪ ܕܘܟܪܢܟ ܡܢ ܠܒܝ ܥܕܡܐ ܠܡܘܬܐ.
7 ܦܪܘܩܢܝ [h]ܡܪܝܐ ܡܢ ܚܛܝܬܐ [i]ܒܝܫܬܐ. ܘܡܢ ܟܠ ܐܢܬܬܐ
ܒܝܫܬܐ ܕܡܟܫܠܐ [k]ܠܫܒܪܐ. 8 ܘܠܐ [l]ܢܫܪܓܢ ܫܘܦܪܗ̇ ܕܐܢܬܬܐ
ܒܘܠܬܐ. ܐܦ ܠܐ ܠܟܠ ܚܛܝܐ [m]ܕܐܝܬ[.] 9 ܘܐܬܩܢ ܥܒ̈ܕ ܐܝ̈ܕܝ
[n]ܩܕܡܝܟ[i]. ܘܗܠܟܬܝ ܢܛܪ ܒܕܘܟܪܢܟ. 10 ܠܫܢܝ ܘܣܦܘ̈ܬܝ ܒܡ̈ܠܐ
ܕܫܪܪܐ ܐܬܩܢ. ܪܘܓܙܐ ܘܚܡܬܐ [o]ܕܠܐ ܡܠܬܐ[o] [p]ܐܪܚܩ ܡܢܝ[q].

[a] This Psalm is quoted in part in the Cambridge MS. Add. 2012 where it is introduced as follows:

ܡܢ ܡܙܡܘܪ̈ܐ ܕܝܠܗ ܕܫܠܝܡܘܢ ܒܪ ܕܘܝܕ

and is rightly numbered as Ps. 58. We may call the fragment Cod. c.

[b] The translation of the difficult opening verses is somewhat paraphrastic, but the Greek can be seen through the Syriac.

[c] Gk. κυρίου θεοῦ. [d] Cod. ܐܚܝܢ [e] Cod. bis ܥܡ

[f] Inc. Cod. c. [g–g] Cod. c transposes. [h] Gk. ὁ θεός.

[i–i] Cod. c om. [k] Gk. ἄφρονα. [l] Gk. ἀπατησάτω με.

[m] A paraphrase for καὶ παντὸς ὑποκειμένου ἀπὸ ἁμαρτίας ἀνωφελοῦς.

[n] = ἐνώπιόν σου for Gk. ἐν τόπῳ σου.

[o–o] A literal rendering of ἄλογον.

[p] Cod. c ܐܒܥܕ

[q] Cod. c adds ܘܠܐ ܐܢܗܘ ܕܬܫܒܘܩ ܒܝܫܐ ܐܝܟ ܚܛܝܬܐ

ܪ¹¹ ... ...

... ...^s... ...¹²... ...

...^t

...¹³... ...^u... ...

...¹⁴... ...^v...

...¹⁵... ...

...

---

r–r A literal rendering of ὀλιγοψυχία.

s Cod. c ܕܝܢ ܐܝܟ   t Cod. c adds ܠ

u Cod. c adds ܐܝܟ

v The translator has omitted the difficult line [ἐν τῷ ἐλέγχεσθαι] ψυχὴν ἐν χειρὶ σαπρίας αὐτοῦ· ἡ δοκιμασία σου; but perhaps ἐν τῷ ἐλέγχεσθαι is latent in ܬܬܕܩܢ, for in Ps. xvii. 27 he renders καὶ ἐλέγξαι by ܘܠܡܟܣܘ. I have added the word ܢܦܫܐ to make the text clear. Wellhausen suggests ܬܬܕܩܢ (cf. Gk. ἡ δοκιμασία σου) which makes the addition of ܢܦܫܐ unnecessary. Cod. c ends here.

PSALM 17 (= Ps. 60).

... ...^a ...¹

...^b ...²

...^c ...³

... ...

...⁴ ...

...⁵ ...

... ...

...⁶ ...^d

... ...

---

a–a Gk. εἰς τὸν αἰῶνα καὶ ἔτι = Heb. לעלם ועד. For the Syriac rendering v. supra, Ps. ix. 20 etc.

b Gk. ὁ χρόνος ζωῆς.   c Cod. ܡܢܝܡ

d Gk. βασίλειον αὐτοῦ and so in v. 7.

ܘܠܐ⁷ ܫܒܚܘ ܠܫܡܟ ܡܝܩܪܐ ܒܬܫܒܘܚܬܐ. ܘܣܡܘ ܡܠܟܘܬܐ
ܚܠܦ ܪܘܡܗܘܢ: ⁸ܐܚܪܒܘ ܟܘܪܣܝܗ ܕܕܘܝܕ ܒܫܘܒܗܪܐ
ᵉܕܫܘܚܠܦܗܘܢ: ܘܐܢܬ ܕܝܢ ᶠܬܫܦܘܠ ܐܢܘܢ: ܘܬܥܩܪ ܙܪܥܗܘܢ
ܡܢ ܐܪܥܐ. ⁹ܟܕ ܢܩܘܡ ܥܠܝܗܘܢ: ܒܪܢܫܐ ܢܘܟܪܝܐ ܡܢ
ܫܪܒܬܐ ܕܠܢ. ¹⁰ܐܝܟ ܣܘܪܚܢܝܗܘܢ ܬܦܪܘܥ ܐܢܬ: ܐܠܗܐ.
ܘܬܬܥܒܫ ܠܗܘܢ ܐܝܟ ܥܒܕܝܗܘܢ: ¹¹ܘܠܐ ᵍܬܪܚܡ ܥܠܝܗܘܢ
ܐܠܗܐ. ʰܦܩܘܕ ܙܪܥܗܘܢ ܘܠܐ ܬܫܒܘܩ ܡܢܗܘܢ ܘܠܐ ܚܕ.
¹²ܡܗܝܡܢ ܡܪܝܐ ܒܟܠܗܘܢ ܕܝܢܘܗܝ ܕܥܒܕ ܥܠ ܐܪܥܐ.
¹³ܐܚܪܒ ܥܘܠܐ ܐܪܥܢ ܡܢ ܟܠ ܕܝܬܒ ܥܠܝܗ. ܣܚܦܘ ܛܠܝ̈ܐ
ܘܣܒ̈ܐ ܘܒܢܝ̈ܗܘܢ ܐܟܚܕܐ. ¹⁴ܒܫܘܦܪܐ ⁱܕܪܘܓܙܗ ܫܕܪ
ܐܢܘܢ ܥܕܡܐ ܠܡܥܪܒܐ. ܘܠܫܠܝ̈ܛܢܗ ܕܐܪܥܐ ܠܒܘܙܚܐ ܘܠܐ
ܚܣ. ¹⁵ܒܢܘܟܪܝܘܬܐ ܡܫܬܒܗܪ ܒܥܠܕܒܒܐ. ܘܠܒܗ ܢܘܟܪܝ ܗ̄ܘ
ܡܢ ܐܠܗܢ: ¹⁶ܘܟܠܡܕܡ ܕܥܒܕ ᵏܐܘܪܫܠܡ. ܐܝܟ ܕܐܦ ܥܡ̈ܡܐ
ܒܓܘܢܐ ܒܡܕܝ̈ܢܬܗܘܢ ˡܠܐܠܗܝ̈ܗܘܢ: ¹⁷ܘܐܚܝܕܝܢ ܗܘܘ ܠܗܘܢ
ܒܢ̈ܝ ܕܕܝܬܝܩܝ ܒܝܢܬ ܥܡ̈ܡܐ ܚܠܝ̈ܛܐ. ܘܠܝܬ ܗܘܐ ܒܝܢܬܗܘܢ
ܕܥܒܕ ܪ̈ܚܡܐ ܘܫܪܪܐ ᵐܒܐܘܪܫܠܡ. ¹⁸ܥܪܩܘ ܡܢܗܘܢ ܐܝܠܝܢ

ᵉ Gk. ἀλλάγματος but the Copenhagen MS. ἀλαλάγματος.

ᶠ Gk. + ὁ θεός.

ᵍ Gk. ἐλεήσεις or ἐλεήσαι.

ʰ The Gk. is ἐξηρεύνησε...καὶ οὐκ ἀφῆκεν...which the Syr. has turned into imperatives. The meaning of ܦܩܘܕ is obscure.

ⁱ The Gk. is ἐν ὀργῇ κάλλους αὐτοῦ, for which the Syr. has read ἐν κάλλει ὀργῆς αὐτοῦ.

ᵏ The translator read ἐποίησεν [– ἐν] Ἰερουσαλήμ and omits ὅσα.

ˡ Reading τοῖς θεοῖς or τοὺς θεοὺς with JLH for which Gebhardt conjectured τοῦ σθένους.

ᵐ This agrees with Gebhardt's reading οὐκ ἦν ἐν αὐτοῖς ὁ ποιῶν ἐν Ἰερουσαλὴμ ἔλεος καὶ ἀλήθειαν. The Gk. MSS. vary between ὁ ποιῶν ἐν μέσῳ ἐν αὐτοῖς ἐν and ὁ ποιῶν ἐν αὐτοῖς ἐν μέσῳ. May it not, however, be the case that the Syr. ܒܝܢܬܗܘܢ stands for ἐν μέσῳ ἐν αὐτοῖς? For ܫܪܪܐ the MS. has ܫܪܪܝܢ (?).

ܕܪ̈ܚܡܝܢ ܗܘܘ ܒܟܢܘܫܬܐ ܕܚܣܝ̈ܐ. ܘܦܪܚܘ ܐܝܟ ܨܦܪ̈ܐ ܕܦܪ̈ܚܝܢ
ܡܢ ܩܢ̈ܝܗܘܢ. [19] ܘܛܠܝ̈ܩܝܢ [n] ܗܘܘ، ܒܡܕܒܪ̈ܐ. ܠܡܦܪܩ ܢܦܫܗܘܢ ܡܢ
ܒܝܫܐ. ܘܝܩܝܪܐ ܗܘܬ ܒܥܝ̈ܢܝܗܘܢ ܬܘܬܒܘܬܗ̇ [o] ܕܢܦܫܐ
ܕܡܬܦܪܩܐ. ܗܘܬ ܡܢܗܘܢ܆ [20] ܒܟܠܗ̇ ܐܪܥܐ ܗܘܐ ܒܘܕܪ̈ܗܘܢ
ܡܢ ܥܘ̈ܠܐ. ܡܛܠܗܢܐ ܐܬܬܚܝܕܘ ܫܡܝܐ ܕܠܐ ܢܚܬܘܢ ܡܛܪܐ
ܥܠ ܐܪܥܐ. [21] ܘܡܒܘ̈ܥܐ ܕܡܢ ܥܠܡ. ܘܐܬܬܚܝܕܘ ܡܢ ܬܗܘ̈ܡܐ
ܘܡܢ ܛܘܪ̈ܐ ܪ̈ܡܐ. ܡܛܠ ܕܠܝܬ ܗܘܐ ܒܗܘܢ ܕܥܒܕ ܙܕܝܩܘܬܐ.
ܘܕܝܢܐ. ܡܢ ܪܫܝܥܗܘܢ ܘܥܕܡܐ ܠܙܥܘܪ̈ܗܘܢ܆ ܐܝܬܝܗܘܢ
ܒܟܠ ܚܛ̈ܗܝܢ. [22] ܡܠܟܐ ܒܥܘܠܐ ܐܝܬܘܗܝ، ܘܕܝܢܐ [p] ܒܡܣܪܒܢܘܬܐ.
ܘܥܡܐ ܒܚܛܝܬܐ. [23] ܚܙܝ، ܡܪܝܐ ܘܐܩܝܡ ܠܗܘܢ ܠܡܠܟܗܘܢ
ܠܒܪܗ ܕܕܘܝܕ. ܒܙܒܢܐ [q] ܕܝܕܥ ܐܢܬ ܐܠܗܐ. ܕܢܡܠܟ ܥܠ
ܐܝܣܪܝܠ ܥܒܕܟ. [24] ܘܚܝܨܝܗܝ، ܒܚܝܠܐ ܕܢܬܒܪ ܫ̈ܠܝܛܢܐ ܕܥܘܠܐ.
[r] [25] ܘܢܕܟܝܗ̇ ܠܐܘܪܫܠܡ ܡܢ ܥܡ̈ܡܐ ܕܕܝܫܝܢ ܠܗ̇ [s] ܠܐܒܕܢܐ.
[26] ܠܡܫܕܝܘ ܥܘ̈ܠܐ ܡܢ ܝܪ̈ܬܘܬܐ. ܠܡܬܒܪܘ ܫܘܒܗܪܐ ܐܝܟ
ܡ̈ܐܢܐ ܕܦܚܪܐ. ܠܡܬܒܪܘ ܒܫܒܛܐ ܕܦܪܙܠܐ ܟܠܗ [t] ܥܘܫܢܗܘܢ܆
[27] ܠܡܘܒܕܘ ܥܡ̈ܡܐ ܥܘ̈ܠܐ ܒܡܠܬ ܦܘܡܗ. ܒܟܐܬܗ ܢܥܪܩܘܢ
ܥܡ̈ܡܐ ܡܢ ܩܕܡ ܐܦ̈ܘܗܝ، [u] ܘܠܡܟܣܘ ܠܚܛ̈ܝܐ ܒܡܠܬܐ
ܕܠܒܗܘܢ.. [28] ܕܢܟܢܫ ܥܡܐ ܩܕܝܫܐ ܗܘ [v] ܕܢܫܬܥܒܪ ܒܙܕܝܩܘܬܐ.
ܘܢܕܘܢ ܫܒ̈ܛܐ ܕܥܡܐ ܕܡܩܕܫ ܡܪܝܐ ܐܠܗܗ. [29] ܘܠܐ ܬܘܒ
ܢܥܒܘܪ ܕܬܒܘܬ، ܫܠܝܬܐ ܒܝܢܬܗܘܢ܆ ܘܠܐ ܬܘܒ ܢܥܡܪ

[n] The translator has referred *ἐπλανῶντο* to the sparrows.

[o] For *παροικίας ψυχή* the translator read *παροικία ψυχῆς*. Cf. note [i] on previous page.

[p] Gk. *ἐν ἀπειθείᾳ*.

[q] Gk. *εἶδες* (JL). Gebhardt conjectures *εἵλου*.

[r] = Gk. *καθαρίσαι*.

[s] Gk. adds *ἐν σοφίᾳ, ἐν δικαιοσύνῃ*: probably by an eye-error to *v.* 31.

[t] Gk. *ὑπόστασιν*. Cf. Ps. xv. 7.

[u] vid. sup. Ps. xvi. 14.

[v] Gk. *οὐ ἀφηγήσεται*.

ܒܝܢܬܗܘܢ ܠܒܪܢܫܐ ܕܝܕܥ ܒܝܫܬܐ. 30ܢܕܥ ܐܢܘܢ ܓܝܪ ܡܛܠ
ܕܟܠܗܘܢ ܒܢ̈ܝܐ ܐܢܘܢ ܕܐܠܗܐ. ܘܢܦܠܓ ܐܢܘܢ ܒܫܪܒܬܗܘܢ
ܒܐܪܥܐ. 31ܘܬܘܬܒܐ ܘܢܘܟܪܝܐ ܠܐ ܢܥܡܪ ܥܡܗܘܢ܂ [x]ܡܛܠ
ܕܕܐܢ ܥܡ̈ܡܐ ܘܐܘܡ̈ܘܬܐ ܒܚܟܡܬܐ ܕܙܕܝܩܘܬܗ. 32ܘܢܩܢܐ
ܥܡܐ ܡܢ [y]ܥܡ̈ܡܐ. ܕܢܦܠܚܘܢܗܝ ܬܚܝܬ ܢܝܪܗ. ܘܢܫܒܚܘܢܗܝ
ܠܡܪܝܐ ܒܓܠܝܐܝܬ ܒܟܠܗ̇ ܐܪܥܐ. 33ܘܢܕܟܝܗ̇ ܠܐܘܪܫܠܡ
ܒܩܕܝܫܘܬܐ ܐܝܟ ܕܡܢ ܩܕܝܡ. 34ܕܢܐܬܘܢ ܥܡ̈ܡܐ ܡܢ ܣܘ̈ܦܝܗ̇
ܕܐܪܥܐ. ܠܡܚܙܐ ܬܫܒܘܚܬܗ. [z]ܟܕ ܡܝܬܝܢ ܐܣܝܪ̈ܐ ܠܒܢܝܗ̇.
ܗ̇ܢܘܢ ܕܐܬܛܪܕܘ ܡܢܗ̇.[z] 35ܘܠܡܚܙܐ ܬܫܒܘܚܬܗ ܕܡܪܝܐ ܗܘ̇
ܕܫܒܚܗ̇ ܐܠܗܐ. ܘܗܘ̣ ܡܠܟܐ ܙܕܝܩܐ ܡܠܦ ܡܢ ܐܠܗܐ
ܥܠܝܗܘܢ܂ 36ܘܠܝܬ ܥܘܠܐ ܒܝܘ̈ܡܬܗ ܒܝܢܬܗܘܢ܂ ܡܛܠ ܕܟܠܗܘܢ
ܩܕ̈ܝܫܝܢ. ܘܡܠܟܗܘܢ ܡܫܝܚܐ ܡܪܝܐ. 37ܡܛܠ ܕܠܐ ܢܣܒܪ
ܡܣܒܪ ܥܠ ܣܘܣܝܐ ܘܠܐ ܥܠ ܪܟܒܗ. ܘܠܐ ܥܠ ܩܫܬܐ. ܐܦ
ܠܐ ܡܣܓܐ ܠܗ ܕܗܒܐ ܘܣܐܡܐ ܠܩܪܒܐ. ܘܠܐ ܢܣܒܪ ܥܠ
ܣܓܝ̈ܐܐ ܒܥܡܡܐ ܕܩܪܒܐ. 38ܡܪܝܐ ܓܝܪ ܘܣܒܪܗ.

Caetera desunt.

[x] The translator read ἔτι as ὅτι.

[y] Gk. λαοὺς ἐθνῶν.

[z–z] The Gk. is φέροντες δῶρα τοὺς ἐξησθενηκότας υἱοὺς αὐτῆς. The Syriac seems to render a Gk. ἐξωσθέντας, which is a better reading, though perhaps it may be a conjecture.